Praise for the First Edition of
The Federal Resume Guidebook

Kathryn Troutman, author of *The Federal Resume Guidebook,* has been helping federal employees with their resumes and application forms for more than 25 years. Now she's helping applicants learn to be concise and reinvention-minded when they get ready to market themselves to federal agencies.

–Brian Friel, *Government Executive Magazine*

Your analysis and justification for using particular approaches clarifies the process and encourages users to really think about what they want to say and how it should be stated.

–Jane Jenkins, coordinator for Career
Learning Center, U.S. Information Agency

You have taken the death of the SF 171 and turned it into a real opportunity for applicants for federal employment. . . . OPM ought to give you a medal for understanding the problem and solving it wisely. Your book is well done and explores all the important issues that face the applicant.

–Morton Leeds, Ph.D., career counselor, former federal
government manager, and job search strategies expert

The Federal Resume Guidebook is the one book that anyone contemplating a job with the U.S. government must have. This guide to the new procedures gives you an excellent overview of the new guidelines along with an easy step-by-step tutorial on constructing your resume within these guidelines. Kathryn has rounded this with great examples and information in the appendices, and tips from many who will be reading the resumes as they come in. . . . All counselors and job search trainers should have copies available for their clients.

–Margaret F. Riley Dikel, Webmaster, The Riley Guide

When the SF 171 was abolished in 1995, applicants were given, for the first time, choices in how best to present themselves for federal jobs. Choices, however, can be overwhelming to applicants seeking the answers to such basic questions as "What does the employer want to know about me? What's important? How much should I say?" *The Federal Resume Guidebook* answers these questions for the applicant. The guidebook clues the applicant in to what is required and essential in applying for the job, and then reveals how to present this material so that it captures the attention of the employer. With the mystery gone as to the content, the applicant is free to highlight his or her accomplishments.

–Paul Krumsiek, Federal Personnel Manager, Department of Justice

We know that the vice president is interested in ways to make the federal job application process easier to understand. Since the use of the resume is a new approach in the way the federal government does business, applicants may need more guidance on resume preparation and content. The Office of Personnel Management has referred to your guidebook, as well as to other publications, in outplacement briefings as an excellent source of reference.

–Mary Ellen Dix, National Performance Review

Troutman notes that a federal resume must contain a series of details–such as an applicant's Social Security number, citizenship status, and names and telephone numbers of previous supervisors–that a traditional resume would not likely include. *The Federal Resume Guidebook* is stuffed with good-looking sample resumes pronounced complete by federal personnel staffing specialists.

–*Government Executive Review*

The Federal Resume Guidebook

SECOND EDITION

Kathryn Kraemer Troutman

Contributing authors:

Michael Singer Dobson, Brian Friel,
Tom Kell, Edward J. Lynch, and Alan Cross

Indianapolis, IN

The Federal Resume Guidebook, Second Edition

Copyright © 1995, 1997, 1999 by Kathryn Kraemer Troutman

Chapter 13 © 1999 by Michael Dobson. All rights reserved. Used with permission.

Part of Appendix D appears in *The Book of U.S. Government Jobs* (Bookhaven Press) © 1996 by Dennis Damp. All rights reserved. Used with permission.

Published by JIST Works, Inc.
8902 Otis Avenue
Indianapolis, IN 46216

Phone: 1-800-648-JIST   Fax: 1-800-JIST-FAX
E-Mail: editorial@aol.com   Web site: www.jist.com

Other books by Kathryn Kraemer Troutman

Reinvention Federal Resumes
The 171 Reference Book
Creating Your High School Resume

See the back of this book for additional JIST titles and ordering information. Quantity discounts are available.

Development editor: Susan Pines

Interior designer and interior layout: Aleata Howard

Interior layout: Carolyn J. Newland

Cover designer: Carol Werner

Appendix resume designs: Bonnie Kraemer Day

Proofreaders: Chuck Hutchinson; Amy Goodwin

Indexer: Sharon Hilgenberg

Printed in the United States of America

02 01   9 8 7 6 5 4

ISBN 1-56370-545-1

Table of Contents

7 The Magic of Page 1—Focusing Your Resume Toward an Announcement, Promotion, or New Career ...123

8 Packaging Your Federal Resume Application 139

9 The New Scannable Format—Writing a Resumix Resume 151

Foreword

Richard Bausch, one of America's finest novelists, teaches creative writing at George Mason University. Recently, I asked him how quickly could he tell whether a student had the talent to be a creative writer. He responded, "within seconds" their writing is "alive."

It is the same for resumes. During over 20 years in the personnel business, I have seen thousands of applications and resumes and have found the same phenomenon as Mr. Bausch—the winning resumes leap out at me.

When reviewing resumes, an employer can pick candidates worthy of interviewing, not after hours of study, but within seconds. So what is it in a resume that tells employers that "this is the one," or that "this is just the person I'm looking for?"

Ms. Troutman provides the secrets to winning resumes in the second edition of *The Federal Resume Guidebook*. She emphasizes the need to know the qualifying experience required for any job and how to find out about it. Her resume formats show how to focus a resume reader's attention on your strengths. Ms. Troutman then coaches you in championing your experiences with action vocabulary that conveys career movement, progression, accomplishment, and vitality.

Additionally, Ms. Troutman alerts you to the vocabulary that will impress the scanner. Yes, human resource offices are becoming more automated. During the next few years, resumes will often be initially scanned with automation, and only those resumes deemed most qualified will be seen by a prospective employer. Ms. Troutman's guidebook lets you know what vocabulary is essential to getting through the perils of this process and gaining a winning shot.

Ms. Troutman's extensive experience in the resume-writing business succinctly teaches you how to construct, step-by-step, the winning resume. More importantly, she helps you learn how to make your resume "alive."

Paul A. Krumsiek
Federal Personnel Manager

Preface

In 1995 I designed what I called a "federal resume" and published *The Federal Resume Guidebook*, the first book written on the new federal application. I am pleased to notice that this format is on the Office of Personnel Management (OPM) Web site at the end of the USAJobs's Resume Builder On-Line Form. The first book sold 10,000 copies and changed the way thousands regard government job applications. This second edition is better than the first, with hundreds of ideas on how you can best present your experience and skills for a promotion or first job in government. I have added more samples and instructions for new college graduates, because the government offers them great job opportunities.

This book is written in an informative, upbeat, and motivating style that does more than teach you how to write a federal resume. I want the book to inspire you to describe what you've accomplished at work and outside work in the best possible way.

The government is moving toward human resources automation where the resume will be the only accepted application, so resume writing for federal jobs is here to stay. Right now it's a dilemma about which application form to use, but more than half of all federal applications are now resumes.

Over the past three years, I have trained thousands of federal workers in resume writing. The participants are enthusiastic about the new resume: "This course gave me great ideas on how to write and reformat my resume." "The information that I gained will last a lifetime. The resource materials are some of the best I've ever seen." "This course should be offered quarterly, with a great amount of publicity so employees will be encouraged to keep their resumes updated and not sit at one job for an extended time."

Is This Book for You?

This book is written for several audiences, including the following:

- ☆ Federal employees seeking advancement
- ☆ Anyone applying for a federal job
- ☆ New and returning college graduates
- ☆ Trainers, career counselors, and human resource managers

What This Book Covers

Your federal resume most likely will be three to five pages long. Why then, is this book over 400 pages long? Because I want to give you lots of samples along with my instructions. This book contains 13 chapters, and each is important to your federal job search.

Chapter 1 describes the federal resume and compares it to the OF 612 and SF 171. Chapter 2 explains how to find job announcements easily through the OPM Web site and other federal services.

Chapters 3, 4, 5, and 6 offer easy-to-follow, resume-writing instructions for your personal information, education and training, other qualifications, and work experience sections. Chapter 7 helps you focus your resume with a dynamic page 1 that responds to "Tell me about yourself." Chapter 8 provides information on packaging your resume. It includes tips on organizing, designing, proofreading, and assembling your application.

Chapter 9 explains which agencies are scanning resumes, how the Resumix scanning system works, and how to write a scannable resume.

Chapter 10 explains what KSAs are and how to write them. In Chapter 11, readers interested in the Senior Executive Service (SES) learn about the new Executive Core Qualifications (ECQ) and how to best apply for the SES.

In Chapter 12, you learn why you need a cover letter and how to write one. Finally, Chapter 13 offers a federal career management strategy that takes just an hour a week but pays big dividends.

The appendixes contain a wealth of reference material, including outstanding federal resume samples for recent college graduates, GS-8 and below, GS-9 and above, Resumix applicants, and private-industry employees who want to convert to government work. You will also find federal occupational information, Resumix job kits, the entire OPM SES qualifications guide, and more. KSA samples and ECQ examples for the SES are also included.

The first edition contained a very popular PC disk with seven federal resumes and templates. You will see a coupon in the back of this book to order this edition's PC disk or CD-ROM by mail or e-mail. The disk can make your resume writing easier by having the format and template on your screen. The disk contains some of the federal resume samples that appear in Appendix A in Word for Windows and WordPerfect formats. You can simply replace text throughout the resume.

Your commitment to getting a promotion or getting hired in government will be tested by finding vacancy announcements and focusing your federal application toward that announcement. Every federal resume, KSA, and cover letter that I write for a client is a challenge. I sincerely

like converting a drab, out-of-date SF 171 into a great-looking, targeted resume. It's a pleasure every time. Some of these federal resumes are in this book and are used with permission.

Thank you for reading this book and for following its ideas. I wish you success in your application. You can write me at resume@resume-place.com.

Acknowledgments

Three years of writing federal resumes have given me the inspiration to rewrite this book and fill it with new enthusiasm, experiences, and success stories. Every federal resume example in this book is real and used with permission, but names have been fictionalized. Since The Resume Place and my Web site specialize in writing, training, and consulting on federal resume writing, I had many successful resumes from which to choose. *The Federal Resume Guidebook,* second edition, would not be the excellent federal resume style guide it is without these real resumes and true success stories.

Thank you to Francine Schlaks, Pat Wine, Mike Rosetti, Patricia Woods, Rob Rottman, Dean Simpkins, Nancy Bienia, Kelvin Jones, Renee McGee, Kevin Mims, Charles Barth, and Giselle Green for allowing me to share their careers and presentations, which will inspire thousands of federal resume writers.

I'd also like to thank federal government personnel and career transition center managers who were early fans of the federal resume and supported my writing, training, and research: Ned Lynch, Dick Whitford, Faith Williamson, Phyllis Day, Kathleen Accetta, Billy Hunter, Leanne Moore, CC Christakos, Paul Krumsiek, Debbie Harlow, Marge Bruning, Mary Jones, Barbara Donnelly, Irene Lieberman, Terrence Hill, Chester Ervin, Suzanne Oprisko, Pat Wood, Sharon Harvey. Thanks also to Claire Gibbons, Antoinette Hawkins, David Hyde, Kate Mercer, Jessica Taylor, Mary Ann Maloney and her staff at the OPM's Office of Communications, and the staff at OPM's Raleigh Service Center who promptly responded to e-mail inquiries.

A special thank you to the writers who contributed valuable research and content: Michael Dobson, Ned Lynch, Brian Friel, Tom Kell, Alan Cross, and Bonny Day. Thanks to JIST Works editor, Sue Pines, for helping me describe in full sentences "how to write a federal resume." Thank you, Sue, for helping me tell thousands how to do what I do everyday.

And thanks to my book promoters, Jill Worth and Scott Thompson at *Federal Employees News Digest,* and www.fedforce.com. for publishing articles and successfully marketing my federal resume books and disks. Thanks to federal Webmaster Pete Brunner at http://safetynet.doleta.gov/resume.htm for linking to my first Web site designed by Brian Lieberman.

And finally thanks to my wonderful children, Chris, Emily, and Lauren, for their patience and loving understanding of my drive to write more than resumes.

CHAPTER 1

What Is a Federal Resume?

A "federal resume" is the best thing that has happened to federal employment in years. Finally, you can write and submit a resume for a federal job instead of completing a "life history" form, known as the Standard Form 171 (SF 171). By writing a federal resume, you will impress HR professionals through an emphasis on accomplishments, results, and skills. Applicants no longer need to use bureaucratic gobbledygook and worn-out position descriptions.

Whether you're seeking a promotion, trying to change to a new series, or attempting to get your first job in government, you can now write a federal job application that gives a great first impression and organizes your qualifications in the most marketable way. You can focus your resume toward a federal job vacancy announcement with new resume sections that help highlight your accomplishments and skills. As Billy Crystal would say, you'll look "mahvelous."

This chapter introduces federal-resume writing, explains why it is the best format to choose for your federal application, and gives some federal resume examples. Upcoming chapters will feature step-by-step, resume-writing instructions; additional lively, professional, and successful federal resume samples; and the rationale for the samples' content and presentation. The goal of this material is to provide inspiration and guidance that will enable you to write a federal resume that will rate you "highly qualified" and get you promoted or hired in government.

Since the federal government changed its rigid application processes, several application formats–including resumes–are acceptable. Most vacancy announcements will give you application options. You'll notice that *resume* is listed first in most announcements. This chapter will review the other application formats for comparison purposes.

The following typically appears in a federal job announcement on "how to apply" for a particular job:

> How to apply: You may submit a resume, OF 612 Optional Application Form for Federal Employment, SF 171 Application for Federal Employment, or any other written format may be accepted. Your application must include all of the information listed in the attached application instructions.

If the agency is an automated one that scans the resumes with optical character recognition (OCR) equipment, you'll see the following in "how to apply":

> How to apply: RESUMIX—ONLY RESUMES WILL BE ACCEPTED.

Refer to Chapter 9 for a full discussion of the Resumix resume. There is a specific format to follow for each automated agency, and the job kit instructions (directions for writing a scannable resume) for the Department of Defense-Washington Service Center, the CIA, and the Immigration and Naturalization Service are included in Appendix E. These agencies are now automated and scan resumes.

What Is Unique to a Federal Resume?

The federal resume is a new federal application. This resume is an application itself and should not be submitted in combination with an SF 171 or the Optional Form 612 (OF 612 is the new, shorter form that is replacing the SF 171). This resume is "federal" because it includes certain information required of federal personnel and is in a specific format. The federal resume averages three to five pages, is chronological, and presents job-related and recent (the last 10 years) employment, education, training, skills, and other qualifications.

The new resume format also introduces a writing style that emphasizes skills, accomplishments, and results. Vice President Gore's Partnership on Reinventing Government program has directed the federal government to become results oriented. The Government Results and Performance Act, signed by the president, mandates agencies to become results oriented and establish methods to measure performance by federal workers. This new attitude toward accomplishments and results must be reflected in your resume if you want to be a successful federal applicant. Only the new federal resume format gives you the opportunity to highlight your accomplishments, results, and skills on page 1 of your document. If the vacancy announcement gives you a choice of format—resume, OF 612, or SF 171—you should select the federal resume as your application.

> **The government's new attitude toward accomplishments must be reflected in your resume.**

HR professionals frequently say that they still prefer the SF 171. Their reasons are valid: Most applicants who use a resume as their application send a private industry resume or a resume that does not include the detail and information the government requires. So, that resume application loses consideration for the job—even if the applicant is highly qualified. Remember that HR professionals have reviewed many lengthy SF 171s for more than 42 years. It's not easy to change. If they cannot find the information easily on the resume, then your application will not be successful. HR professionals have to review hundreds of applications, and they appreciate an easy-to-read, job-related resume in reverse chronological order with all compliance details. Compliance details consist of information that the government and the vacancy announcement require on a resume.

It's not easy to find the instructions for writing your resume and application in the job announcements. In Chapter 2, you'll study federal job announcements, look for their buried but critical instructions on what to include, analyze these details closely, and learn how to incorporate them into your resume presentation. If your federal resume includes the necessary compliance details, is targeted toward a vacancy announcement, and you are truly well qualified, you could be a serious candidate for the position.

Here is the first part of a resume for federal employee Susan Lieberman, who is applying for a new position. Page 1 of her resume is attractive and interesting. Her profile statement makes her look outstanding. If you were the hiring manager, wouldn't you read on with great interest?

SUSAN C. LIEBERMAN
9080 Rogers Avenue
Alexandria, VA 22209
Home: (703) 888-9090   Work: (703) 666-8989

Social Security No: 000-00-0000
Citizenship: United States
Federal Civilian Status: Contract Specialist, GS-1102-13
Veteran's Preference: Not applicable

Objective: Contract Specialist, Announcement No: FAA-90999

Profile:

Award winning contract specialist and manager with nine years' experience in a large federal science agency with a $250 million contract budget.

Professional Experience:

National Institutes of Mental Health (NIMH)   August 1991 – present
5600 Fishers Lane   Beginning Salary: $45,000
Rockville, MD 20857   Current Salary: $57,000
Supervisor: Tom Milliton (301) 443-9999   40 hours per week
Yes, you may contact present employer.

(continued)

Unlimited Contracting Officer authority responsible for all pre-award and post-award functions on NIMH contracts, most of which are complex and for significant amounts crossing multiple fiscal years.

Pre-Award:

- Serve as expert advisor to program officials in the conceptualization and development of contract requirements.

- Establish an acquisition plan for each requirement that identifies clearances and includes performance milestones.

- Review draft Statement of Work (SOW) and revise unclear or ambiguous requirements to ensure no offeror receives unfair advantage. Recommend appropriate method of competition to the Branch Chief and prepare necessary Determinations and Findings for appropriate approvals.

How Does a Federal Resume Differ from a Private Industry Resume?

A federal resume is not a private industry resume. Special personal information is required for government security reasons. The following is the mandatory information that you typically would not include in your private industry resume:

☆ Social Security number

☆ Supervisor names and telephone numbers

☆ Beginning and ending salaries

☆ Street address, city, state, and zip code for employers

☆ Military status

☆ Zip codes for colleges

☆ High school name and the year you graduated

The Office of Personnel Management (OPM) flyer OF 510, *Applying for a Federal Job,* lists "what your resume should include" and is reprinted in almost every vacancy announcement. Read it carefully. For you to become qualified for your desired federal position, this information must be easy to find on your federal resume.

How Does a Federal Resume Differ from the SF 171?

The SF 171 was officially eliminated as of January 1995 by the OPM. The long, green form is no longer being printed. But the form is available on software if someone really wants to prepare an SF 171. The SF 171 software, called *Quick and Easy,* is available at most computer stores.

OPM and its Interagency Task Force determined that the federal HR professionals did not have time to spend up to 30 minutes on each application. Some SF 171s were up to 80 pages long with binders, tabs, and tables of contents. The weight of the paper that resulted from a job announcement was overwhelming. The only way to fix the problem was to eliminate the form.

One of the options the task force selected was a federal resume. A federal resume requires certain specific information that was on the SF 171. The differences between the SF 171 and the resume are listed below:

> A federal resume requires certain specific information that was included on the SF 171.

SF 171	Federal Resume
Four to 80 pages	Three to five pages
Requires special software	Requires your favorite word processing package
Rigid, chronological format	Flexible format
Impersonal and unattractive	Personal and attractive
Bureaucratic and lengthy job descriptions	Shorter job descriptions with focus on accomplishments
Page 1, the first impression, was a form	On page 1, you can put your best foot forward and emphasize information as desired
Lots of wasted space in the form	No wasted space

Following are excerpts of the SF 171 for a contract specialist. The SF 171 did not allow this candidate to emphasize his best qualifications.

Application for Federal Employment - SF 171

Read the instructions before you complete this application. *Type or print clearly in dark ink.*

Form Approved.
OMB No. 3206-0012

GENERAL INFORMATION

1 What kind of job are you applying for? Give title and announcement no. (If any)

Contract Specialist/Procurement Analyst, GS-1102

2 Social Security Number
999-99-9999

3 Sex
[X] Male   [ ] Female

4 Birth date (Month, Day, Year)
8/13/57

5 Birthplace (City and State or Country)
Washington, DC

6 Name (Last, First, Middle)
LIEBERMAN, BRIAN MARCUS

Mailing address (Include apartment number, if any)
35578 Parkside Drive

City
Kensington

State
MD

ZIP Code
32888

7 Other names ever used (e.g., maiden name, nickname, etc.)
n/a

8 Home Phone
Area Code Number
(301) 787-8989

9 Work Phone
Area Code Number Extension
(202) 787-7878

10 Were you ever employed as a civilian by the Federal Government? If "NO", go to item 11. If "YES", mark each type of job you held with an "X".

[ ] Temporary [X] Career-Conditional [ ] Career [ ] Excepted

What is your highest grade, classification series and job title?
GS-1102-13, Contract Specialist

Dates at highest grade: FROM Aug. 1988 TO Present

AVAILABILITY

11 When can you start work? (Month and Year)
2 weeks notice

12 What is the lowest pay will you accept? (You will not be considered for jobs which pay less than you indicate.)
Pay $ per   OR Grade 13

13 In what geographic area(s) are you willing to work?
Washington Metropolitan Area

14 Are you willing to work:

	YES	NO
A. 40 hours per week (full-time)?	X	
B. 25-32 hours per week (part-time)?		X
C. 17-24 hours per week (part-time)?		X
D. 16 or fewer hours per week (part-		
E. An intermittent job (on-call/season		
F. Weekends, shifts, or rotating shifts		

MILITARY SERVICE AND VETERAN

15 Are you willing to take a temporary job lasting

A. 5 to 12 months (sometimes longer

B. 1 to 4 months?

C. Less than 1 month?

16 Are you willing to travel away from home for:

A. 1 to 5 nights each month?

B. 6 to 10 nights each month?

C. 11 or more nights each month?

MILITARY SERVICE AND VETERAN

17 Have you served in the United States Military Ser only active duty was training in the Reserves or N answer "NO". If "NO", go to item 22..

18 Did you or will you retire at or above the rank of m ant commander?

THE FEDERAL GOVERNMENT IS AN EQUAL OPPOR
PREVIOUS EDITION USABLE UNTIL 12-31-90

Page 1

FOR USE OF EXAMINING OFFICE ONLY

Date entered register

Form reviewed:
Form approved:

Option	Grade	Earned Rating	Veteran Preference	Augmented Rating

[ ] No Preference Claimed
[ ] 5 Points (Tentative)
[ ] 10 Pts. (30% Or More Comp. Dis.)
[ ] 10 Pts.(Less Than 30% Comp. Dis.)
[ ] Other 10 Points

Initials and Date

[ ] Disallowed [ ] Being Investigated

FOR USE OF APPOINTING OFFICE ONLY
Preference has been verified through proof that the separation was under honorable conditions, and other proof as required.

[ ] 5-Point [ ] 10-Point–30% or More Compensable Disability [ ] 10-Point–Less Than 30% Compensable Disability [ ] 10-Point–Other

Signature and Title

Agency   Date

MILITARY SERVICE AND VETERAN PREFERENCE (Cont.)

19 Were you discharged from the military service under honorable conditions? (If your discharge was changed to "honorable" or "general" by a Discharge Review Board, answer "YES". If you received a clemency discharge, answer "NO".)
If "NO", provide below the date and type of discharge you received.

[ ] YES [ ] NO

Discharge Date (Month, Day, Year)   Type of Discharge

20 List the dates (Month, Day, Year), and branch for all active duty military service.

From	To	Branch of Service

WORK EXPERIENCE If you have no work experience, write "NONE" in A below and go to 25 on page 3.

23 May we ask your present employer about your character, qualifications, and work record? A "NO" will not affect our review of your qualifications. If you answer "NO" and we need to contact your present employer before we can offer you a job, we will contact you first.

[ ] YES [X] NO

24 READ WORK EXPERIENCE IN THE INSTRUCTIONS BEFORE YOU BEGIN.

- Describe your current or most recent job in Block A and work backwards, describing each job you held during the past 10 years. If you were unemployed for longer than 3 months within the past 10 years, list the dates and your address(es) in an experience block.
- You may sum up in one block work that you did more than 10 years ago. But if that work is related to the type of job you are applying for, describe each related job in a separate block.
- INCLUDE VOLUNTEER WORK (non-paid work)–If the work (or a part of the work) is like the job you are applying for, complete all parts of the experience block just as you would for a paying job. You may receive credit for work experience with religious, community, welfare, service, and other organizations.
- INCLUDE MILITARY SERVICE–You should complete all parts of the experience block just as you would for a non-military job, including all supervisory experience. Describe each major change of duties or responsibilities in a separate experience block.
- IF YOU NEED MORE SPACE TO DESCRIBE A JOB–Use sheets of paper the same size as this page (be sure to include all information we ask for in A and B below). On each sheet show your name, Social Security Number, and the announcement number or job title.
- IF YOU NEED MORE EXPERIENCE BLOCKS, use the SF 171-A or a sheet of paper.
- IF YOU NEED TO UPDATE (ADD MORE RECENT JOBS), use the SF 172 or a sheet of paper as described above.

A Name and address of employer's organization (Include ZIP Code, if known)
Department of the Navy
Naval Information Systems Management Center
Contracting Directorate, Building 176-4
Wash, DC 20374

Dates employed (give month, day and year)
From: 8/88 To: Present

Average number of hours per week
40

Number of employees you supervise
0

Salary or earnings
Starting $39,501 per year
Ending $63,734 per year

Your reason for wanting to leave
Command Disestablishment

Your immediate supervisor
Name: Cmdr John Grine

Area Code Telephone No.
(202) 433-7000

Exact title of your job
Contract Specialist

If Federal employment (civilian or military) list series, grade or rank, and, if promoted in this job, the date of your last promotion
GS-1102-13

Description of work: Describe your specific duties, responsibilities and accomplishments in this job, including the job title(s) of any employees you supervise. If you describe more than one type of work (for example, carpentry and painting, or personnel and budget), write the approximate percentage of time you spent doing each.

Warranted Contracting Officer for Information Technology. Warranted Small Purchase Contracting Officer. Project Manager and served concurrently as Procuring and Administrative Contracting Officer. Team Leader and senior contract specialist. Procure through both pre-award and post-award processes. Experienced on a variety of Information Technology (IUT) contracts, including complex computer and telecommunications and technical support services, generally multi-million dollar in value and acquired for multiple agencies and installed and maintained at multiple locations, often overseas. Secret Clearance. Member of the Navy Acquisition Professional Community, Level III, February 1994. Procurement Contracting Officer for the Official and Unofficial Long Distance Telephone and Operator Services for Guantanamo Bay Naval Station, Cuba. Awarded

Continued on a Separate Page

B Name and address of employer's organization (Include ZIP Code, if known)

Dates employed (give month, day and year)
From: To:

Average number of hours per week

Number of employees you supervised

Salary or earnings
Starting $ per
Ending $ per

Your reason for leaving

Your immediate supervisor
Name

Area Code Telephone No.

Exact title of your job

If Federal employment (civilian or military) list series, grade or rank, and, if promoted in this job, the date of your last promotion

Description of work: Describe your specific duties, responsibilities and accomplishments in this job, including the job title(s) of any employees you supervised. If you describe more than one type of work (for example, carpentry and painting, or personnel and budget), write the approximate percentage of time you spent doing each.

Page 2   IF YOU NEED MORE EXPERIENCE BLOCKS, USE SF 171-A (SEE BACK OF INSTRUCTION PAGE).

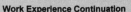

Work Experience Continuation

LIEBERMAN, BRIAN MARCUS
999-99-9999
09-28-1998

A) Department of the Navy - Page 1

Contract Specialist/Procurement Analyst, GS-1102

$38 million, 10-year contract, without protest 4 months after issuance of RFP. This was the first long distance telephone service contract awarded at NISMC. Served as Procuring Contracting Officer and Project Manager for the Base Telecommunications System for NAWCAD Patuxent River. The Navy had been trying to award a contract for the last 10 years unsuccessfully to replace the antiquated telephone system at Patuxent River Naval Base. Due to the reorganization, it was imperative that the project be awarded since the old phone system would not be able to handle the increased personnel. The RFP was issued allowing proposers to bid on services or equipment solutions. Identified contractual requirements needed when developing the Plan for Action and Milestones(POA&M). Prepared, reviewed and approved all contractual inputs into approvals for the RFP, amendments/supplements, the Source Selection Plan (SSP), the acquisition strategy and all regulatory approvals. Assured that the source selection criteria set forth in the approved SSP are properly addressed in the RFP. Assured that the proposals are requested on a basis which permits verification of their price credibility. Determinining responsibility of offerors and preparing all documentation supporting the official contract file.

How Does a Federal Resume Differ from the OF 612?

The OF 612 was designed to replace the SF 171. It consists of two pages, and the instructions state that you cannot add attachment pages. Parts of the form are the same as the SF 171. Another form was created to replace page 4 of the SF 171. Called the Declaration for Federal Employment (OF 306), it asks personal questions about felonies, court martials, arrests, and government debt. The OF 306 is not usually required until the hiring agency is interested in interviewing you for a position.

The OF 612 contains similar information to the federal resume, but since it is a rigid form, the presentation is not as effective and professional as the resume. The OF 612 is considered by most to be too short and too much like the SF 171. Why use a form when you can write an attractive and complete federal resume?

The OF 612 is a very short form and has space for only three positions, which is limiting. Here is a comparison:

OF 612	Federal Resume
Two pages–no attachments	Any length–average is three to five pages
Wasted space with the form	Productive use of space
Rigid, chronological format	Page 1 can be maximized and organized as desired
Space for only three jobs	Space for more than three jobs if needed
Education is on last page	Education can be highlighted
Little space for other qualifications	Unrestricted space for qualifications
Format is a form	Format is yours

Here is part of the OF 612 for a management analyst.

Form Approved
OMB No. 3206-0219

OPTIONAL APPLICATION FOR FEDERAL EMPLOYMENT - OF 612

You may apply for most jobs with a resume, this form, or other written format. If your resume or application does not provide all the information requested on this form and in the job vacancy announcement, you may lose consideration for a job.

1 Job title in announcement	2 Grade(s) applying for	3 Announcement number
Program Expert	GS-0301-14	9700-703

4 Last name	First and middle names	5 Social Security Number
LITTLE	EMILY ANN	898-88-9999

6 Mailing address	7 Phone numbers (include area code)
20090 Woodland Road	Daytime (202) 787-8888

City	State	ZIP Code	
Ft. Washington	MD	20907	Evening (301) 787-7777

WORK EXPERIENCE

8 Describe your paid and nonpaid work experience related to the job for which you are applying. Do not attach job descriptions.

1) Job title (if Federal, include series and grade)

Management Analyst GS-0343-13/7

From (MM/YY)	To (MM/YY)	Salary	per	Hours per week
1/20/85	Present	$65,555	year	45

Employer's name and address	Supervisor's name and phone number
Office of General Counsel, General Services Administration	Susan Schmidt
18th & F Sts., NW, Washington, DC 20405	(202) 777-7777

Describe your duties and accomplishments

System Administrator for the Office of General Counsel (OGC) responsible for the management of the Local Area Network (LAN) for OGC and the Office of Equal Employment Opportunity. Custom design of the computer system to meet changing needs. Project Leader for system development. Supervision of LAN contract staff. Custom designs the computer system to meet ongoing needs and requirements of the office and individual users. Prepare written contract deliverable, reviews and evaluates contractor-prepared deliverables, and accepts or rejects deliverables. Procures hardware, software, supplies and hardware maintenance. Ensure accurate accounting of equipment/software inventory. Approve transfer of equipment

Continued on a Separate Page

2) Job title (if Federal, include series and grade)

From (MM/YY)	To (MM/YY)	Salary	per	Hours per week
		$		

Employer's name and address	Supervisor's name and phone number

Describe your duties and accomplishments

　　　NSN 7540-01-351-9178　　　Optional Form 612 (September 1994)
U.S. Office of Personnel Management

Work Experience Continuation

LITTLE, EMILY ANN	1) Management Analyst GS-0343-13/7 - Page 1	898-88-9999
Program Expert	9700-703	GS-0301-14

between property accounts. Serve as expert computer advisor and provide high-level technical assistance and advice to OGC Central Office and regional staff. Conduct analytical studies of the OGC local area network, make recommendations, and implement all modifications. Prepare high-quality written technical reports. Make presentations to the General Counsel, executive staff and GSA officials. Prepare GSA contracts for legal research. Prepare OGC data for input in the Federal Productivity Measurement Program, Bureau of Labor Statistics. This project requires thorough data gathering, south analyses and logical conclusions and recommendations.

What Else Should Go with Your Federal Resume?

The federal resume application package usually requires a supplemental statement known as *KSAs*: Knowledge, Skills, and Abilities that relate to the announcement. Chapter 10 will give examples and instructions for writing these mandatory statements. Examples of KSAs are *ability to communicate orally and in writing* and *ability to plan, organize, and coordinate work plans*.

You can also write a cover letter that will summarize your most significant skills and experiences. In a cover letter, you can tell the hiring manager why you believe you are an excellent candidate for the position. Chapter 12 shows you how to write a good cover letter for government positions.

Other forms that are required for submission with your federal resume are listed in the job announcements. The following announcement excerpt shows an example of the various forms and information required. You will need to get this information for your application. Each announcement may ask for different forms and information, so read the list carefully. You can call the telephone number on the application to ask questions about the unfamiliar forms.

How to apply:

☆ Application for federal employment (resume/OF 612/SF 171).

☆ Your most recent SF 50 (notice of personnel action) verifying competitive status and grade promotion potential for candidates who are serving or who have served at the grade of the advertised position.

☆ All status candidates who wish to be considered for status or non-status referral must submit two (2) applications.

☆ Your most recent performance appraisal.

☆ A supplemental statement addressing the Knowledge, Skills, and Abilities listed in the announcement (mandatory).

☆ A cover letter stating why you are well qualified for the position (optional).

What Are Benefits of a Federal Resume?

The following is a review of the features and benefits of a federal resume.

Looks Great

As mentioned earlier, the federal resume averages three to five pages, is easy to read, and looks attractive. Remember that the HR professionals study resume packages all day long; they appreciate an easy-to-read presentation. You want them to enjoy reading and looking at your resume.

The new federal resume application will not permit attachments of recommendations, training certificates, or supervisory evaluations (except the most recent). The average type size on your resume should be 11 point, with the headings in 12 point. Your name can stand out by using 14 or 16 point type. Margins are usually 1 or 1.5 inches, and it's good to include white space between major paragraphs to increase readability. See Chapter 8 for more information on packaging your resume.

> HR professionals study resume packages all day long and appreciate an easy-to-read presentation.

The federal resumes presented in this book are job-winning examples. They are "federal" because they include the compliance details required by federal HR professionals. Otherwise, they would be sharp, well-organized, and focused resumes in the private industry, too.

Provides a Flexible Format

Using your favorite word processing program to create a resume instead of filling out a form is more flexible and creative. The SF 171 wasn't known for being a personal sales piece. The federal resume is better for content and presentation. No one looks great with his or her career listed on a form—either the SF 171 or the OF 612. As long as the resume includes all required information, you're a solid competitor. As the saying goes, you never get a second chance to make a first impression. On the next page is the start of a highly skilled statistician's resume. His qualifications are emphasized in his expertise, education, and professional highlights sections. His SF 171 was not as impressive as this resume.

Helps Career Changers

Do you want to change series? Do you want a promotion? The federal resume can be your career change tool. You can target the announcement with your relevant experience, education, and skills on page 1. Chapter 7 discusses focusing your resume for a promotion, series change, or entry into government work.

FREDERIC ALVIN WINSTON JR.

2100 Connecticut Avenue, N.W., Apt. 403
Washington, D.C. 20008-5903
Daytime: (301) 444-5555 (voice)
Evening: (202) 333-4444 (voice/fax)
e-mail: Frederic.A.Winston.Jr@ccmail.census.gov

Objective: Statistician, GS-12, Announcement No: 444-87988

Social Security Number: 233-33-3333
Citizenship: United States
Federal Civilian Status: Survey Statistician, GS 1530-11, 7/95 to present
Military Status: Not applicable

EXPERTISE

SAS programming:
- SAS Programming, STAT Techniques, Linear Modeling
- Statistical Methodology, Experimental Design

Statistical design, testing and analysis:
- Process modeling and control/sample design
- Linear and nonlinear regression analysis
- Hypothesis testing, Detection of outliers, Optimization

Computer software skills/knowledge:
- SAS (UNIX - STATSUN/LAMAR & PC/WINDOWS VERSIONS)
- SPSS (DOS/WINDOWS)
- dbase IV, LOTUS 1-2-3, Quattro Pro, WordPerfect, Latex, Windows 95

EDUCATION

M.S. Degree in Statistics — Colorado State University, Fort Collins, CO 80523-1992

B.A. Degree in Physics — Gallaudet University, Washington, D.C. 20002-1980

PROFESSIONAL HIGHLIGHTS

United States Department of Commerce
U.S. Bureau of the Census, Governments Division, Suitland, MD 20233   1/89-Present
SURVEY STATISTICIAN, GS 1530-11   Current Salary: $32,000/year
Supervisor: Lewis Andrews (301) 444-4444 (permission to contact)

Prepared elementary-secondary school finance data files for two different fiscal years for Census and NCES with separate sets of documentation for each.

SAS Programming
- Developed SAS programs to merge with very accurate documentation.
- Created and maintained well-documented SAS program files that defined the relationship between complex data items.
- Program files served as specifications, but are executable programs that convert data.

Highlights Your Background as Desired

The federal resume format can help you highlight your background as you so desire. Here are some examples:

☆ **Personal information:** Who are you? Your personal information can catch the attention of the reader. Don't let the reader forget your name. You can make your name, address, phone numbers, and compliance details stand out. You can select the type font, type size, format, and presentation that will set the tone of your resume.

☆ **Education:** What if you've just completed your degree and want to highlight the degree, courses, and projects? What if you've finally earned your master's degree, and the knowledge you have gained will give you the expertise required for a position? What if you have completed a career development program with a rotational assignment that gave you valuable experience for an advanced grade or series change? The resume will allow you to list your education and professional development on page 1, following your profile. See the sample for Steven R. Tyler in Appendix A.

☆ **Previous experience:** What if your current position is a downgrade or not relevant, and your previous position is more important for your career? You can highlight the skills from the previous experience in the profile, skills, and accomplishments sections on page 1. What if you were on a task force that was challenging and impressive and gave you more experience than your current position? You can highlight the task force or detail experiences in an accomplishments section on page 1. That way, the reader can see this experience quickly and be impressed with the relevance of your experience to the position. See the sample for Emily Anne Layton in Appendix A.

The federal resume can support unique experiences by giving you the opportunity to list and describe them on the first page. The SF 171 and OF 612 required that the information be chronological and buried where it belongs on the form.

The sample on the next page is for Kevin Quinn, who is applying to the Census Department to help with the Y2K problem after 14 years in the U.S. Navy in computer work. He is highlighting his critical skills, accomplishments, and experience in a great first-page presentation.

Kevin R. Quinn
1002 Rivers Edge
Easton, MD 20603
(301) 888-8888
kevinquinn@net.net

Social Security Number: 222-33-9999
Citizenship: United States
Veteran's Preference: GS7, Petty Officer 2nd Class, Data Processing Tech

OBJECTIVE: To obtain the position of Computer Specialist for the Department of Commerce at the Census Bureau.

SKILLS SUMMARY

Over 14 years of Desktop Support, User Support, Help Desk and Computer Operations experience while serving in the United States Navy.

- Extensive experience with PC hardware, software and operating systems both in stand-alone and networked environments. Able to communicate effectively with technical peers and end users to resolve technical issues.

- Supervised, managed and trained personnel for Desktop/PC and LAN Support, Help Desk, and Computer Operations, as well as time management and production scheduling.

- Effective team-builder with strong leadership skills and proven track record at setting and achieving realistic goals for self and others. Keeps mission of command and division in perspective and does not lose sight of overall picture.

- Provided top-notch customer service at all commands achieving over 98% satisfaction rate at the Naval Computer and Telecommunications Area Master Station.

EMPLOYMENT HISTORY

1/83-3/98   United States Navy

Naval Computer and Telecommunications Area Master Station   **9/95-3/98**
9625 Moffet, Norfolk, VA 23511-2784. 48 hours/week. Petty Officer 2nd Class, Data Processing Technician. Supervisor Mark Jones, (606) 777-7777.

Automated Data Processing Technician   *Supervisor may be contacted*

Responsible for installation, upgrade, maintenance, and repair of PCs, peripherals and associated software. Supervised five personnel providing desktop and user support to 5,000 users for MS Word 6.0, WordPerfect 5.0/6.0, MS-DOS (to v6.22), Windows 95, Windows 3.1, Norton Utilities, McAfee, cc:Mail and PC Tools in a Novell NetWare 3.x LAN environment. As Help Desk Supervisor personally handled 20-50 trouble calls on a daily basis.

Provided Level I and II Help Desk support for communications and COTS issues to seven sites on a global basis including Puerto Rico, Alaska, Italy and U. S. Naval vessels afloat. Help Desk handled over 300 trouble calls daily and was in operation 24 hours a day, 7 days a week. Provided routine hardware and software maintenance and changes to PCs, LAN, and all software as needed.

Focuses the Resume with a Profile Statement

Every resume can benefit from a profile statement. It is your introduction and the answer to the question, "Tell me about yourself." Your hope is that the reader will be impressed and continue to read. The profile should be brief and perfectly targeted to the announcement.

Here's the profile of an applicant for a senior program manager position, summarizing an extensive career with the Department of Health and Human Services. He's summarizing his expertise (programs and civil rights), his executive leadership ability (strategic perspective), his management expertise (policy and programs), and his involvement in major programs in civil rights, disability rights, and accessibility standards for protected classes. This paragraph is packed with information for a fast read. A profile statement can be written for anyone, first-time federal applicants as well as existing federal employees—from GS5 through Senior Executive Service (SES).

Profile

Program manager and administrative officer with thirty years' experience in the development and application of innovative programs and civil rights policies. Strong strategic perspective with the ability to balance short-term priorities against long-term organizational goals. Coherent record of effective policy development and program management. Broad experience promoting and monitoring federal programs to assure civil rights, disability rights, and accessibility standards for protected classes.

Emphasizes Accomplishments and Results

The new focus in government is on accomplishments and results. With the new resume format, you can present your most significant accomplishments, results, and skills on page 1 and in your positions descriptions. You can present yourself as an outstanding candidate—not just a good employee—who knows his or her job, agency, mission, purpose, and customer needs and who works quickly and efficiently to achieve job objectives.

If you are highly accomplished, you can list accomplishments on page 1. You will be telling the reader, "These are the accomplishments of which I am most proud." You will look like a government innovator and impress the hiring managers with your ability to work outside the box. You have initiative, drive, new ideas; you also get things done, make things better, care about your job and your customer, and achieve results.

Here are the accomplishments of another senior program manager with Health and Human Services who has established many new systems,

programs, and policies that have improved housing and housing communications throughout the United States. He's applying for Senior Executive Service positions. (This is an optional section.)

Recent Accomplishments

- Conceived and currently developing a new Field Evaluation System (FES) that decentralizes HUD responsibilities to the field, provides more effective customer service and *for the first time,* a performance measuring process for field operations.

- Developed and implemented a nationwide communications program linking headquarters and field personnel on a regular basis. This monthly conference call program for approximately 100 Office of Fair House & Equal Opportunity (FHEO) field and headquarters staff was rated as *"essential and effective"* and is the model for present nationwide conferencing. This program was created to keep personnel updated on the political, administrative and programmatic issues affecting them during a period of great uncertainty for HUD (and indeed all) federal employees.

- Organized HUD's Office of the Deputy Assistant Secretary (DAS) for Policy and Initiatives during a period of department-wide downsizing to provide more efficient and streamlined coordination between HQ and 38 field offices nationwide.

- Appointed Departmental Disability Program Manager. Created and published a monthly newsletter, the *HUD Disability Update,* and was responsible for ensuring that the department met the needs of its staff members with disabilities.

- Negotiated contract with TARGET Center, USDA, to give hands-on experience to HUD managers and staff with disabilities.

Here is a sample accomplishments section within a position description:

Senior Procurement Analyst, GS-1102-14

Established the Contracts Business Review Office

Principal advisor to the Executive Director on practices and policies associated with the solicitation, evaluation, and award of major information technology and telecommunications.

Review, analyze, and provide independent assessments of best-value source selections including technical/cost tradeoff analysis and cost realism analysis. Most recently:

- PC LAN+, $300M.

- New Technologies for Office and Portable Systems (NTOPS), $176M.

- Improved contract quality, streamlined source selections, and dramatically reduced protests of awards. This was accomplished by:

    Developing in-process, interactive reviews to disclose compromises to source selections throughout the acquisition cycle. Quality of reviews eliminated two layers of management oversight.

    Identifying major factor in protests of support service contracts and formulating revised policy. There have been no successful challenges to source selections in the past six years.

For novice federal applicants, the page 1 accomplishments section is helpful to emphasize job-related private industry accomplishments. The following is an example from a man who is in the produce distribution business and is seeking a position in the USDA as a food produce inspector.

ACCOMPLISHMENTS

- Established new, more efficient buying procedures for corporation, saving 15% in costs and improving productivity. Restructured product prices and costs in line with market conditions, increasing sales by 5%.

- Successful operations experience with Mazo-Lerch Co., Inc. ($85 million annual sales), involving staff management, sales and marketing strategies, and inventory control for all facets of the operation. Improved inventory tracking system, which reduced product shrinkage by 20%.

- Restructured the operations process to consolidate like-activities, achieving more efficiency and control of specific department functions.

- Developed good working relationships with end-users, key players and major leaders in the produce industry. Increased customer satisfaction and reduced customer complaints.

- Increased overall corporate sales by 20% through more efficiency and operations control.

Highlights Critical Skills and Job-Related Information in the Position Descriptions

What are your critical skills? What critical skills do you have that the agency needs? Make a list that tells the reader what you have to offer. Make it clear, easy to find, and written in plain English. How do you know which skills to highlight? The skills required for the position are usually in the vacancy announcement. You can match your skills to the announcement and create a highly targeted list for page 1. The statistician's resume on page 11 lists his critical skills clearly.

The person whose skills are shown next is a private industry employee, a marketer, applying for a marketing specialist position with the U.S. Postal Service. The duties and responsibilities in the announcement match her critical skills in private industry for Nabisco Foods. The Postal Service has products, retailers, and customers too!

CRITICAL SKILLS

- Managing national accounts with outstanding success

- Meeting customer needs and acting as highly effective sales consultant

- Analyzing historical, competitive, product and program sales

- Packaging, pricing and positioning successful product mix

- Designing cooperative advertising and promotions

- Devising new ways of doing business and selling products

- Implementing new programs

- Training motivated sales representatives

Taking the Next Step

Your resume is a picture of you: highly qualified, experienced, professional, and outstanding in a certain field. The process of writing your resume will be positive and motivating. Not only will you feel good about marketing yourself to a new position, you will want to achieve more so that your resume will get better and better.

Now that you have an overview of the federal resume, the next step is to find a federal vacancy announcement. Chapter 2 will give you information about how to find vacancy announcements. That chapter will also tell you how to read, analyze, and understand the information in the announcement.

The New Federal Employment Process— Search, Analyze, and Apply

Thanks to technology and the federal government's efforts to modernize the way it hires employees, finding and applying for a federal job is now much easier than it used to be. To show how serious it was about making the process easier, the federal government scrapped the cumbersome, lengthy job application form it had used for decades and permitted applicants to use resumes, as explained in Chapter 1. Doing away with the intimidating and highly structured SF 171 was only one of many changes the government made to create a hiring system that is more flexible, responsive, and applicant friendly. Now, as the OPM says in its *Straight Talk on the Federal Job Search*, you can forget what you have heard about the complexities in finding a federal job. "We have made the process simple! Your job search for federal career opportunities is now a three-step process."

OPM has developed the Federal Employment Information System to assist you in your job search. The system is composed of the user-friendly components described next in Step 1. By using the system, you have access to not only federal job listings but also some state and local government job listings and some from the private sector. The system provides current information that is updated daily and available 24 hours a day, seven days a week.

Step 1: Find the Job You Want

Use any of the following components of the Federal Employment Information System to search for job opportunities.

OPM's Worldwide Web Site: www.usajobs.opm.gov

This Internet-based system, called USAJOBS, provides access to the Federal Jobs Database of worldwide opportunities; full-text job announcements; answers to frequently asked federal employment questions; and access to electronic and hard copy application forms. To use this system, you will need a personal computer with a modem and access to the Internet.

The Career America Connection

This is a telephone-based system that provides instant access to current worldwide federal job opportunities, salary and employee benefits information, student employment programs, special recruitment messages, and more. You can also record your request to have application packages, forms, and other employment-related literature mailed or faxed to you. To access the Career America Connection, call (912) 757-3000 seven days a week, 24 hours a day. A Telephone Device for the Deaf (TDD) is available at (912) 744-2299. For an up-to-date list of local phone numbers for Career America Connection, call the above number and request Federal Employment Info Line fact sheet EI-42, *Federal Employment Information Sources.*

OPM's Federal Job Opportunities Bulletin Board (FJOB)

This computer-based bulletin board system provides current worldwide federal job opportunities, salaries and pay rates, general and specific employment information, and more. You must have a personal computer with a modem to dial up this system at (912) 757-3100. Many of the jobs announced on the FJOB have complete text announcements attached to them that you can download, view online, or have mailed to you.

You can also access this bulletin board via the Internet at fjob.opm.gov for Telnet or ftp.fjob.opm.gov for File Transfer Protocol. Information about obtaining federal job announcement files via Internet mail should be directed to info@fjob.opm.gov.

Federal Job Information Touch-Screen Computers

Kiosks with touch-screen computers are located throughout the nation in OPM offices, federal office buildings, and other locations. Using the touch-screen computers, you can access current worldwide federal job opportunities, online information, and more with the touch of a finger. You can also use them to request that application packages, forms, and other employment-related literature be mailed to you.

For an up-to-date list of touch-screen computer locations, use one of the components of the Federal Employment Information System to request Federal Employment Info Line fact sheet EI-42, *Federal Employment Information Sources.*

FedFax Service

This facsimile service does not contain vacancy announcements or job listings, but it does allow you to obtain a hard copy of employment-related information at any fax machine in the world, 24 hours a day, seven days a week. Simply use a touch-tone telephone or fax machine and select the information or form you wish to have faxed to you. FedFax is available at the following numbers: Atlanta, (404) 331-5267; Denver, (303) 969-7764; Detroit, (313) 226-2593; San Francisco, (415) 744-7002; and Washington, D.C., (202) 606-2600.

Full-Text Announcements

You can obtain full-text vacancy announcements from OPM's Web site (www.usajobs.opm.gov), the Federal Job Opportunities Bulletin Board, or federal job information touch-screen computers. In many cases, you will be able to complete an application online and submit it electronically. The Federal Employment Information System is updated daily, so check it often for current listings.

Take advantage of the system's automated features. Remember, any requests you make that require manual operations, such as assembling information and mailing it to you, will take additional time for processing.

Other Sources

Although the Federal Employment Information System just described is the most comprehensive and efficient way to search for a federal job opportunity, it is not the only way. Following are some other sources of information about federal job vacancies you might want to include in your search for job opportunities with the federal government.

Agency announcements. Through individual agency personnel offices, agency bulletin boards, agency in-house employee newsletters, and increasingly through agency Web sites and other online information systems (including touch-screen computers), you can find job opening announcements. These sources are particularly valuable if you seek opportunities with a specific agency or if you know that one or more specific agencies are actively seeking people with your qualifications. This is sometimes the case, for example, when the Department of Veterans Affairs seeks nurses for DVA hospitals or when the Immigration and Naturalization Service seeks border guards.

Newspaper ads. In the Washington, D.C., area, the *Washington Post* lists positions almost every Sunday. Major metropolitan papers in other areas of dense federal employment will too. If a phone number appears in an ad, call to get a copy of the actual announcement.

Professional journals. Jobs requiring highly specialized skills such as nursing, banking, data processing, and technical writing can sometimes be found in publications of professional associations.

Job fairs. Government agencies sometimes hold or send representatives to job fairs. This does not happen with great frequency. When it does, you'll want to be ready to stand out from other applicants by having copies of a good federal resume written according to the guidelines in this book. You'll also want to be ready with a "sound bite"–a short statement of what your skills are and how you can contribute to the organization. You may be lucky and get to say more to the representative at the job fair. Very often, though, job fairs are crowded, and you have only a few seconds to get your point across.

Federal agencies usually use newspaper ads, notices in professional journals, job fairs, and other special recruitment activities as supplements to the Federal Employment Information System. Specifically, agencies use these other recruiting techniques when they are actively looking for people, usually people with specialized skills, to fill vacancies. You, on the other hand, are looking for a vacancy that matches your skills and interests. The best–the most reliable and consistent–way to do that is through the Federal Employment Information System described previously in this chapter. Although you might learn of a federal job vacancy in some other way, your best bet is to use the automated components of the system designed to help you find federal job opportunities.

The grapevine. Do you know someone who works in government? Who does this person work for? What is this person's job? Is this individual's agency growing or downsizing? Is it hiring? What kinds of people does the agency hire? How can you apply? Does the person you know have any clout with hiring managers? These are the questions you should ask your neighbor, golf partner, and fellow churchgoer. This person's agency might be adding a new program where it needs to hire more program managers, contract specialists, and computer specialists. This person might not know that you would like to work for the government and that you have expertise in a particular area. Network. Meet and talk with as many people as you can. You never know where you'll find a good lead.

> Often you can learn about a job opportunity through informal contacts.

Often you can learn about a job opportunity through informal contacts and then go to the Federal Employment Information System to get specific information. Federal employees and others who work in areas of high federal employment will tell you that the informal grapevine should not be overlooked as a job source. Think long range. Listen for new programs and initiatives, especially those that will require specialized technical skills. Watch news sources for federal offices and agencies that are moving or building new facilities. While existing employees are offered opportunities to move to the new agency or program site, many choose not to, thus creating opportunities for new employees. When an imminent relocation or new program is announced, you may find that you have time to master or expand technical skills of interest to that potential employer. You may have as much as six months or a year before the change. Find out what skills will be needed. Enroll in a course or technical training to make yourself more attractive professionally. Then, when the job openings are announced, you will be ready.

Reading and keeping your eyes open. Read federal newspapers, union newsletters, the federal page in your newspaper if it has one, the federal page in the *Washington Post* (available online at www.washingtonpost.com), and *Government Executive Magazine* (also available online at www.govexec.com) to stay on top of what's going on in government. You might see that a federal agency is relocating to your town or that an agency is taking on new duties. Like private-sector corporations, government organizations relocate, grow, expand, and change functions. By being aware of these changes, you can position yourself to take advantage of job opportunities that the changes might bring about.

> It's very, very important that you go over a job announcement carefully.

Step 2: Obtain and Analyze the Vacancy Announcement

Once you have found a job opportunity that interests you, get a copy of the vacancy announcement. As it is described in Step 1, you can do this directly through OPM's Web site, www.usajobs.opm.gov; OPM's Federal Job Opportunities Bulletin Board; or the federal touch-screen computers. You can also call the phone number in the ad or use any component of the Federal Employment Information System to leave your name and address and request a copy by mail. However you do it, get a copy of the vacancy announcement as soon as you can and study it thoroughly. Don't be intimidated by it. The announcement might look long and hard to read, but it really isn't once you know what to look for. It's very, very important that you go over it carefully. It's chock-full of information you need to know if you seriously want to get the job.

Hint: If the vacancy announcement is in tiny type and difficult to read, enlarge it. If it's in electronic form, display it on your screen or print it out in a larger font. If it's in hard copy form, recopy it on a photocopier that has an enlargement feature.

Sample Vacancy Announcements and Analyses

Next you'll find two typical vacancy announcements. One is for a secretary, with recruitment and selection handled directly by the hiring agency. The other is for a program analyst, with recruitment and selection handled by OPM's Service Center Center in Raleigh, North Carolina. For the second job, applicants can make a fully automated online application with Form C. Both were real job vacancies available to anyone via OPM's Web site, www.usajobs.opm.gov, in August 1998.

Announcement 1: Secretary, GS-0318-7/8

Here's a section-by-section analysis of the vacancy announcement for a secretary. This is an agency-serviced announcement requesting written KSAs and accepting your choice of a resume, OF 612, or SF 171.

USAJOBS FEDERAL–OPEN TO EVERYONE

CONTROL NO BE4530

SECRETARY (OFFICE AUTOMATION)

OPEN PERIOD 08/07/1998 - 08/27/1998

SERIES/GRADE: GS-0318-07/08

PROMOTION POTENTIAL: GS-08

ANNOUNCEMENT NUMBER: OS-98-139

DUTY LOCATIONS: 0001 WASHINGTON, DC

HIRING AGENCY: HHS, Ofc Sec Health and Human Services

REMARKS: No further information provided.

CONTACT: CARROL DUGGINS

PHONE: (202) 619-0146

INTERNET ADDRESS: WWW.DHHS.OS.GOV

BROGRAM SUPPORT CENTER

P.O. BOX 14840

SILVER SPRING, MD 20911-4840

First, for each job announcement in USAJOBS, a summary block precedes the full announcement. This summary provides essential information about the vacant position that helps you determine whether to look more closely at this announcement. It tells you it is a USAJOBS listing and a federal job vacancy. (USAJOBS also lists some state and local job vacancies as well as some from the private sector.) The control number will help you locate this announcement in USAJOBS if you want to come back to it later. Otherwise, this number is not very important to you.

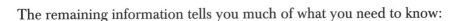

The remaining information tells you much of what you need to know:

☆ The vacancy is for a secretary who will be working with office automation equipment such as a computer with word processing and other software. The vacancy is open from August 7 through August 27.

☆ "Series/grade" refers to the federal government's system for defining jobs and establishing the rate of pay. This job, like most federal civil service jobs, is in the General Schedule (GS) pay system. It is in the 318 series (secretary) at the grade 7 or 8 level. If you're already a federal employee, you probably understand what this means. If you're new to the federal civil service, you might want to find out more about job classification and pay. The USAJOBS Web site is a good place to start. For example, under "General Information" and then "Federal Salary and Benefits," you can look up "General Schedule Pay." There you would learn that in August 1998, basic pay for a GS-7 position was $24,734 per year, and basic pay for a GS-8 position was $27,393. Locality pay adjustments, the Web page said, could increase those amounts by 5.6 to 12 percent. As mentioned earlier in this chapter, USAJOBS is part of the OPM's Web site. From OPM's home page (www.opm.gov), you can select "index" and then "classification" if you'd like to learn more about this subject.

☆ The announcement number *is* very important to you. This number tells the hiring agency exactly for which job you are applying. You must include this number in your application package. Put it on both your resume and cover letter.

☆ The job is located in Washington, D.C.

☆ The hiring agency is the headquarters office (the Office of the Secretary) of the U.S. Department of Health and Human Services. Direct agency recruitments usually require a resume, OF 612, or SF 171, plus written KSA statements.

☆ This announcement provides no information under "remarks." If the position were a temporary or part-time one, that would probably be noted here.

☆ The final item in this summary section provides the name and telephone number of a person you can call if you have any questions. For example, you might want to double-check the mailing address with Ms. Duggins before you copy "*B*rogram Support Center" on your envelope. You also can go to the hiring agency's Web site (www.dhhs.os.gov) and find out about the Office of the Secretary.

The full vacancy announcement then follows. If you're still interested in applying for this position, the full announcement repeats the information summarized at the beginning and provides more specifics.

> Department of Health and Human Services
>
> Program Support Center
>
> Human Resources Service
>
> Personnel Operations Division

This is the full name of the personnel office issuing the vacancy announcement. It is probably not the office in which the vacant position exists. (Here you learn that it is the "*P*rogram Support Center" and don't have to call Ms. Duggins about *that*. Hey, mistakes like this are bound to happen—at least until they can get *you* on the job.)

> APPLICATIONS MUST BE POSTMARKED BY THE CLOSING DATE
>
> Announcement Number: OS-98-139
>
> Opens: 08-07-98
>
> Closes: 08-27-98

Closing dates are important. This application must be *postmarked* by the closing date. Say it is now August 26, 1998, and you're seeing this for the first time. What do you do? You could call Ms. Duggins and ask if the closing date is likely to be extended. Sometimes open periods are extended. It's worth a shot.

If she says no, then you'll have to slap something together tonight and get it postmarked by August 27. Otherwise, forget about this job and go on to another announcement. Fortunately, you are a well-organized person whose resume is already in your computer. All you need to do is make some minor changes, print out a fresh copy, and the job is practically yours. Of course don't stop reading here; check if KSAs are needed for this application.

> Relocation Expense: No
>
> Supervisory/Managerial Position: No
>
> Bargain Unit Position: Yes

The government is not willing to pay relocation expenses to fill this position. It is assuming it can find a qualified person for this job in the Washington, D.C., commuting area and save the taxpayers' money by not paying for moving expenses. You also learn that the job is not a managerial one. Finally, the job is in the bargain*ing* unit. (Another little

typo and another instance in which you might want to look up more information, this time on labor-management relations in the federal government.) Being in the bargaining unit means the job is covered by an agreement between the office of the Secretary and the union or other organization the Office recognizes as the official representative of its employees. When you get the job, you won't have to join that organization. But you'll be represented by it and protected by the terms of its agreement with management anyway.

> Competitive Status: No
>
> Number of Vacancies: One (1)
>
> Promotion Potential: To GS-8

You don't need to have "competitive status" to apply for this job. Once you have successfully held a federal job for at least one year, you'll earn competitive status and can apply for jobs open only to federal employees or former federal employees who have earned status within the competitive civil service.

We're talking about only one job here. Sometimes one vacancy announcement is used to fill several identical jobs.

It may be only one job, but it is a job with *promotion potential*. That means the hiring agency can bring you on as a GS-7 initially and then, after you have become more proficient and experienced, promote you to GS-8. Many vacancy announcements say "none" for promotion potential. If this one had said "none," it would mean you'd stay a GS-7 for as long as you were in this position. You would be eligible for pay raises—annual pay adjustments and step increases. But you wouldn't be promoted. To become a GS-8, you'd have to find, compete for, and be hired to fill another position, one classified at the GS-8 level. You'd leave your old GS-7 position behind, and the Office of the Secretary would have to hire someone else.

> Organizational Location and Duty Station:
>
> DHHS, OS, Office of the Assistant Secretary for Planning and Evaluation, Office of Health Policy, Division of Health Financing Policy, Washington, D.C.

Just in case you thought "Office of the Secretary" meant a snug little place with deep carpet just outside a Cabinet member's door, here's a more detailed description of your new job's location: It's in Washington, D.C., and it's in the Office of the Secretary of the Department of Health and Human Services. But between the "DHHS, OS" and the

"Washington, D.C." are three more organizational levels. (Hey, if you hate bureaucracy, you probably shouldn't be looking for government work. On the other hand, if you are fascinated by large organizations and how talented and dedicated people make them work, stay with me. Uncle Sam needs you.)

> Area of Consideration: ALL SOURCES NON-STATUS APPLI-CANTS INCLUDED

This represents both good news and bad news. The good news: If you're trying to get into the federal government from the "outside," you have a shot. The bad news: A huge number of people will apply, including people with many years of experience inside government, inside *this* office. Your application is going to have to be very special to stand out.

> Duties and Responsibilities: The incumbent independently performs a variety of secretarial and administrative duties requiring a knowledge of the problems and activities of the office. Specific functions include but are not limited to: screening all callers and visitors; making arrangements for meetings and conferences including space, time, participants, and similar matters; maintaining control on incoming and outgoing correspondence; keeping supervisor's calendar; searching, assembling, compiling, and summarizing highly specialized materials and information from a variety of office files and sources; making all arrangements for travel; composing and drafting memoranda, correspondence, and similar material concerning general inquiries; typing highly technical and complex materials into draft or final form.

This is what your new organization will be expecting you to be able to do. Be sure your resume reflects your abilities to carry out the duties and responsibilities of the position. The language and keywords in the description should be reflected in your resume.

> SMOKE FREE WORKPLACE

This is good news if you hate secondhand smoke. It could be bad news if you're a smoker.

> Qualification Requirements:
>
> Fifty-two (52) weeks of specialized experience directly related to the line of work of the position to be filled which has equipped the

> applicant with the particular knowledge, skills, and abilities to successfully perform the duties of the position. To be creditable, specialized experience must have been at least equivalent to the next lower grade level.

This is what you need to qualify for this job. If you're already a federal employee, you need to have been in a GS-6 position—or a position equivalent to a GS-6—for at least a year. What if you've never been a federal employee? How do you know if your experience is "equivalent to the next lower grade level"? You can contact the OPM and ask for information on qualification standards (its Web site has little useful information on this topic but much on classification). Or you can call Ms. Duggins. She should be able to explain it for you or to send you the information you need—the subject is "qualification standards."

Evaluation Criteria:

1. Ability to effectively organize the flow of administrative/clerical processes in an office.

2. Ability to organize and design a filing system.

3. Ability to make arrangements for such things as travel, conferences, and meetings.

4. Ability to locate and assemble information for various reports, briefings, and conferences.

5. Ability to compose nontechnical correspondence.

6. Skill in operating word processing equipment.

The Evaluation Criteria are more commonly known as KSAs, or Knowledge, Skills, and Abilities statements. This is the criteria by which the hiring agency will evaluate your application. Your package should include a statement on each of the criteria that demonstrates clearly to the evaluators that you have the abilities they are seeking. Be specific. Cite examples. Although this announcement says that KSAs are not mandatory, include them if they're listed in the announcement. See Chapter 10 for more on KSAs.

Where to mail applications: DHHS, PSC, Personnel Operations Division; P.O. Box 14840; Silver Spring, Maryland 20911-4840.

Where to hand carry applications: DHHS, PSC, Personnel Operations Division; 8455 Colesville Road Suite 700; Silver Spring, Maryland 20910.

When your application is complete, this is where to mail it or deliver it–in person or by messenger or delivery service. But before you do, be sure you have carefully followed these instructions:

HOW TO APPLY

YOU MAY APPLY FOR THIS VACANCY WITH A RESUME, THE OPTIONAL APPLICATION FOR FEDERAL EMPLOYMENT (OF-612), SF-171, OR ANY OTHER FORMAT YOU CHOOSE. YOUR APPLICATION OR RESUME MUST CONTAIN THE FOLLOWING:

JOB INFORMATION: Announcement number, title and grade(s) of the job for which you are applying.

PERSONAL INFORMATION: Full name; mailing address (with zip code); day and evening phone numbers; Social Security number; country of citizenship (most federal jobs require United States citizenship); Veterans preference (if claiming veterans preference, please attach DD-214 and if 10 points, also attach SF-15); reinstatement eligibility; highest federal civilian grade (give job series and dates held–verify with SF-50).

EDUCATION: High school (name, city, state, and zip code, if known); date of diploma or GED; colleges or universities attended (name, city, state, and zip code, if known); major, including type of degree(s) and year(s) received (if no degree, show total credits earned and indicate semester or quarter hours). Send a copy of your college transcript only if the job vacancy announcement requests it.

WORK EXPERIENCE: Give the following information for your paid and nonpaid work experience related to the job for which you are applying: job title (include occupational series, if applicable, and employer's name and address); duties and accomplishments; supervisor's name and phone number (indicate if we may contact your current supervisor); starting and ending dates (month and year); hours per week, and salary of each specific work experience.

OTHER JOB-RELATED QUALIFICATIONS: training (course titles and dates); skills (e.g. typing, computer, language, machine, etc.); certificates and licenses; honors, awards, and special accomplishments (e.g. publications, memberships in professional or honor societies, leadership activities, public speaking engagements and performance awards).

IF YOUR RESUME OR APPLICATION DOES NOT PRO-
VIDE ALL THE INFORMATION REQUESTED ABOVE, YOU
MAY NOT BE CONSIDERED FOR THE POSITION.

ADDITIONAL INFORMATION TO SEND:

- YOUR MOST RECENT SF-50 (NOTICE OF PERSONNEL
  ACTION) VERIFYING COMPETITIVE STATUS AND
  GRADE PROMOTION POTENTIAL FOR CANDIDATES
  WHO ARE SERVING OR WHO HAVE SERVED AT THE
  GRADE OF THE ADVERTISED POSITION(S).

- ALL STATUS CANDIDATES WHO WISH TO BE CON-
  SIDERED FOR STATUS AND NON-STATUS REFERRAL
  MUST SUBMIT TWO (2) APPLICATIONS.

- YOUR MOST RECENT PERFORMANCE APPRAISAL.

- A SUPPLEMENTAL STATEMENT ADDRESSING THE
  RANKING FACTORS LISTED IN THE ANNOUNCE-
  MENT (SUBMISSION IS ENCOURAGED BUT NOT
  REQUIRED).

The ranking factors mentioned here are the "evaluation criteria" discussed earlier. Although not required, an effective supplemental statement addressing these criteria is one way to make your application stand out. You could cover the evaluation criteria in your resume. Chapter 10 on KSA writing will help you immensely in writing the ranking factors (which are the same as KSAs).

The remaining sections of the announcement discuss the method that will be used to evaluate your application and other highly specialized topics that may not apply to you. Be sure to read these item and to ask Ms. Duggins if you have any questions.

Announcement 2: Program Analyst, GS-343-12/13

The following is a detailed look at a vacancy announcement for a GS-12 or 13 program analyst position. Like the announcement for the secretary position, it is an actual announcement from www.usajobs.opm.gov. And, like all announcements on USAJOBS, it begins with a summary section.

The OPM in Raleigh is handling candidate screening for the DOT. OPM uses an automated process, which requires Form C or an online supplemental qualifications statement, plus either an online or paper resume. Completing Form C is easier than writing KSAs. You can choose to do Form C with pencil and paper or online at USAJOBS.

USAJOBS FEDERAL–OPEN TO EVERYONE

CONTROL NO AR1726

PROGRAM ANALYST

OPEN PERIOD 08/10/1998 - 09/08/1998

SERIES/GRADE: GS-0343-12/13

PROMOTION POTENTIAL: GS-13

ANNOUNCEMENT NUMBER: AR1726

DUTY LOCATIONS: 0001 WASHINGTON, DC

HIRING AGENCY: DOT, U.S. Coast Guard

REMARKS: PCS/RELOCATION EXPENSES ARE NOT AUTHORIZED. APPLICANTS WHO FILE THE ONLINE RESUME MUST ALSO COMPLETE AND FILE EITHER THE ONLINE SUPPLEMENTAL QUALIFICATIONS STATEMENT OR A HARD COPY FORM C IN ORDER TO BE CONSIDERED. SEE FULL TEXT VACANCY ANNOUNCEMENT FOR DETAILS.

CONTACT: USAJOBS BY PHONE

PHONE: (919) 790-2822

INTERNET ADDRESS: RALEIGH@OPM.GOV

U.S. COAST GUARD

C/O US OFFICE OF PERSONNEL MGT

RALEIGH SERVICE CENTER

4407 BLAND RD. #200

RALEIGH, NC 27609

This position is open to all applicants. You don't have to be a federal employee to apply. The control number is for reference within the USAJOBS listing only. It's not very important to you.

This announcement is for a program analyst, GS-0343-12/13. This string of letters and numbers tells those familiar with the federal civil service that the job is in the General Schedule pay system and that it has been classified in the 0343 series (program analyst) at the 12 or 13 level. If you are unfamiliar with all this, you probably should take some time to learn

more about it. More information on classification and pay is available from the OPM Web site (www.opm.gov) and from the personnel office issuing this announcement.

The personnel office issuing the announcement is identified under "contact," the last item in the summary box. Unfortunately, the contact information provided on this announcement, unlike the one for the secretary position, does not include a specific name. That's because this is an OPM-serviced recruitment. You can e-mail the Raleigh Service Center with questions. (The phone number provides a recording about the job.)

The OPM is a human resource center for government agencies now. You will see many announcements handled by the OPM, with more automated features.

After "series/grade," the announcement tells you that this job has promotion potential. That means, if you hire into this position as a GS-12, you can be promoted to GS-13 without further competition. If you're already a GS-13 and would be willing to take the job as a lateral transfer, the hiring agency can bring you into the position as a GS-13. However, once you've reached the GS-13 level in that position, you can't be promoted in that specific position. That is, you'll be eligible for annual pay adjustments and step increases, but you cannot promoted to GS-14. To do that, you'll have to find and compete successfully for another position, one at the GS-14 level.

Competition among many applicants for any given job is a general principle in the U.S. civil service. Finding a GS-12 position with promotion potential to GS-13 is somewhat unusual. Its promotion potential makes this job particularly well worth applying for. However, it also makes it harder to get. You'll be competing with experienced candidates from outside the federal civil service as well as current and former federal employees who are or were program analysts at the GS-11, GS-12, and GS-13 levels.

This job announcement was open from August 10 to September 8, 1998. Of course, it's closed now. So in actual practice you'd skip this one and move on. But assume the dates are in the near future. Maybe even too near. Say it closes tomorrow. You could decide not to bother with it, or you could contact the hiring agency and ask if the open period is likely to be extended. You might get lucky. Otherwise, you'll have to find a way to get your application package to OPM's Raleigh, North Carolina, service center before close of business tomorrow. You could complete Form C online and fax your resume. Be aware that the fax will be busy during official hours.

The announcement number is AR1726. This is the important number. You should put this in your cover letter or on your resume and preferably both. It is the number everyone uses to identify this particular job. (In this case, it is also the "control number." But that's not always true. The secretary announcement had different control and announcement numbers. The announcement number is the one you need to care about.)

The job is located in Washington, D.C. The 0001 means only one job is being filled with this announcement (as opposed, apparently, to 9,999). Anyway, I used the e-mail address to ask. Someone responded promptly: "It means there is one vacancy." (I also asked why a recorded job announcement was listed as a contact number, but no one responded to that.)

The hiring agency is the U.S. Department of Transportation (DOT), U.S. Coast Guard. The remarks tell you that the government will not pay to relocate you to Washington, D.C. They also tell you that you can file for this job electronically as well as by mail. (Here's the answer if you need to get your application in right away.) You can apply for this job online, but the online resume might be too brief. It's better to mail or fax your federal resume. The block following the summary block tells you how to submit an online resume. But if you do that, the remarks point out, you'll have to also submit an "online supplemental qualifications statement," which is discussed in the body of the announcement.

If you don't want to do the online supplemental qualifications statement, you can submit Form C. Form C is a machine-gradeable form available from any OPM office, including the one in Raleigh identified as this announcement's contact. The announcement includes instructions for filling out Form C, but it does not include the form itself.

The rest of the vacancy announcement repeats the address of the hiring personnel office—the OPM Raleigh Service Center, the title of the vacancy announcement, the announcement number, and the opening and closing dates. It provides the additional information that the exact deadline is 5 p.m. on the closing date:

U.S. Office of Personnel Management

Raleigh Service Center

4407 Bland Road, Suite 200

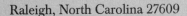

Raleigh, North Carolina 27609

Phone: (919) 790-2822; Fax #: (919) 790-2824

E-Mail: RALEIGH@OPM.GOV

VACANCY ANNOUNCEMENT FOR PROGRAM ANALYST, GS-0343-12/13 WITH THE U.S. COAST GUARD, WASHINGTON, DC

ANNOUNCEMENT NUMBER: AR1726

OPEN DATE: 08/10/98
CLOSING DATE: 09/08/98

●● Your completed application MUST be received in the Raleigh Service Center by 5:00 PM on the closing date, 09/08/98, to receive full consideration. ●●

The announcement next provides more specific information about the position. You should read this information carefully and have it in mind when you write your resume and complete Form C or the online supplemental qualifications statement.

ABOUT THIS POSITION: This position is located in the Program Development and Implementation Division, Office of Boating Safety. The incumbent assists in the daily administration of the Program Development and Implementation Division to ensure Division programs and projects are technically sound and consistent with U.S. Coast Guard goals and Congressional intent. The incumbent will provide technical leadership and continuity necessary for planning, directing, and executing the Division's program development and implementation operations. Additionally serve as technical advisor for the Program Development and Implementation Division on matters related to acquisition and procurement. PCS/RELOCATION EXPENSES ARE NOT AUTHORIZED.

The following seems clear enough:

BASIS OF RATING: Competitors will be rated on the basis of the extent and quality of experience and training relevant to the duties of the position, based on information contained in their applications and their responses to the questions on the Supplemental

(continued)

(continued)

Qualifications Statement found in the following pages. Answers to the questions MUST be provided on the Form C (by mail) or via the Internet at the OPM Web site (see below). INCOMPLETE APPLICATIONS MAY RESULT IN A LOWER OR INELIGIBLE RATING.

> **An HR professional "grades" your application much as a teacher grades an essay test.**

This statement says your application will be rated on the quality of your experience and training relevant to the duties of the position—*based on the information you put in your application package.* But what does the agency mean by "rated"? And who does the rating?

You've probably heard of civil service examinations; written tests used to be widely used in filling civil service jobs. You'd sit down and take a test, just like in school. The test would be graded, and you'd get a numerical score. If you were among the top scorers, you'd be called in for an interview. If you didn't score well, you'd know not to expect a call.

Although written tests are still used in filling some positions, most professional-level jobs like this one are filled on the basis of "rating" application packages. Basically, an HR professional grades your application much as a teacher grades an essay test. The review of your package *is* the exam. You want to earn as many points from the rater as you can. And remember, all that rater has to go on is what you tell him or her in your application.

So, your package has to be as thorough and complete as you can make it. Submitting an incomplete application, as a practical matter, is completely out of the question. As noted above, a vacancy announcement like this will result in hundreds of application packages flooding into the processing personnel office. If your package is not complete—and completely convincing—it won't make the cut. You won't stand a chance of getting the job—no matter how well qualified you are—if the rater does not understand from your application package and from that package alone how well qualified you are.

TO APPLY BY MAIL, YOU MUST REQUEST APPLICATION MATERIALS BY CALLING (919)790-2822, and leave your name, address, and the announcement # of the position you wish to apply for; OR WRITE: U.S. Office of Personnel Management, Raleigh Service Center, 4407 Bland Road, Suite 200, Raleigh, North Carolina 27609.

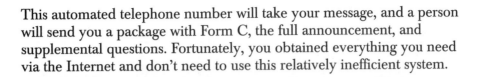

This automated telephone number will take your message, and a person will send you a package with Form C, the full announcement, and supplemental questions. Fortunately, you obtained everything you need via the Internet and don't need to use this relatively inefficient system.

> TO APPLY VIA THE INTERNET (HTTP://WWW. USAJOBS.OPM.GOV): You can use your computer to access our Internet site where you can search for current job openings and file an application online instead of completing the Form C by mail. After completing the questionnaire online, you MUST send your resume and any other required forms (except the Form C) to our office, listed above. If sending your resume from the Web site, you MUST complete the Supplemental Qualifications Statement online also. If applying online, you MUST do so before midnight Eastern Time of the closing date.

Not only did you get this announcement from the Internet, but you can submit your entire application package electronically. You can also prepare your resume and the supplemental qualifications statement the old-fashioned way—on paper—and mail it. The former offers the advantage of speed and convenience. The latter gives you more time for polish and review. If you opt for electronic submission, you should take the time, if you have it, to prepare and review your package offline. Having a third party review your package before you send it could make the difference between your getting that interview or not. A minor point: Electronic submission gives you until midnight of the closing date. Hard copy has to be in by 5 p.m.

Next, read the following instructions. If you have any questions about them, contact the hiring office. The business about a "DD-214" and "veterans' preference" applies only to people who have served in the U.S. Armed Services. If you're a veteran and you don't understand this, you should find out more about it before you apply.

> **Be sure to put the announcement number on every page of your package and on the envelope.**

The point about putting the announcement number on the package bears repeating. *Be sure to put the announcement number on every page of your package and on the envelope.*

> PLEASE CHECK THAT THE FOLLOWING MATERIALS ARE INCLUDED IN YOUR APPLICATION PACKAGE & SEND THEM TO THE ADDRESS SHOWN ABOVE: your completed
>
> *(continued)*

(continued)

Form C (unless applying electronically—see above); your application/ resume; a list of your college courses, if relevant; your DD-214 if claiming veterans' preference; and your SF-15 and proof of preference if claiming 10-points veterans' preference. If you fax your application to us, please try to do so after regular business hours and do NOT include certificates, references, or other information/documents not specifically requested. BE SURE TO WRITE THE ANNOUNCE-MENT NUMBER ON THE FRONT OF YOUR APPLICATION TO ENSURE ITS QUICK PROCESSING.

The next lines are something you should probably ask about before applying. It seems to be boilerplate medical information. At least it was probably so regarded by the person who apparently tossed it into this vacancy announcement. Does this job have medical requirements? If so, what are they? Why aren't they spelled out? It's something you'd probably want to clarify before proceeding, unless you like surprises.

MEDICAL REQUIREMENTS: Eligibles are subject to meeting the medical requirements of the position, if any. This determination will be made at the time of appointment.

The next paragraph makes a good point: You don't have to be paid to earn experience the HR professional will give you credit for. Volunteer service relevant to the job you're applying for counts.

CREDIT FOR VOLUNTEER SERVICE: Credit will be given for appropriate unpaid experience or volunteer work on the same basis as paid experience, provided it is directly related to the job for which you are applying. To receive proper credit, you must show the actual time spent in such activities.

Picky, but clear:

NOTE: Only education or experience acquired before the filing deadline will be considered.

The next description of Qualification Requirements is probably clear—if you're already a federal employee. If, however, you're not sure what work experience is "equivalent to" the GS-11 or GS-12 levels, you may want to find out more about "qualification standards." Ask an HR professional. Qualification standards define the characteristics an *individual* must have at the various GS levels. These are different from the "classification standards" that describe the characteristics of *positions* at the various GS levels.

QUALIFICATION REQUIREMENTS:

This position may be filled at either the GS-12 or 13 levels. To qualify, applicants must have:

At the GS-12 level:

Completed 1 year of full-time work experience (equivalent to the GS-11 level in the federal service) serving as a liaison responsible for coordinating program initiatives with various states, boating organizations, boat manufacturers, national nonprofit/boating agencies, and federal agencies to ensure goals are met in implementation of a national Recreational Boating Safety Program; providing technical and analytical support on recreation boating safety matters; and developing standards for evaluating the effectiveness of program initiatives in meeting program objectives.

At the GS-13 level:

Completed 1 year of full-time work experience (equivalent to the GS-12 level in the federal service) serving as a liaison responsible for coordinating program initiatives with various states, boating organizations, boat manufacturers, national nonprofit/boating agencies, and federal agencies to ensure goals are met in implementation of a national Recreational Boating Safety Program; providing technical and analytical support on recreation boating safety matters; developing standards for evaluating the effectiveness of program initiatives in meeting program objectives; developing detailed responses to complex proposals to ensure completeness and compliance with an organization's existing policy; and analyzing technical proposals and interpretations of rules, regulations and standards for their impact on a program.

Unless you are a "surplus or displaced federal employee," the following guidelines don't apply to you. If you are and have questions, contact the servicing personnel office.

PRIORITY CONSIDERATION FOR SURPLUS OR DISPLACED FEDERAL EMPLOYEES

THE CAREER TRANSITION ASSISTANCE PROGRAM (CTAP) AND THE INTERAGENCY CAREER TRANSITION ASSISTANCE PROGRAM (ICTAP) grant priority consideration to displaced federal civilian employees. If you are an employee of the Transportation Department who has received a Reduction in Force (RIF) separation notice or a Certificate of Expected Separation within the last year, then you are eligible to apply under the CTAP. If you are a displaced federal employee from a different agency, then you may be entitled to receive special priority selection under the ICTAP. To receive this priority consideration you must:

1. Be a displaced federal employee. The following categories of candidates are considered displaced employees. You must submit a copy of the appropriate documentation such as RIF separation notice, letter from OPM or your agency documenting your priority consideration status with your application package.

    A. Current or former career or career-conditional (tenure group I or II) competitive service employees who: (1) Received a specific RIF separation notice within the last year; or (2) Separated because of a compensable injury, whose compensation has been terminated, and whose former agency certifies that it is unable to place; or (3) Retired with a disability and whose disability annuity has been or is being terminated; or (4) Upon receipt of a RIF separation notice retired on the effective date of the RIF and submits a Standard Form 50 that indicates "Retirement in lieu of RIF"; or (5) Retired under the discontinued service retirement option; or (6) Was separated because he/she declined a transfer of function or directed reassignment to another commuting area.

    B. Former Military Reserve or National Guard Technicians who are receiving a special Office of Personnel Management (OPM) disability retirement annuity under section 8337(h) or 8456 of title 5 United States Code; or

2. Be applying for a position at or below the grade level of the position from which you have been separated. The position must not have a greater promotion potential than the position from which you were separated.

3. Have a current (or last) performance rating of record of at least fully successful or equivalent. This must be submitted with our application package. (This requirement does not apply to candidates who are eligible due to compensable injury or disability retirement.)

4. Occupy or be displaced from a position in the same local commuting area of the position for which you are requesting priority consideration.

5. File your application by the vacancy announcement closing date and meet all the application criteria (e.g., submit all required documentation, etc.).

6. Be rated well-qualified for the position. To be considered well-qualified you must earn the score cutoff of 90 which distinguishes well-qualified candidates from minimally qualified candidates on the rating criteria developed for the position.

The following statement appears to be a footnote. It isn't. The asterisks are meant, along with all the capital letters, to call attention to the statement. It's an important operating principle of the federal personnel system—possibly the *most* important operating principle. In your job hunt and federal career, you will hear people speak of the "merit system." This, basically, is what they're talking about:

∗∗ APPLICANTS FOR FEDERAL EMPLOYMENT WILL RECEIVE CONSIDERATION WITHOUT REGARD TO ANY NON-MERIT FACTOR SUCH AS RACE, COLOR, RELIGION, SEX, SEXUAL ORIENTATION, NATIONAL ORIGIN, MARITAL STATUS, AGE (WITH AUTHORIZED EXCEPTIONS), POLITICAL AFFILIATION, OR DISABILITY. ∗∗

Next are the very important Form C instructions. Form C can be completed online or on paper and then mailed.

FORM C INSTRUCTION SHEET

You should use the following instructions to help you complete Form C (Qualifications & Availability Form). The instructions are numbered to match the section numbers on Form C. (If applying online, ignore #1 & #2.)

(continued)

(continued)

1. Write your NAME on the Form C.

2. Write PROGRAM ANALYST.

3. AR1726 (If you are applying online, you will need to enter the control number, AR1726. Then, you will be asked to enter the Vacancy Identification Number, AR81726.)

4. 0343 D

5. 81726

6. Enter 12 or 13 for the lowest pay grade you are willing to accept. Coding 12 will allow us to consider you for both positions if qualified.

7a-d. Leave blank

7e. Question 1: Are you currently an employee of this agency who has been declared surplus AND is requesting special priority selection consideration under that agency's Career Transition Assistance Program (CTAP)? Y = YES, N = NO.

7e. Question 2: Are you a displaced federal employee who is requesting special priority selection consideration under the Interagency Career Transition Assistance Program (ICTAP)? Y = YES, N = NO. [NOTE: If you answer YES to either question 1 or 2, you must meet the CTAP or ICTAP eligibility requirements AND submit supporting proof documentation. Refer to the Special Selection Priority Consideration Provisions for Surplus or Displaced Federal Employees section, earlier in this announcement for additional information.]

8. 001

9. 675 (This position is with the U.S. Coast Guard in Washington, D.C.)

10-11. Self-explanatory

12. Enter a telephone number where you can be reached and the best time of day to contact you.

13-16. Self-explanatory

17. See the Supplemental Questionnaire (below) for instructions for this section.

18-22. Leave blank

23. Use this section to mark your entitlement to veteran preference. If you are not entitled to veteran preference, mark "No preference claimed." Please note: Except for disabled veter-

ans, those whose entire period of military service began on or after October 15, 1976, must have: at least 24 months of continuous, active duty service, AND have served in a campaign or expedition for which a campaign medal has been authorized; OR, have served at least 1 day during the period 08/02/90 through 01/02/92 AND have 24 months of continuous, active duty service, or been a reservist activated during that period. Persons who retired from military service at the rank of major, lieutenant commander, or higher are not entitled to veteran preference except as disabled veterans. You must include a copy of your DD-214 with your application to receive veterans preference. (NOTE: Recent changes in the law also authorize the Armed Forces Expeditionary Medal for service in Bosnia during Operation Joint Endeavor (November 20, 1995–December 20, 1996) and Operation Joint Guard (December 20, 1996–to be determined). The Secretary of each military department must decide which members are eligible. The award of the Armed Forces Expeditionary Medal is qualifying for veterans preference. More information on veterans preference is available in the Vets Guide that can be found on the Internet at www.opm.gov.

24. Self-explanatory

25. Enter the dates of your military service. If you have no military service, leave this section blank.

26. You must sign and date this form certifying the accuracy of the information you provided.

Kick back for a few minutes, because the hard part is about to begin.

The following are continuing instructions for filling out Form C. You will need a number 2 pencil to darken the ovals completely. The supplemental qualifications statement and Form C are your first job interview. Take these questions seriously. Remember that you will be graded. Form C appears in Appendix C. Call to get an original, because it will be scanned.

This supplemental statement, along with a well-crafted resume, can make the difference between getting an interview and having your package tossed in the stack. Take your time. Give it your very best shot. Get help with it if you can. Good luck!

SECTION 17–SUPPLEMENTAL QUALIFICATIONS STATEMENT

In this section, you will answer questions that are especially relevant to this position. Please follow the directions in filling out Form C and be sure to use a #2 pencil to mark your responses, completely blackening each oval you choose and completely erasing any mistakes or stray marks. Also, PLEASE DO NOT SEPARATE THE PAGES, FOLD, STAPLE, OR PAPER CLIP YOUR FORM C, AND DO NOT SUBMIT PHOTOCOPIES OF YOUR FORM C AS THEY CANNOT BE PROCESSED BY OUR COMPUTER SCANNER. WARNING! YOUR ANSWERS WILL BE VERIFIED AGAINST INFORMATION PROVIDED IN YOUR APPLICATION OR BY REFERENCE CHECKS. BE SURE THAT YOUR APPLICATION MATERIALS CLEARLY CORROBORATE YOUR RESPONSES TO THE FOLLOWING QUESTIONS BY ADDRESSING SPECIFIC ASPECTS OF YOUR EXPERIENCE OR EDUCATION RELEVANT TO THIS POSITION. IF YOU EXAGGERATE OR FALSIFY YOUR EXPERIENCE AND/OR EDUCATION, YOU MAY BE REMOVED FROM EMPLOYMENT CONSIDERATION. YOU SHOULD MAKE A FAIR AND ACCURATE ASSESSMENT OF YOUR QUALIFICATIONS.

QUALIFICATION REQUIREMENTS

1. This section will be used to determine if you possess the background needed to qualify for this position. From the descriptions below, choose the letter beside the statement that BEST describes your background relevant to this position. Darken the oval corresponding to that letter in Section 17, number 1, on the Form C. SELECT ONE LETTER ONLY. FAILURE TO RESPOND TO THIS QUESTION WILL RESULT IN YOUR BEING RATED INELIGIBLE.

    A. I have 1 year of full time work experience (equivalent to the GS-11 level in the federal service) serving as a liaison responsible for coordinating program initiatives with various states, boating organizations, boat manufacturers, national nonprofit/boating agencies, and federal agencies to ensure goals are met in the implementation of a national Recreational Boating Safety Program; providing technical and analytical support on recreation boating safety matters; and developing standards for evaluating the effectiveness of program initiatives in meeting program objectives.

B. I have 1 year of full time work experience (equivalent to the GS-12 level in the federal service) serving as a liaison responsible for coordinating program initiatives with various states, boating organizations, boat manufacturers, national nonprofit/boating agencies, and federal agencies to ensure goals are met in implementation of a national Recreational Boating Safety Program; providing technical and analytical support on recreation boating safety matters; developing standards for evaluating the effectiveness of program initiatives in meeting program objectives; developing detailed responses to complex proposals to ensure completeness and compliance with an organization's existing policy; and analyzing technical proposals and interpretations of rules, regulations, and standards for their impact on a program.

C. My background does not match any of the above choices.

RANKING CRITERIA

For each task in the following group (numbers 2–24), choose the statement from the list below (A–E) that best describes your experience and/or training. Darken the oval corresponding to that statement in Section 17, on the Form C. Please select only one letter for each item.

A. I have not had education, training, or experience in performing this task.

B. I have had education or training in performing this task, but have not yet performed it on the job.

C. I have performed this task on the job. My work on this task was monitored closely by a supervisor or senior employee to ensure compliance with proper procedures.

D. I have performed this task as a regular part of a job. I have performed it independently and normally without review by a supervisor or senior employee.

E. I am considered an expert in performing this task. I have trained others in the performance of this task or am normally the person who is consulted by other workers to assist them in doing this task because of my expertise.

● ● ● ● ● ● ● ● ● ● ● ● ●

2. Serve as a liaison responsible for coordinating program initiatives with states, boating organizations, boat manufacturers, national

(continued)

(continued)

nonprofit aquatic/boating agencies, and federal agencies to ensure goals are met in implementation of a recreation boating safety program.

3. Provide technical and analytical support on recreational boating safety matters.

4. Develop rationale and procedures to support technical and programmatic changes to applicable provisions to increase the effectiveness of a recreational boating safety program.

5. Develop detailed responses to complex proposals, ensuring completeness and compliance with organizational policy.

6. Prepare issue papers, special analyses, and reports on technical programmatic and developmental issues.

7. Develop and formulate awareness and implementation projects and coordinates in-depth review of all aspects of project management to ensure that organization intent for a program is implemented.

8. Develop standards for evaluating the effectiveness of program initiatives in meeting program objectives.

9. Develop program policies, processes, objectives, and strategies necessary to direct a program at a national level.

10. Assist in the development of a mutually acceptable project plan, which typically includes identification of the work to be done, the scope of the project, and deadlines for its completion.

11. Determine the appropriate course of action to achieve designed goals, and for carrying out the planned strategy to complete assignments.

12. Inform management of potentially controversial findings, issues, or problems with widespread impact.

13. Use computers to generate tables and spreadsheets.

14. Prepare oral and written reports and presentations, concisely and effectively, using learned evaluative and analytical methods and techniques.

15. Write narrative reports, memoranda, and correspondence.

16. Conduct briefings for managers.

17. Identify problems, gaps, and duplications, and take appropriate action to resolve such problems.

18. Recommend future administrative management goals and program direction for training and educational programs.

19. Develop standardized procedures, guidelines, and protocols for enhancing organizational operations.

20. Modify and/or adapt guidelines to fit the needs of program requirements.

21. Identify, monitor, track, and provide analysis of an organization's emerging program initiatives.

22. Recognize when issues have reached sufficient significance that they require management participation and/or attention.

23. Make recommendations on various processes and functions of an organization's program policy including analyzing new or proposed guidelines to determine impact on program operations.

24. Present recommendations to managers and negotiate solutions to disputed recommendations.

Using the OPM supplemental qualifications statement with Form C is easier than writing KSAs. You won't, however, be able to customize the information for your experience.

Step 3: Follow the Application Instructions

Once you have obtained and analyzed the vacancy announcement, follow the instructions it contains. You can apply for most jobs with a resume. You can, in most cases, also use the OF 612. However, the resume provides greater flexibility in presenting your qualifications and is rapidly becoming the format preferred by government employers. The OF 612 was developed primarily to help people—applicants and personnel specialists alike—make the transition from a highly structured form to the more flexible resume. For jobs that are unique or are filled through automated procedures, the vacancy announcement will specify special forms or provide special instructions.

Although the federal government does not require a standard application form for most jobs, it does require information usually not contained in a resume you'd submit to a nonfederal employer. The form OF 612 collects this information from you. When you use a resume to apply, you have to remember to include the following.

☆ **Job information:** Announcement number, title, and grade.

☆ **Personal information:** Full name, mailing address (with zip code), day and evening phone numbers (with area code), Social

Security number, country of citizenship, veterans' preference, reinstatement eligibility, highest federal civilian grade held.

☆ **Education:** High school name, city, and state; colleges or universities names, cities, and states; majors and type and year of any degrees received (if no degree, show total credits earned and indicate whether semester or quarter hours).

☆ **Work experience:** Job title, duties and accomplishments, employer's name and address, supervisor's name and phone number, starting and ending dates (month and year), hours per week, salary, and whether your current supervisor may be contacted. Prepare a separate entry for each job.

☆ **Other qualifications:** Job-related training courses (title and year), job-related skills, job-related certificates and licenses, job-related honors, awards, and special accomplishments.

Just Follow the Steps

That's really all there is to it. Three simple steps: find the vacancy, get the announcement, and do what it says.

The next chapters will tell you how to write a competitive, targeted federal resume section by section. You will get instructions and samples to make your application package stand out and help you get hired.

CHAPTER 3

Getting Started

To help you get started on your federal resume, the following section answers the questions frequently asked at my federal resume-writing workshops and on my Web site. After your basic questions are answered, you'll start writing your federal resume with job information and personal information.

Q. *I'm a federal employee. How am I going to edit my 20-plus page SF 171 down to a four- or five-page resume? That seems impossible.*

A. You will learn how to edit the work experience and training sections. You will also be gaining a great deal of white space that was lost to the form. Creating a four- or five-page federal resume will not be difficult with the resume-writing instructions in this and the next few chapters.

Q. *I'm a novice federal applicant. Why can't I just use the resume I have now to apply for a federal job?*

A. The federal resume is different from your private industry resume. If you submit your private industry resume, you will lose consideration for the job.

Q. *Where do I start with writing my federal resume?*

A. With this book, your SF 171 or existing resume, and your computer.

Q. *What do I save from my SF 171?*

A. You'll edit your SF 171 into a resume section by section in this and the following chapters.

Q. How far back should I go with my positions?

A. Ten years of employment with the compliance details; prior to ten years with a basic chronology if the positions and career history will be of interest to the hiring manager.

Q. How many pages should the resume be?

A. Three to five pages is the average length of the new federal resume.

Q. What resume format is generally used?

A. Reverse chronological format, with the most recent position first.

Q. Are the KSAs included in the resume?

A. The KSAs (Knowledge, Skills, and Abilities) are usually a separate mandatory statement required by each vacancy announcement. They are not part of the resume. They are separate answers to questions in the announcement that will demonstrate how qualified you are to perform a certain position. Your federal application package will include a resume, cover letter, KSAs, and other special forms required by the announcement. Chapter 10 will review how to write KSAs according to the vacancy announcement. You will write your KSAs based on the resume information you have developed.

If you have other questions not answered in this book, you can e-mail me at resume@ari.net.

Background on Federal Resume Writing

Federal resume-writing basics appear in the directions of every federal vacancy announcement and in the OPM's OF 510 brochure, *Applying for a Federal Job.* The federal government application process requires certain information be included in your resume.

Applying for a Federal Job

United States Office of Personnel Management

Here's what your resume or application must contain

(in addition to specific information requested in the job vacancy announcement)

JOB INFORMATION

- ❑ Announcement number, and title and grade(s) of the job you are applying for

PERSONAL INFORMATION

- ❑ Full name, mailing address *(with ZIP Code)* and day and evening phone numbers *(with area code)*
- ❑ Social Security Number
- ❑ Country of citizenship *(Most Federal jobs require United States citizenship.)*
- ❑ Veterans' preference *(See reverse.)*
- ❑ Reinstatement eligibility *(If requested, attach SF 50 proof of your career or career-conditional status.)*
- ❑ Highest Federal civilian grade held *(Also give job series and dates held.)*

EDUCATION

- ❑ High school
  - Name, city, and State *(ZIP Code if known)*
  - Date of diploma or GED
- ❑ Colleges or universities
  - Name, city, and State *(ZIP Code if known)*
  - Majors
  - Type and year of any degrees received *(If no degree, show total credits earned and indicate whether semester or quarter hours.)*
- ❑ Send a copy of your college transcript only if the job vacancy announcement requests it.

WORK EXPERIENCE

- ❑ Give the following information for your paid and nonpaid work experience related to the job you are applying for. *(Do not send job descriptions.)*
  - Job title *(include series and grade if Federal job)*
  - Duties and accomplishments
  - Employer's name and address
  - Supervisor's name and phone number
  - Starting and ending dates *(month and year)*
  - Hours per week
  - Salary
- ❑ Indicate if we may contact your current supervisor.

OTHER QUALIFICATIONS

- ❑ **Job-related** training courses *(title and year)*
- ❑ **Job-related** skills, for example, other languages, computer software/hardware, tools, machinery, typing speed
- ❑ **Job-related** certificates and licenses *(current only)*
- ❑ **Job-related** honors, awards, and special accomplishments, for example, publica–tions, memberships in professional or honor societies, leadership activities, public speaking, and performance awards *(Give dates but do not send documents unless requested.)*

> **THE FEDERAL GOVERNMENT IS AN EQUAL OPPORTUNITY EMPLOYER**

Applying for a Federal Job, OF 510, is the flyer that lists the information your resume must contain.

You will learn here and in the next few chapters how to package the required information into a succinct, job-related, compliant, and good-looking federal resume. You will see many examples of each required section of the federal resume. Now that the SF 171 fill-in-the-blanks format is eliminated, these explanations and samples of the important required information will be your federal resume-writing guide. By following my samples and directions, you will learn how to organize and format information to best present your experience for a specific position, satisfy requirements, and aesthetically please the HR professionals and the hiring manager.

The First Two Sections of a Federal Resume

> The easiest way for you to build your federal resume is section by section.

The easiest way for you to build your federal resume is section by section. You should build your federal resume a section at a time, without consideration for length. Later you will edit, rewrite, focus, and format the material. Now it's time to learn about the first two sections of your federal resume.

Job Information

```
JOB INFORMATION

❑ Announcement number, and title and
   grade(s) of the job you are applying for.
```

From OPM: the job information your federal resume must contain.

Every federal resume must include information about the job for which you're applying. Use the job title listed in the announcement as your objective. The vacancy announcement number should be listed on every page of your application, including the envelope.

"Grade" is the job's level of difficulty. If the job announcement specifies several grades (for example, GS 9/12), indicate only the highest grade(s) you are seeking. If you aren't sure which grade you're qualified for, list the entire range indicated in the announcement. Here's an example:

Objective: Secretary (Office Automation), GS-301-6/7
Announcement Number: 9015-NAR-001

Personal Information

PERSONAL INFORMATION

❏ **Full name, mailing address** *(with ZIP Code)* **and day and evening phone numbers** *(with area code)*

❏ **Social Security Number**

❏ **Country of citizenship** *(Most Federal jobs require United States citizenship.)*

❏ **Veterans' preference**

❏ **Reinstatement eligibility** *(If requested, attach SF 50 proof of your career or career-conditional status.)*

❏ **Highest Federal civilian grade held** *(Also give job series and dates held.)*

From OPM: the personal information your federal resume must contain.

The personal information listed above is required on a federal resume. If you are a first-time federal resume writer and former SF 171 writer, you will be impressed with how outstanding your personal information can look with white space, professional-looking type fonts, and headline size type. This information gives the first impression about you, so select a format that you like.

> **HR professionals will appreciate the time and effort it took to create an excellent package.**

Private industry resume writers have always enjoyed the opportunity to create stand-out resumes, and they start with your personal information at the top. It is believed that a resume's appearance can make a difference in hiring and build personal confidence in the job search. HR professionals will appreciate the time and effort it took to create an excellent, job-related package.

If you are a novice federal applicant, you will not be impressed with the additional information required for the federal resume. You might think this information will clutter your resume. You will not be accustomed to including your Social Security number, citizenship, veterans' preference, and highest grade held on the top of your resume. The federal resume is a transition from a lengthy, detailed application form and still includes some specific personnel information required on the earlier form. You will need to include all of the required information if you wish to be a serious candidate for a federal job. Just be thankful that you don't have to complete the SF 171.

Whichever type of federal applicant you are, page 1 of your resume must include the required personal information, or you may lose consideration for a federal job.

Special Instructions on Each Item

Full name, mailing address, day and evening phone numbers. You can also include your e-mail address at home or work (preferably at home for federal employees). In some agencies, your office e-mail is considered government property, similar to government postage, letterhead, and envelopes. Do not use government property for job applications, or your resume will be rejected.

Social Security number. Most vacancy announcements require this. Sometimes, however, it is not required. Read your announcement carefully.

Country of citizenship. Most federal jobs require United States citizenship. If you are not a U.S. citizen, give your country of citizenship.

Federal civilian status/reinstatement eligibility. Were you ever a federal civilian employee? If yes, write your highest civilian grade and give the job series, the grade level, and the dates you held that grade. Be sure to write the highest grade held, not the current or last grade. Here's an explanation of federal civilian personnel terms:

☆ *Reinstatement eligibility for current and former federal employees* means you are eligible for reinstatement based on career or career-conditional federal status. If you are eligible for reinstatement, attach Standard Form 50 as proof if the announcement requires it.

☆ *Status* means you are currently in a federal civilian job, or you formerly held a federal job and may be reinstated or rehired without competing again.

☆ *Career-conditional* is the initial appointment and leads to a permanent or "career" position after three years of satisfactory service.

Read your job announcement carefully to determine if the position is open to anyone or only to candidates with status. Sometimes the announcement will say "area of consideration" is "nationwide." In this case, the job is open to both status and non status applicants.

For example, if you are a current or former federal employee, write the following:

Federal Civilian Status: Writer-Editor, GS-301, 11/9, April 1993 to present

If you are not a current or are a former federal employee with no federal status, write the following:

Federal Civilian Status: N/A

Veterans' preference. Do you claim veterans' preference? If you have never been in the military, write "N/A" and leave the section at the top of the resume so that the HR professionals will not look for military experience. If the answer is yes, write the name of military service, dates, rank, and if you were honorably discharged.

Example if the answer is yes:

> **Veterans' Preference:** 5 point preference, U.S. Army, Sergeant, April 1991–April 1995, Honorably Discharged.

Example if the answer is no:

> **Veterans' Preference:** N/A

Generally, you will get 5 points added to your application evaluation rating if you were honorably discharged. Ten points are added if you are disabled, and in some cases if you are a spouse, widow, widower, or mother of a disabled veteran. If you claim 5 points, attach your DD-214 or other proof. If you claim 10 points, attach an Application for 10-Point Veterans' Preference (SF 15) and required proof.

Also write one of the following if they are applicable to you:

- ☆ 5-point preference based on active duty in the U.S. Armed Forces.

- ☆ 10-point preference for noncompensable disability or a Purple Heart.

- ☆ 10-point preference based on a compensable service-connected disability of more than 10 but less than 30 percent.

- ☆ 10-point preference based on wife, widow, or widower preference.

- ☆ 10-point preference based on a compensable service-connected disability of 30 percent or more.

How the Points Help Veterans Get Federal Jobs

Veterans meeting the criteria for preference and who are found eligible (achieve a score of 70 or higher either by a written examination or an evaluation of their experience and education) have 5 or 10 points added to their numerical ratings depending on the nature of their preference. For scientific and professional positions in grade GS-9 or higher, names of all eligible candidates are listed in order of ratings, augmented by veterans' preference, if any. For other positions, the names of 10-point preference eligible candidates who have a compensable, service-connected disability of 10 percent or more are placed ahead of the names of all other eligible candidates on a given register. The names of other 10-point preference eligibles, 5-point preference eligibles, and nonveterans are listed in order of their numerical ratings. More information on veterans' preference and employment programs can be found on OPM's Web site at http://www.usajobs.opm.gov/b2a.htm.

You will see examples of how to organize and present your reinstatement eligibility and veterans' preference in the samples that follow. The statements you will write on your resume are much simpler than the explanations just given.

Job and Personal Information Samples

The following three examples show how to format the job information and personal information sections.

EXAMPLE 1

KELVIN LEWIS GREENE
5008 Greenery Court
Ft. Collins, CO 90909
Home: (316)-899-9999
Work: (316)-888-8989
Email: kgreene@aol.com

Social Security Number:	222-22-2222
Citizenship:	United States
Federal Civilian Status:	Not Applicable
Veteran's Preference:	Five Points, Petty Officer 2nd Class, U.S. Army, 8/91-8/95, Data Processing Tech
OBJECTIVE:	Computer Specialist, Announcement Number 39-9809 Department of Commerce. Census Bureau.

EXAMPLE 2

ROBERTA E. SPENCER
124 3rd Street, NE, Apt. 301
Washington, DC 20002-3456
Home: (202) 567-8910
Work: (202) 267-9976, ext. 1001
email: rspencer@aol.com

Social Security Number:	345-87-6540
Citizenship:	United States
Veterans' Preference:	N/A
Federal Civilian Status:	Public Affairs Specialist, GS-12
OBJECTIVE:	Federal Aviation Administration International Aviation Operations Specialist AWA-AIA-96-137910590

EXAMPLE 3

RONALD B. AUGUSON

PERSONAL INFORMATION

Address:	3456 Hensley Road
	Pasadena, CA 90909
Telephones:	Home: (316) 779-5328
	Office: (316) 208-7654
	Email: rauguson@mindspring.com
Social Security Number:	925-24-5748
Citizenship:	United States
Reinstatement Eligibility:	Supervisory Criminal Investigator, GS-1811-14,
	April 1991 - present
Veterans' Preference:	U.S. Navy, June 1961 - August 1964
	5-point preference based on active duty in the U.S. Armed Forces.

OBJECTIVE	Supervisory Criminal Investigator, GS-1811-15
	USDA Announcement 97-23

You're off to a good start on your federal resume. In the next chapter, you will learn what to include in the education and training sections.

CHAPTER 4

Writing Your Educational Background

Your educational background is an important part of your federal resume. The amount of information you provide, the way you present the information, and the organization of this section can impress the HR professionals and hiring managers. The HR professionals are looking for specific degrees, majors, courses, and specialized training to determine whether you are qualified for the position. Some federal jobs require degrees. Other federal positions will accept specialized or generalized experience in place of college degrees. The federal job announcement is clear about the qualifications for the position. Read the "Specialized or Generalized Qualifications" section of the announcement to see whether you have the necessary educational qualifications for the position.

Here is the education information that must be on your federal resume, according to OPM brochure OF 510 and most announcements:

EDUCATION

❏ High school

    Name, city, and State *(ZIP Code if known)*

    Date of diploma or GED

❏ Colleges or universities

    Name, city, and State *(ZIP Code if known)*

    Majors

    Type and year of any degrees received

    (If no degree, show total credits earned and indicate whether semester or quarter hours.)

❏ Send a copy of your college transcript only if the job vacancy announcement requests it.

From OPM: the educational information your federal resume must contain.

Considerations for Organizing Your Educational and Training Background

One of the best features of using a resume instead of the SF 171 is that you can place your education section before work experience, if you wish to highlight a recent degree or course work. For recent and returned college graduates, you can include your educational honors, awards, scholarships, grade-point average, activities, significant courses, major papers or theses, and assistantships with each college listing. The HR professional will appreciate reviewing your entire educational background in a concise, organized format.

> **HR professionals will appreciate reviewing your educational background in a concise, organized format.**

Education is usually a separate category from training. In the education category, you will list your high school and college education and degrees. Your training, professional development, and continuing education (three suggested headings for this section, all with similar meanings) can be listed separately. You can combine the education and training sections if you wish to improve their presentation.

If you possess extensive job-related training, you can create functional headings for the training list. Many federal employees receive considerable training in computers, management, leadership, supervision, accounting, budget, contracts, and project management.

The OF 510 does not mandate inclusion of classroom hours, but some vacancy announcements will ask for classroom hours. Read the announcement to determine the information required, or include the hours just in case. Some announcements will want transcripts; others will not. College students and recent graduates can attach a course list if courses are significant in showing qualifications and performance for a particular federal job. A course list is especially helpful if your major qualifications for the job are your education, research papers, and courses. See Appendix A for a course list example.

Education Section Samples

Next, you'll find 12 examples of how to organize, present, and highlight your education and training sections. Not all of the samples include high school information, but you should provide it on your resume if mentioned in the job announcement. Next you'll find the samples arranged by the following federal applicant groups:

☆ No college degree

☆ Recent college graduates or those with new degrees

☆ GS-9 through GS-14 (current federal employees and first-time federal applicants)

☆ GS-15 through Senior Executive Service

No College Degree

According to Dennis Damp in *The Book of U.S. Government Jobs*, 63 percent of all federal workers do not have a college degree. The education level is dependent upon the position. In many cases for general administrative and management positions, you can replace a college degree with a certain number of years of specialized or generalized experience. You can read the qualifications required for each position in the announcement.

> Sixty-three percent of all federal workers do not have a college degree.

EXAMPLE 1: APPLICANT FOR GS-5 BORDER PATROL AGENT

This high school graduate worked as a border patrol agent on a contract basis in his senior year of high school and is seeking a permanent position with the Immigration and Naturalization Service. This is a combined education and training section.

> **EDUCATION AND TRAINING:**
> USDA Work Conference, 1998
> USDA APHIS VS Tick Identification and Awareness, 1998, 4 hours
> Federal Law Enforcement Firearms Training, 1998. Qualified to carry firearms.
> Pesticide School, 1998
> Graduated Carrizo Springs High School, Carrizo Springs, TX 78834, 1998

EXAMPLE 2: GS-8 SECURITY ANALYST WITH SPECIAL TRAINING

This current federal employee does not have a bachelor's degree but has completed a four-year government internship in computer programming analysis. High school information was not required by this announcement.

EDUCATION

USDA Graduate School   Fall 1998
Troubleshooting and maintaining the IBM PC, XT, AT and Compatibles, 40 classroom hours

Personnel Information Systems Command, Alexandria, VA   1992 - 1996
Internship, Computer Programmer Analyst, GS-334. Received extensive on-the-job training; see course list below.

Montgomery College, College Park, MD 20912   1988 – 1991
Completed 52 credit hours toward A.A. in Business Administration

PROFESSIONAL TRAINING

Security Systems
Internet and Systems Security: Attacks and Countermeasures, July 1997
PC/DACS for DOS and Windows, Utimaco Mergent, April 1997

Programmer Intern Training, Personnel Information Systems Command, Alexandria, VA, 1992-1996

Programming:
       Cobol: Structured Programming I, II, III
       MVS JCL and Advanced JCL
       CICS Programming

Database Management:
       Datacomm DB, ISPF, MS-DOS, DATA Reporter, Data Query, VSAM,
       DATA Collection Techniques

Security:
       Automated Information Systems Security

Word Processing and Graphics:
       Microsoft Windows 95
       Word for Windows

Project Management:
       Leadership
       Microsoft Project 4.0
       C4 Planning and Implementation Seminar
       Customer Relations

Systems Analysis

Recent College Graduates or Those with New Degrees

The education section for these job applicants is listed before the employment history.

EXAMPLE 3: NEW COLLEGE GRADUATE AND FIRST-TIME FEDERAL APPLICANT

This college graduate is pursuing a GS-7/9 position in aviation operations with the FAA.

EDUCATION

Bachelor of Arts, with Honors, AVIATION MANAGEMENT   June 1997
        University of California-Los Angeles, CA 98099

Aviation Planning: Aviation Forecasting, Airport Master Plan Development, Environmental Impact Assessment

Airport Design: Airport Capacity and Aircraft Delay, Runway Design, Taxiway and Apron Design, Aircraft Approach and Departures Paths, Airport Pavements, Terminal Building Development, Heliport Design

The National Airspace System

Advanced Computer Applications: SIMMOD and INM

Aviation Safety

Airport Management: NPIAS, Licensing and Certification, Maintenance, Emergency Plans, Security (FAR), Financial Management, Economics, Leases, Public Relations

---

EXAMPLE 4: NEW COLLEGE GRADUATE AND FIRST-TIME FEDERAL APPLICANT

This new graduate is seeking law enforcement positions. On his resume, the applicant included an extensive professional development training list and course descriptions.

EDUCATION

University of Maryland—Baltimore County, Baltimore, MD 21228
B.S. Degree, *Magna Cum Laude,* May 1997
GPA: 3.85/4.0
Major: Emergency Health Services—Paramedic Track
Semester Academic Honors: Fall 1996, Spring 1996, and Fall 1997
Member of Phi Kappa Phi National Scholastic Honor Society

Calvert Hall College High School, Baltimore, MD 21286
College preparatory, diploma, June 1993

PROFESSIONAL DEVELOPMENT

Specialized Training and Education in Controlled Dangerous Substances
University of Maryland—Baltimore County, Baltimore, MD, Spring 1997

University-level course in Medical Emergencies covering drug identification, pharmacology of illicit and prescription drugs, and treatment of drug-related emergencies. Included Controlled Dangerous Substance lecture given by Maryland State Police—Narcotics Division. The course also covered the 1970 Controlled Substances Act and schedule stratification of drugs according to their medical use and abuse potential.

Basic Police Training Course

Eastern Shore Criminal Justice Academy, Salisbury, MD, May 1996

Intensive one-month law enforcement training program for Ocean City Police Department recruits. Topics covered: firearms, PR-24 Police Baton, restraining devices, DWI, criminal law/investigation, report writing, constitutional law, domestic violence, drug identification, and court testimony.

Stevenson Volunteer Fire and Ambulance Company, Stevenson, MD, June 1995—Present

Active volunteer in community receiving extensive training and certifications. Currently certified as a NREMT-P, Nationally Registered Paramedic, Registry 4PO855719. Also, currently certified by the American Heart Association in ACLS—Advanced Cardiac Life Support, PALS—Pediatric Advanced Life Support, and CPR—Cardiopulmonary Resuscitation and Emergency Cardiac Care. Certified in the State of MD as Emergency Medical Technician.

Computer Related Skills and Training, Baltimore, MD, September 1996—Present

Knowledge of software packages including Microsoft Windows, Microsoft Works, WordPerfect, and a variety of multimedia application programs. Also familiar with Internet, email, and scanning technology.

EXAMPLE 5: RETURNING COLLEGE GRADUATE AND FIRST-TIME FEDERAL APPLICANT

This person is seeking a GS-9 international trade specialist position with the Department of Commerce. She included an extensive course list with her application; see the next page.

Educational Background

GEORGE MASON UNIVERSITY, FAIRFAX, VIRGINIA , 20989
       M.A. – INTERNATIONAL TRANSACTIONS, JANUARY 1997
          CONCENTRATION IN DEVELOPMENT ECONOMICS
         GPA 3.75/4.00
         Courses taken include Economic Analysis (macroeconomic theory and policies); International Finance and the Global Economy; Approaches to International Transactions (encompassing accounting for investments and foreign exchange); and Data Identification Analysis (quantitative methods). *See attached course descriptions.*

PRAIRIE VIEW A&M UNIVERSITY, PRAIRIE VIEW, TX 90909
       B.A. – ACCOUNTING, MAY 1980
         G.P.A. 3.56/4.00; National Dean's List, 1978-80

ARLINGTON BAPTIST HIGH SCHOOL, ARLINGTON, TX 90101
       GRADUATED 1977

Professional Development

American Management Association, Washington, D.C., 80 classroom hours, July, 1998

       Professional training in Corporate Financial Analysis: capital budgeting, financial forecasting, evaluating capital investment proposals, cash flow analysis, break-even analysis, cost-benefit analysis, income statement analysis, management contingencies factoring in risk, and more.

This list of international courses was provided on a separate sheet:

GEORGE MASON UNIVERSITY

1996-97 International Transactions Courses (INTL)

Offered by International Institute

Approaches to International Transactions
National economic policy and international trade, investment, and finance. National income accounting, balance of payments, and factors affecting foreign exchange rates. Comparison of national strategies for growth and development and in using political and economic analysis to assess the reasons for the choice of a national economic strategy and its relative effectiveness.

International Transactions and Culture
Examines and applies the major dimensions of cultural analysis to international transactions. Cultural perspectives that influence the flow of peoples, messages, goods, capital, and technology across national and cultural boundaries.

Economic Analysis for International Transactions
Foundation in international economics and the fundamentals of international trade, finance and transactions. The course focuses on alternative approaches to understanding the international economic system. Topics covered include problems in trade theory, exchange-rate determination, balance of payments, debt appraisal, and economic development.

Research and Analysis Methods
Qualitative and quantitative research and analysis of international trade and transactions. Develop tools for statistical analysis of data and includes use of computers for analyzing and displaying information. It covers major data sources as well as literature and indexes related to international transactions.

International Trade and Technology
Science and technology policies and international trade, with an emphasis on their relationships and interactions. The roles of science and technology as economic drivers are assessed, and the strategies employed by companies and governments to link research and development to economic growth and competitiveness are explored.

International Financial Institutions and Globalization
Roles of financial institutions in the international financial system. International finance; international, regional, and national financial organizations; and financial markets. Key policy issues such as the environment and externalities, equity issues and sectoral imbalances, the international debt crisis, and financial challenges facing the new and developing states are discussed.

International Business Operations and the Multinational Corporation
International business environment and the challenges facing companies of all types and sizes in conducting operations in an increasingly interconnected global marketplace.

International Trade Relations
Examines the role of the United States in the world economy and the evolving global trading system. Particular attention is given to domestic trading institutions.

EXAMPLE 6: GS-12 CURRENT FEDERAL EMPLOYEE COMPLETING MASTER'S DEGREE AND SPECIAL TRAINING

This federal employee is working on a master's degree and a DAWAI Certificate in Procurement and Acquisitions as part of a Career Track Program in Procurement with grade-level potential to GS-15. Note that the personal pronoun "I" is acceptable in federal resumes and KSAs.

EDUCATION

Master of Arts in Procurement and Acquisitions Management, 1998; GPA: 3.8
WEBSTER UNIVERSITY, Bolling AFB, Washington D.C.

Honors:
Distinguished Graduate
Thesis: Alternative Dispute Resolution

Defense Acquisition Workforce Improvement Act (DAWAI) - level I and level II certified
DEFENSE ACQUISITION UNIVERSITY, 1997; GPA: 4.0
Honors:
Distinguished Graduate for Automated Information Systems
Honor Graduate for Government Contract Law
Distinguished Graduate for Intermediate Contracting

Bachelor of Science Degree in Political Science, 1995; GPA: 3.5
BALL STATE UNIVERSITY, Muncie, Indiana
Minor in Military Science

Honors:
Dean's List and G.T.E. Academic All-American and scholar athlete award
in college football

RELEVANT COURSE WORK:
Information Technology Contracting, Information Systems Security, Computer Resources and Information Management, Contracting Fundamentals, Contract Pricing, Government Contract Law, Intermediate Contracting, Intermediate Contract Pricing, Congressional Research Training, Library of Congress Training, Negotiations, Logistics, Pricing, Operations Management, Security Management, Analysis of Management Systems, Proposal Preparation

SPECIALIZED TRAINING:
In addition to the skills I have learned as a contract specialist, I have also taken the following specialized training: Defense Acquisition University, Small Business Contracting, Commerce Business Daily Transmissions Using the Internet, Service Contract Act, Trade Agreements Act, HTML/Internet Programming and Usage, Defense Acquisition Workforce Improvement Act, Government Ethics, Security in the Workplace, Procurement Integrity Act, Blanket Purchase Agreements, Privacy Act and Freedom of Information Act, Communications with Congress and Department of Defense Heads. (All of the above training took place from 1994 to 1997 and lasted from 2 hours to 4 weeks).

GS-9 through GS-14

EXAMPLE 7: PRIVATE INDUSTRY PROFESSIONAL PURSUING FIRST POSITION IN GOVERNMENT

After working in private industry, this individual is applying for a position as a GS-9 marketing specialist with the U.S. Postal Service. Notice how she lists her graduate school hours. She has not completed the degree.

EDUCATION

Graduate Studies, MORGAN STATE UNIVERSITY, Baltimore, MD, 21229
Completed 12 hours in Marketing Management
Courses: Strategic Planning, Writing a Business Plan, Economics I, 1997-1998

BS., Psychology, MORGAN STATE UNIVERSITY, Baltimore, MD, 21229, 1996

SPECIAL TRAINING

Microsoft Office including Word for Windows, PowerPoint, Excel and Microsoft Mail.

Spanish as second language - intermediate level

Dale Carnegie Graduate Assistant (November 1996/February 1997)

Dale Carnegie Course (October/November 1995)

Effective Business Writing (September 1991)

Licensed Maryland Real Estate Sales Person (June 1990)

Effective Oral Presentations (November 1988)

Accountability Team Selling (December 1987)

Accountability Seminar/Sales Negotiations (October 1987)

Accountability Seminar/Strategic Planning (October 1987)

EXAMPLE 8: PRIVATE INDUSTRY APPLICANT APPLYING FOR FIRST FEDERAL JOB

The following applicant is seeking a GS-9, health-care administration position with the Veteran's Administration.

EDUCATION

Yale University, Divinity School / Graduate School, New Haven, CT 90909
M.A., Pastoral Counseling, 1979

Yale University, Lay School of Religion, New Haven, CT 89898
Fellowship, 1976 – 1977

Goucher College, Social Work, Baltimore, MD 21229
B.A., 1976 (Recipient of Scholarship)

Northwestern High School, Baltimore, MD, 21229, Graduated 1972

PROFESSIONAL TRAINING

- **SMS Medical Practice Computer System**—report generation; system utilization; conversion processes; training; and optimum use of the system to manage information for the practice.
- Microsoft Suite (Advanced Excel and Word 7.0) , Windows 97, Internet and E-mail, QuickBooks 5.0, Online Banking—1997 to present

EXAMPLE 9: GS-12 PUBLIC AFFAIRS SPECIALIST AT FAA SEEKING CAREER CHANGE THROUGH A CAREER DEVELOPMENT PROGRAM

This employee is seeking a career change toward aviation operations management with the FAA. The professional training section is categorized into major areas of training: aviation technical, management, and communications. The Career Development Program described in the following example is the USDA Graduate School's Executive Potential Program (EPP). This program offers motivated federal employees classroom training, rotations, mentors, and specialized training in a new career area. In this case, the applicant received valuable aviation operations experience.

EDUCATION & TRAINING:

Bachelor of Arts	*University of California-Los Angeles*	June 1971
	(Speech & Communications) Los Angeles, CA 95701	

Associate of Arts	*Simi Valley Community*	June 1969
	Los Angeles, CA 95701	

Diploma	*Robert Fulton High School*	June 1967
	Queens, NY 10065	

PROFESSIONAL DEVELOPMENT/TRAINING:

U.S.D.A. Graduate School, Career Development Program   1997-1998

Aviation Executive Potential Program (EPP)

Mentor: Charlene Perry (707) 554-0900

Successfully completed developmental assignments emphasizing leadership and management potential. Formalized classroom training included leadership styles, managing conflict, empowerment, stress, and cultural diversity management. Cluster group assignments focused on improving performance management in a team environment.

Assistant to FAA's International Liaison Officer for 60 days in planning and performance of multinational meetings developing protocols to shift air traffic control technology over Pacific Ocean routes. Coordinated media presence in three-day international meetings, securing substantial favorable coverage for the U.S. government and the agency. (40 hours per week, April-May, 1998)

Assisted the Resident Agent-in-Charge with the U.S. Customs Office for 30 days. Managed public affairs for international smuggling conference, providing important coverage for new international law enforcement protocols governing movement of passengers and freight. Supported operation through media expertise and technical familiarity with airspace system operations. (40 hours per week, February, 1998)

Other Professional Courses

Aviation Technical Courses:
Detail, FAA Civil Aviation Security Office (1997)
Introduction to Emergency Readiness (1997)
Air Traffic Control History (1996)
Managing Public Communication, FAA Center for Management Development (1996)

Management Development Courses: (All 1995)
Seven Habits of Highly Effective People   The Quality Advantage
Management Skills for Non-Supervisors   Investment in Excellence
Discovering Diversity/Valuing the Diverse Workforce   Thinking Beyond the Boundaries

Communications Training:
Public Involvement Training (1991)
Collateral Duty Recruiter Training (1990)
Constructive Communications (1988)
Communications Training Workshop (1989)

GS-15 through Senior Executive Service

EXAMPLE 10: GS-15 SPECIAL ASSISTANT PURSUING SES POSITION

This applicant's professional training section emphasizes leadership and management training.

EDUCATION HISTORY

MAS Management   Johns Hopkins University, Baltimore, MD 21229   1988
BA History   University of Maryland, College Park, MD 21229   1971
Springbrook High School, Silver Spring, MD, graduated 1966

PROFESSIONAL TRAINING

Team Building and Coaching Skills for Managers, 1998
Certified Trainer, William Bridge's Seminars on Managing Organizational
        Transitions, 1998
Appearing at Your Public Best, Georgetown University, 1997
Certified Trainer for Pritchett & Associates, Business as Unusual, 1995
Seven Management and Planning Tools, Goal/QPC, 1994
Workshop for Team Leaders & Team, OPM, 1993
Management Effectiveness Seminar, Career Track, 1991
Front Line Leadership, Zenger-Miller, 1990
Training prior to 1990 available upon request

EXAMPLE 11: SES PERSONNEL DIRECTOR APPLYING FOR ANOTHER SES POSITION

The "other training" section emphasizes the applicant's desire for growth.

EDUCATION:

M.B.A., Georgetown University, Washington, DC 20006	1978
M.A., Howard University, Washington, DC 20009	1971
B.A., Goucher College, Baltimore, MD 21229	1968
Leadership for a Democratic Society	October 2-28, 1996
Federal Executive Institute	
Executive Development Seminar	
Management Development Center	August 2-13, 1993

OTHER TRAINING:

Association for Computer Training and Support Computer Training and Support Conference	1992
American Society for Training and Development ASTD National Conference	1991
Federal Quality Institute Federal Conference on Quality & Productive Improvement	1990
Department of Energy Equal Employment Opportunity for Managers	1989
Office of Personnel Management Annual OPM Governmentwide Training Conferences	1985-1987
Harvard University Workshop on Case Teaching and Simulation	1985

EXAMPLE 12: GS-14 INSPECTOR GENERAL SEEKING PROMOTION

This candidate wants to move to a GS-15 position.

EDUCATION

MA	***Western Carolina University*** Cullowhee, North Carolina 29978	*Criminal Justice*	January, 1972
BS	***James Madison University*** Harrisonburg, Virginia 25350	*Sociology*	May, 1969
	General Beedle State University Pierre, South Dakota 76543	*Liberal Arts*	1965-1966
	Sacred Heart High School Dubuque, Iowa 65449	Graduated	1964

PROFESSIONAL TRAINING

Federal Law Enforcement Training Center   Washington, DC
       Criminal Investigations   1998

Federal Law Enforcement Training Center   San Francisco, CA
       Procurement Fraud   1997

Federal Law Enforcement Training Center   Washington, DC
       Law Enforcement   1995

You're ready to move on to writing about your other qualifications and skills.

CHAPTER 5

Writing About Other Qualifications and Skills

Outside your 9 to 5 position, you have another life. That's what "other qualifications" are: your other life. You have special interests, maybe a few memberships, some community involvement, activities with your kids, speaking engagements, writing, and leadership involvement. You might speak other languages, travel extensively, or volunteer your extra time somewhere meaningful. The HR professional and the hiring manager might be impressed or interested in what you do outside work. There's no guarantee that this information will get you qualified for a position. But many outside-of-work activities demonstrate leadership, public speaking, organization, planning, people skills, and the ability to manage time and resources. Those are valuable skills on any job.

In private industry, the personal interests section of the resume has been many recruiters' favorite. This section makes it easy to get an interviewee talking about sports such as tennis, golf, and sailing; special interests such as youth events; travel to favorite places; and avocations such as gardening or cooking.

Your resume's goal is to get you interviewed. If your other qualifications keep the hiring manager interested in your resume, they're beneficial to include. For more than 40 years, the SF 171 was totally impersonal and boring; now it's time to write about your qualifications gained outside work, if you think your experiences are valuable and will contribute to your candidacy. Note that you would not actually use the heading of "Other Qualifications." See the examples in this chapter for the types of headings to use.

Here is the federally required information for the "other qualifications and skills" section, according to OPM brochure OF 510:

OTHER QUALIFICATIONS

- ❏ **Job-related** training courses *(title and year)*
- ❏ **Job-related** skills, for example, other languages, computer software/hardware, tools, machinery, typing speed
- ❏ **Job-related** certificates and licenses *(current only)*
- ❏ **Job-related** honors, awards, and special accomplishments, for example, publica– tions, memberships in professional or honor societies, leadership activities, public speaking, and performance awards *(Give dates but do not send documents unless requested.)*

From OPM: the "other qualifications" information your federal resume must include.

SF 171 Material Transformed into a Federal Resume

The other qualifications section for former SF 171 writers could be the information contained in Attachment A to Item No. 31 and "Other Qualifications and Skills" from Page 3 of the SF 171. This page would have included memberships, awards, community and civic activities, and other experiences that did not have a specific "block" in the SF 171. You might be able to copy and paste your Attachment A into your federal resume file and then continue to develop these sections in your new federal resume.

Private Industry Resume Sections Convert Easily into a Federal Resume

For individuals applying for the first time to the federal government, other qualifications are normal resume sections that may be included in your current private industry resume. You can copy and paste this information from your private industry resume into your federal version.

Notice the number of times "job related" is repeated in the government requirements. The emphasis in the new federal resume is for recent and job-related information. HR professionals are looking for skills, accomplishments, and professional involvement that are job related so they can determine if you are qualified for a specific federal position. It is important to present your entire background.

Examples of the Other Qualifications Section

The following examples show the kinds of other qualifications information you can provide in your federal resume. These other qualifications include the following:

☆ **Job-related training courses:** Training was covered in the discussion of a federal resume's education section. Please refer Chapter 4 to review the training information.

☆ **Job-related skills:** Job-related skills can be shown through a list of training courses and certifications. Some examples in this chapter show separate skills sections, and others give training and certification lists that demonstrate specialized skills.

If you are writing a Resumix (scannable) resume, your skills list will become one of the most important parts of your resume because the computer will be searching for your skills. An example of a Resumix skills section is included in this chapter. Resumix resumes are discussed in Chapter 9.

☆ **Job-related certificates and licenses:** Many times, the specialized skills are listed near certificates and licenses. Only certain positions require specific certificates or licenses, so licenses and certificates will not be included in every resume.

EXAMPLE 1: GS-7 COMPUTER SPECIALIST SEEKING A GS-8 POSITION USING COMPUTER SKILLS

This federal employee is making sure her skills stand out.

COMPUTER SKILLS

Networks:	Networking with Novell Software 3.12, Windows NT
Operating Systems:	Windows NT, Windows 95, MS/DOS 5.0, Wang and IBM
Programs:	Word 6.0, Word Perfect, PageMaker, MultiMate, Lotus 1-2-3, VSO

EXAMPLE 2: GS-7 PARK RANGER/INTERPRETER USING A COMBINATION SECTION OF TRAINING AND CERTIFICATION

This federal employee has extensive training and uses it every day.

PROFESSIONAL TRAINING & CERTIFICATION

CERTIFICATION:
- Marine Life Naturalist
- Emergency Medical Technician
- Red Carded for Wildland Firefighting and Timekeeping
- American Red Cross CPR Instructor
- Federal Level Two Structure Firefighter
- Hazardous Material—Awareness Level

TRAINING:

Emergency Medical Services
Emergency Medical Technician, continuing education hours
HIV/AIDS Awareness, 2 hours, January 1995
Red Cross CPR Instructor, 12 hours, February 1993
VAVRS—Extraction Course, 16 hours, October 1991
Emergency Medical Technician, 120+ hours, August 1991

Wildland Firefighter
Personal Time Recorder, April 1993
Fire Business Management Principles, November 1992
Introduction to Fire Dispatch, August 1992

Structural Firefighter
Federal Type II Structure, Certified, June 1995
Hazardous Materials Training, 16 hours, October 1993

Search and Rescue (SAR)
Rapelling /Patient Packaging, 8 hours, August 1993
SAR Basic Refresher, 4 hours, August 1992
Basic Winch Training, 3 hours, July 1991

Dispatch
B.C.I./N.C.I.C Certification, 24 hours, April 1992
V.C.I.N./N.C.I.C. Certification, 16 hours, December 1991

Cross Training in Other NPS Divisions
Resource Management (eradication of exotics/feral animal removal, endangered species monitoring), 150+ hours, 1993-present.
Haleakala Wilderness Area Fenceline Inspection, 32 hours, October 1995

Resource Management
Marine Life Naturalist, 20 hours, June 1996, Kipahulu Biological Reserve, Eradication of Exotics/Feral Animal Removal, 40 hours, February 1994

Supervision
Orientation to the National Park Service, 36 hours, April 1995
Personnel, Ethics, and Conduct, 16 hours, February 1994
Sexual Harassment in the Workplace, 8 hours, Summer 1992

EXAMPLE 3: RESUMIX SKILLS SUMMARY FOR AN EQUAL EMPLOYMENT OPPORTUNITY SPECIALIST

This employee is with a Department of Defense Agency. The skills summary contains many keywords and phrases found in the vacancy announcement and in her position description.

SKILLS SUMMARY

EEO/affirmative action and discrimination complaint processing, Writing, Analytical skills, Fact-finding, Case management, Oral communications, Negotiations, Stress management, Community liaison, Public Affairs, Corps of Engineers Early Resolution Program, EEO program evaluation, Reports. EEO Executive Orders, Public Laws and Civil Rights Act; AR 690-600, CEERP, Career Program-28.

HQ, US Army Corps of Engineers, Office of Public Affairs Representative and Recorder, Special Emphasis Program Committee; Member, Office Managers Advisory Committee; Recorder, Special Emphasis Training Committee.

Office Management, Organization, Efficient Systems, Files Management, Systems System Design: Exceptional Performance Rating and Cash Award (1990)

Town Planning Commission Chair, Middletown, VA (1981-1985). Sensitive rezoning hearings, Presentations, Fact-finding, Negotiations, Mediations, Hearings, Reports, Leadership.

EXAMPLE 4: NEW COLLEGE GRADUATE APPLYING FOR LAW ENFORCEMENT POSITIONS

Licenses & Certifications:
> NREMT-P, Nationally Registered Paramedic, Registry 4PO00000
> ACLS-Advanced Cardiac Life Support
> PALS-Pediatric Advanced Life Support
> CPR-Cardiopulmonary Resuscitation and Emergency Cardiac Care, American Heart Association
> EMT-Emergency Medical Technician. Certified in the State of MD
> Nationally Registered Paramedic, Registry 4PO855719
> Firefighter II, National Professional Qualifications Board

EXAMPLE 5: GS-12 CONTRACT SPECIALIST WITH THE DAWAI CERTIFICATION

Certification:

Defense Acquisition Workforce Improvement Act level I and level II certified, 1998

EXAMPLE 6: APPLICANT FOR *FAA* AVIATION OPERATIONS POSITION

LICENSES & CERTIFICATIONS:
Private Pilot, Instrument Rating

COMPUTER SKILLS:
ATP, AIRPAC, FLIESOFT, A/P DIRECTORY, SOURCE BOOK, AVITAT, INM, SIMMOD, Word, Excel, PowerPoint
Awarded for developing a new system database.

EXAMPLE 7: PRIVATE-INDUSTRY APPLICANT FOR *GS-13* SANCTUARY MANAGER

The position sought is with the National Oceanic and Atmospheric Administration.

LICENSES:
• U.S. Coast Guard Licensed Master, 100 Gross Tons
• Professional Association of Dive Instructors: SCUBA Instructor

EXAMPLE 8: *GS 10-12* OPERATING ACCOUNTANT, *NIH*

The certification "CPA" is written after this applicant's name at the resume's top. The licenses and specialized knowledge include a listing of special accounting functions and regulations.

GEORGIA T. SAMPSON, CPA

Licenses and Specialized Knowledge:
♦ Licensed CPA, May 1997
♦ Conversion of PMS 272 to Electronic PMS 272
♦ Federal regulations analysis and presentations with PowerPoint
♦ Cash Management Improvement Act of 1990 and Single Audit Act
♦ Microsoft Office
♦ OMB Circular A-133-revised
♦ Cost Principles Applicable to Grants and Contracts with State and Local Governments (OMB Circular A-87)
♦ Treasury's Central Accounting Requirements
♦ Appropriation Law
♦ Mandatory Grants

Memberships:
♦ Association of Government Accountants, Montgomery-Prince George's Chapter
♦ Maryland Association of Certified Public Accountants, Inc., Capital Area Chapter

EXAMPLE 9: REGISTERED NURSE AND FEDERAL APPLICANT

This nurse is applying for International Health Program Management.

Licensure:
Registered Nurse, Connecticut State Board of Nursing, 1990
Critical Care RN Certification (CCRN), Connecticut, 1989
ASPO Lamaze Natural Childbirth Certification Course, Newark, N.J., 1988
RN Licensure, Massachusetts State Board of Nursing, 1987
Aero Medical Life Support Certification, Miami, FL, 1986

EXAMPLE 10: NEW COLLEGE GRADUATE WITH ECONOMICS DEGREE

This person is an applicant for a labor economist position with the U.S. Department of Labor.

Summary of Skills Developed from B.S. Degree Program in Economics:

Economics

- Utilize knowledge of economic relationships to advise senior researchers
- Apply money, banking, and foreign exchange principles to current research

Econometrics

- Prepare economic and governmental forecasts
- Provide information to support policy decision making

Computers

- Mini-tab and SAS statistical software
- Data compilation, statistical analysis
- Spreadsheet and report production
- Internet and Microsoft Suite for research and report production

Written Language

- Construct clear, concise, audience specific reports
- Conduct extensive research to support team-oriented work projects

Public Speaking

- Design and present informative, demonstrative or persuasive speeches
- Deliver animated conference level presentations with visual aids
- Interview specialized professionals and executive on economic research

EXAMPLE 11: CONSULAR ASSISTANT, DEPARTMENT OF STATE, MOSCOW, RUSSIA

LANGUAGE PROFICIENCY

Russian: 3/3 Level. Moderate speaking and writing. Able to interpret and translate adoption and legal documents and correspondence for both Americans and Russians.

INTERNATIONAL TRAVEL

Extensive travel in over 50 countries. Lived in Australia for the entire year of 1989. Lived in Italy for 3 months in 1990. Lived in Russia for 2 years from 1/95 to present. Traveled more than 2 months in over 10 countries.

EXAMPLE 12: GS-7 SECRETARY/OFFICE AUTOMATION WITH THE IMMIGRATION AND NATURALIZATION SERVICE

Languages

Bilingual, English and Spanish; reading, speaking, typing

EXAMPLE 13: GS-9 SECRETARY/OFFICE AUTOMATION, NIH

Web Development Skills: Trained and experienced in HTML and Adobe Acrobat for programming and posting office travel schedule, program information and mission statement to office Web site. Self-taught in both programs with experience for the past 10 months in compiling data, editing, programming and posting more than 300 pages of documents viewed by internal and external customers. Skilled in Internet research, e-mail management and creating links from other Web sites of interest to our customers.

EXAMPLE 14: GS-13 COMPUTER SPECIALIST

EXPERTISE: UNIX Professional
Certified C Programmer
Informix 5.0 and 7.0
Sun O/S / Solaris 2.5
Systems Administration Integration Management
Sun Hardware

PROFESSIONAL TRAINING:

UNIX/C Certificate Program, 1994

George Washington University, Ashburn, VA
Completed 250 course hours in UNIX Systems Administration, C Programming, Networking with TCP/IP, Shell Programming

System Administrator for Solaris, Sun Educational Centers (present)

EXAMPLE 15: MATHEMATICIAN, STATISTICIAN, AND SAS PROGRAMMER

Expertise

SAS programming:
- SAS Programming
- STAT Techniques
- Linear Modeling
- Statistical Methodology
- Experimental Design

Statistical design, testing and analysis:
- Process modeling and control/sample design
- Linear and nonlinear regression analysis
- Hypothesis testing
- Detection of outliers
- Optimization

Computer software skills/knowledge:
- SAS (UNIX - STATSUN/LAMAR & PC/Windows versions)
- SPSS (DOS/WINDOWS)
- dBASE IV, Lotus 1-2-3, Quattro Pro, WordPerfect, Latex, Windows 95

Job-Related Honors, Awards, or Special Accomplishments

Your honors, awards, and special accomplishments may be important in qualifying you for certain positions. This section includes such items as publications, memberships in professional or honor societies, leadership activities, public speaking, performance awards, and dates received. Here is an overview of the items you can list and describe on your federal resume:

> **Your special accomplishments may be important in qualifying you for certain positions.**

☆ **Honors and awards** demonstrate career or educational excellence and recognition.

☆ **Professional memberships** will demonstrate involvement, motivation to learn about specific industries, and knowledge of state-of-the-art industry information through reading newsletters, attending conferences, and attending meetings.

☆ **Public speaking and presentations** will show communications skills before groups and the ability to write and present information orally.

☆ **Publication lists or written works** will illustrate your ability to research, write, edit, use computers, and study a specific topic area.

☆ **Collateral duties** in your federal job can be listed in this section. These additional responsibilities may lead to new careers and positions. The responsibilities you carry out 5 to 20 hours per week may provide the skills you need to make a career change.

☆ **Community or civic activities** will demonstrate personal interest, dedication, and time committed to helping others. You may have valuable responsibilities, such as leading groups, planning, promoting and coordinating events, managing budgets, negotiating contracts, directing volunteers, and achieving organizational goals.

☆ **Special accomplishments** are covered in Chapter 7.

The following examples show various resume sections of honors, awards, memberships, public speaking, and publications that you can follow when you write your federal resume.

Example 16: GS-15 Special Assistant

HONORS AND AWARDS

Cash Award for Outstanding Performance
Assistant Secretary's Excellence Award, 1997, 1995
Assistant Secretary's Teamwork Award, 1995
Assistant Secretary's Citation, 1995
Cash Award for Outstanding Performance, 1994
Federal Leadership Award, 1993
Deputy Director's Award, 1992
Special Service Award, 1990
Administrator's Citation, 1988
Quality Step Increase, 1988 and 1987
Cash Awards for Outstanding Performance, 1985 and 1984

PROFESSIONAL ASSOCIATIONS / LEADERSHIP POSITIONS

Former member of the Federal Managers' Association
Currently on Board of Directors and Past President, Lone Tree Townhouse Association
Past Member of Toastmasters International
Member of National Child Support Enforcement Association

PUBLICATIONS, SPEECHES, ARTICLES

Frequent guest speaker/trainer at numerous state and local CSE conferences and workshops.
"Improving Program Performance Through Management Information," DHHS, 1986.

Example 17: GS-12 Procurement Specialist

AWARDS:

Outstanding Performance Appraisal Review System award, 1996, 1997
Quality Salary (Grade) increase, 1994, 1995, 1996
Tac-4 Contract Recognition award from Vice Admiral
Tac-4 Protest Recognition award from Rear Admiral
Outstanding achievement award for 1995 Navy Contracting Intern Training Conference
Navy Intern Conference Letter of Commendation from Assistant Secretary of the Navy
Distinguished graduate for Contracting 201, 211 and 241 courses
United States Government Outstanding Scholar Program recipient
Letter of Commendation from FISC executive officer for outstanding customer support
G.T.E. Academic All-American, all-conference academic team in college football
College Scholars of America
Letter of appreciation from U.S. Senator Carl Levin for outstanding constituent support

LEADERSHIP AND ACTIVITIES:

Civilian Leadership Development Program, College Football team captain for over 100 players, National Contract Management Association, Ice Hockey team captain responsible for organization of 20 teammates, Benevolent and Protective Order of Elks, Friends of the National Zoo, Sons of the American Revolution, NISMC blood drive coordinator, Soil and Water Conservation Society, Government Ethics Representative, High School class president responsible for class reunion of over 300 people, Ball State University Alumni Association and Varsity Club

EXAMPLE 18: GS-13 FACILITIES PLANNING SPECIALIST

PROFESSIONAL ACTIVITIES/AWARDS/SKILLS:
- Performance award for Space 20 Report Task Force (NARA), 1998
- Performance award for Archives II Project (NARA), 1997
- Served as jury member, U.S. Air Force Design Awards, 12/95
- Professional member of Council of Federal Interior Designers (CFID)
  National Secretary; Executive Board Member, 1/95
- Knowledgeable in computer software to support project management and
  planning programs.
- Expert knowledge of the latest developments in designing space, furniture and
  furnishings for Federal Government archives, offices and public services.

EXAMPLE 19: GS-7 BORDER PATROL AGENT

HONORS AND RECOGNITIONS
> Lone Star Farmer, Carrizo Springs High School, 1985
> FFA Officer, 1982-1985
> Texas High School Rodeo State Finalist (Calf Roping and Team Roping), 1984, 1985
> Texas High School Region 8I Champion Team Roper, 1984, 1985

EXAMPLE 20: GS-12 PUBLIC AFFAIRS SPECIALIST

PUBLICATION:
Published annual magazine, <u>Texas Hunting Directory.</u> Magazine was a compilation of available hunting leases and public hunting lands in Texas. This one-man operation involved location research, writing and soliciting articles of interest, advertising sales, typesetting and pasteup, printing and distribution, 1995.

EXAMPLE 21: GS-9 AVIATION OPERATIONS

Specialized Knowledge:

- Corporate Aviation: 91 vs. 135
- Aviation regulations: 61, 91, 135 121
- Advisory Circulars
- FAA Orders
- Taxes: Sales/Use, Income
- FAA Enforcement Actions
- Airman Certification
- Maintenance: AD's, MPRM's
- Aircraft Valuations
- Insurance: Aircraft Pilots
- Legal Assistance: Accidents/incidents
- Corporate Status; Legal Research
- Aviation Sales
- Title/Escrows and Liens
- Marketing Surveys

Professional Affiliations:

National Business Aviation Association
American Association of Airport Executives
Aircraft Owners and Pilots Association
Florida Institute of Technology School of Aeronautics Alumni Association

EXAMPLE 22: GS-12 FAA PUBLIC AFFAIRS SPECIALIST

RECENT PROFESSIONAL PUBLICATIONS:

Co-author, *Woman & Minorities in Aviation in Hawaii,* Hawaii Office of Education, 1994
"Aviation Progress in the Pacific," *FAA World*, October 1995
"Safety Basics for the Novice Pilot," *Aviation Education News*, Fall 1993
Our Hawaii, marketing book used worldwide by private corporation in Hawaii, 1988
The Air War in the Pacific, (Honolulu, Air Force Historical Association), 1987

CONFERENCES ATTENDED:

Hawaii Conference on Women and Minorities
National Congress on Aviation & Space Education
Civil Air Patrol Commanders' Call Conference
National Association of Travel Agents

PROFESSIONAL MEMBERSHIPS & AFFILIATIONS:

Air Traffic Advisory Committee
Air Force Association
Hawaii Aerospace Development Corporation
Federal Women's Program
Civil Air Patrol Aviation Education and Professional Development Committee
Honolulu Chamber of Commerce

HONORS & AWARDS:

Outstanding Performance Ratings seven consecutive years	1989 - 1995
National Award for Excellence in Aerospace Education from Civil Air Patrol (Brewer Award)	1995
Participant in Women's Executive Leadership (WEL) Program	1995
Special Recognition Award from Kauai Council of Girl Scouts in Honolulu, Hawaii	1994
FAA Employee of the Year Award (Category III, GS-12 and above)	1993
Certificate of Achievement from Federal Executive Association	1993
Chuck Yeager Regional Award for Excellence in Aerospace Education from Civil Air Patrol	1992
Award of Notable Achievement, Dept. Of Defense (for Completion of History Program)	1987
Public Relations Society Association Award (for corporate newsletter)	1983
International Film Festival Award (for production of educational film)	1979
National Pacesetter Award (for California Office of Education publication)	1977

EXAMPLE 23: GS-12 CONTRACT SPECIALIST

AWARDS:
- Outstanding Performance Awards 1996, 1995, 1994, 1993, 1992, 1987, 1988, 1984
- Honor Graduate, Defense Acquisition Contracts Basic, Army Logistics
- Management Center
- Honor Graduate, Defense Acquisition Contracts Advanced, Army Logistics Management Center
- Member Acquisition Professional Community, Certified Level 3

EXAMPLE 24: GS-13 EDUCATION SPECIALIST

PROFESSIONAL MEMBERSHIPS

Phi Delta Kappa

Association for Supervision and Curriculum Development

Association for the Education of the Visually Handicapped

Founding Member of The Association for Severely Handicapped (TASH)

RECENT PUBLICATIONS AND PRESENTATIONS

District Improperly Used Formula to Determine Existence of LD, *The Special Educator, Vol. 12, No. 2 (August 16, 1996), 24 IDELR 400 (SEA MD 1996).*

Limited Services for Private School Student Sufficient, *The Special Educator, Vol. 11, No. 22 (June 7, 1996) 23 IDELR 1236 (SEA MD 1996)*

Neither Separate School Nor Tiny Tots Program Was Appropriate, *The Special Educator, Vol. 11, No. 9 (November 1995), 23 IDELR 152 (SEA MD 1995).*

Coauthored appeals decision as member of three-judge panel, Somerset County Public Schools 21 IDELR 942 (SEA MD 1994). Decision later featured in *The Special Educator, Vol. 10, No. 12 (January 21, 1995).*

Letting Go, *Council for Exceptional Children, D.V.H.,* Vol. XXXIX, No. 2 (Winter 1994).

Transition 2000: Defining Future Roles of Residential Schools for Sensory Impaired Students, paper presented to The Council of Exceptional Children, (1992).

EXAMPLE 25: GS-15 INTERNATIONAL TRADE SPECIALIST

DELEGATIONS: *Official U.S. Representative to:*

ECO ASIA 94, Environment Congress for Asia and the Pacific	Tokyo 1994
Third Pacific Rim Fisheries Conference,	Beijing 1994
Science and Technology for Regional Sustainable Development	Tokyo 1994
International Whaling Commission	Kyoto 1993
International Convention for Conservation of Atlantic Tuna	Tokyo 1993
Symposium on Conservation and Sustainable Use of Wildlife	Kyoto 1992
Convention on International Trade in Endangered Species	Kyoto 1992
Council for Southeast Asia Fisheries Development	Tokyo 1992

HONORS AND AWARDS

Department of Justice   1990
    For litigation support and technical contributions in cases before Ninth Circuit

Department of Commerce Group Service Award   1982
    For legal support to development of interagency administrative support units in region

National Academy of Public Administration/American Society for Public Administration   1980
    National nominee for negotiations resolving fishing rights in Northwest U.S. and Canada

PUBLICATION

"Managing United States Marine Fisheries," THE NATURAL RESOURCES LAW MANUAL, (American Bar Association, 1995).

MAJOR REGULATIONS

Federal statute and implementing regulations for U.S.-Canada Salmon Agreement
Marine fisheries regulations for Pacific Coast/continental U.S.
Lead drafter of regulations and policy documents for Pacific Fisheries Management Council
Drafted regulations, position and policy papers of International Pacific Halibut Commission

PROFESSIONAL MEMBERSHIPS

Oregon State Bar
    Environmental, international, natural resource, administrative, and governmental law sections
Federal Bar for the Ninth Circuit Court of Appeals and two Federal District Bars
American Chamber of Commerce in Japan
Japan-America Society of Washington
Australia-New Zealand American Society.
United States Pacific Fisheries Management Council
U.S. Department of Justice Task Force recommending resolution of environmental and natural resource problems and to improve relations with Indian tribes.

FOREIGN LANGUAGES   Spanish, Samoan

Sports, Activities, and Special Interests

You might wonder why this information should go on your federal resume. This is certainly new information from writing the SF 171. This information will not help you qualify for the position, but if the hiring manager is an avid golfer, sailer, or an Orioles sports fan, you'll give that manager a short vacation from the serious side of candidate reviews. These outside activities usually show leadership, communications ability, organizational skills, creativity, entrepreneurial spirit, planning, management, budgeting, mentoring, counseling, teamwork, and interpersonal relations skills. Outside activities also show energy, interest, enthusiasm, community spirit, involvement, caring, giving of time, the ability to manage multiple functions, and commitment and service to others. That's a lot. If this information makes your resume stand out, then include it, just in case.

> **Give the manager a short vacation from the serious side of candidate reviews.**

EXAMPLE 26: GS-13 PROCUREMENT AGENT

Avid youth softball league coach, volunteer and fan with 2 children, ages 12 and 14, active in the community league, schedule practices, more than 25 games per season. Supervise, train and coach a team of 18 middle school youths in softball skills and team spirit.

Member of Getaway Sailing Club Race Team sailing J-23's on a weekly basis in the Baltimore Harbor. Successfully won 3 out of 3 races as Captain. Trained team and manage practices.

Member of Semi-Pro Men's Tennis League, Capital Hills, Washington, DC (1995-present). Active player of Men's Singles and Doubles achieving a regional championship out of 5 states.

Media, Quotes, Articles, and Public Speaking

If you've been quoted in a newspaper, spoken before a class or association on your area of expertise, been interviewed on the radio, or done something brave or incredible, write it in your resume and include it again in your KSA statement. The popular KSA statement, "Ability to communicate orally and in writing" can be answered with detailed statements regarding your public speaking and articles.

EXAMPLE 27: VARIOUS APPLICANTS

Quoted and featured in newspapers on the subject of resume writing, small business management and politically related career change processes in The Washington Post, The Baltimore Sun, Warfield's Business Weekly, Patent Publishing Co., FEW News & Views.

Community leader. Subsequent to a terrorist bomb attack on our office building in Riyadh, Saudi Arabia, November 13, 1995, recognized as the community leader for the organization of family support efforts, casualty visitation, donations, and counseling services.

Publications, speeches, articles. Frequent guest speaker/trainer at numerous state and local CSE conferences and workshops. "Improving Program Performance Through Management Information," DHHS, 1986.

Travel Experience

If you travel through your work or on your own extensively, it may be of interest to the hiring manager. Many job applicants travel so much in their work they forget to mention it. If you travel extensively in your work, tell the reader where you travel and for what reasons.

EXAMPLE 28: VARIOUS APPLICANTS

INTERNATIONAL TRAVEL:
Extensive travel in over 50 countries. Lived in Australia for the entire year of 1989. Lived in Italy for 3 months in 1990. Lived in Russia for 2 years from 1/95 to present. Traveled more than 2 months in over 10 countries.

TRAVEL:
Traveled extensively as Project Manager and Technical Support since 1995 to more than 100 customers in Europe, The People's Republic of China and throughout Asia.

CHAPTER 6

Writing Your Work Experience

Now you are ready to start writing the most important and most difficult part of the federal resume–your work experience section. This chapter will cover writing about work experiences for the federal resume based on the following: the SF 171; a private industry resume; part-time and small business positions; and unpaid experiences. You also will be introduced to the "writing partner" concept. Sometimes it's good to talk about your job announcement and your related job experiences and skills so that you are inspired to write a focused federal resume. Finally, this chapter will teach you how to make your job descriptions follow the HR professionals' Factor Evaluation System (FES), which ensures that you have covered all important elements.

Allow time to write your work experience section. You can't fly through it without much thought. After you have finished the work experience section, there will be one more resume-writing chapter. It is Chapter 7, which shows you how to focus your resume toward an announcement.

The Importance of the Work Experience Section

Why is the work experience section so important? Steve McGarry, an official with the OPM, says that the first goal of the federal resume is simply to see that the candidate meets the basic qualifications for the vacancy announcement (for example, academic degrees, years of experience, areas of expertise, technical capabilities). The KSAs tell if a candidate is qualified to perform the specific position. The federal resume is more of a technical document. HR professionals want the hard facts–not a life story–that allow them to screen the resume quickly and see basic qualifications.

Here is the federally required information for the work experience section, taken from OPM brochure OF 510:

WORK EXPERIENCE

❑ Give the following information for your paid and nonpaid work experience related to the job you are applying for.
(Do not send job descriptions.)

  Job title *(include series and grade if Federal job)*

  Duties and accomplishments

  Employer's name and address

  Supervisor's name and phone number

  Starting and ending dates *(month and year)*

  Hours per week

  Salary

❑ Indicate if we may contact your current supervisor.

From OPM: the work experience information your federal resume must contain.

This simple list is deceptive, especially the "duties and accomplishments" line. Just three words will translate into hours of thinking and writing and pages of text. Those three words are what you do at work—and a major part of your resume.

An Overview of Your Work History

As you think about and possibly get overwhelmed with your work history, you're probably wondering how much you have to write, how many years back you have to go, and how many jobs should be included. Here are quick answers to these questions and a review of what's most important in the federal resume:

☆ **The last 10 years.** You will need to cover 10 years of work experience and include all compliance details (as listed in the OF 510 snippet shown above).

☆ **Your current position.** Most of your time and energy will be spent writing this description (if it is your highest level and most job-related position). You could budget one to five hours for writing it. The length of the description will be from three paragraphs to a full page. If you have been in your current position for five years, most of the difficult, important writing will be over.

☆ **Writing your work experience section.** You generally can follow the list below, but you won't necessarily use all the headings. You can adapt this list for writing about your major, most recent positions:

- Compliance Details
- Introduction
- Duties & Responsibilities
- Accomplishments/Projects/Teams/Collateral Duties

☆ **The length of the second job description.** This will be approximately half of that for the first position, unless it is your most job-related position.

☆ **For earlier positions within the last 10 years.** You will not follow the list above; just give compliance details and a few descriptive lines.

☆ **Prior to the last 10 years.** It will be your choice if you wish to show a short chronology of your early career. If your experience is job related, then you need to describe those positions in detail so that you will qualify for the new position.

☆ **Remember to include paid and unpaid work experience related to the job for which you are applying.** You can include on your resume the following: community and civic leadership positions, association or nonprofit leadership positions, teaching, consulting, and small business experiences. At the end of the chapter, I'll give you examples of these types of work experiences.

Getting Psyched to Write

Before you start writing, find as much information as you can that contains descriptions, keywords, and details about your jobs. This will save time and refresh your memory about the varied responsibilities you have had. You will also need this data to complete the compliance details for each job for the last 10 years: dates, titles, supervisor names and telephone numbers, salaries, hours per week, duties, and accomplishments.

Another reason you are researching your existing written material on your work experience is to dig up what has been written about you, including evaluations, letters of commendation, and awards. You need to gather all of the positive, complimentary comments, so that you can create a description of your responsibilities and accomplishments that will impress the HR professional and inspire the hiring manager to want to meet you.

Writing a great resume for yourself requires positive thinking. You will be selling yourself with your resume. Say this out loud if you're not convinced that you're an outstanding employee right now:

> I am an excellent employee who performs many job-related tasks very well, accomplishes the established goals, has knowledge of the agency programs and services, continues to learn, gives outstanding service to customers, is efficient and productive, shows initiative, and is a valuable member of my organization.

This statement is about you. Read it out loud slowly once again. Think about it. When your federal resume is finished, you're going to say, "Wow, I'd hire myself!"

When you write the descriptions of your positions, the HR professional or hiring manager should be thinking positive thoughts about you too, which will result in keeping the attention on your application so you can rise to the next level of consideration. Enough inspiration—you're motivated or you wouldn't have read this far in the book. Let's think about the audience for a moment.

Your Resume's Audience

In the private sector, the audience for a resume is the hiring official. Personnel staff may do some preliminary screening, but that is all. The hiring official hires whomever she or he wishes, and the personnel staff simply process the paperwork. In the federal government, the HR function is much more complex. Since the founding of the Civil Service and the overturning of the "spoils system," a goal of the federal personnel process is to ensure that the most qualified candidate is selected and that political and personal influences on the process are minimized, at least for so-called "statutory" positions. You must take seriously the role of HR professionals in the process and realize that your federal resume must meet different audiences' needs.

HR professionals will determine if your stated qualifications fit the formal requirements of the position and, if so, will classify you as "qualified." Depending on the number of qualified applicants, they usually will perform a deeper evaluation to select the "best qualified" candidates. Only the best-qualified candidates are forwarded to the selecting panel or official (your potential supervisor-to-be). The selecting official has some discretion in choosing the candidate she or he likes most from among the best qualified. Do not assume the HR professional is an expert in your career field, although many are quite knowledgeable. Help the reviewer understand and interpret your qualifications. Make the reviewer's job easier, and you will get more benefit of the doubt. Confuse or obscure your qualifications, and you will earn a lower score than your experience otherwise merits.

When the hiring official sees your federal resume, it is in a folder along with resumes from other highly qualified candidates. The hiring official does not normally have to interview all highly qualified candidates. Who gets interviewed? Qualifications are important, of course. But so is the "feel" the hiring official gets from the resume. Is the applicant a positive person? Is he hard working? Will I like him? Will she fit my team? Is she going to be a threat to my job? Show your final version to friends, and ask how they feel about the person on that piece of paper.

Researching Your Work Experience

Now go to your desk, files, bookcases, computer, and briefcase and gather this information so you can begin to write: latest resume, SF 171, OF 612, SSA 45, DC 2000, and any other agency employment forms. This will be helpful information for the chronology, overview, and compliance details. Also look for the following information:

☆ **Position descriptions (PD) for the last two positions.** Beware of depending on the PD for the duties and responsibilities of your job. Is the PD up-to-date? Does it really say what you do? You should not write directly from the PD; this could result in a 171 life-history document. The resume is not going to be as long, and it will be directed more toward accomplishments. Use the PD so that you will include the most important aspects of your jobs.

☆ **Supervisory evaluations.** Look for the text and keywords in the evaluations. Also read the evaluations to find out where your strengths are.

☆ **Independent Development Plans.** Many critical skills, key-words, and accomplishments included in the IDP can be used in your resume.

☆ **Annual Achievements List** (if you write one). This is great information for the accomplishments portion of your job description and also for KSA statements.

☆ **Agency brochures and mission statements** (from the Web site or your office). This is excellent information for the introduction portion of the description. The agency information will also remind you who your customers are, the mission of your organization, and the role you play in achieving that mission. Your agency's annual report may also be helpful.

☆ **Letters of commendation and appreciation awards.** Read these letters and awards to remind yourself of your value as an employee. The awards and letters are written by others about you and your accomplishments. These descriptions can be great resume material.

☆ **Vacancy announcements.** These are outstanding places to find keywords, phrases, and information to use in your federal resume and KSAs.

☆ **Access Packages** (DOD employees). The material in the Access Package is similar to resume material, only reformatted and presented differently.

☆ **Transcripts of college courses and college course catalog descriptions.** If you are a recent college graduate or a returned college graduate, you may need to describe your courses. You can find keywords and language in the course descriptions that may help you write your critical skills.

☆ **Training certificates.** You need these to remember titles of courses and dates. You will create a course list for the training section of the resume.

Researching Federal Agencies

Background information on your potential employer can be very helpful. Information about federal agencies will help you write your work experience section with more confidence, and your interviews will go much more smoothly. If you are seeking your first government job, read the *U.S. Government Manual,* agency Web sites, and the budget to get a good perspective on departments, agencies, and programs. If you are a current federal employee, read your job description in the Qualifications Standards and your agency's Web site to review its mission. Here are more details on where to find information on federal government jobs and agencies:

☆ **Qualifications Standards.** If you have time or access to your local Federal Agency Personnel Office or Federal Job Information Center, you can find the Qualifications Standards Operating Manual (formerly called the X-118). The "Qualifications Standards" list basic descriptions of each major government position, which can help you write your work experience section and KSAs. Another reason to check the official standards is for keywords. If you use the same language as the official standards for your series, it's easier for the staffing specialist to determine that you possess the needed experience.

☆ **Agency Web sites.** If you have access to the Internet, go to the Web site of the federal agency advertising an open position. You can read and print the mission statement and gain an understanding of the organization. You can also find information about its programs, services, and customers so that you can focus your federal resume and KSAs toward meeting its goals. Identify areas in the federal government where you would like to work. You may be moving from position to position within your own agency or trying to get in for the first time. Distinguish yourself from the

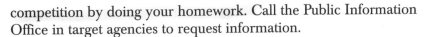

competition by doing your homework. Call the Public Information Office in target agencies to request information.

☆ ***The United States Government Manual***. This is a giant guideline and resource for agencies and programs. It is available at the Government Printing Office (GPO).

☆ **The federal budget**. If you are willing to work harder than the average person and really want an edge, get a copy of the federal budget. This hefty tome is packed with information, although it's hard to extract. Among the information in the budget is a table of expected employment levels in agencies and programs. You can discover which agencies are getting more people and which are scheduled for major shrinking.

What if you are just answering a specific announcement or two? You may not need to do all this research, but it may benefit you anyway. You will be far more impressive on paper and in an interview if you have done your homework on an agency's mission, programs, and future.

> You will be far more impressive on paper and in an interview if you have done your homework.

Getting Help from a Writing Partner

Instead of relying solely on written research materials to compose your work experience section, you could devise new material by asking a coworker or friend to interview you on your work activities. I use this approach in my office and workshops. I have found that what people say about their work activities is downright interesting and the real thing. Can you find someone to quiz you about your job? Can you find someone who will encourage you to talk about your challenges, responsibilities, and accomplishments at work? If you can, you'll find something new to write in your work experience section.

The writing partner can ask questions about your job and write the answers on a separate sheet. Soon you will start talking about your job's challenges and problems (potential KSA material), the new programs, the customers, meeting the organization's mission, and so on. If you get excited about your job and recognize that your work is important and valuable, then you will write an interesting description of your work.

Let your writing partner use the following list when interviewing you. The person should write the answers on a separate sheet and then give it to you. The answers will help you write your job descriptions or at least help you clarify your thoughts about your work.

Sample Writing-Partner Interview Questions

☆ What does your organization do? (Mission)

☆ What do you do all day long? (This information is for your duties and responsibilities section. An example is, "Talk to customers, use the computer, travel, and write. Major areas are telephones 20%; administrative 50%; writing and e-mail 15%.")

☆ Are you really busy? (The answer to this implies the level of work you handle. Can this be quantified in any way?)

☆ Who are your customers? (The answer should be titles–not people's names–and descriptions of who they are and include both internal and external customers.) The government is customer focused now.

☆ How do you communicate with others? (Telephone, e-mail, fax, in person, travel.)

☆ Do you use a computer to do your work? (List specific programs.)

☆ What is the hardest part of your job? (You know this one.)

☆ What do you like the most about your job? (Think hard about this.)

☆ Have you done anything at work this past year that makes you really proud? (Important: This is the accomplishments question for your resume now and for your KSAs later.)

Converting Your SF 171 into a Succinct Federal Resume

You've gathered your information, read it all, and been interviewed by your writing partner. It's time for you to start writing and typing.

The first step in writing should be to get everything on paper. A famous newspaper editor told a young reporter, "Don't put more fire into your work. Put more of your work into the fire." Write it all, go into excruciating depth, and cut from there. Your first draft should be a life-story approach, which you will edit profusely. Write everything, but be sure not to send it yet. Here is an example of how to start:

1. **What the job was or is.** Write like you speak, at least in this draft. You might write something like this:

   I set up local area networks for offices in IRS headquarters.

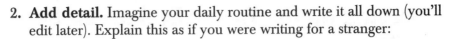

2. **Add detail.** Imagine your daily routine and write it all down (you'll edit later). Explain this as if you were writing for a stranger:

> I set up local area networks for offices in IRS headquarters. Basically, my boss tells me which department is next. I go to the department and do a survey. I talk to the department head and others. I draw a map of the office and look at how I can run wires. I figure out when to do this so it won't interrupt anybody. Then I come in and actually run the wires and plug them in. I install the network software, and sometimes put in a server. Then I debug it and help people with their technical questions as they get used to it. I also answer telephone calls and sometimes troubleshoot systems I put in previously.

3. **Did you leave out any steps?** Reread your draft and add to it if necessary.

4. **Next, quantify everything.** Put in numbers that help flesh out the picture. How many, how big, how much?

> I set up **1-2** local area networks **per month** for offices in IRS headquarters. Basically, my boss tells me which department is next. I go to the department and do a survey. I talk to the department head and others. I draw a map of the office and look at how I can run wires. **The offices usually have 15–20 workstations.** I write up the work order and requisitions to buy the hardware and software. **The cost of a project is normally $10,000– 15,000.** I figure out when to do this so it won't interrupt anybody. Then I come in and actually run the wires and plug them in. I have to go through ceilings, drill through walls, and do other work. I install the network software and sometimes put in a server. Then I debug it and help people with their technical questions as they get used to it. I also answer **5-10** telephone calls **per day** and sometimes troubleshoot systems I put in previously **(usually at least once a week).**

5. **Now that you have a good general description, look for accomplishments.** Are there any tasks you've done that are special? What problems have you solved? Have you received awards or recognition?

> The LAN for the Office of the General Counsel earned me a Letter of Commendation. I had to take on this project on a rush basis, because they had gotten funding to tie into the Tax Court database. The lawyers were working all hours, and I had to work unusual shifts to fit in the work. They changed requirements on me six different times and also added four new lawyers, each of whom had to be added to the network. I had to ensure compatibility with non-IRS software, debug a particular mess in one in-house software package, and deal with management problems. In spite of everything, I met a ridiculous deadline and came really close on the budget. The IRS General Counsel made sure I got a letter saying, "I wish all our support people had your positive attitude."

14 oracle projects (instances)

13 Informix Dynamic Server 2000

1 9iAS

Focusing on the Factor Evaluation System (FES)

Now you can analyze the lengthy description of your job against the Factor Evaluation System (FES) criteria. These criteria are used by the OPM to assign grades to a position by applying the official classification standards. The nine FES factors are useful to you because they form a handy and logical checklist to ensure your job descriptions are effective and persuasive. When you have written a draft of your federal resume job description, you want to make sure that you have addressed the various questions that personnel staffing specialists may have.

> **Every position possesses the nine common factors.**

The FES is a technique for comparing apples to oranges. How can HR professionals determine that an accountant and a program analyst are both GS-12 positions? They do that by realizing that every position, regardless of subject, possesses the following nine common factors.

The FES criteria for each position:

1. Knowledge required for the position
2. Supervisory controls
3. Guidelines
4. Complexity
5. Scope and effect
6. Personal contacts
7. Purpose of contacts
8. Physical demands
9. Work environment

Analyzing Your Work Experience Section to Make Sure It Covers All FES Components

1. **Knowledge required for the position.** What level of knowledge is required? Knowledge can be general ("a general knowledge of agency policies concerning computer procurement") or specific ("a detailed knowledge of Novell and Token Ring network design and implementation sufficient to design and install a network of up to 20 nodes with a central server"). This is a powerful factor, and it explains, for example, why an entry-level lawyer is of a higher grade than an extremely experienced secretary. Make sure you explain the level of knowledge required:

   > To do this job, I need to know LAN systems in great detail, especially Token Ring. I know how to determine hardware and

software requirements on my own, how to plan an installation start-to-finish, how to troubleshoot almost all technical problems, and how to do the actual work of installation. I also have to know agency policies on ADP to advise offices on what I can and can't do, and how people elsewhere are solving specific problems so I can do the same. I have to know about IRS and office missions and goals to do the work. I have to know how to implement customized solutions based on the technology.

2. **Supervisory controls.** Everything else being equal, a person who has to check with the boss before spending $25 is of a lower grade than a person who gets a general assignment and runs with it. While job description language may go into a lot of detail, do not overemphasize this area in your writing. A few keywords ("substantial independence," "apply own judgment," "general guidance," "independently plan and execute") are all you need in your descriptive copy:

> I set up 1–2 local area networks per month for offices in IRS headquarters. Basically, my boss tells me which department is next, **and I do the rest of the work independently, calling only if I run into a policy issue.**

3. **Guidelines.** If you can look up the answers to all your problems in a book, you cannot be handling very complicated problems. The availability and applicability of guidelines to your specific situation constitute another determining factor. What is there for you to use? General agency guidelines, detailed technical manuals, vendor instructions? Are the guidelines current, or are they inadequate and frequently inapplicable? Do you need to apply independent judgment and make difficult decisions?

> There is quite a lot of technical documentation available. Most of the time I can find an answer to technical issues by doing research, but computer documentation is hard to read, badly indexed, and subject to interpretation. When I find an answer, I often have to use my judgment in deciding just how I'm going to make it work in the real world. Frequently, when I do the work, I end up creating my own answers.

4. **Complexity.** What factors make this work complex, or is it really a simple job? Remember, simple and complex are in the eyes of the beholder. If you have 15 years' experience in highly technical work, hold a Ph.D., and are generally considered a national expert, you may think the problems and situations in your work are simple. An outsider, comparing your work to that of other people, would conclude that your job was highly complex. Do not sell yourself short. Some of your complexity issues are dealt with in knowledge and guidelines. Specific complexity issues include having to make decisions with insufficient data, dealing with competing interests and demands, changing of basic

systems, and responding to Congressional or public controversy or pressure. Complexity can relate to office politics, but you have to be careful in choosing your words:

> . . . I talk to the department head and others. **Often, I find that people in the department have strong and conflicting ideas about what they want and need. Sometimes, there is a lot of resistance about installing a LAN at all.**
>
> The offices usually have 15–20 workstations. **They are older offices and often have problems taking the new wiring.** I write up the work order and requisitions to buy the hardware and software. . . .
>
> **Every project I've ever done has posed at least a couple of unique technical challenges that made me go outside the standard procedures.**
>
> . . . I had to take on this project on a rush basis, because they had gotten funding to tie into the Tax Court database. **The lawyers were working all hours, and I had to work unusual shifts to fit in the work. They changed requirements on me six different times, and also added four new lawyers, each of whom had to be added to the network. I had to ensure compatibility with non-IRS software, debug a particular mess in one in-house software package, and deal with management problems. In spite of everything, I met a ridiculous deadline and came really close on the budget.**

5. **Scope and effect.** Scope and effect tell us how vast the work is. The example has already described much of this information; it is highlighted below for your study:

> I set up 1–2 local area networks per month **for offices in IRS headquarters.** Basically, my boss tells me which . . . **The offices usually have 15–20 workstations. . . The cost of a project is normally $10,000–$15,000. I figure out when to do this so it won't interrupt anybody. Then I come in and actually run the wires and plug them in. I have to go through ceilings, drill through walls, and do other work. I install the network software and sometimes put in a server. Then I debug it and help people with their technical questions as they get used to it. I also answer 5–10 telephone calls per day and sometimes go troubleshoot systems I put in previously (usually at least once a week).**

6 and 7. Personal contacts/purpose of contacts. These are really two different factors. The level of your work contacts tells something about your grade. A secretary for a branch chief is a lower grade than the secretary for a cabinet secretary, because the ability to work effectively with VIPs is a specialized job skill. For most people, the purpose of contacts is more important. Who you talk with and what you talk about are both important:

> I go to the department and do a survey. **I talk to the department head and others, usually working with branch chiefs (GS-13 and higher), and sometimes with senior agency officials at the SES level, listening to their objectives, offering technical solutions and options, and helping them gain familiarity and comfort with the new technology. Often, I find that people in the department have strong and conflicting ideas about what they want and need. Sometimes, there is a lot of resistance about installing a LAN at all. I have to deal with this in a diplomatic manner.**

> . . . and sometimes put in a server. Then I debug it and **help people with their technical questions as they get used to it. I also answer 5–10 telephone calls per day from people at all grade levels in numerous departments** and troubleshoot systems. . . .

> . . . and **deal with management problems such as lawyers trying to tell me how to program and wanting last-minute changes based on something they'd read in a magazine.** In spite of everything, I met . . .

> **The IRS General Counsel made sure I got a letter,** saying "I wish all our support people had your positive attitude."

8 and 9. Physical demands and work environment. Again, you can lump together these two factors, because they do not apply to the majority of office positions. If there are unusual physical demands or the work environment is hazardous, this can increase your grade if the demands and environment are relevant to your new position. For most applications, ignore this.

Congratulations! You have now completed a first draft. It's too long and not written powerfully, but it's the first step. Take the rest of the day off and start again after your draft has had a chance to cool down.

Rewriting

James Michener once said, "There are no great writers—only great rewriters." You will use a "bulleted format" for rewriting. Your job description will begins with a general overview paragraph (one to two sentences) to describe the work. Then a series of bullet points will follow, each helping to make the case for your qualifications. Remember to anchor your copy in the FES. You need not address each FES factor—only those that are key to your goals. Let's try it.

Computer Specialist

June 1991-present

INTERNAL REVENUE SERVICE, Washington, D.C.

- Establish 1-2 local area networks per month for offices in IRS headquarters, with independent responsibility for planning and executing projects of significant technical complexity, ranging from 15-20 workstations with budgets up to $15,000.

- Working directly with operating department heads, consult with them on management needs and technical solutions using cutting-edge PC technology.

- Independently solve complex technical problems in network implementation, normally not covered in manuals or published sources, using strong skills and good judgment to respond to unique technical challenges.

- Advise on sensitive management issues including technology resistance and agency policies regarding ADP, with diplomatic and interpersonal skills.

- Personally perform complex technical installations including running wires through older facilities, linking workstations of numerous brands and capabilities, installing software, and debugging setups.

- Ensure that department work continues uninterrupted during the installation process.

- Troubleshoot the full range of technical issues related to LAN installations by telephone and in person.

- Recognized as technical authority on Token Ring network; maintain high level of knowledge and skill relating to both technical and policy/agency issues.

Special Project/Accomplishment

- Working around the clock during a period of staff expansion and major projects, ensured compatibility of network with non-IRS software, debugged a non-LAN system to make it work, and dealt with a continual stream of last-minute change requests.

- Achieved on-schedule delivery and kept add-on requirements to minimal additional costs.

- Received a Letter of Commendation for successfully completing an interagency linking system for a LAN in the Office of the General Counsel, IRS. The General Counsel wrote, "I wish all our support people had your positive attitude."

But a few of the points are not necessary, and others can be consolidated. See the next version on the facing page. As a final step, use the power of the computer to shrink the actual size of the sample without cutting any more words. Appearance counts!

Computer Specialist

June 1991-present

INTERNAL REVENUE SERVICE, Washington, DC

- Establish 1-2 local area networks per month for IRS headquarters offices. Independently plan and execute projects of significant technical complexity, ranging up to 20 workstations and budgets up to $15,000.

- Consult with senior department heads on management needs and cutting-edge technical solutions. Advise on sensitive management issues including technology resistance and agency ADP policies, with diplomatic and interpersonal skills.

- Independently solve complex technical problems in network implementation, normally not covered in manuals or published sources, using strong skills and good judgment to respond to unique technical challenges.

- Personally perform complex technical installations including running wires through older facilities, linking workstations of numerous brands and capabilities, installing software, and debugging setups.

- Troubleshoot the full range of technical issues related to LAN installations by telephone and in person.

- Recognized as technical authority on Token Ring network; maintain high level of knowledge and skill relating to both technical and policy/agency issues.

Special Project/Accomplishment

- Working around the clock during a period of staff expansion and major projects, ensured compatibility of network with non-IRS software, debugged a non-LAN system to make it work, and dealt with a continual stream of last-minute change requests.

- Received a Letter of Commendation for successfully completing on-schedule an interagency linking system for a LAN in the Office of the General Counsel, IRS. The General Counsel wrote, "I wish all our support people had your positive attitude."

A good federal resume can be three or five pages in length, as opposed to a traditional private-sector resume, which seldom exceeds two pages. Remember that previous positions will be described in progressively less detail.

Examples of Work Experience Sections Converted from SF 171s

Next, you'll find some examples of work experience sections that you can follow.

Before: SF 171 Copy

This SF 171 was written by an EEO specialist GS-260-9. The target job was GS-11, general personnel or management.

Scope of Responsibility

As an **Equal Employment Opportunity Specialist** with the Federal Trade Commission, provide guidance and oversight to eleven EEO counselors in serving a 2,700-person staff. Extensive responsibility in training, program development and implementation, budget, and reporting.

Specific Duties, Responsibilities, and Accomplishments

Legal and Regulatory Issues: Analyze and interpret applicable laws, regulations and decision impacting the EEO work environment.

Identify new issues and developments in EEO, personnel and labor law.

Interpret Equal Employment Opportunity Commission and Federal Trade Commission policies as they relate to EEO and Affirmative Action programs.

Provide technical, procedural and legal guidance to counselors on EEO complaint processing issues.

Program Development and Implementation: Conduct research, program development, program implementation, and training activities.

Appointed to coordinate the development of the agency's upward mobility program. Developed comprehensive program package, including format, procedures, and policy objectives. Designed recruitment strategies to increase the participation of women and minorities in career development programs. This key effort has been advanced substantially during this period.

Developed Auxiliary Orientation Program for New Employees on career development, EEO, and related issues.

Prepare and deliver briefings and presentations to managers, employees and labor unions on Affirmative Action Program requirements and progress.

Consult with managers in goal-setting and implementation of Affirmative Action Program objectives.

Conduct statistical analyses of workforce data and prepare a variety of reports.

Casework: Oversee and analyze work of EEO Counselors.

Review all reports from EEO Counselors for timeliness, quality and accuracy of information, and clarity; edit and correct reports as necessary.

Brief supervisors on issues addressed in reports; develop suggestions and effect settlements as appropriate.

Analyze Reports of Investigation and official records. Write Proposed Dispositions and draft Final Agency Decisions (which are normally upheld), and support findings with appropriate documentation.

AFTER: NEW FEDERAL RESUME

EEO Specialist GS-260-9

11/94 to present

FEDERAL TRADE COMMISSION, Washington, DC

- Manage agencywide EEO effort. Train and supervise eleven EEO counselors in serving a 2,700-person staff. Extensive responsibility in training, program development and implementation, budget, and reporting.

- Analyze and interpret laws, regulations and policies impacting the EEO work environment. Identify new issues and developments in EEO, personnel and labor law. Consult with key agency managers.

- Interpret policies and provide technical, procedural and legal guidance to counselors on EEO complaint processing issues. Conduct research, program development, program implementation, and training activities.

- Brief and advise managers, employers, and labor unions on EEO and Affirmative Action issues. Deliver numerous presentations agencywide. Research and author statistical and compliance reports.

- Analyze Reports of Investigation and official records. Write Proposed Dispositions and draft Final Agency Decisions (which are normally upheld), and support findings with appropriate documentation.

Key Accomplishments

Developed agency upward mobility program. Developed comprehensive program package; designed recruitment strategies; achieved measurable results. Developed orientation for new employees on career development, EEO, and related issues.

Before: SF 171 Copy

This SF 171 belonged to a logistics management specialist GS-346-12. His target job was a logistics or contracting position, GS-13.

SCOPE OF RESPONSIBILITY

Manage and administer a $28 million logistics support contract for telecommunications equipment, serving as Contracting Officer's Technical Representative (COTR), with broad responsibility for developing logistics support strategies, concepts and schedules for overall Integrated Logistics Support (ILS) considerations. Review and analyze pricing data for peculiar support equipment to render technical opinions on cost and necessity. Provide technical support to contract modifications with large potential dollar impact. Chair conferences and meetings; prepare and deliver briefings; interface with contractor management; ensure quality and contract performance.

SPECIFIC DUTIES AND RESPONSIBILITIES

Conduct complex and advanced logistics planning, which involves a multidisciplinary approach impacting on supply, procurement, contracting, accounting, and other activities. Coordinate and integrate these diverse program elements to ensure that full ILS support is provided.

Manage and coordinate government and contractor efforts for this $28 million program to provide ILS for field telecommunications equipment. Serving as COTR, interface directly with contractors and government officials in all the functional activities impacted by the program. Ensure that program meets system maintenance, technical data, support, equipment, supply support, and related goals and objectives.

Hold a leadership role in all activities related to the contract. Participate in program management reviews, source selections, maintenance demonstrations and technical reviews. Chair logistics guidance conferences, provisioning conferences, and logistics support record reviews.

Conduct financial analysis and review of pricing data for support equipment. Develop and render technical opinions on man-hours and other cost elements. Provide technical support and research in complex contract modification negotiations involving significant dollar cost increases and changes to scope of work.

ACCOMPLISHMENTS

Developed and presented reports and briefings to higher management, including a Logistics Management Review, Program Management Responsibility Transfer (PMRT) document to transfer program logistics responsibilities, and other materials.

Wrote the logistics section of a production statement of work. Wrote the ILS Support Plan for telecommunications equipment. Expedited the response to requests and inquiries from contractors and government activities. Analyzed LSA documents as part of an LSAR review concerning maintenance tasking, identification of parts and support equipment, and achievement of contractual logistics objectives.

Reviewed Support Equipment Documents (SED) to ensure test equipment capabilities met support requirements without incurring increased life-cycle cost or special procedures. Validated the accuracy of technical manuals by field observation of technical performance. Updated the Air Force Logistics Management Information System (ALMIS) database.

On very short notice, organized a conference at a contractor facility that resulted in the identification of problems and development of remedies, thus ensuring smooth transition from development to production of telecommunications equipment.

AFTER: NEW FEDERAL RESUME

Logistics Management Specialist GS-346-12

8/92 to present

DEFENSE MAPPING AGENCY, Washington, DC

- Manage and administer a $28 million logistics support contract for telecommunications equipment.

- Conduct complex and advanced logistics planning, which involves a multidisciplinary approach impacting on supply, procurement, contracting, accounting, and other activities.

- Manage and coordinate government and contractor efforts for this $28 million program to provide for field telecommunications equipment, serving as COTR.

- Chair or facilitate management reviews, source selections, maintenance demonstrations, technical reviews, and logistics support meetings.

- Conduct financial analysis and review of pricing data for support equipment. Render technical opinions. Advise in complex contract negotiations involving significant cost increases and changes to scope.

ACCOMPLISHMENTS

Ensured test equipment capabilities met support requirements without incurring increased life-cycle cost. Validated the accuracy of technical manuals. Updated the Air Force ALMIS database. Organized a contractor conference on short notice to ensure smooth transition from development to production.

Before: SF 171 Copy

The applicant in this example is a supervisory communications specialist GM-393-14. Her target position is GM-15 or SES. (This SF 171 copy continued for another page.)

SCOPE OF RESPONSIBILITY

Appointed Acting Director, U.S. FTS2000 Service Oversight Center (SOC-B), with direct management responsibility for creating this office and associated policies and programs in the management of the FTS2000 Federal telecommunications network contract, covering the total aspect of all telecommunications services provided by GSA to all Federal agencies on a nationwide basis, described by GSA officials as *"unprecedented in the Federal government in terms of scope and responsibility"* Received outstanding performance ratings and bonus for each rating period.

Specific Duties and Responsibilities

Transition Management/Creation of the Center

Administered the development, staffing, organization and creation of the entire SOC, involving over 70 employees in grades ranging from GS-2 through GS/GM-14, through an organizational structure of subordinate divisions and branches, with an annual budget of $20 million and responsibility for a contract totalling $300 million.

Coordinated the transition from the existing FTS network to the new range of FTS2000 services, including switched voice service, switched data service, switched digital integrated service, packet switched data, video transmission service and dedicated transmission service.

Conducted extensive study and analysis of policy and program issues, needs and alternatives relating to the organizational and administrative requirements to accomplish a smooth transition and to implement FTS2000 management and oversight functions.

Managed and directed the staffing of the center, including review, evaluation, interviewing, and selection of personnel. Initiated training for all personnel to ensure ability to perform their assigned technical, administrative, and contract management functions.

Developed a network of agency agreements, designated agency representative (DAR) officials, and service ordering and acceptance programs for FTS2000. Developed and implemented billing management interfaces and procedures to ensure accurate information for verification of contractor invoices.

Managed the technical implementation and conversion from FTS to FTS2000 to ensure conversion completion accuracy and schedule adherence. Verified and accepted transitioned service delivery points after each cutover phase.

Serve as <u>Contracting Officer's Technical Representative</u> (COTR) for the FTS2000 contract. managed and directed facilities test and acceptance activities; ensured accurate technical procedures and full compliance of Center Support Systems with the FTS2000 contract.

Conduct extensive liaison with senior officials of all Federal agencies and programs in the implementation of FTS2000; regularly coordinate with senior GSA program officials at SES and political appointee levels. Prepare and deliver reports, briefings, and other support materials.

<u>Technical/Contract Management</u>

Provide executive technical direction and oversight to a system of unprecedented scope, complexity and responsibility, involving the full range of voice and data communications services for all Federal agencies.

As COTR (previously, Alternate Contracting Officer's Technical Representative), oversee and monitor the performance of contractor's network management, system control, and customer service system. Train subordinates in the techniques of oversight management and contract compliance.

Review and approve technical data, plans, and activaties submitted by the contractor, and examine their performance through independent sampling as well as through contractor-supplied data.

AFTER: NEW FEDERAL RESUME

Acting Director, FTS-2000 Center GM-14

8/90 to present

GENERAL SERVICES ADMINISTRATION, Washington, DC

Created this office, covering the total aspect of all telecommunications services provided by GSA to all federal agencies on a nationwide basis. Described by GSA officials as *"unprecedented in the federal government in terms of scope and responsibility."* Received outstanding performance ratings and bonus for each rating period. Commended *for "exceptional managerial capability and knowledge of the FTS-2000 program to accomplish his assigned tasks in an outstanding manner."*

- Administered the development, staffing, organization and creation of the center, involving over 70 employees, an annual budget of $20 million, and a contract totaling $300 million.

- Coordinated the transition from the existing FRS network to the new range of FTS-2000 services, with comprehensive responsibility for state-of-the-art technical issues of unprecedented scope, complexity, and responsibility. Managed all contract issues, verification, and acceptance, serving as Contracting Officer's Technical Representative (COTR).

- Conducted extensive liaison with senior officials of all federal agencies and programs on the most complex technical issues of communications and management.

- Resolved complex agency/contractor problems impacting millions of dollars as well as the federal government's telecommunications capabilities.

Expanding Your Job Descriptions and Converting Your Private Industry Resume

The private industry resume job descriptions are usually too short for a federal resume. They do not cover all of the FES factors. And they certainly don't cover all of the elements in the announcement. Since government is accustomed to receiving lengthy applications with details that describe a position thoroughly, you will have to expand your descriptions for a federal resume. You will also need to cover all of the duties, responsibilities, and KSAs listed in the federal job announcement. The federal resume may serve as an application and an interview since you may not meet the hiring manager in person (maybe, maybe not). And keep in mind the hiring manager may not understand your private industry job and how it relates to government. *You* have to interpret these responsibilities and skills and explain your job in terms of the needs of the federal agency. That's the challenge!

EXAMPLE 1: FOOD DISTRIBUTION BUYER SEEKING POSITION AS USDA PRODUCE INSPECTOR

BEFORE: PRIVATE INDUSTRY DESCRIPTION

Produce Buyer/Merchandiser, U.S. Food Service   11/97 – 4/98

Purchased fresh fruits and vegetables for national retailers. Managed inventory, ensured quality control. Researched and selected vendors purchasing $4-5 million in sales. Trained and directed warehouse supervisors. As Produce Buyer/Merchandiser for U.S. Food Service ($5 billion in sales), responsible for procurement, quality control, inventory management of database, pricing and marketing of fresh fruits and vegetables. Directed sales meetings and provided customer services.

The above description did not mention the following, which are details that need to be included to qualify for the food inspector position:

Developing new FOB buying procedures and competitive pricing; systems for cutting costs and increasing productivity. Analysis of pricing methods, outsourcing vendors, analyzing pricing, interpreting results in relationship to marketing practices.

AFTER: FEDERAL RESUME DESCRIPTION

Here is the job description rewritten for a federal resume:

U.S. FOOD SERVICE   11/97 - 04/98
8024 Telegraph Road, Severn, MD 00000   Salary: $51,189 - 51,189
Supervisor: Nathanial Waters; may be contacted   (plus company car)
Phone: (410) 666-9090   40 hours/week

Produce Buyer/Merchandiser
As Produce Buyer/Merchandiser for U.S. Food Service ($5 billion in sales), responsible for procurement, quality control, inventory management of database, pricing and marketing of fresh fruits and vegetables.
- Established and implemented new FOB buying procedures by cutting out the middle man and setting up a direct-purchasing program, which resulted in saving 15 percent in costs and increasing productivity. To accomplish this, I researched, negotiated, and selected vendors (4-5 million in sales) for this branch in order to get the best for less. Also, sourced out to vendors locally.
- Created new competitive FOB pricing for produce. Restructured cost and sale pricing to make it more in line with market conditions, resulting in a 5 percent increase in sales. This was accomplished by studying and analyzing aspects of produce pricing methods and price interrelationships of markets to determine effects; interpreting the results of such analyses related to the marketing of produce; and contacting representatives of the produce industry, trade associations and other groups in gathering economic and marketing information.
- Controlled proper inventory levels for maintenance of inventory database.
- Trained warehouse supervisors on inspection procedures.
- Directed sales meetings, advised sales staff & customers, and sustained relationships with industry leaders.

EXAMPLE 2: ENGINEER AND SCIENTIST WITH LAW DEGREE SEEKING GS-13 OR HIGHER POSITION

This candidate is looking at federal engineering, science, and patent law positions.

BEFORE: PRIVATE INDUSTRY DESCRIPTION

SCHWENKS CONSULTING, Marina del Rey, CA
President, 1983 - 1996

Research Scientist/Consultant, PRC Environmental Management, Inc. Wrote a preliminary draft of an Environmental Impact Statement for Southeast Asia. I wrote the Research Proposal that evaluated, suggested and studied different approaches to developing a methodology to determine the preferred industries, from existing industries and identification of a list of preferred industries, for the future development of the economy in Barelang, Indonesia.

Financial Analysis of Innovative Sites Clean-up Technologies. National Energy and Environmental Quality Division. Prepared an analysis paper for the Twenty-First Annual National Energy and Environmental Quality Division Conference. I was the principal scientific/economist and wrote and had published the "Financial Analysis of Innovative Site Clean-up Technologies"—the basis for the Conference Session: New Approaches to Cleaning up Contaminated Sites.

Consulted on all aspects of improving profitability and financial security, including economic risk analyses for all types of investment portfolios and brokerage services for stock and stock options.

Researched and recommended potential investment opportunities including oil and gas ventures; environmental planning enterprises; and various types of real estate development projects.

Entertainment Industry Technical/Science Consultant. Provided creative consultation for story development for the film industry. Researched scientific and technical analysis for special effects and plot development. Supervised the scientific elements of pre- and post-production work.

AFTER: FEDERAL RESUME DESCRIPTION

SCHWENKS CONSULTING, Marina del Rey, CA
President, 1983 - 1996
Supervisor: None

Ending Salary: $120,000; Starting: $40,000

- **Developed and led firm conducting scientific, operational and economic assessments of natural resource and mineral sites.** Performed financial assessment and strategic engineering evaluations of investment options. Reviewed assets and performance of over-the-counter oil and gas firms in the western U.S. and provided guidance to investors and firms. Supervised work of ten mineral engineers, financial analysts, and operations research professionals to produce analytical reports of resource capacities, extraction strategies, and operational factors. Comprehensive site evaluations included seismic assessments, optimization studies, strategic and operational plans incorporating environmental mitigation strategies. Wrote and presented reports providing strategic assessments, problem resolutions, and advice regarding management approaches to maximize performance. Developed and sustained corporate growth through twelve-year period.

- **Real estate investment and development.** Assessed wide array of oil and gas ventures, and managed acquisition, renovation, leasing, and sale of investment properties. Assisted in acquisition of properties for environmental management and multi-purpose developments.

- **Cinema support.** Researched scientific and technical factors to support development of special effects and to enhance plots of major movies.

EXAMPLE 3: CHARTER BOAT CAPTAIN SEEKING POSITION AS MANAGER OF MARINE SANCTUARY

The desired position, sanctuary manager, GS-301-13, is with the National Oceanic and Atmospheric Administration in Texas.

BEFORE: PRIVATE INDUSTRY DESCRIPTION

Senior Captain, Capree Ventures, Inc., Freeport, TX, 12/95 to present

Licensed Captain of the research vessel CAPREE in the Gulf of Mexico. Perform installation and maintenance on the mooring buoy system at the Flower Gardens Banks National Marine Sanctuary. Responsible for all aspects of vessel operation including training and evaluation of employees, procurement and operational readiness of equipment, and coordination with shore based support regarding replenishment, repairs, and scheduling.

AFTER: FEDERAL RESUME DESCRIPTION

SPREE VENTURES, INC. 12/95 to Present
1203 N. Avenue J 60 to 80 hours per week
Freeport, Texas 77541 $4,500 per month
Supervisor: Roger Sterrin. Yes, you may contact.
Tel: (409) 222-3333
Position: SENIOR CAPTAIN

Spree Ventures, Inc., operates scientific research and diving motherships in the Gulf of Mexico with most activity centered on the Flower Gardens Banks National Marine Sanctuary. The company also performs all installation and maintenance work done on the mooring buoy system at the sanctuary.

As Senior Captain of the research vessel CAPREE, I spend an average of five days per week at the Flower Gardens Banks NMS when conditions permit. Having intimate knowledge of the topography, flora, fauna, history, and regulations regarding the sanctuary has increased my effectiveness in dealing with the scientific and recreational user groups who are our clients. In addition to the responsibility for safe navigation of the ship, I exercise independent authority for the following:

- Responsible for all aspects of vessel operation including training and evaluation of employees, procurement and operational readiness of equipment, and coordination with shore-based support regarding replenishment, repairs, and scheduling.

- Utilize knowledge of scientific research procedures used in the marine environment as well as technical and recreational diving skills expertise to make sound judgment decisions involving feasibility and safety.

- Resolve conflicts that sometimes arise when multiple user groups are aboard the vessel.

- Enforce sanctuary regulations aboard ship, as well as operational policy.

- Implement rescue/evacuation procedures in the event of accident or sickness. This involves communication and coordination with elements of the U.S. Coast Guard, shore-based hospital facilities, and medical personnel aboard ship.

- Maintain good client relations through positive interaction and expression of interest in their activities. Communicate with sanctuary manager, other NOAA officials, and project directors to keep informed on issues related to the Flower Gardens NMS. Give informative presentations about the Marine Sanctuaries Program to user groups, and have given interviews to print and television media about the Flower Gardens.

- Direct team efforts to solve unexpected problems that are often encountered when new technology is being tried in marine research.

- Company headquarters has received numerous letters and e-mails from clients who complimented the crew of SPREE as a well-run organization. Rodale's Scuba Diving, a national magazine, has consistently rated SPREE as one of the top vessels of her kind in the world.

Special Issues on the Work Experience Section

The following questions and answers address common situations in writing the work experience section.

What if my best job is not my most recent job?

The traditional career path, in which each subsequent position is better than its predecessor, does not describe as many people as it once did. When this happens, put the primary effort into your most *relevant* job, not your most *recent*.

What if I am applying to jobs in lots of different series? Do I need to rewrite the federal resume each time?

In general, one properly thought-out federal resume will work for just about every job for which you apply. I once had a client who had two career ideas: a spy for the CIA or a career in military music. If your career goals are that diverse, write two (or more) federal resumes, each with the appropriate focus (see Chapter 7). For most people, however, one is sufficient. Remember, the KSAs are the primary opportunity you have to tailor your background to the specific position.

With the use of PCs, you can create a few different approaches to your most recent or relevant jobs and paste and print each time for different announcements. Do not do this unless you see a strong need. You can spend your time better in the job hunt by uncovering more job leads.

What about really old jobs?

As you move back in your career, write less and less about each position. Jobs more than 10 years old can be summarized thus: "Previous experience includes entry-level computer programming jobs with Smith Corp. and various part-time positions during high school and college." Put that at the end of your resume.

Writing Your Part-Time and Small Business Job Descriptions

If you have part-time and small business paid experiences, you can list this experience as a full job—with the compliance details—or you can mention your experience under "other qualifications" (see Chapter 5). Just remember that the OF 510 states you should include only "job related" positions and experience in your resume. If you are using and developing skills in this job, then you could include this experience and a short description. Here are two examples:

Vice-President and Bookkeeper, B&D Service Center, Milwaukee, WI, 1995-present; 10 hours per week.

Manage the accounting and bookkeeping for spouse's business on a part-time basis. Utilize QuickBooks 5.0 to maintain A/R, A/P, payroll for 3 individuals, and general ledger. Prepare billings for customers and collect monies owed.

Amway Distributor, San Francisco, CA, 1997 – present; 6 hours per week. Promote and sell household and personal environmentally correct products to friends and neighbors. Skilled in presentations, ordering, inventory, customer services and marketing. Achieved recognition as Outstanding Sales Representative for the Quarter.

Writing About Unpaid Work Experiences

The federal job announcement instructions give you the opportunity to describe paid and unpaid work experiences that are related to the position for which you are applying. In some cases, you will want to include the number of hours you worked in these unpaid positions and activities. If you would like to include a supervisor's name and telephone with the activity, you may do so. These other work experiences may be used as statements for KSAs as well. Examples are shown next.

Federal Collateral Duty and Leadership Positions

Many federal employees perform more than one job—a "full-time paid job" and "collateral duty." These additional roles may be as a Federal Women's Program Manager, Equal Employment Opportunity Officer, Hispanic Program Manager, Recreation Officer, American Red Cross Blood Donor Coordinator, or United Way Representative. You should describe your responsibilities, skills, and accomplishments just like you would for a paid position. You should write the hours per week and dates for these activities in order to get credit for your experience.

These collateral duty positions involve many skills and abilities, including leadership, communications, coordination, conference and meeting planning, budget management, recruitment, promotion, agenda setting, problem solving, public relations, agency representation, and public speaking. Here are two samples of unpaid experiences on a federal resume:

> **Conference Chairperson, Federally Employed Women, Inc.** Planned and managed the regional training program attended by more than 2,500 people U.S.-wide. Planned agenda, lead a volunteer board and committees, and managed a budget of $1.5 million. (10 hours per week, Jan. 1997-Jan. 1998)
>
> **Primary Member of the Special Emphasis Planning Committee (SEPC).** Utilize my knowledge of Executive Orders, Public Laws and Civil Rights Acts as an organizational liaison between managers and the federal employee, receiving and transmitting information regarding employee needs and concerns. Interview employees and report to the director at organizational staff meetings. Ensure that the objectives of the EEO program, the Affirmative Employment Plan, are met.

Volunteer Teaching

Many people are invited to teach a class for high school or college. You could be an adjunct professor, presenter, guest speaker, or panelist. This experience demonstrates expertise, communications skills, visibility, and the ability to be a professional representing a group or field.

> **Volunteer Trainer, Catonsville High School,** Catonsville, MD. Recruited by Director of School-to-Work Program to teach resume writing to all levels of English classes for the entire school for two years. Developed a curriculum and subsequently wrote a book, *Creating Your High School Resume* published by Jist Works in Indianapolis. The book will be used as a text in high school classrooms. (1997-present)

Community Service and Volunteer Positions

Here are some ideas for examples of what people do outside work. Being an active member or leader of a community, town, school, or nonprofit organization can set you apart from your competition. The resume reader might remember you specifically because of your unique "outside interests."

If you are looking for examples for KSA statements demonstrating "ability to communicate orally," or "ability to plan and coordinate projects," or "ability to negotiate and resolve problems," you could describe your outside activities, skills, and accomplishments as an organizational leader.

Chair for the Town Planning Commission, Middletown, VA, 1995-1997 (10 hours/week)

Analyzed rezoning and zoning hearing petitions. Demonstrated knowledge of the zoning requirements, public laws and historical value of the community. Mediated and facilitated meetings and lead significant decision-making impacting the future business and residential community.

Member of the Catonsville 2000 Urban Planning Committee. Reviewed plans to improve the downtown village infrastructure following a development plan prepared by a professional engineering firm. Presented the plan to the community with more than 500 in attendance. Developed graphics and budget presentations for expenditures of more than $2.5 million over 5 years to improve the traffic flow and beauty of the community. (1997-1998)

Mentor and Counselor, House of Ruth, Seattle, Washington. Received training in stress management, listening skills, intervention training and crisis management in order to provide individual and family counseling. Volunteer 5 hours per week to assist and counsel families who are temporarily residing in group homes. (1997-1998)

President/Trustee, The McLean Orchestra, McLean, Virginia

Interim Executive Director (1995); President and Board Member since 1990)

Administered a 17-member board; promoted fundraising for $250K budget. Founded community string ensemble for young musicians; obtained grant and oversaw promotion and marketing.

Fundraiser, Project Cradle, University of Miami Hospital, Miami, Florida, Christmas, 1997. Successfully raised $7,000 and donations of Christmas presents for pediatric AIDS clinic for 300 young patients.

Troop Leader, Girl Scout Troop 26, Nantucket, RI (1996-present). Managed a group of 25 Girl Scouts with successful track record in achieving badges, managing successful Girl Scout Cookie Campaigns and many camping events. Mentored the girls in badge achievement, as well as school, career, and interests.

Vice President, Parent Teacher's Association, Hillcrest Elementary School, Baltimore, MD (1997-present). Co-directed PTA meetings, planned the annual fund-raising event that raised $250,000 for a new playground through a new auction /festival format. Coordinated the efforts of 30 volunteers for the festival attended by more people than any time in the history of the school (35 years).

The next chapter is on focusing your resume toward your job objective or announcement. Keep reading; it will be worth it when you're done.

CHAPTER 7

The Magic of Page 1— Focusing Your Resume Toward an Announcement, Promotion, or New Career

One key to success with a federal application is focusing your resume toward a specific announcement, promotion, or career change. You will learn in this chapter how to focus your resume with optional federal resume sections: profile statement, critical skills, and accomplishments list. These sections are placed on page 1 of your resume. You can choose to write one or all three sections. These focusing sections are challenging to write, especially the profile statement. If you are on a tight deadline and cannot take the time to write the focusing sections, they are not mandatory. You can come back when you have time to focus your application and objectives and write these sections. Even though you place these three sections on page 1 of your resume, you write them last because they summarize your entire resume for your audience.

Later in this chapter, you will see examples of federal job applicants' use of the various focusing sections. I've also included the rationale behind each focusing section.

When you finish your focusing sections, you will be finished writing your resume. Then it's time to edit, format, and proofread your resume. The next chapter will review these last steps and explain where to place your various resume sections.

Overview of the Three Types of Focusing Sections

Next, you'll find a brief description of each of the three focusing sections that I recommend for your resume.

Profile Statement

The profile statement addresses the interviewer's statement, "Tell me about yourself." The federal resume format allows you to strengthen your application by summarizing your qualifications in an opening profile statement, an option that the old SF 171 never permitted. This section on the federal resume provides an opportunity to develop a precise and targeted response to an announcement. Private industry resumes almost always include a profile statement to introduce the reader to the applicant's qualifications and background. It is a helpful introductory paragraph for the HR professional. Do you want the reader to be interested in you and keep reading your resume? Then you need a profile statement on your resume. Here is the profile for a GS-5 accounting aide who is emphasizing administration, not accounting work. She wants a promotion and to move into another series.

> Secretary/Administrative Assistant/Accounting Aide with seven years' solid experience in federal government offices. Experienced in Taxpayer Services, Quality Assurance, and Planning and Special Programs Departments. Able to effectively support 5 to 15 professionals with projects, word processing, correspondence, schedule and telephone management. Completed ten months of professional secretarial training.

Critical Skills

What are the critical skills in the announcement? You can include your critical skills on page 1 so that the HR professional can quickly see that you have the necessary skills for the job. The critical skills section is especially useful for technical positions in which certain skills are mandatory. Do you have specific expertise that is required for your desired position? Then make a list, and place it on page 1. These are the critical skills that support the profile statement for the GS-5 accounting aide above. She looks very qualified for a GS-6 or GS-7 position as an administrative assistant or secretary with this list. The basic skills in accounting are left out. She is determined to leave the accounting field.

Critical Administrative Skills:

- Programmatic and technical support.
- Producing accounting and budget reviews and reports.
- Utilizing computerized management information system for input, research, and updating.
- Tracking information to support programs.
- Monitoring and maintaining client files.
- Administrative and computer problem solving, researching discrepancies.

- Editing, formatting, and proofreading written documents in WordPerfect and Word 6.0.

- Coordination of projects; monitoring deadlines.

- Handling multiple projects.

- Detail oriented, efficient, able to design administrative systems to improve location of information and accessibility.

- Word processing with WordPerfect 8.0, Windows, Lotus 1.2.3, keyboard 70 wpm.

Accomplishments

Do you have an accomplishment that demonstrates you are an excellent and valuable employee to your office? Was this project challenging, interesting, and successful? Did it result in new methods or processes in your agency? Would you like this accomplishment to stand out? Do you want to impress someone with your abilities and experience in a particular area? Then you can write a three-to-five-line statement focusing on the results of your accomplishment. You can include between three and eight statements before the list becomes too long.

Here are two examples of accomplishments shared by participants in my federal resume-writing workshops:

Saved the agency $50,000 in printing fees by recommending and coordinating in-house printing of large biannual publication. Received a Superior Performance Award and $250 cash bonus for recommendation. (Position: records management technician)

In just 90 days, negotiated and managed a sole-source multimillion-dollar contract using new Acquisition Reform practices. Received Letters of Appreciation from my supervisor and the vendor for streamlining the process and meeting the acquisition and budget deadline. (Position: procurement specialist)

It's important to mention that your resume accomplishments can be the same as your KSA accomplishments, except that these accomplishments are expanded in your KSAs. As you are writing accomplishments, be aware that the length of your resume's accomplishments section must be brief and written differently than the same examples in your KSAs. Chapter 10 on KSA writing will give you examples of KSAs and tell you how to write your KSAs.

The resume accomplishment section includes the following:

☆ Description of the situation or project

☆ Result

The KSA follows the CCAR method:

☆ Context

☆ Challenge

☆ Action

☆ Result

Here are the two accomplishments from the resume workshop participants written as KSAs:

> (Context) Recognized the opportunity to use in-house duplicating equipment to produce a biannual 300-page document with 450 copies, instead of the normal contract printing arrangement. (Challenge) Recommended to management that in-house equipment be used, and (Action) set up a system to manage the production process and meet the printing deadline. (Result) Saved the agency $25,000 with each printing of this document, as well as other documents typically contracted out. (Award) Received a Superior Performance Award and $250 cash bonus for recommendation.

> (Context) Selected to procure Penguin Missiles for my agency in a very tight window of time. With an unexpected budget overage of $100 million, (Challenge, Action, and Result) I negotiated and successfully purchased through a sole source contractor the Penguin missiles in just 90 days using new Acquisition Reform practices. (Recognition) Received Letters of Appreciation from my supervisor and the vendor for streamlining the process and meeting the acquisition and budget deadline.

On your KSAs, be sure to omit the words *context, challenge, action, result,* and *recognition.*

Targeting Each Announcement

You should target each announcement by changing your profile statement. It will take only about an hour or so to customize each federal resume for each announcement.

Read and analyze the duties and responsibilities section of the announcement. Read between the lines too! If you don't understand the position description, go to the agency's Web site and find out the agency's functions and programs. Think about the agency's and the hiring manager's needs. You are applying for this job; you will be the person who will perform this job. Whatever problems or special situations exist in this office, you will be the person who will solve them. Chapter 2 reviews how to analyze the announcement in more detail. Reading, understanding, and valuing the information in the announcement are important when you are focusing your resume.

> **Match your profile statement to the announcement the best you can.**

Some vacancy announcements are printed with very small type and absolutely no formatting, making them almost unreadable. You can enlarge your announcement so that you can study the content more easily. *Be sure to read the announcement more than once.*

You must match your profile statement to the announcement the best you can. The example here is a vacancy announcement for an aviation operations specialist and the profile of an FAA public affairs specialist who wants to move into aviation operations. Her profile highlights her job-related responsibilities and skills.

Vacancy announcement language: Responsible for planning and developing policies and activities related to the FAA's international program; analyzing data; conducting studies that support those policies and activities; organizing, executing, and managing activities; implementing the FAA's international policies and programs; and supporting the overall activities of the Division and office.

Federal resume profile statement targeting the duties of this position: Aviation communications professional with over 15 years' experience demonstrating organizational skills, award-winning media relations, and development and maintenance of positive relationships among government employees, industry representatives, and academia. Recent assignments include special project involving Pacific region air transportation technology and multiple agency missions. Adept at reviewing, analyzing, and maintaining government and private industry programs, budgets, and collateral materials with international effects.

You can have more than one version of your federal resume by rewriting the profile. You can have your various versions saved in your computer ready for applications. The profile can be changed for each field of work. For instance, one federal applicant would be qualified for and interested in the following positions: training director, educational specialist, and human resources specialist. Each profile would be slightly different, highlighting the specific language of the announcement.

The Focusing Sections Can Help You Change Careers

If you read the announcement carefully, you will see specific language for each position. For instance, you may have skills and be qualified for budget analyst, financial analyst, and program analyst positions. The profile statement should focus on one announcement at a time. The budget analyst position, for example, will focus on budgets, reports, finance, analysis, negotiations, and management. They keywords of the announcement should be reflected in your profile or summary statement.

Highlighting Skills from Prior Jobs

Would you like to change careers? Would you like to highlight skills and experience you gained *before* your current position? Would you like to *play down* your current job title and responsibilities? Would you like to highlight a new degree or training you've received?

> It's easy to emphasize certain skills and accomplishments with one of the focusing sections.

It's easy to emphasize certain skills and accomplishments with one of the focusing sections. Look at the sample below. This job applicant is currently a security technician. Her job is being contracted out to private industry, and she needs to leave the security field. Luckily, she had rather extensive accounting and administrative experience before taking her DoD job. I have highlighted her accounting and administrative skills in this scannable DoD resume format. This skills-based resume was successful, with the scanner picking up 120 accounting-related skills. You'll learn more about scanning, Resumix resumes, and "hits" in Chapter 9.

PROFILE
Accounting and Administrative professional expertise in systems, accounting, and security.

CRITICAL SKILLS

Administration: office operation and management, personnel training and supervision, human resources and personnel records management.

Bookkeeping and Accounting: error and discrepancy identification, account reconciliation and analysis, payroll preparation, report preparation.

Security Assistant: data collection and audits, reviews, processing, disbursement of personnel security investigation within strict compliance with Department of Defense guidelines, technical guidance, policy and procedure interpretation, direction of a team of Security Clerks, regulatory compliance, and achieve time and quality of work objectives.

Personal qualities include being able to formulate accurate analyses, handle details, work with precision, solve problems, and make sound decisions. Also can work independently or as an effective team leader.

Computer Skills: Microsoft Word, Microsoft Excel, Internet Explorer, Netscape Communicator.

Highlighting a Recent Degree

Have you gone back to school to get the training you need to change your career? Would you like to highlight your recent degree before you start describing your work history? The following applicant returned to school after years as a credit and collection specialist in private industry. She is now qualified for an economist or international trade specialist position in government. Her critical skills section describes skills gained in her graduate program. Since she does not have work experience as an economist, her education and skills are critical. This resume included a list of her relevant graduate courses.

Critical Skills:
- Analyze international development economics
- Understand international economic relationships
- Apply money, banking, and foreign exchange principles to economic analysis
- Compile data and write clear, concise reports
- Statistical analysis and spreadsheet and report production
- Perform research to support team-oriented work projects
- Budget management, forecasting, and cost analysis

Education:

George Mason University, Fairfax, Virginia
MA, International Transactions
Concentration in Developmental Economics, January 1997
> GPA 3.75/4.00
> Courses taken include Economic Analysis (macroeconomic theory and policies); International Finance & the Global Economy; Approaches to International Transactions encompassing accounting for investments and foreign exchange; and Data Identification Analysis (quantitative methods). (See attached course descriptions.)

Howard University, Washington, DC
> **B.A., Accounting, May 1986**
> G.P.A. 3.56/4.00; National Dean's List, 1978-80

More Profile Statement Examples

The following five profile statements are for applicants seeking a promotion in the same field.

Biochemical research director: Biochemical research director with extensive experience in the oversight and development of national research programs. Effective record establishing and nurturing research teams of national prominence to promote scientific and technological progress. Strong commitment to developing new instrumentation technologies. Solid record in applied research. More than 85 publications in leading refereed journals. Seeking to build on experiences managing research grant programs in biomedical or biophysical sciences.

Geochemical engineer and financial analyst: Experienced geochemical engineer and financial analyst with extensive environmental research skills. Broad experience includes seismic, geochemical, and business assessments of mineral development and agricultural properties, natural resource evaluations, oceanic and watershed research, and missile research abatement. Technological consulting includes innovative special effects for futuristic movies. Advanced law student seeking opportunities to apply scientific and business experiences in a position involving natural resource management responsibilities.

Business and marketing executive: Senior marketing executive with background in information technology solutions and services for both commercial and government sectors. Central to success in both arenas is the proven ability to communicate clearly and concisely the issues, challenges, and technical substance associated with the integration of complex information technology solutions. Skilled in planning, organizing, implementing, and monitoring of Integrated Logistics Support (ILS) of major systems acquisitions, including operational and training systems. Experience includes effective participation in Logistics Reinvention and Modernization (LR&M) Industry Steering Group and Joint DoD Industry Digital Information Interchange Task Group. Seeking opportunity to build upon knowledge of emerging technology requirements in defense contracting arena.

FBI agent: Experienced investigator with extensive record coordinating successful operations with federal, state, and local law enforcement organizations. Extensive record of organizing and presenting evidence to prosecutors in concise formats, supported by detailed background and written analyses. Consistent and reliable witness in numerous cases, including federal (civil and military), state, and local prosecutions. Active in community organizations promoting sporting and athletic competitions. Seeking opportunities to continue conducting background investigations on a contract basis.

Environmental expert: National Expert in Environmental Management Systems—voluntary programs and U.S. regulatory systems. Seven years' experience as Counsel to the U.S. Environmental Protection Agency, Office of Enforcement and Compliance Assurance. Experienced in designing performance measures, directing audits, writing national policies, advising on cost devising strategies for compliance and interpreting enforcement policies. Principal advisor to the EPA Administrator; member of U.S. Delegate on international environmental commissions and technical advisory groups. Law degree and ISO 14000 lead Auditor Candidate.

The next set of profile statements is for applicants who desire a career change.

Executive who has experience doing business with the government and who is emphasizing marketing research and program management instead of general management: Highly accomplished professional with over twenty years' experience in marketing research, strategic planning, project management, contract negotiations, and product development. Special expertise in applying marketing techniques to reduce social problems. Clients are federal agencies such as the Environmental Protection Agency, the Food and Drug Administration, and the Equal Employment Opportunity Commission; nonprofit organizations; and corporations.

Classroom teacher who wants to leave the classroom and change her career toward educational program management in government: Accomplished professional with eleven years of experience as an elementary school special education teacher. Achievements include serving as chair of current school's Local Screening Committee; initiating, planning, and coordinating programs such as a support group for parents of students with Learning Disabilities and Attention Deficit Disorder; serving as current school's "designated administrator"; teaching preschool hearing-impaired students; and developing and implementing technology-based learning programs. Strong management, public relations, leadership, presentation, and writing skills.

JD candidate who is interested in legislative work: Successful political campaigner with expertise as an analyst, fundraiser, and events planner/coordinator for local, statewide, and national races.

Juris Doctor Candidate with experience as a Legislative Coordinator for the Senate of Maryland; as a Law Clerk for Patrick A. O'Doherty, Esq. of Baltimore; and as a Judicial Intern for the Honorable Christian M. Kahl, Circuit Court of Maryland, Baltimore County.

Accomplished Legislative Coordinator for the State of Maryland Senate, Select Committee 11 (Baltimore City Senate Delegation—1998 session).

Outstanding leader and public speaker. Strong advocate and appointed leader for higher education issues.

Information systems specialist who wants a promotion to project manager: Experienced information systems professional with solid record as a team leader and contracting officer's technical representative on major information systems design and development projects. Consistent record of effective support for major Department of Education programs and excellent customer service optimally to process and support Department-wide information systems. Background includes frequent interaction with executive branch IRM policy officials to facilitate development and modification of data systems to support Department of Education mission.

Federal Resume Case Studies with Page 1 Focusing Sections

The applicants in the seven resume case studies that follow focused their resumes toward a specific position with the use of the profile statement, critical skills section, or accomplishments section. The primary objective of a resume's first page is to target your area of interest and keep the reader's eyes on the page. Keep them turning the pages of your resume just like a Dean Koontz thriller.

CASE STUDY 1: CRITICAL SKILLS

Computer operator, GS-7: Rachel's federal job objective is to get promoted to a GS-9 and get involved in computer systems. Rachel is highlighting her highest-level computer skills in a profile and skills list. The announcement mentioned problem solving and system solutions and modifications—so that's the first skills section under the profile. The announcement also wanted a team player who could communicate very well with customers. The computer software and hardware are listed on page 1 for easy reading.

Rachel T. Jones

4000 – Eighth Street, SW
Washington, D.C. 20017

Home: (202) 888-8888
Work: (202) 666-6666

Social Security No.: 600-00-9999
Citizenship: U.S.
Federal Status: Computer Operator GS-7; **TOP SECRET CLEARANCE**
Veterans Preference: None

Profile:

As a Computer Operator and member of computer support team provide e-mail, computer system, hardware, software, networking management and upgrading to more than 300 users within the Office of the Secretary, Department of State.

Provide System Solutions, Modifications, and Problem Solving:
Assist with resolving critical problems in existing or planned systems/projects (LAN or e-mail)
Anticipate systems changes and prepare users for changes
Make minor modifications to computers, networks, and e-mail systems
Provide technical advice to management and program office officials seeking ADP support services
Using innovative methods and techniques for problem solving
Analyze interrelationships of pertinent components of the system

Member, Project/Support Service Team:
Carry out project assignments, meeting deadlines, providing quality service to customers
Sequence of actions necessary to accomplish the assignment
Responsible for at least one segment of the overall project
Assist in development and maintenance efforts

COMPUTER SKILLS:

Networks: Networking with Novell Software 3.12, Windows NT

Operating Systems: Windows NT, Windows 95, MS/DOS 5.0, Wang and IBM

Programs: Word 6.0, Word Perfect, PageMaker, MultiMate, Lotus 1-2-3, VSO

Case Study 2: Profile Highlighting Education, Travel, and Languages

Consular assistant, Department of State: John summarized his entire professional career in the first paragraph. He covered his language skills, international experience, private-industry background, and his broad program background. His objective is to stay in the international field and stay overseas, but change his position.

JOHN T. PHILLIPS

Permanent Address: P.O. Box 1111, Savannah, GA 22209

Work Telephone: 011-7-096-909-8989
Permanent U.S. Telephone: (708) 900-0999
Fax: 011-7-565-78878
email: john.phillips@dos.us-state.gov

Objective:	Federal Law Enforcement Agencies
Social Security No:	444-44-4444
Citizenship:	U.S.
Veteran's Status:	N/A
Federal Status:	Consular Assistant - Immigration Unit, Department of State, US Embassy Moscow, Russia

Profile: Recent college graduate with 18 months' Department of State experience at the American Embassy in Moscow requiring almost fluent Russian language skills; 8 years in private industry management; 2 summers in Department of Interior Park Service volunteer programs. Skills include case, database, and international services management; writing and editing; excellent communications and interpersonal skills; and problem-solving abilities. Adept at learning complex U.S. and foreign government regulations, interpreting laws and processes to customers, and ensuring compliance with procedures. Recognize the importance of quality, efficiency, and service in customer-oriented government agency that involves international travel, substantial constituent financial investment, and highly sensitive personal/family/emotional (and sometimes, political) issues.

EDUCATION

University of Tennessee, Knoxville, TN 37996
B.A., Russian   December 1993
Dean's List   GPA: 3.2/4.0

Gornyii Institute, St. Petersburg, Russia   Summer 1993
Intensive Russian Language Program, 40 hours per week, 12 weeks

English Valley High School, N. English, Iowa 52316
Graduated   1982

LANGUAGE PROFICIENCY

Russian: 3/3 Level. Moderate speaking and writing. Able to interpret and translate adoption and legal documents and correspondence for both Americans and Russians.

INTERNATIONAL TRAVEL

Extensive travel in over 50 countries. Lived in Australia for the entire year of 1989. Lived in Italy for 3 months in 1990. Lived in Russia for 2 years from 1/95 to present. Traveled more than 2 months in over 10 countries.

CASE STUDY 3: CRITICAL SKILLS

Secretary, GS-8/10: Margaret is highlighting all of her skills (except secretarial). She no longer wants to be a secretary. She wants to be more diverse in her responsibilities, especially toward writing, editing, and training. She has highlighted her skills and accomplishments in these areas on page 1.

Margaret D. Kraemer

5000 Williamsburg Pike, #1107
Falls Church, VA 22041

Office: (703) 777-8989
Home: (703) 787-8888
E-mail: m.kraemer@audit.navy.mil

SSN: 200-00-0000
Federal Civilian Status: GS-8/10, 4/87
Citizenship: United States Citizen
Veteran's Preference: 5 points, SFC, US Army Reserve
Security Clearance: SECRET

PROFILE

Executive secretary, office manager, and instructor/writer with over 25 years' Federal, National Guard, and Army Reserve experience. Excellent communications, organizational, and administrative skills. Valued by senior executives for ability to independently manage offices, improve systems, meet deadlines, and implement new administrative procedures.

Office Reorganization and Design of Administrative Processes Experience

- As Executive Secretary, Naval Audit Service HQ (1989 to present) have developed and improved office administrative systems for decreased staffing and growing audit report production requirements. Improved workflow, file management, and communication methods that meet deadlines, maintain quality, and ensure satisfaction by 10 audit managers plus the Director.

- As an Administrative Assistant to the Director of the Internal Security Division, IRS, wrote new procedures governing timekeeping and processing requests for personnel actions, reducing errors and processing time. Successfully managed an extensive travel and premium pay budget for investigative staff.

Writing and Editing Experience

- Edited the Department of Energy (DOE) *D.O.E. This Month*, a monthly newsletter distributed to all Departmental headquarters and field offices. (7 years)
- Edited the *Public Information Field Report* (on key programs, events, and issues) for daily distribution to 50 top Headquarters officials and 300 field public information officers departmentwide. Increased *Field Report* coverage 30% in one month.

Training Experience

- Senior instructor/writer for the 2970th U.S. Army Reserve Forces School, Ft. Belvoir, VA. Courses include Basic Computer Operation and Concepts of the Tactical Area Army Computer System–(TAACS), Document Security Methods, Office Management.

Computer Skills

- MS Word, PowerPoint, Excel; WordPerfect; Lotus 1-2-3; Ventura; cc:Mail; GENUS; TAACS

CASE STUDY 4: QUOTING A SUPERVISOR IN A PROFILE

Department of Interior park ranger: Carolyn's profile is directed toward quality, experience, and knowledge in the National Park Service. The profile is impressive and interesting to read with the supervisor's quote.

CAROLYN D. O'CONNOR

Permanent Address:
P.O. Box 310
Kula, HI 96790

Local Address:
National Park Service
Haleakala National Park
PO Box 369, Makawao, HI 96768

Evening: (808) 744-4324

Daytime: (808) 572-9306 (ext. 5510)

Social Security No: 000-00-0000
Citizenship: United States
Federal Status: Park Ranger, GS-025-07/01, 8/20/95
Veteran's Preference: Not Applicable

PROFILE:
More than five years of experience in four different National Parks. Highly qualified in a wide range of skills from those involved in creating original interpretation programs to radio dispatch, emergency medical service, firefighting, and administrative support using various computer software applications. Effective supervisor and trainer. Energetic, creative, anxious to learn about and participate in all aspects of work at our National Parks. A former supervisor writes: *"Carolyn's performance has been outstanding. She learned the park operations and resources quickly and is able to execute her duties independently without close supervision. She consistently exceeds expectations and does more than what is required for the job.... Her motivation, initiative, proactivity, and reliability have been truly exemplary. She is an employee of high caliber and dedication."*

CASE STUDY 5: ACCOMPLISHMENTS

Travel office director: John is a private industry entrepreneur. He has owned and operated a successful travel agency for 25 years. He would like to obtain a position in government managing an agency's travel office where he can depend on a salary and a regular work week. The three significant accomplishments would be supportive of the travel office manager duties.

Significant Accomplishments

♦   Created and maintained government airfare program for Federally Funded Research & Development Centers (FFRDC). Saved participating agencies over $149 million in air, hotel, and car expenses compared to commercial travel costs. Enhancements included trip leg cost measurements, average per mile costs, and per diem compliance.

♦   Provided route planning and passenger support that retained schedule requirements and yielded lowest cost per mile traveled. Anticipated air traffic and weather delays and planned routes accounting for season, weather, and aircraft availability based on daily Internet updates.

♦   Managed 300-400 international and domestic reservations per day to include changes due to business and weather delays.

CASE STUDY 6: ACCOMPLISHMENTS FOR CAREER CHANGE

Public affairs officer, GS-12: Roberta is trying to leave public affairs and move into international aviation operations. The three accomplishments highlighted on page 1 emphasize her operations experience. The recent accomplishments list is optional but quite interesting because her accomplishments stand out.

ROBERTA E. SPENCER

124 3rd Street, NE,
Washington, DC 20002

Home: (202) 567-8910	Work: (202) 267-9976

Social Security Number: 345-87-6540
Federal Civilian Status: Public Affairs Specialist, GS-12

Veteran's Status: N/A
Citizenship: U.S.

OBJECTIVE: International Aviation Operations Specialist, AWA-AIA-96-1379-10590

PROFILE: Aviation communications professional with over 15 years' experience demonstrating organizational skills, award-winning media relations, and development and maintenance of positive relationships among government employees, industry representatives, and academia. Recent assignments include special project involving Pacific region air transportation technology and multiple agency missions. Adept at reviewing, analyzing, and maintaining government and private industry programs, budgets, and collateral materials with international effects.

RECENT ACCOMPLISHMENTS

- Facilitated international meetings of Chinese, Filipino, Indian, and Pakistani media briefings after negotiations of air traffic control protocols for Pacific Ocean flights. Prepared briefing materials and agendas, organized presentations, and ensured complete media access to technical officials. Presentations resulted in major international coverage for innovative technologies in air commerce.

- Completed developmental assignment with U.S. Customs Service to publicize strengthened enforcement of smuggling laws with regard to major Asian nations. Coordinated presentations for international meetings involving Malaysian, Pakistani, and Filipino governments and presenting resolution of complex international negotiations.

- Published articles in *FAA World* describing agency perspective on success of international negotiations. Reported advances in air traffic control technology, new agreement with the People's Republic of China for maintenance of aircraft consistent with FAA standards, and new international smuggling accord.

PROFESSIONAL EXPERIENCE:

FEDERAL AVIATION ADMINISTRATION
800 Independence Avenue, SW
Washington, DC 20591
Supervisor: Roger Sperrin (202) 267-9975

October 1991 to Present
40 hrs./week
Starting Salary: $35,136
Current Salary: $47,154

You may contact present employer.

Deputy Public Affairs Officer, GS-12/4

October 1993 to Present

CASE STUDY 7: PROFILE AND ACCOMPLISHMENTS

Staff accountant, GS-10-12: This resume is targeting management, leadership, challenge, and career change. Beatriz is currently a GS-12 staff accountant who wants a different job in government. She does not want to be an accountant any longer; she wants a management position.

Beatriz Mendes

SSN: 444.44.4444
Federal Civilian Status: US Citizen
Staff Accountant, GS-510-12, June 1995–Present
Veteran's Preference: n/a

Objective

Special Assistant to the Deputy Director, GS-301-12/13
Announcement Number 97-02-JJJ

Profile

Financial management and accounting professional with 30 years' public and private sector experience in business development, risk assessment, program and grant development and management, and budget analysis. Extensive background with state and federal government agencies, profit and nonprofit organizations. Acute analytical ability. Strong background in strategic planning to support organizational goals and mission requirements. Superb people and communication skills with proven ability to lead and inspire others. Generous team player. Nationwide professional network in and out of government.

Recent Accomplishments

- Appointed Supervising Lead Accountant for the Office of Community Oriented Policing Services (COPS) with day-to-day management responsibility for 12 staff accountants and technicians, and overseeing the grants, program, and operational budgets.
- Represented COPS at the 1996 US Attorney's Conference. Created and presented 2 seminars at the session to 100 representatives from US Attorney's offices.
- Created and conducted, *in Spanish and English,* a grants management seminar to government and law enforcement officials from Puerto Rico.
- Appointed Federal Women's Manager for the Office of Justice Programs.
- Demonstrated the Grant Application Analysis Process to Attorney General Reno, COPS Director Brann, OJP's Financial Management Director Schwimmer, and others.

Packaging Your Resume Is Next

Congratulations. You have just finished the final resume-writing section. You have now produced your personal and job information, education and training, other qualifications, work experience, and focusing sections. The next step to completing your federal resume is to organize the sections, fix up the format, edit the material, and proofread it. Chapter 8 will discuss type fonts, sizes, and spacing, as well as options for organizing sections of your resume. You're almost finished with a federal application that will get results.

Packaging Your Federal Resume Application

Get ready to make your federal resume package look like a million dollars! Now that you have written your personal and job information, education and training, other qualifications, work experience, and focusing sections, you need to put it all together and make it look great. This chapter will give you suggestions for organizing your resume sections and turn you into a resume designer. I'll also cover grammar and proofreading, with an emphasis on consistency, and give you a detailed checklist to review before you mail the application package.

It's always a debate about what is more important—content or presentation. For government jobs, the content has to be more important. But if the content is excellent and the presentation is terrible, then the package may not be successful. So, your resume package has to make a stand-out presentation. The presentation of your total document is what impresses your audience and sells your skills.

Organizing Your Resume Sections

Federal resumes are chronological resumes with the most recent information listed first—in all sections. Here are two suggested resume organizations for your resume.

Resume organization for technical applicants, in which the emphasis is on licenses, certifications, and educational training:

- ☆ Personal and job information
- ☆ Profile
- ☆ Critical skills and/or accomplishments
- ☆ Licenses and certifications
- ☆ Education and training (this can move after professional experience if experience is more important than education)

☆ Professional experience

☆ Other qualifications (memberships, publications, presentations, community associations, special interests, travel, and so on)

Resume organization for a position that does not require specific education or licenses to perform the job (professional experience would be listed before education in this case):

☆ Personal and job information

☆ Profile

☆ Critical skills and/or accomplishments

☆ Professional experience

☆ Education

☆ Training

☆ Other qualifications

Professional experience versus education—which section is your best seller? If your education is outstanding and can be written in a small amount of space, you may want to list it first. The experience section will still start on page 1. If your education is not recent, and your experience is more impressive and relevant, then write the experience section first. You will have to look at the two sections and your job objective to decide which section you will list first.

Formatting Your Federal Resume

An attractive yet readable resume is an important part of your federal job search. The following are the main points to consider as you design and format your resume.

> An attractive yet readable resume is an important part of your job search.

Type font: Favorite resume type fonts are Times or Arial, but if you have access to or prefer another type font (such as Bookman, Souvenir, or Century Gothic), use it so that your resume will be distinctive. You should create your entire package in the same type font. The following two examples show how different a resume can look because of type font. The first example is in Arial; the second is in Times.

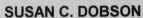

SUSAN C. DOBSON
1390 Florence Road
Mount Airy, MD 21771

Home: (301) 888-9090
SS#: 000-00-0000
Federal Status: Waste Management Scientist, GS-1301-14
3/22/95 to present

Work: (301) 888-8888
U.S. Citizen
Veteran's Preference: N/A

Objective: Program Analyst, GS-0343-15/15
                  Announcement #WA-GS-8-0769

SUSAN C. DOBSON
1390 Florence Road
Mount Airy, MD 21771

Home: (301) 888-9090
SS#: 000-00-0000
Federal Status: Waste Management Scientist, GS-1301-14
3/22/95 to present

Work: (301) 888-8888
U.S. Citizen
Veteran's Preference: N/A

Objective: Program Analyst, GS-0343-15/15
                  Announcement #WA-GS-8-0769

Type size: Text should be 11 point. Use 10 point if you are trying to tighten up the copy for nice page breaks. Headings can be 12 or 13 point type. Your name can be 14 to 18 point type, in bold caps, uppercase and lowercase letters, or small caps.

Joe Friday
2500 Rolling Road
Baltimore, MD 21228
Home: (410) 555-1212 ♦ Office: (410) 844-1212

Social Security Number: 000-00-0000
Veteran's Preference and Federal Civilian Status: N/A
Country of Citizenship: USA
Vacancy Announcement Number: 898-99-999
Job Title: Law Enforcement Officer

EDUCATION
   University of Maryland - Baltimore County, Baltimore, MD 21228
   B.S. Degree, *Magna Cum Laude,* May 1994

Headings: Be consistent with your resume headings and sections. Your major resume section headings can be in bold caps or bold uppercase and lowercase letters. Be consistent with every heading.

BOLD CAPS	**Bold Upper and Lower**
PROFILE	Profile
CRITICAL SKILLS	Critical Skills
ACCOMPLISHMENTS	Accomplishments
PROFESSIONAL EXPERIENCE	Professional Experience
EDUCATION	Education
TRAINING	Training

Employers, job titles, college names, and degrees: The type style for employers' names should be different than the one for your job titles. The type style for the college name should be different than the type style you use to list your degree.

EDUCATION
University of Maryland - Baltimore County, Baltimore, MD 21228
B.S. Degree, *Magna Cum Laude,* May 1994

PROFESSIONAL EXPERIENCE
Rehoboth Beach Police Department   5/96 – 8/96
6501 Coastal Highway, Rehoboth Beach, MD 21842
Sgt. John W. Kraemer, Supervisor; Telephone: (410) 555-1212
Salary: $8.28/hour
Hours: 40+ hours/week

Probationary Police Officer
- Enforce laws pertinent to the Maryland Annotated Code, Maryland Motor Vehicle Law, and local ordinances.

Margins and tabs: You can start your resume with 1.25 inches all the way around the resume. If you need more space, then you can make the margins on the left and right 1 inch. If absolutely necessary, you can make the top and bottom margins .75 inch. The best amount of white space around the resume is 1 to 1.25 inches.

Tabs must be consistent throughout the resume. Two or three tabs are acceptable, but more than that will make the resume look disorganized to the reader. Indenting the text makes the resume easier to read and makes it easy to see the number of employers at a glance.

The following resume is formatted with these three tabs:

☆ Left margin: major headings

☆ Tab 1: names of employers and job titles

☆ Tab 2: descriptive text

☆ Tab 3: bulleted text

PROFESSIONAL EXPERIENCE:

DEPARTMENT OF THE NAVY, Washington, DC 20350   9/80 to present
Secretary of the Navy (Administration Office)

CORRESPONDENCE ANALYST/EXPEDITER (GS-8)   2/92 to present
Allan Grisolm, Supervisor (703) 744-4324   40 hours/week
Supervisor may be contacted

Responsible for analyzing, prioritizing, and making decisions for the appropriate handling of correspondence for professional staff within the Administrative Office of the Secretary of the Navy, the Department of Defense, and other agencies.

- Maintain awareness of events, programs, priorities, and issues in order to perform responsibilities.

Headers, footers, and page numbers: Your entire federal application should look like one package. Many federal announcements ask that you put the vacancy number on each page of your application. You can add a header or footer on your resume with the following information:

John T. Smith, SS# 222-22-2222
Candidate for Program Analyst, Vacancy Annct: 98-88-8888

Or, to save room, do the following:

John T. Smith, SS# 222-22-2222, Vacancy Annct: 98-88-8888

Be sure to include page numbers on every page of your word-processed application package. Page 1 should not include a page number.

Line breaks: When you are writing the text of your resume, try not to have a "widow" on a single line. This takes up valuable space and does not look good. Here's an example:

Support two agents in the Planning Programs Department with special audits.

Edit this line by taking out one word equal in size to the word *audits*. This will make your resume look tighter.

Page breaks: Use the Page Preview before you print your resume. Be careful that you do not have one, two, or three lines hanging over the next page from the previous paragraph. There are many things you can do to the resume to edit one or two lines:

- ☆ Check for widows.
- ☆ Delete white spaces (but be consistent throughout the resume).
- ☆ Consolidate two lines if they can be combined.
- ☆ Change the page margins to expand the line length. (If you have 1.25 inches, change the margin to 1 inch right and left.)

Length: Your federal resume will average three to five pages. Federal job announcements will not give you a specific length unless you are writing a Resumix resume. I will cover the Resumix resume instructions in Chapter 9. Some federal resumes for professionals and senior executives can be longer than five pages. A list of publications, speaking engagements, projects, and other professional information may be added to demonstrate capabilities for a senior executive or technical position. Even if the federal resume is seven or eight pages, that is still much shorter than the previous application format, which could have been 20 to 30 pages.

Justified versus flush left text: This format decision is a personal preference. Justified means that the text is even on both the right and left. Flush left means that the text is flush on the left side and uneven on the right. Here are the pros and cons of each:

- ☆ Justified text is neat in appearance but can leave large white spaces between words if you are not using hyphenations.
- ☆ Flush left text will not have the large white spaces between words, but you will not have the neat appearance of justified paragraphs.

Here is an example of justified text:

Duties & Responsibilities:

- ◆ Demonstrated thorough knowledge of National Housing Act, D.C. Relocation Act, and DHCD policies and procedures.
- ◆ Identified needs of individuals and families based on legal, economic, and social basis and recommended many practical solutions through reports, meetings, and periodic updates.
- ◆ Conducted home visits to obtain relocation assistance information; demonstrated thorough knowledge of program assistance available from multiple public and private agencies; discussed socioeconomic factors; and obtained data relating to family composition, age, living conditions, size, income, employment, and related problems.

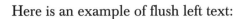

Here is an example of flush left text:

Duties & Responsibilities:

♦ Demonstrated thorough knowledge of National Housing Act, D.C. Relocation Act, and DHCD policies and procedures.

♦ Identified needs of individuals and families based on legal, economic, and social basis and recommended many practical solutions through reports, meetings, and periodic updates.

♦ Conducted home visits to obtain relocation assistance information; demonstrated thorough knowledge of program assistance available from multiple public and private agencies; discussed socioeconomic factors; obtained data relating to family composition, age, living conditions, size, income, employment, and related problems.

Grammar, Consistency, and Proofreading Tips

> **Proper grammar and spelling are just as important as your resume's look.**

Proper grammar and spelling are just as important as your resume's look. Keep in mind the following pointers.

Verb tenses: Make sure that your verb tenses are the same throughout each section of the resume. One of the biggest challenges of using verb tenses can be found in writing a description of your current position. If you have both present and past responsibilities that are part of your current position, how can you have both present and past tense in the same description and have consistent tenses? Here are some suggestions.

☆ Separate the present tense from the past tense with a separating phrase:

Maintain awareness of events, programs, priorities, and issues in order to perform responsibilities.

Create abstract of the correspondence using key words, cross-references, and relationships to other correspondence and programs.

Track documents and maintain information concerning action items and deadlines.

Review and ensure quality control of documents for the Secretary of the Navy's signature.

Previously until 10/97:

Representative for an Information Systems Group. Provided information to users concerning system and application updates.

> Liaison with congressional offices, Department of Navy heads, and other inquiring individuals concerning correspondence and documents flowing through the Administrative Office.

☆ Even though this drives English grammar experts crazy, list all current responsibilities first; then list the past responsibilities. If you have held a position for a lengthy period, it is not unusual that certain responsibilities have ended, but it would be inaccurate to use the present tense.

☆ If previous responsibilities could be considered accomplishments, you can pull these statements out of the duties description and highlight them in an accomplishment section.

If you still can't figure out how to handle this verb tense dilemma, find an English grammar expert to help you fix the verbs so that they are both accurate and correct.

Proofreading: Of course, if you're using a word processing program, use your spell checker. But beware–the spell checker will not find every error. Simple spelling errors that can be missed include *lien* and *line*, *Bethesda* and *Beheads*, *golf* and *gold*, and *trial* and *trail*. I learned the golf and gold error because of a client's special interest section, which included tennis, gold, travel, and gardening. The trial and trail words are watched carefully in legal resumes.

Read the resume for context line by line with a ruler to review the spelling of your name, address, zip code, telephone numbers, proper names, supervisor's name, inappropriate words, and inconsistencies with grammar and punctuation.

If you are not a good proofreader or editor, find a person who can do this for you. Even if you are a good proofreader, it is helpful if someone else can read the resume. This is a valuable effort. Finish your package a day ahead so that someone else can read it and you can still make corrections.

Packaging Your Application

Your resume, cover letter, and supporting material should be packaged in this order:

☆ Cover letter

☆ Resume

☆ Executive Core Qualifications (for SES packages)

☆ KSAs

☆ Last supervisor's evaluation

✮ SF 50, DD 215, Form 15, and other required forms

✮ Course list (if needed)

Paper and Envelope Considerations

The best resume paper is a 20- or 24-pound weight paper. Use a good quality paper that is 100 percent recycled or 25 percent cotton bond. A light ivory or bright white make the best presentation. Grays, blues, and speckled sheets will not fax, scan, or copy well. The color names to look for include Colonial White, Ivory, White Wove, and many others.

The best styles of paper are called linen, wove, laid, and so on. Linen has a nice linen-like effect. A wove finish is usually very flat, and the type prints very clearly. A laid finish has lines in it that create a unique look. You can examine each style and decide which you like the best.

Envelopes measuring 9 x 12 inches should be used so that the contents do not need folding. Any color envelope will work. It is not necessary to purchase colorful envelopes. They will not be seen by any decision maker. Important: Type or neatly print the vacancy announcement on the bottom left corner of the envelope.

Checklist for Your Resume Application Package

Personal information and job information sections:

❑ Check your name, address, phone numbers, e-mail address, Social Security number, job title, and announcement number.

Education section:

❑ Check college names, degrees, majors, dates, cities, states, and zip codes.

❑ Check high school name, address, zip code, and dates.

Training section:

❑ Check course titles and dates.

Work experience section:

❑ Check the compliance details for each job in the last 10 years: street addresses, zip codes, supervisors' names, telephone numbers, hours worked per week, salaries, permission to contact present supervisor.

Format and type font:

- ❑ All margins and tabs are consistent.
- ❑ All type fonts, sizes, and styles are consistent.
- ❑ All lines have periods or not.
- ❑ Page breaks are okay.
- ❑ Line breaks are okay.
- ❑ All major headings have colons or not.

Proofreading:

- ❑ Spell check the entire document.
- ❑ Proofread the entire document.
- ❑ Have another person proofread the entire document.

The total application–are all the following pieces there?

- ❑ Cover letter
- ❑ Federal resume
- ❑ ECQs and/or KSAs
- ❑ Other documents as required by the announcement; read "How to Apply" in the announcement to ensure that you include all required documents.
- ❑ Sign the resume if the announcement asks for an original signature.
- ❑ Unnecessary attachments are not included.

Duplicating:

- ❑ Quality is perfect–either laser or high-quality photocopy.

Envelope:

- ❑ It is neatly typed and includes the vacancy number.
- ❑ All elements are unfolded in the envelope and not stapled (in case the agency is scanning).
- ❑ Federal employees: Do not use government postage or paper for your application.
- ❑ It includes enough postage for the weight.
- ❑ It is postmarked by the deadline on the announcement.

Disk:

❑ Save your application on disk so that you can easily edit it for the next application.

❑ Save on a PC disk as a backup if you are writing at work or a friend's house.

I am sure that your federal resume is outstanding-looking and that you are proud of your work. It's possible that you are so impressed that you are thinking, "Is this really me?" That's the reaction I've seen many times when a federal job applicant dedicates time and effort to writing a federal resume. If you're not impressed yet, find an editor, designer, or writer to help until you are impressed with your resume presentation. The Resume Place provides consultation, editing, and review services. See a description at www.resume-place.com.

CHAPTER 9

The New Scannable Format—Writing a Resumix Resume

Because automated resume readers are helping federal agencies hire employees, you may never write a resume the same way again. In this chapter, you will learn which federal agencies are using computers to read resumes; how computers read, or "scan," resumes; how to write a "scannable" resume; and how to submit a resume by e-mail or on the World Wide Web.

For more and more jobs in the Defense Department, the Air Force, the Army, and other agencies, you *must* submit a scannable resume. This resume even has a name, the Resumix resume. The automated agencies will not accept SF 171s, OF 612s, or any other resume format. Technically, the government has a policy that any of those formats should be accepted. But if the agency is an automated agency, it can accept resumes only. So for your sake, please, read on.

Introduction to Scanning

Terrence Hill is a self-described "automation fanatic." He loves computers, and he thinks computers can take care of many tasks that people take care of now.

You should care about this, because Hill will help Uncle Sam hire you. He's an HR professional in the federal government. And he's not the only HR professional who likes computers.

As the federal government cuts back its human resources staff, agencies are turning to computers to help managers hire new employees. At the same time, computers are becoming more adept at doing the things HR professionals do. Like reading resumes.

> **In some places, hiring a new employee will soon be a completely paperless, completely digital process.**

Government agencies receive stacks and stacks of resumes every year. In the past, HR professionals would scour through them all. A few hundred resumes into the stacks, when their eyes started to cross and their necks began to cramp and their paper cuts began to deepen, those HR professionals became unhappy campers.

Now that agencies' human resources offices are cutting back staff, there are fewer HR professionals to do all the same work–advertise job vacancies, receive resumes, review resumes, enter applicant information into databases, set up interviews, and answer applicants' questions, not to mention all the things HR professionals do for people who are already working for the government (payroll, benefits, vacation, health insurance, retirement information, training, counseling, career assistance). So they have to automate something. Remember how un-fun reviewing resumes is? Well, then, guess what's getting automated first?

You got it. Resumes.

Terrence Hill–the automation fanatic–helped set up a computer system that processes resumes electronically at the Justice Department. Now he's setting up a similar system at the Federal Deposit Insurance Corporation.

This is no one-man show. In fact, more and more HR professionals in the federal government are turning to technology to help them hire new employees. From the Immigration and Naturalization Service to the U.S. Patent and Trademark Office to the Defense Department, the government is starting to automate the hiring process. In some places, hiring a new employee will soon be a completely paperless, completely digital process.

Even if you're totally technophobic, don't get scared. You're going to see how to prepare your resume for the electronic eye, in a way that all those bits and bytes are going to help you get the federal job you want. Before you read how to prepare a scannable resume, you'll learn which agencies are using automated resume systems and how computer programs actually read resumes.

Which Agencies Are Using Computers to Read Resumes?

Many private-sector companies are using computers to process resumes. It's not uncommon for corporations to maintain databases of hundreds of thousands of resumes. For example, Electronic Data Systems, a major technology company based in Plano, Texas, keeps a computer database of 200,000 resumes. When a position opens, managers search the database to find potential candidates. Automated systems save human resources departments hours of work and a lot of money; some companies' recruiting costs have been cut in half by switching from human eyes to computer eyes.

Computerized resume programs are not entirely new to the government. In fact, President Clinton's transition team used one after the 1992 election to process the thousands of resumes eager Democrats sent to Washington at the dawn of the Clinton administration. For the most part, though, government agencies stuck to the laborious process of reading resumes one-by-one.

Now the resume revolution in the federal government is beginning. The most important battlefield is at the Defense Department, home to half the federal government's civilian employees. The Army, Navy, Air Force, and Defense agencies are installing computer systems to process resumes. By the spring of 2000, civilian Defense Department employees throughout the world will be hired using scannable resumes. Initially, 12 sites are testing scannable resumes: Washington Headquarters Services, the Defense Information Systems Agency, one Defense Finance and Accounting Service personnel office, six Army regions, two Navy regions, and the Air Force Personnel Center.

The Justice Department's Justice Management Division and the Immigration and Naturalization Service are leading the resume revolution outside the Defense Department (DoD). A rule of thumb to follow in federal management is that where goes DoD, so goes the rest of the government. Be watching for more agencies to jump on the automation bandwagon. (The job announcement will tell you if an agency is automated.)

How Computers Read, or "Scan," Resumes

The most widely used computer system for processing resumes is called *Resumix*. Resumix has been around since 1988, when a group of computer whizzes experimenting with artificial intelligence came up with a computer program that could read resumes. They decided to go into business for themselves. Since the Defense Department is using their software, I'll describe how Resumix reads your resume.

> This process has not been perfected, so say no to fancy fonts, underlines, and shading.

Assume that you sent your resume to an agency in the mail (later in the chapter you'll learn about e-mail and the World Wide Web). A clerk at the agency feeds your resume into a scanner, which captures your resume as an image, essentially snapping a high-definition photograph. Then software called *OCR* (Optical Character Recognition—don't worry, you won't be tested on this later) goes over the image, identifying letters and numbers and punctuation. The OCR software then creates a text file of your resume. As you can guess, this process has not yet been perfected, which is why in the next section you'll say no to fancy fonts, underlines, and shading.

Once your resume has been scanned into the system, it becomes one of the files in the agency's database of resumes. Then the Resumix brain, the artificial intelligence part of the program, turns on.

Artificial intelligence programs use "rules" to figure out what words and phrases mean. The more rules a program uses, the better the program understands and can process text. Resumix uses 140,000 rules, which means it can give human HR professionals a run for their money. In addition, the software's programmers have taught Resumix how to recognize more than 10 million resume terms. So, the program can look at words and determine their meanings by the context of the sentences around them. For example, Resumix can tell the difference between Ada—the first name, ADA—the American Dental Association, and ADA—the Americans with Disabilities Act, based on the context surrounding those three letters. Since the program is designed to process resumes, it understands resume formatting. For example, it knows which section is education and which section is work experience.

The software analyzes your work-related skills. Based on the skills you've included in the resume, Resumix places you in job categories. For example, if your resume lists contract negotiation, market-based research, writing work statements, and Federal Acquisition Regulations (FAR) training as some of your skills, a government-tailored Resumix would recognize you as a procurement specialist.

When managers are looking to fill a position, they can search the Resumix database for specific skills or within job categories. The system then ranks applicants based on how well their resume matches the manager's requirements. The more hits a manager's search makes with your resume, the higher you appear on the manager's list. If you've written your resume with this process in mind, you will have a better chance of coming up at the top of the manager's search results.

This process is pretty amazing, isn't it? Now that you have a basic explanation of how automated resume systems work, you next look at how you can maximize your resume for the digital age.

How to Write a "Scannable" Resume

Three basic rules make scannable resumes different from regular resumes:

* ☆ You must format your resume so that the scanner can easily read it.

* ☆ You must use keywords and phrases when you write your resume to maximize the number of hits the software matches during a hiring search.

* ☆ You must follow specific instructions in agencies' job kits or on vacancy announcements to the letter. Each human resources

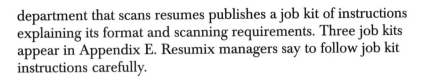

department that scans resumes publishes a job kit of instructions explaining its format and scanning requirements. Three job kits appear in Appendix E. Resumix managers say to follow job kit instructions carefully.

Format

Here are some guidelines for formatting a scannable resume:

☆ If you're going to submit your resume on paper, type with black ink on 8½ x 11-inch white bond paper printed on one side only.

☆ Use a laser printer and submit a clean original.

☆ Do not staple, fold, bind, or punch holes in your resume. Place it in a large manila envelope.

☆ Avoid faxes. If you must fax, set your machine to the finest resolution.

☆ Use a minimum margin of one inch on all sides of your printed resume.

☆ Use Courier typeface (10 to 12 point) or Times New Roman typeface (12 point). Use boldface and/or capital letters for section headings.

☆ Do not use any of the following: vertical or horizontal lines, graphics, boxes, two-column format, fancy treatments such as *italics*, <u>underlining</u>, shadows, or bullets.

☆ Avoid acronyms or abbreviations. Use only acronyms that are well established and commonly understood.

☆ Use white space and line breaks. Resume readers recognize emptiness as a break between sections or topics.

Maximizing Hits

Despite all my gee-whiz talk earlier about artificial intelligence, it is just that: artificial. The computer thinks differently than an HR professional does. A basic difference between a person and a machine is that the person appreciates presentation. People give style points. As far as the computer's concerned, you can keep your style to yourself. Just the facts, please, that's all. Similarly, a computer will not be impressed with how well rounded you are unless a manager specifies a variety of skills during the hiring search. Typically, the computer wants to put you in a category by figuring out what most of your skills have in common.

> Strike a balance between writing like a robot for the computer and writing like a human for the manager who will hire you.

At the same time you're trying to impress the computer, keep in mind that eventually human eyes will be laid on your resume. So even though you're writing for the computer, you don't want to sound like a computer. You must strike a balance between writing like a robot for the computer and writing like a human for the manager who will eventually hire you. Don't just write "personnel policies, regulations development, recommendations" in order to cram in keywords. Go ahead and write "Developed and recommended personnel policies and personnel regulations." All the keywords are there for the computer, and a sentence structure is there for the humans.

It's important for you to think carefully about every word you write on a scannable resume. This takes some getting used to, so here are five rules of thumb and some examples to demonstrate those rules.

Rule 1: Skills, Skills, Skills

Over the span of your career, you've learned how to do many things. Think about your most important skills and what you do very well. Before you write your resume, make as long a list as you can of every relevant skill you have. Then include these skills in your resume. Most agencies' resume job kits will tell you to list your most relevant skills in a summary of skills section at the top of your resume. (At the Defense Department's Washington Services Center, resumes used to be limited to 80 key skills, but that limit is now 200.)

Here's an example of a traditional SF 171 job description:

> Multifaceted administrative/data management position with ultimate responsibility for the collection, audit, review, processing, and disbursement of personnel security investigation information within strict compliance to DoD guidelines. Receive, open, review, and process large volumes of military, industrial, and civilian personnel investigative requests. Analyze requests. Investigative packets are subject to audit in several critical areas including the appropriateness of the investigation (based on type and scope of requirements), completeness of the questionnaire, and the verification of response.

Here's what you'd write on a scannable federal resume skills section:

> Coordinate personal clearance services for government and Defense Department customers, including military, industrial, DOD civilians, government contract employees. Casework coordinator for 55 to 65 new cases per day for investigative team. Procure and update files; respond to file inquiries; review quality control.

Rule 2: Be Concrete

Labels and keywords are your best bet. In traditional resumes and SF 171s, you use fancy phrases and long-winded explanations to sell yourself. But in a scannable resume, you need to just spit it out. You need to include as many skills as you can in a scannable resume, so briefly and clearly describe a skill, and then go on to your next skill.

The following example is from a management analyst with the Department of Energy, Small Business Technology Transfer (SBTT) and Small Business Innovation Research (SBIR) programs.

Before:

As the Administrative Coordinator for both the SBIR and SBTT programs, held responsibility for the completion of all administrative tasks to support the programs. This includes assigning tasks to as many as three DOE staff persons and serving as the contract representative for the support services contract. This requires monitoring the work of the contractor which has six employees to assure that their data management system is complete and accurate, and that all applications are processed in an accurate and timely manner. Also responsible for developing operating procedures and policies for both of these programs. This requires making recommendations to the management staff on suggested policy and procedure improvements.

After:

Analyze, design, and manage the implementation of administrative operating procedures used for evaluating 2000 small business research and development grant applications each year to assure maximum operating efficiency of this $470 million per year program.

Manage support services contract consisting of six full-time employees and technical consultants. Manage all contract issues, verification, and acceptance while serving as the Contracting Officer's Technical Representative (COTR).

Rule 3: Include Specifics

Managers will be conducting searches to see what computer programs you have experience with, what certifications you have, what management systems you understand, and so on. If you're a computer programmer who knows COBOL, a manager will want to know that. A good trick to use: If you're tailoring your resume to a specific job vacancy, make sure you use the key phrases and words in the duties and responsibilities section of the vacancy announcement.

This GS-7 computer operator is applying for GS-8 positions in which she will be performing a higher level of computer support to internal customers. Notice she lists the specific computer programs with which she is familiar.

SUMMARY OF SKILLS

As a Computer Operator and member of computer support team, provide e-mail, computer system, hardware, software, networking management and upgrading to more than 300 users within the Office of the Secretary, Department of State.

Provide System Solutions, Modifications and Problem-Solving:

Assist with resolving critical problems in existing or planned systems/projects (LAN or e-mail)

Anticipate systems changes and prepare users for changes

Make minor modifications to computers, networks and e-mail systems

Provide technical advice to management and program office officials seeking ADP support services

Use innovative methods and techniques for problem-solving

Analyze interrelationships of pertinent components of the system

Member, Project / Support Service Team:

Carry out project assignments, meeting deadlines, providing quality service to customers

Sequence of actions necessary to accomplish the assignment

Responsible for at least one segment of the overall project

Assist in development and maintenance efforts

COMPUTER SKILLS:

Networks: Networking with Novell Software 3.12, Windows NT

Operating Systems: Windows NT, Windows 95, MS/DOS 5.0, Wang and IBM

Programs: Word 6.0, Word Perfect, PageMaker, MultiMate, Lotus 1-2-3, VSO

EXPERIENCE:

U.S. Department of State   1988 to present

Computer Operator; GS-7 (9/96 – present) $26,069/year

Office of the Secretary

2201 C Street, NW, Washington, D.C. 20520

Supervisor: John Smith (202) 666-9090   May be contacted.

Provide technical support for critical information systems for the Secretary of State and over 800 users at the Secretariat level. Manage the electronic mail system and imaging and Local Area Networks (LANs).

Rule 4: Use Industry Jargon

When managers are looking for prime candidates, they'll search for buzzwords in their areas of expertise. If you know them, put them in your resume. You should also include detailed information about specific projects, including title, budget, and scope. The following is a project list for a computer specialist with the Department of Education. The resume also includes a separate list of responsibilities for each IT project.

Major IT projects have included:

Program System Support (PSS) Year 2000 Independent Verification & Validation (IV & V). Ensured that the 11 mission-critical student financial aid program systems are assessed, renovated, tested, validated, and implemented for Year 2000 compliance. Validate 15 non-mission critical programs.

Selected projects include:

Title IV Automated Technical Support Contract – multi-year contract budgeted over $750,000 per year.

General Electronic Support (GES) – Multi-year Wide Area Network (WAN) telecommunications support contract is in excess of $2 million per year. WAN covers over 1,000 destinations in the Continental US and its territories.

Lead Analyst – Joint Application Design session for the Postsecondary Education Participation System (PEPS). Budgeted for $2.5 million per year. Directed the design and development of system architecture to support Postsecondary Education Financial Aid Delivery Systems.

Database Administrator – Lotus Notes Tracking Systems – Directed the design, development and implementation of two Lotus Notes Tracking Systems.

Rule 5: Be Brief, But Don't Cram

Remember, computers like white space. It helps the automated readers recognize breaks between sections. And again, someone will read your resume. Most vacancy announcements or job kits will give you a page limit, but there's no need to try to get everything into one page. In Appendix A, you'll find a complete scannable resume. Note the clean format.

Follow Instructions

OPM has granted agencies broad leeway in the requirements it places on applicants. Every agency has developed its own slightly different format for scannable resumes. For example, Defense's Washington Human Resource Services Center allows three-page resumes, while the Army limits them to two pages. Justice allows four pages. Defense is not accepting faxes anymore, but other agencies still allow them. While Justice asks applicants to put the job announcement number on the resume, INS, Defense, and Army ask for the resume, followed later by a separate "self-nomination" for specific positions.

What Happens to Your Resume in the Database

Each human resources department maintains and uses its database differently. Because they're in the beginning stages of building federal employee resume databases, the hiring managers are not searching the databases for candidates–yet. At this point, if you are interested in an advertised position on a Web site and your resume is already in the agency's database, you use a special self-nomination sheet found in the job kit. You will then forward the nomination by e-mail or fax. The HR staff will pull your resume for consideration for the position. The job kit will tell you how to nominate yourself for a position or how your resume will be managed in the particular agency's database. A sample of the self-nomination sheet appears in Appendix E.

Bottom Line: Read Directions Carefully

Keep in mind also that federal resumes require information that private-sector resumes don't. In some cases, you'll still have to submit supporting documents like SF 50 forms for current or former federal employees. For instance, the Air Force looks for SF 50s for federal employees, DD 214s for former military, SF 15s for veterans, and college transcripts. The government is in the opening scenes of the resume revolution, so expect baggage from the old regime to remain for some time.

Automated Agencies Using Scannable Resumes

The following agencies scan resumes. Also listed are Web site addresses for obtaining the agencies' job kits. The sites also list job announcements.

Agency	How to Get a Job Kit
Defense Department	http://www.hrsc.osd.mil
Human Resource Services	
National Capital Region	
Defense Finance and Accounting Service–Kansas City Center	Send an e-mail message to rdfas-kc@cleveland.dfas.mil with the subject: Send Job Kit

Air Force Personnel Center	http://www.afpc.af.mil/palacecompass/applican/AFJOB1.HTM
Army Civilian Personnel	http://www.cpol.army.mil
U.S. Army Europe	http://www.chrma.hqusareur.army.mil/Resumix/
Army—North Central Region	http://ncweb.ria.army.mil/cpoc/resumix/jobkits/jobkits.htm
Army—Pacific Region	http://www.cpol.army.mil/pac/jobkit.htm
Army—South Central Region	http://www.cpol.army.mil/scr/emp-center/stairs1.htm
Army—West Region	http://www.cpoc.army.mil/resume/resumekit.htm
Army—Northeast Region	http://www.cpol.army.mil/ner/resumix/resumix.htm
Immigration and Naturalization Service	See Appendix E.
Justice Department	No job kit. Resume instructions are included in vacancy announcements.

How to Submit a Resume by E-Mail or on the World Wide Web

Just when you thought the process couldn't get any more automated, it did. With e-mail or the World Wide Web, you can automate the resume process on your end as well. We are getting closer and closer to the day when you will get hired without ever touching a piece of paper.

Why would you want to go paperless? For starters, faxing is risky business. If you're susceptible to Murphy's Law, every time you send a resume by fax, the machine on the other end runs out of toner or sends ugly black streaks up and down the left side of your resume. DoD isn't even accepting faxes anymore. Postal mail is safer and cleaner, but it's slower and more expensive. If you see a job vacancy announcement on Thursday and the closing date is Friday, your best bet is to submit your resume electronically to make sure it gets there on time.

Plus, you have to admit, it's pretty cool that you can submit your resume this way. Before you started reading this chapter, did you ever think you might be applying for a job online? You're on the cutting edge!

First, let's talk about e-mail. Agencies accepting e-mail resumes have very stringent requirements. As always, read the vacancy announcement or job kit carefully for instructions, but as an example, look at how Defense's Washington Human Resource Services Center handles e-mail:

☆ E-mails must be sent to resume@hrsc.osd.mil.

☆ The subject line of your e-mail must have the word "resume" in it.

☆ The body of the message must begin with 10 "@" signs in a row, like this:

@@@@@@@@@@

You must include your resume in the body of the message. Do not send it as an attachment. Different mail systems handle attachments in different ways, often garbling the attachments and making them unreadable. You can just cut and paste your resume into the e-mail message.

Here's a warning about cutting and pasting: Cutting and pasting sometimes inserts invisible breaks at the ends of lines in paragraphs, which, even though you can't see them, mess up the computer system's ability to read the resume. So, to be safe, you should go to the end of each line within a paragraph and press the Delete key to get rid of those invisible characters.

Once you send your resume by e-mail to DoD, you will receive a confirmation message that it has been received and processed by Resumix. Once that happens, you must submit a self-nomination form for the position you are seeking. The self-nomination form is on the DoD Web site at www.hrsc.osd.mil/empinfo.htm.

Self-nomination forms are the way you get yourself considered for specific jobs with most agencies. You may wind up applying for several jobs over several months, but remember that most agencies will let you have only one resume in their databases.

The job kits won't tell you this, but you can update your resume at any time, though some personnel offices process updates only once a month. By updating your resume, you can tweak it to emphasize the job skills listed in a specific vacancy. And by all means, update your resume whenever you gain a new skill by attending training, completing courses, or learning new skills on-the-job. The more relevant skills you have on your resume, the better. So don't be afraid to update and resubmit your resume. Just remember that the previous version will be replaced by the new one.

> **The job kits won't tell you this, but you can update your resume any time.**

Now here's how to apply on the Web. One advantage the Web has over all other forms of submission is that Web forms are in fill-in-the-blank format. If you fill in every blank, you know you have hit all the information the agency is looking for. Many of

the online resume builders also allow you to view the resume before you send it, giving you time to print it out for your records, save it to disk, and review it for errors.

The Army and DoD have their own online resume builders, and the Patent and Trademark Office has online applications for patent examiners. You're going to look at how to submit resumes on the Web via OPM's USAJOBS site. USAJOBS is the only government-wide database of federal job vacancies on the Web. The site includes 7,000 job listings a month from every corner of the government. Several agencies are also paying OPM to sponsor special vacancy listings available only to internal employees. The second announcement in Chapter 2 was for an OPM vacancy.

In April 1998, USAJOBS set up an online resume builder. People could submit their resumes online into an OPM database of potential hires. By June, more than 19,000 people had created online resumes on USAJOBS. The only problem was, nobody was looking at the resumes. They were just sitting there. And for the most part, they're still just sitting there. (Don't lose heart! DoD, the Army, the Air Force, INS, and other agencies are actively using their resume databases. Only the OPM resume database was a complete dead end.)

In the middle of June, some of the resumes started moving. A handful of job vacancy announcements was linked to the resume builder, where applicants could complete resumes, click Submit, and ship their resumes off to the agency offering the job vacancy. By the end of June, 154 job vacancies were marked as accepting online resumes. A total of 247 applicants responded by submitting their resumes through the USAJOBS resume builder.

Admittedly, that's a tiny percentage of all the job vacancies in government. But it is a start. As agencies increasingly rely on USAJOBS to post their job vacancies, more and more will start accepting resumes through the Web site as well.

Here's how the USAJOBS system works: You search the USAJOBS database until you find a job vacancy that piques your interest. As you read the vacancy announcement, you notice an animated envelope sealing itself on your screen. Next to the envelope is a hyperlink that reads Submit Resume Online. You print out the vacancy announcement and then click on the link and go to the online resume builder.

First, the system prompts you to create a personal password so that only you can access your resume to make changes. Then, you create your resume by filling in the blanks labeled Name, Address, Objective, and so on. If the vacancy announcement requests any special information, the resume builder has a blank marked Miscellaneous, where that information goes.

If you click View, you see what your resume will look like to the hiring manager. If you want to make changes, you click Edit to return to the resume. Once you're satisfied, you click Submit, and off your resume goes to the hiring agency.

The next time you search for a job vacancy and discover that you can submit a resume online, all you have to do is click on that animated envelope, enter your password, and return to the resume you already created. You can make changes to the resume to reflect the new vacancy announcement and then ship it off as well.

The USAJOBS system automatically reformats your resume to match the requirements of different agencies. If the agency wants your Social Security number directly beneath your name, that's where it will appear. If another agency wants your Social Security number directly above your name, then that's where it will appear. That saves you the trouble of reformatting resumes for each different agency.

OPM keeps resumes in its database for six months, after which they are deleted.

Online resume builders are clearly in their infancy. However, you should look for more and more job vacancies on the Web connected to resume builders as agencies push for a paperless end-to-end hiring process.

You're Ready for the Resume Revolution

So there you have it. You now know how to write and format a scannable resume, or as they call it in DoD, a Resumix (Resumix is to scannable resumes as Kleenex is to tissue paper). You now know where to find resume job kits. And you know how the computers actually read your resume. You can wow your colleagues and friends with your newfound knowledge.

The person who will benefit most from this knowledge is you. You should now be confident and ready to take on digital resumes. Keep this book by your side as you create your first scannable resume. Refer to the sample resume in Appendix A. And remember to read job kit and vacancy instructions very carefully.

You are now on the front lines of the resume revolution. Crack your knuckles, take a deep breath, and charge forth!

CHAPTER 10

Boosting Your Employment Chances with Great KSAs

Your new federal resume will qualify you to get in the race for a federal job or a promotion. But once you're in the race, another portion of your application will give you the boost you need to win. That portion is known as the KSA statements. KSA stands for Knowledge, Skills, and Abilities.

Like OPM's Steve McGarry said in Chapter 6, the first purpose of the federal resume is to see that the candidate meets the basic qualifications for the vacancy announcement (for example, academic degrees, years of experience, areas of expertise, technical capabilities). The KSAs tell whether the person is qualified to perform the specific position.

KSA statements are the one-half to full-page descriptions of the relevant, superior knowledge, skills, and abilities you write and attach to your resume. Well-written KSA statements convince readers you have what it takes to succeed in the position for which you're applying. An excellent set of KSAs puts you in the final heat of the job race. Poorly written KSA statements guarantee that you won't get the job. KSAs are extremely important.

You may have heard rumors about KSAs: what they are, how HR professionals "grade" them, and how to write them. In this chapter, I'll give you the real heads-up on KSAs; show you how to identify requests for KSA statements in job vacancy announcements; explain how to write KSA statements with basic rules, helpful tips, and examples; and show you how to format your KSAs.

An In-Depth Look at KSAs

KSAs are supplemental statements to your application that give specific examples of paid and nonpaid work experience, education, training, awards, and honors that support each major work area of an announced position. There are usually four to six KSAs listed on each announcement.

> **A good set of KSAs can set you apart from your competition.**

KSAs are usually written in the first person (*I did this and that*) and, as mentioned previously, are typically one-half to one full page each. So a complete set of KSAs will average two to five pages if five statements are requested. First-level HR professionals grade or "rate" them. If you pass this level, your application can go to the hiring panel or the hiring manager. KSA statements are usually mandatory to be considered for a position. A good set of KSAs can set you apart from your competition.

KSAs are also a writing test and an elimination tool. KSAs require an ability to communicate in writing, an ability to understand instructions, skill in using a computer to produce the document, an ability to interpret the announcement, knowledge of an agency's or organization's mission and purpose, and the ability to interpret the special needs of the hiring organization. If you sharply write about your experiences in each KSA statement, hiring managers will "rate" you very well.

Definition of Knowledge, Skills, and Abilities

Here's how the government defines knowledge, skills, and abilities:

☆ **Knowledge.** An organized body of information, usually of a factual or procedural nature, which, if applied, makes adequate performance on the job possible.

☆ **Skills.** The proficient manual, verbal, or mental manipulation of data, people, or things. Observable, quantifiable, measurable.

☆ **Abilities.** The power to perform an activity at the present time. Implied is a lack of discernible barriers, either physical or mental, to performing the activity.

Sometimes announcements request *KSAOs,* which means *"Other" Personal Characteristics.* According to the government, the *O* stands for a special, specific personality factor or aptitude or a physical or mental trait needed to do the work, which appears either in addition to or to a greater extent than what is generally expected of all employees in all jobs.

How Agencies Grade KSAs

HR professionals have a "rating and ranking" system for each KSA statement. Your statements can range from Superior to Not Acceptable. By writing your statements in sufficient detail so that the reviewer can determine the level of your knowledge, skill, or ability, you can convince the hiring staff to rank you as Superior.

Crediting plans (the name of the HR professionals' rating systems) vary from job opening to job opening. Because the plans are personnel tools, they are most often not public information. So you probably won't know which KSAs the hiring managers consider the most important. Just remember when you're writing the KSAs that you are being graded. You want to achieve maximum points for each KSA.

> **Remember when you're writing the KSAs that you are being graded.**

A GS-7 secretary position may have the following crediting plan. (The actual points given to each element are confidential.)

1. Ability to maintain and plan schedules, respond to changes in scheduling in order to maintain supervisor's calendar, and assure smooth flow of office operation. ____ **points**

2. Skill in utilizing word processing programs and other automated programs in order to prepare correspondence and reports and to track the status of such documents. ____ **points**

3. Ability to communicate orally in order to receive and direct calls and to give technical assistance. ___ **points**

4. Ability to independently plan and carry out multiple assignments under short deadlines and to provide substantive support on special projects. ___ **points**

5. Ability to acquire and apply knowledge of the responsibility of various administrative and program offices in order to refer calls and correspondence to appropriate offices and to coordinate and review the format, grammar, and organization of various work products from these offices. ___ **points**

A KSA by Any Other Name Is Still the Same

Deep in the text of the dense federal vacancy announcement, you will find instructions for writing additional statements that will further describe your ability to perform the job. You already know what they're called: KSAs.

Agencies don't always call these statements "Knowledge, Skills and Abilities." Sometimes agencies refer to them as Quality Ranking Factors, Narrative Factors, Supplemental Statements, and so on. Announcements might ask for a separate sheet of paper with a response to three to five elements, factors, or knowledge, skill, and abilities statements.

Each announcement will be different in content, instruction, detail, format, and font type. You will have to become accustomed to looking for the KSA requirements—especially to determine if they are mandatory or require separate sheets of paper.

Federal Job Announcement Examples with KSA Requirements

In this section, you'll find parts of three federal job announcements that give requirements for KSA statements. I have placed footnotes in each announcement where I want you to notice particular instructions and information. Analyzing the instructions and responding correctly can make a difference in your candidacy for the position.

Job Announcement Example 1

Position: AGRICULTURAL PROGRAM SPECIALIST, GS-1145-09/12

DEPARTMENT OF AGRICULTURE (USDA)

USDA, Farm Service Agency

SPECIALIZED EXPERIENCE

Specialized experience is experience that demonstrated the following:

Knowledge[1] of the laws and regulations governing agricultural stabilization and conservation programs and of the particular application of national policies and objectives at the State level; Understanding of farming practices and customs in the United States, and of the economic needs of farm communities at the State level; Knowledge of current State and Federal agricultural trends; and Ability to establish and maintain effective relationships with representatives of public and private organizations, farmers' associations, and others, and to interpret regulations, programs and policies affecting them.

Examples of qualifying specialized experience include:[2] Agricultural extension work as a subject-matter specialist, county agent or assistant or associate county agent. Teacher of vocational agriculture. District Director, State program specialist, or county office employee performing duties in the operational phases of farm programs such as production adjustment, price support, and conservation. Experience at the county, district or State government levels in the operational phases of farm programs of the type carried out through such agencies as the Soil Conservation Service, Farmers Home Administration, or related programs.

Knowledges, Skills, and Abilities Required (Mandatory):[3]

For each of the criteria listed below, describe specifically and accurately the relevance of each of the following: experience, training, education, and awards.

You should include specific tasks performed,[4] the dates you performed them, and where you were working at the time.

Knowledge of FSA farm programs and operations.

Knowledge of the FSA county office workload and work measurement system.

Ability to analyze and interpret written material.

Ability to communicate in writing.

Ability to communicate orally.

Notes:[5] There are no special forms for these statements. They may be submitted on plain paper with your name and the announcement number at the top. Candidates who do not submit the supplemental statement will not be considered.

Supplement on plain paper, in narrative format, information which concisely addresses each of the knowledge, skills and abilities listed under Ranking Factors. Include work experience, education, and training that clearly demonstrates how well you possess each element. Current Federal employees applying for promotion under this announcement will not receive further consideration if KSA narrative is not submitted.

Please submit the following:

- Application

- Performance Appraisal

- Supplemental KSA (knowledge, skills and abilities) Statements[6]

Author's Comments

1. This announcement is very specific; it tells you the knowledge required very clearly.

2. Tasks—very unusual, but the announcement gives you examples of tasks to support the KSAs.

3. For Knowledge, Skills and Abilities, notice the word *mandatory*. That means mandatory, or don't apply.

4. Again, it tells you to write about specific tasks.

5. Very detailed instructions about how to write the KSAs/Ranking Factors.

6. KSAs are referred to here as Supplemental Statements.

Job Announcement Example 2

Legal Secretary, GS-7

FDIC

JOB INFORMATION CENTER

WASHINGTON, DC 20429 9990

QUALITY RANKING FACTORS (DESIRABLE KNOWLEDGE, SKILLS, AND ABILITIES):[1]

1. Knowledge of administrative policies, procedures, and requirements of a legal office.

2. Skill in controlling correspondence, maintaining a suspense system, and following up on assignments.

3. Skill in locating, analyzing, and summarizing information from files and documents in order to respond to correspondence or telephone calls.

4. Skill in composing and preparing routine correspondence.

5. Ability to establish and maintain a filing system.

EVALUATION METHODS:[2] Applicants will be evaluated on the basis of information provided in their application package as to their experience, training, self-development, and awards; knowledge, skills and abilities; and, performance appraisals. Failure to provide specific information as to your qualifications for the position to be filled (including any selective and/or quality ranking factors described in this vacancy announcement) could result in disqualification.[3]

Author's Comments

1. These KSAs are called Quality Ranking Factors.

2. Evaluation methods are provided.

3. These KSAs are mandatory.

Job Announcement Example 3

TYPE OF POSITION: COMPUTER ASSISTANT, GS-0335-7

SALARY: $26,075-$33,893 PER ANNUM

LOCATION: Information Technology Division, VAMC, CHARLESTON, SC

RATING AND RANKING:[1] The following KSAOs[2] (Knowledge, Skills, Abilities, and Other Characteristics) will be used to further evaluate applicants who meet the qualification requirements described by determining the extent to which their work or related experience, education, training, awards, and outside activities, etc. indicate they possess the knowledges, skills, and abilities described below. All applicants should address each KSAO listed, providing clear, concise, accurate, detailed information that shows level of accomplishment or degree to which they possess the knowledge, skills, and abilities.[3] KSAOs (job elements for wage grade jobs) can work to your advantage. It is important that you put time and effort into developing responses to these evaluation factors that are relevant only to this job vacancy.[4] Qualified promotion candidates will be evaluated using a rating guide developed on the KSAO concept (job element for wage grade jobs). All relevant information available on each qualified candidate, taken as a whole, will be evaluated against each rating factor or job element, as appropriate, to determine the amount of credit to be granted. Information on how to respond to KSAOs is available to Human Resources Management Service.[5]

☆ Knowledge of electronic principles and mechanics of the computer, related components, and auxiliary and peripheral equipment.

☆ Ability to apply computer logic and communication protocols.

☆ Knowledge of operating systems such as Windows 95, Windows NT, and application packages, etc. Consideration is given to scope of knowledge of these systems and application packages.

☆ Ability to train others in computer applications.

☆ Ability to problem solve, evaluate and analyze problems and propose and implement working solutions in Local Area Network environment.

☆ Skill in the installation, repair, and maintenance of electronic digital computer systems, auxiliary, or peripheral equipment. Please provide examples.

Author's Comments

1. This announcement gives many details of rating and ranking for your information.

2. The KSAs are referred to as KSAOs. "Other characteristics" represents the fourth letter here.

3. Detailed instructions on the importance of showing the level of accomplishment.

4. Emphasis on the importance of these "evaluation factors" and that they should be relevant to this position.

5. There is a KSAO rating guide that is available at the Human Resources Management Service. You could call this office and get a copy of the crediting plan on these KSAOs.

How To Write Great KSAs

A Department of Justice HR professional told me, "I want to see one or two good examples for each KSA." HR professionals want to read meaningful, interesting statements with concrete examples describing your skills. Three basic rules of thumb are as follows:

☆ Give at least one good example per KSA.

☆ Make every example different for each KSA statement.

☆ Your KSA statements should be one-half to one page each—no more, no less.

> HR professionals want to read meaningful, interesting statements with concrete examples describing your skills.

Here's an example of a bad KSA statement made great. The KSA is "skill in research and providing information to internal and external customers":

> **Too short and general:** As a Library Technician I research information for customers, provide assistance to databases, and maintain library materials.

> **Rewrite with specifics about program, customers, skills, and results:** As a Library Technician at the National Agricultural Library, I am part of the new Customer Service focus being implemented at Agricultural Research Service to improve response time for information and materials to internal and external customers. For example, I am ensuring on-site delivery of material from the general collection within 20 minutes of request. Because of my knowledge of the library collection and understanding most of my customers' needs, I am providing books and articles in response to e-mail, fax, mail, telephone, TDD or Ariel (electronic delivery) requests within 2 to 4 days.

For "ability to communicate orally," don't just write, "I answer the phone all day, take messages, and forward calls. I also communicate with employees in the office about projects and administration. I communicate orally at least 50% of the day." Anyone can say that. This statement will not separate you from your competition. In fact, you will not get any points at all. A better way to tell the reader how well you communicate is this detailed paragraph:

> As the only Secretary to the Assistant Chief of Dermatology,[1] I receive all incoming phone calls from her direct staff (20 department heads at NIH), academic professors, investigators, and legislators.[2] I screen the calls by asking the subject of their inquiry and answer as many questions as I can[3] knowing my supervisor's schedule, current projects, and meetings. I take detailed notes and forward as many calls directly to the appropriate department heads as possible, saving my supervisor's time. I handle more than 15 inquiries per hour of which 10 I handle myself.[4] Approximately 50% of my day is spent speaking with staff and others by telephone, in person, and by e-mail. I am knowledgeable of my department's current programs,[5] which at the moment is the "Population Control" project that has been approved by Congress and is being set in motion throughout the nation from this office. Most of the phone calls are related to this new program at this moment. I keep up-to-date on the activities, schedule and issues so that I can answer questions and understand the status of the program. I enjoy providing responsive customer service to our internal and external customers—professional staff, investigators, vendors and the public.[6] I answer their questions, find information and followup as fast as I can

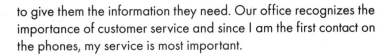

to give them the information they need. Our office recognizes the importance of customer service and since I am the first contact on the phones, my service is most important.

Author's Comments

1. Title of position and office—give a reference to the position and organization.

2. Who you support in the office—describe the geographic or personnel scope of the office.

3. What you do—action statement.

4. Quantifiers of what you do—performance measures if possible.

5. Specialized knowledge—the knowledge you have to be able to do your job.

6. Customer service statement—remember the customers you serve.

The personnel reviewer and hiring manager can see that this smart secretary knows what is going on in her office. She doesn't just answer the phones; she listens to the questions, finds answers, and can give answers because she is aware of her office's mission. She also knows, based on who is calling, what kind of information the person probably wants. She reads information about her office's new programs and gives the information with confidence. She's more than a secretary; she's a public information officer, a public relations officer, an administrative officer, and probably a computer specialist too! Her excellent KSA statement has given her a mega-advantage over all the other secretaries who have applied.

Important Elements of the KSA Statement

The following sections describe the important elements of KSA statements.

Write Your Statement in First Person as a Narrative Statement

This writing style is similar to writing a letter. This person could have written the preceding statement to her mother:

Dear Mom,

How are you doing? To answer your question about what I do at work, here's just part of what I do:

As the only Secretary to the Assistant Chief of Dermatology, I receive all incoming phone calls from her direct staff (20 department heads at NIH), academic professors, investigators, and legislators. I screen the calls by asking the subject of their inquiry and answer as many questions as I can knowing my supervisor's schedule, current projects, meetings . . . .

Write About a Specific Situation, Project, or Task

OPM recommends that if you are writing an accomplishment KSA, you should include the context, the challenge, your action, and the result. The same CCAR model is used for writing SES Executive Core Qualfications.

1. **Context:** Write about the individuals and groups with whom you worked and/or the environment in which you worked.

2. **Challenge and Action:** Describe a specific problem or goal and the actions you took to address a challenge.

3. **Result:** Give examples of results. If you can include numbers to quantify the result, please do that.

To illustrate this formula, study the KSA examples written by an equal employment specialist, GS-7. The bracketed numbers in the two examples below correspond to the formula above.

Skill in applying analytical techniques and procedures:

My ability to apply analytical techniques and procedures has been demonstrated in my current position over the last 5 years as the Executive Assistant to the Chief of Public Affairs. [1:] The critical function of the command is to respond to sensitive and highly visible public affairs that directly affect the public's perception of the Corps of Engineers. [2:] In producing correspondence, communicating with external and internal offices, and assisting with major projects, I analyze situations, projects and procedures in order to [3:] support the office mission the most efficiently and professionally.

Previously as the Secretary, U.S. Army Corps of Engineers, [1:] I was tasked with developing ways to improve the efficiency of the office. [2:] I analyzed administrative functions and job tasks, information sources and correspondence and reporting systems. [3:] As a result, I reorganized administrative functions, designed and improved correspondence handling system with the use of an Excel spreadsheet to track files, and reorganized the physical layout of the office.

Knowledge of Executive Orders, Public Laws, and Civil Rights Acts pertaining to EEO as they relate to EEO complaints:

As a [1:] Primary Member of the Special Emphasis Planning Committee (SEPC), I utilize my knowledge of Executive Orders, Public Laws, and Civil Rights Acts. I am an organizational liaison between managers and the federal employee receiving and transmitting information regarding employee needs and concerns. [2:] I interview employees and report to the director at organizational staff meetings. [3:] I am also responsible for ensuring that the objectives of the EEO program, the Affirmative Employment Plan, are met.

Include Job-Related Education, Courses, Training, and Awards

In addition to writing paid and nonpaid work examples for your KSAs, you should also include job-related training, educational courses, awards, and memberships. Overall, you need to look like you can perform well in the specific KSA area.

Include Buzzwords

Buzzwords will result in a higher grade on your application. The verbs that you select to describe your knowledge, skills, and abilities can demonstrate your level of expertise. Look at a few ways to describe your responsibilities, skills, and abilities, and the ratings that will result from each:

> **Buzzwords will result in a higher grade on your application.**

KSA statement: Ability to use regulatory material.

- ☆ Superior: interpret regulatory material.
- ☆ Good: research regulatory material.
- ☆ Satisfactory: apply regulatory material.
- ☆ Barely acceptable: recognize regulatory material.

KSA statement: Ability to schedule work.

- ☆ Superior: schedule work to accomplish agency mission.
- ☆ Good: schedule work to accomplish project goals.
- ☆ Satisfactory: schedule work to accomplish unit objectives.
- ☆ Barely acceptable: schedule work to accomplish own work.

KSA statement: Ability to communicate in writing.

- ☆ Superior: write technical reports.
- ☆ Good: write critiques.
- ☆ Satisfactory: write letters.
- ☆ Barely acceptable: write internal communications.

KSA statement: Ability to plan, organize, and schedule work.

- ☆ Superior: process action to meet project goals.
- ☆ Good: process action to meet given objectives.
- ☆ Satisfactory: process action using established precedent.
- ☆ Barely acceptable: process action using procedural instructions.

Five Approaches to KSA Statements

Here are some ways to approach KSA statements:

☆ Describe a specific *situation*.

☆ Give an *overview* of your experience.

☆ Give an example of relevant *education* or *training*.

☆ Describe an *award* given for specific accomplishments.

☆ Describe an experience in your previous jobs in the *history* format.

Don't feel tied to one approach. Feel free to combine different types in a single statement. Each KSA statement, for example, can be made up of paragraphs giving an overview, describing a situation (one or two of these), discussing relevant education, and describing an award or recognition. Next, you'll find examples of the five types of KSA statements.

Situation KSA

This specific example demonstrates your knowledge, skill, or ability in a certain area. This is an example of a nonpaid work experience KSA statement for a budget analyst, GS-9.

Ability to perform effectively and maintain composure in tension-filled situations:

As a member and Chairman of the Middletown, Virginia, Town Planning Commission, I directed sometimes tension-filled Rezoning Meetings that affected the commercial activity of the town, but would also affect the residential character of the town. I was successful in mediating controversial rezoning issues concerning the Main Street. I also chaired many sensitive hearings, acting as sounding board for long-time residents. The rezoning activities involved local media coverage and required skills in problem-solving and public relations.

Overview KSA

This introductory, summary KSA statement is for a secretary, GS-7.

Skill in expressing ideas orally in a form that is clear, logical, and grammatically correct:

As a Secretary to 3 senior government executives, I have developed a clear, logical, and grammatically correct writing style that is trusted by my supervisors. I am skilled in communicating clearly both orally and in writing. My supervisors depend on me to communicate priorities and significant information to department heads, congressional offices, and the public. I am sensitive to public affairs issues, politically accurate responses, and tense situations. I speak and write with excellent grammar.

The next KSA was written by a security specialist, GS-12.

Knowledge of the theories, principles, practices, and techniques of Automated Information Systems (AID) security for U.S. government computer systems and installation:

As a result of experience in both Army and Navy operations, in overseas as well as with U.S.-wide computer systems, I have maintained extensive knowledge of U.S. government computer systems. In addition, due to widely varied experience, I have cultivated a network of top computer experts in the U.S. and abroad who regularly inform one another about latest updates and developments in sophisticated systems.

Education/Training KSA

The following is a statement of related education and training that supports the KSA. The employee is chief of medical technical equipment, GS-12.

A general knowledge of the mission, organization and activities of a health care facility:

Education and Specialized Training:

Currently enrolled (with 42 hours earned) in dual degree Bachelor's program at Howard University, Washington, DC, in Business Management and Computer Sciences.

Earned well over 1,500 hours training with advanced medical technology and equipment (see complete listing attached to federal resume).

In earlier career, completed over 400 hours as firefighter in fire safety, prevention and emergency medical care.

Award/Recognition KSA

An award or recognition indicates the quality at which duties have been performed that demonstrate a KSA. The record of the award must contain sufficient information about relevant behaviors or activities to show that the KSA was demonstrated at some level. The following KSA was written by an environmental specialist, GS-13.

Knowledge of federal hazardous materials transportation regulations:

At the conclusion of a recent Safety Review by the Office of Motor Carriers, I was commended for knowledge of regulations and programs developed for the company. In addition on my most recent performance evaluation, I was cited for having "excelled at meeting new challenges and improving the performance of the Fleet Safety Programs."

The next example was for a foreign affairs officer, GS-13.

Ability to plan and direct program activities:

Commended on most recent Performance Review for being "only division officer who planned and managed two town meetings, one month apart, in St. Louis and San Francisco. The results were outstanding. The St. Louis event drew over 350 citizens (despite the floods) and great media coverage. The San Francisco meeting, with a record-breaking attendance of 1,300, was the first such meeting in over 13 years. Both the Secretary and the spokesperson commented publicly on their tremendous success."

Historic KSA

The following summary of past experience supports the KSA for a vocational rehabilitation specialist, GS-12.

Ability to promote the rehabilitation program and to negotiate contracts and agreements with prospective employers and training facilities:

My work in vocational rehabilitation for the department has spanned over 20 years, and, through regular positions and special assignments, I have gained a broad understanding of the department's mission, goals and programs. As a result, for the past three years I have been selected to speak on panel presentations regarding "Effective Client Strategies" at the annual National Rehabilitation Hospital Conference.

Here is another historic KSA example, this one for an inspector general, GS-12.

Skill in the analysis of complex multi-million dollar financial transactions:

For the past ten years, I have managed cases that involve individuals charged with economic crimes as well as local and national businesses charged with such offenses as money laundering and procurement fraud. For example, I serve on task force investigations in complex . . . .

Recommended KSA Format

Here is the federally recommended setup for each KSA. Follow this format when you write your own KSAs. The fonts and paper you use should match your resume. See Appendix B for more examples.

Department of Health and Human Services

Program Support Center

Division of Supply Management, Quality Assurance Branch

Perry Point, MD

Announcement Number: 98P-01

Title of position: Project Coordinator, GS301-12

Candidate: Thomas Richard Smith, SS: 000-00-0000

KNOWLEDGE, SKILLS, AND ABILITIES

Knowledge of theory and principles of management, organization and administrative procedures of a Medical Supply Center.

As the Center Project Coordinator from 1985 until present, I have demonstrated my expert knowledge of theory and principles of management, organization, and administrative procedures of the Supply Service Center. I am currently coordinating seven major clinical NIH drug studies, and serve as the facilitator for the Veterans Administration's central mail order pharmacy program (CMOP). This is a large service contract disseminating products to ten distribution centers.

Examples of Good KSAs

To help you get started with your own KSAs, carefully read the three KSA examples that follow. What approaches do they take? Are all the basic elements there?

Expert knowledge of the occupational area of specialization, its governing laws, regulations, methodologies, and/or policies to provide sound and authoritative technical guidance on all issues related to the assigned program:

I serve as the Office of General Counsel's LAN and System Administrator; team leader and technical advisor for the Legal Automated Workload System (LAWS); and the author of the Annual Information Technology Strategic Plan.

My expertise in the area of Information Technology within the OGC is communicated with staff outlining resources assigned to programs, reviewing capabilities and assigning tasks to two contractors who are LAN Engineers, a GS-12 Program Analyst and a GS-11 Management Analyst. I directly consult with our clients (attorneys) to determine their IT needs and provide quality support and assistance.

I have examined the training needs in four areas: managerial, legal, computer and clerical support and made training recommendations to increase the effective use of our new systems and equipment. To date more than 98% of the administrative staff and 92% of the legal staff have received system training.

Skill in applying analytical techniques and procedures:

My ability to apply analytical techniques and procedures has been demonstrated in my current position over the last 5 years as the Executive Assistant to the Chief of Public Affairs. The critical function of the command is to respond to sensitive and highly visible public affairs that directly affect the public's perception of the Corps of Engineers. In producing correspondence, communicating with external and internal offices, and assisting with major projects, I analyze situations, projects and procedures in order to support the office mission efficiently and professionally.

Previously as the Secretary, U.S. Army Corps of Engineers, I was tasked with analyzing office operations and procedures and making decisions to reorganize many administrative functions. By analyzing the correspondence and reporting systems, I redesigned an improved correspondence handling system.

As the Chair for the Town Planning Commission, Middletown, VA, I analyzed rezoning and zoning hearing petitions. Utilizing knowledge of the zoning requirements, public laws and historical value of the community, I mediated and facilitated meetings and led significant decision-making impacting the future business and residential community.

Ability to plan, organize and manage projects;
Ability to communicate orally;
Ability to negotiate and give presentations:

Note: Here is a KSA statement that could cover any of the above three KSAs. This example involves planning, communicating, and negotiating. You could choose any of the three KSAs to use with this example. Also notice the Results and Recognition statement at the end of this KSA. It is clear what the results were from his effort. He received a well-deserved recognition for his initiative.

In January 1996 following the notification that SAMHSA would receive a dramatically reduced budget, I recognized that important programs would be discontinued, including a much needed drug-abuse program for the Kickapoo Reservation Indians in the State of

Texas. As the Federal Program Manager, I took the initiative to communicate the situation with the State of Texas to turn over funding to the State. I traveled to Texas on several occasions to negotiate directly with the State of Texas Project officer to ensure that the State appreciated the severity of the situation and the change in federal funding. I prepared a briefing booklet for State Representatives giving them the data on the 1,300 eligible adults on the Reservation and the fact that 2/3rds of the total population participated in the program.

Results: successfully achieved a cooperative agreement with the State with commitments of $500,000 per year. I also discovered an additional $400,000 from carry-over from previous year. Additionally brought in 4 other state agencies to assist with service provision and additional funding and support.

Recognition: Received Secretary's Award for Distinguished Award

Time to Practice

Now you have a firm grasp on what a KSA statement is, how to locate requests for KSAs in a vacancy announcement, what hiring managers are looking for in KSAs, the basic elements of great KSAs, and five ways to approach writing them. It's time for you to practice writing your own. Be sure to refer to the examples in this chapter as you draft, rewrite, and perfect your KSAs. Also see Appendix B for more KSA examples.

CHAPTER 11

Applying for the Senior Executive Service

The Civil Service Reform Act of 1978 created the Senior Executive Service (SES) in an effort to develop a corps of highly qualified federal managers who would be able to perform a range of functions at the highest levels of government. Rather than follow traditional career paths through single agencies, the idea behind the SES was that well-trained managers should be able to move between agencies and that a broad background on the part of federal managers would counteract some of the inbreeding associated with people spending entire careers in a single agency. Also, managerial service within government would not be the dominant criteria for gaining a senior position in federal agencies. The U.S. federal service, unlike nearly all professional government officials around the world, remains open to the possibility of people entering on the basis of experience gained outside government service.

A Profile of the SES

The SES has changed in many ways during the past 20-plus years, but it still constitutes the leadership cadre of the federal service. Of the 7,500 members of the SES, 88 percent are career civil servants. The remainder are noncareer (usually political) appointments or limited-term appointments. More than three-quarters of the SES are based in the Washington, D.C., metropolitan area. The skills mix of the SES reflects the requirements of federal agencies. Thirty-nine percent are in administrative or management fields. Another 13 percent provide legal services. Engineering, science/math, and other fields each account for 12 to 14 percent. Twenty percent of the SES are women, and 12 percent are minorities.

The first word of "Senior Executive Service" fits: It is a senior service, with 32 percent of its membership eligible for immediate retirement. Retirement remains the primary method of attrition in the SES. In 1996, 443 SES members did retire, or about 7 percent of the SES workforce. Turnover is low, but more than 500 SES positions are filled each year.

The 1993 National Performance Review recommended that the SES develop a "corporate perspective" that supports government-wide cultural change. The Clinton administration has announced intentions to attempt further modifications of the SES. In 1997, the Office of Personnel Management revised the Executive Core Qualifications (listed later in this chapter) used as the foundation of the SES. Under the guidance of the President's Management Council, the administration is conducting an extensive review of the SES and has made a commitment to introduce legislation that will bring additional changes to this corps.

> The 1993 National Performance Review recommended that the SES develop a "corporate perspective" that supports government-wide cultural change.

In many senses, the vision of the SES as a mobile corps of flexible executives remains the model around which the OPM endeavors to guide the SES's future development, even though the mobile model has largely not been implemented in practice.

Who Should Apply?

In the majority of cases, new members of the SES rise through career development ladders within single agencies or departments. They might serve within diverse components of the agency during their careers, but the federal service generally still adheres to the principle that advancement is related to development within a profession. A new SES manager in the Environmental Protection Agency's water program, for example, is more likely to come from within that program than from any other program within the EPA. Although most agencies have SES attorneys, an attorney experienced in immigration law is unlikely to transfer into an SES position in the antitrust division at the Department of Justice. Demonstrating relevant skills through an extended career is the surest route to enter the SES, and that is usually done most credibly at the agency where the promotion will be achieved.

New entrants to the SES who rise through career ranks frequently have 15 to 20 years' experience within their agencies. They largely have at least a college education and frequently possess graduate degrees and other forms of professional development training. Many will be identified and nurtured—or mentored—through their agency's SES candidate development programs or through other well-recognized channels, such as the Federal Executive Institute and the Women's Executive Leadership Program. Their experiences will include broadening through a couple of detail assignments at other agencies. Nearly all successful SES applicants will have a succession of outstanding performance evaluations and demonstrate a record of developing other people to ensure that their organizations continue to work well in their successors' hands. In addition to this sustained superior performance, it usually helps to have pulled one or two major projects out of the fire under emergency or unusual circumstances.

If the preceding description fits you, consider applying for the SES. Position vacancies for SES positions are found on the Web site at www.USAjobs.opm.gov. The vacancy list is updated regularly. Many individual agencies will advertise SES positions on their Web sites.

Requirements for Successful Applications

Applications for positions in the SES require—in addition to a strong resume—statements addressing as many as three sets of qualifying factors listed in the vacancy announcement. But first and foremost, entry into the SES requires the establishment of Executive Core Qualifications—the combination of managerial skills that are the precondition for entry into the SES. Unless the resume and the statements demonstrate possession of the Executive Core Qualifications, even exceptional technical qualifications will not be enough to develop a successful SES application.

The five Executive Core Qualifications (ECQs) are as follows:

- ☆ Leading Change
- ☆ Leading People
- ☆ Results Driven
- ☆ Business Acumen
- ☆ Building Coalitions/Communication

In addition to the Executive Core Qualifications, each agency can define sets of both mandatory and desirable technical qualifications for any SES position advertised. They vary according to the requirements that the agency defines as appropriate to the position. For example, an applicant for assistant administrator of the Federal Aviation Administration for airway facilities must be able to demonstrate professional knowledge of the design and engineering of radio navigational systems. Firsthand flying experience in the air navigational system might strengthen those qualifications, but that would be a desirable, rather than a mandatory, technical requirement.

More than managerial responsibilities, SES core qualifications require a demonstration of leadership potential. These descriptions of executive abilities cannot stand in isolation. As one personnel officer responsible for SES positions commented, "I want to know not merely what the applicant claims to have done; I need to know when and where it was done to make the case credible." This HR professional reported receiving as many as 60 applicants for each advertised SES announcement. Another Cabinet department advertised more than 40 SES positions in 1997 and received an average of 47 applicants per position.

Nearly one-third of applications are rejected for not meeting fully the advertised qualifications for the position. Of the rest, effective statements of ranking factors can make the difference between being grouped among the "well qualified," who gain interviews for the position, and the "qualified," who do not get to the interview stage. Of the nearly 35 "qualified" applicants in the departmental analysis, for example, the "well qualified" list usually numbered between 7 and 12 applicants. At the SES levels, then, the competition is intense, and several competitors might have inside tracks.

There is no substitute for substantial experience in gaining an SES position. Many SES members have 25 to 30 years of experience. As with most federal positions, the important dimension of an application responds to the question, "What have you done lately?" Federal personnel officers and selecting officials are most interested in the development of progressively responsible performance at or near the level for which one is applying. Typically, the SES applicant will be able to describe five to seven years of experience at the GM-15 level.

At any agency, advertisement of an SES opening indicates some organizational change—even if it is the retirement of an experienced executive or the creation of a new position to address some weakness identified by agency leaders. Knowing the agency is important, and any SES statement will be strengthened if the applicant knows what the agency leadership perceives as the needs of the position. The knowledge need not be gained from inside the agency, but the applicant bears the burden of demonstrating that experience and knowledge gained elsewhere provide enough background to perform effectively. Under these conditions, any candidacy is strengthened if the rating officials reviewing the applications—usually made up of other senior executives at or above the level being considered—know many of the individuals, and the application effectively reaffirms accomplishments that are already well-known to the agency's leadership. Successful applicants must demonstrate an ability to think at least two bureaucratic levels above the advertised position. An SES appointment will usually require the approval of an agency head, so a senior executive applicant must be able to speak that executive's language.

See Appendix G for the OPM's *Guide to SES Qualifications*.

Writing Executive Core Qualifications

Writing Executive Core Qualifications is no different from any other writing challenge: Well-written material that keeps the reader's interest gets more attention than sleeper prose. Still, the challenge of consolidating 20 years of accomplishments into five pages is significant—especially if there are too many successes to fit in the allotted space. The normal SES package is composed of a cover letter, federal resume, technical and managerial factors, and ECQs. The package can be put into a small portfolio or folder. Here are some basic principles to remember when writing successful ECQ statements:

> The challenge of consolidating 20 years of accomplishments into five pages is significant.

☆ The basics of effective writing still apply. Use the active voice. Your responses must convey what you did and what difference it made. Avoid passive constructions and bureaucratic phrasing: "I decided and directed" *not* "I was given responsibility for." Some scanner software that performs initial reviews of qualifications is programmed to read nouns that identify key skills. If you believe that an SES package might have to pass through a scanner, use more nouns and skill categories than you might otherwise include. See Chapter 9 for details on writing a scannable resume.

Here's an example of a nonscannable profile statement:

Profile:

Senior program manager with twenty-year background creating and managing innovative, cost-effective large-scale and long-term programs. Extensive governmental reengineering and streamlining experience. Strong strategic sense with the ability to balance short-term priorities against long-term organizational mission and goals. Excellent communication, leadership and negotiation skills. National network of professional contacts in and out of government.

Here's a scannable profile statement with emphasis on the nouns and key skills the scanner would search for in a senior government executive.

Profile:

Senior Program Manager. Reengineer. Innovator. Strategist. Communicator, Negotiator, Connected. Mission Planner. Leader. Cost Analyst. Budget Manager. Sets goals, priorities. Organizational representative with government and industry.

☆ Where technical skills require knowledge, Executive Core Qualifications require effective application of what you know. Effective statements require more than an explanation of your personal growth. On each account, describe the difference that you made in terms of effects on other people, other organizations, and agency policies. If you have been responsible for interagency coordination, it needs to be brought to the evaluators' attention.

☆ This is not the place to write about how you developed skills. Many of the KSA statements written for lower-level positions are effective where they show "progressive responsibility"—that is, how you gained increasingly complex skills or moved up the ladder. The SES needs people who can demonstrate, through what they have already done, that they are in a position to take charge, now. Well-qualified applicants must be able to describe effective responsibilities while heading programs. OPM materials suggest citing recent education and training that enhanced your skills in particular factors. If you do, make the link specific and stress the recency of it. Every lawyer has a law degree; that does not make every lawyer a leader. Although a developmental approach to explaining how you developed skills might work well in writing KSAs for lower-level positions, SES positions need to demonstrate executive performance. How you got there is a story for some other time.

☆ What have you done for me lately? The SES needs people who are ready to lead in today's environment. Use recent examples as much as possible. Three years are fine, but if you have to go back more than five years, the achievement needs to be spectacular. If an applicant's responses to Executive Core Qualifications dwell on accomplishments at the GM-13 level, the description will be less favorably received than comparable accomplishments at the GM-15 level.

☆ Be concise. OPM seeks one to one-and-a-half pages for each qualifications statement. You are writing executive summaries, not biographies. If you need more than one page, make certain that every word is important to convey your full leadership abilities. As much as possible, avoid repetition by relying on different achievements for each of the statements.

☆ Be specific. Use precise numbers to describe budget, personnel, dates (time frame), and other factors. Avoid the "various," "numerous," and "several " phrases that make people guess about how much. You need to convey enough familiarity with the results and the ways in which they were achieved so that your reader can easily grasp the full context of the environment and the achievement.

Make selections in describing particular achievements. Consider the following examples:

> As a senior investigator in an FBI District Office, an agent assembled a team to address a major smuggling operation. He conceived the investigative strategy, coordinated participation from other federal enforcement agencies as well as state and local law enforcement agencies, and directed preparations that resulted in 15 arrests, 12

convictions, and the seizure of more than $3 million in assets for the agencies involved.

Should that story be related as "Results Driven," "Building Coalitions/ Communication," or "Leading People"?

> As a senior financial manager at an agency operating both with appropriated funds and fee receipts, the applicant identified a substantial source of new revenue that did not quite fit into statutory categories that yield fee revenues—resulting in a major portion of agency services being provided for a limited populace that might have been charged a fee with a small change in the law. This manager developed the proposed statutory change, then worked with senior management to gain support for the legislation at the department, OMB, and congressional levels—yielding additional revenues from user fee accounts.

Does the achievement count as "Business Acumen" or "Building Coalitions/Communication"?

> Congress enacts a major new program, requiring a shift in the agency's mission—at least in the eyes of many agency managers. A program analyst within the policy office develops and articulates a rationale—consistent with the legislative history—and organizes a policy-planning team to give the new legitimacy within the agency. She then provides effective support in the development of budgets, personnel classifications, and an operational strategy to get the organization running within months of the deadline established in legislation.

Does this get listed under "Leading Change," "Results Driven," or "Business Acumen"?

In each case, a candidate with genuine likelihood of success will have numerous achievements in each category and have to make selections based upon which factors most deserve elaboration in order to achieve the best possible presentation for the advertised position. For a technical professional in a low-visibility program, experience speaking for the agency before congressional committees and staff could be rare—so any credible claim should be mentioned in that category. For an attorney who has been managing development of congressional testimony during his entire career, the same experiences could be written with an emphasis on program accomplishment or evaluation aspects of the same event.

In describing your achievements, attempt to provide different examples to highlight each of the qualification factors. Nothing can substitute for reviewing the core qualifications as a group, sorting through your resume and supporting notes, and making hard choices about where your achievements fit into the factors.

> **Effective statements combine breadth of accomplishments, clear indications of exceptional training, and a record of supervising others in the successful completion of tasks.**

In short, successful presentations of Executive Core Qualifications are most effective if they are consistent continuations of other elements of the federal application package. They should summarize—concisely—a record that demonstrates readiness for the responsibilities that the successful applicant will fulfill. Effective statements of the Executive Core Qualifications will combine breadth of accomplishments, clear indications of exceptional professional training, and a record of supervising other people in the successful completion of substantial tasks.

Remember, most SES applications are reviewed by agency Executive Resources Boards whose members are frequently familiar with both the challenges that will be reported in the statements and the conditions facing the agency at the time. The responses need to remind people of these accomplishments in a credible, consistent way.

OPM's Recommended Format

In announcing its new formulation of the Executive Core Qualifications, OPM recommended a format for applicants to consider in presenting their statements. These factors include the following:

Challenge. What was the specific problem you faced that needed resolution?

☆ It should be at a large organizational level, with agency-wide, government-wide, or national effects.

☆ It should require more than individual actions. Leadership means, at minimum, that you have the ability to get other people to follow when you set direction.

Context. Define the other factors (people, institutions, procedures) that made the challenge of executive caliber.

☆ It should include redefinition of goals, changes in conditions, some requirements to gain other people/organizations to comply with your changed direction.

☆ Be specific in terms of factors that made the challenge substantial: resources, people, laws, regulations, deadlines, complexity.

Action. What did you do that made a difference?

☆ Express your achievement in a team environment, but focus on your role within the team.

Result. What difference did it make?

☆ Performance and accountability are the critical factors. Your participation needs to be seen as the critical factor that accomplished something that someone else wanted and/or needed done.

Now you will review the ECQs from the OPM and the traits that should be covered in these statements.

Leading Change—*The ability to develop and implement an organizational vision that integrates key national and program goals, priorities, values, and other factors. Inherent to it is the ability to balance change and continuity—to continually strive to improve customer service and program performance within the basic government framework, to create a work environment that encourages creative thinking, and to maintain focus, intensity, and persistence, even under adversity.*

This statement needs to articulate an understanding of the mission and vision of the organization that you have led. Think up the organizational ladder. Describe your achievements in terms of how the head of the agency would have seen the challenge and why it should have been considered important.

If you have participated in major transformation of an organization—for example, taking a nuclear weapons program from a production focus to an environmental clean-up mission—this is the time to highlight your account of how you achieved the change.

Do not minimize the continuity factor here. It is important to realize that sometimes missions change even when authorizing laws and regulations do not. Convey the scope of the challenge, and describe your role in transforming the organization.

Leading People—*The ability to design and implement strategies that maximize employee potential and foster high ethical standards in meeting the organization's vision, mission, and goals.*

Leading people includes supervisory responsibilities, but they should be expressed in terms of coaching, mentoring, and motivating for success. Communications skills and the ability to convey instructions, delegate responsibilities, and achieve professional development among subordinates all should be stressed here.

Working across organizations is vital. Within an agency, critical is your ability to reach out, gain the support of other organizations, integrate the working of other managers, and represent the organization so that others come to rely on the role that your team plays in the achievement of defined objectives. Your ability to lead people should lead the reader to expect strong comments related to coalition building in the fifth factor.

Workforce diversity is part of the Leading People factor. Government requires an ability to work with all races, creeds, sexes, colors, religions, and nationalities. This factor should affirm a solid commitment to the professional development of women and minorities, describe affirmative employment achievements, and discuss overcoming challenges. Recruiting and retaining highly qualified people constitute one dimension of the presentation. Demonstrating your ability to train other team members who are highly regarded in the organization is a big help.

Diversity also should highlight the need to integrate a complex range of professional skills. Scientific, human resources, legal, public affairs, and other talents need to be melded to achieve complex missions. If you are a mathematician, how did you get your public affairs office to understand the importance of what you accomplished? If your skill is legal, how did you develop a mastery of the technology that your agency uses?

Results Driven—*Stresses accountability and continuous improvement. It includes the ability to make timely and effective decisions and produce results through strategic planning and implementation and evaluation of programs and policies.*

This factor should rely upon presentation of strong numerical achievements. Wherever possible, cite before and after data. In defining challenges, use indicators of performance that were considered unsatisfactory (that is, what is it you had to change?). In describing the results, compare the differences and describe the resources that you brought to bear to make a difference.

Changes need not only be in terms of results, but in terms of context. If your actions built alliances, strengthened relationships, or overcame resistance, that, too, is a result.

Mention successes in changing organizations—sustaining productivity in light of reduced resources. Mention policies and procedures you developed to incorporate new assignments while sustaining the organization's current productivity.

Describe methods you developed for defining nonessential factors and reducing or eliminating paperwork and other burdens on citizens while sustaining results. If you changed OSHA from measuring compliance with rules to measuring reductions in accident rates, or reductions in time lost to illness and injury, this change in focus should be highlighted here.

What changes did you institute—for example, monitoring mechanisms—to identify future opportunities for improvement and to provide incentives to sustain the improved performance?

What measures did you take to correct performance problems that preceded your leadership?

Business Acumen—*Involves the ability to acquire and administer human, financial, material, and information resources in a manner that instills public trust and accomplishes the organization's mission, and to use new technology to enhance decision making.*

Budget data, numbers of people, size of the constituency served, and methods of reducing costs/increasing efficiency should be highlighted here. Familiarity with procedures for establishing and justifying budgets, securing resources, and managing finances should be identified here.

Demonstrate the effective use of information technology for your activities. The critical factors here are not the abilities to use word processors and spreadsheets, but to define System Development Life Cycle strategies and other factors associated with the acquisition and management of technology resources. The Executive Review Board has to recognize that you know how to apply information technology to the design and management of the organization that you will supervise.

If you have success resolving major material weaknesses—financial management and accounting procedures, security deficiencies, or potential vulnerabilities of organizations that you have identified and overcome—this is the place to discuss those achievements.

Building Coalitions/Communication—*The ability to explain, advocate, and express facts and ideas in a convincing manner, and negotiate with individuals and groups internally and externally. It also involves the ability to develop an expansive professional network with other organizations and to identify the internal and external politics that impact the work of the organization.*

Where the Leading People factor addresses your ability to communicate down the organizational chart, this one emphasizes your ability to reach out to other organizations. This factor should highlight ability to work with nongovernmental organizations, the media, professional associations, and at least other substantial organizations within your department.

Written and oral communications are both required here. The question should not focus on your ability to write, but on your ability to set direction for others who will draft the correspondence, memoranda, speeches, and other material.

Working on interagency committees and coordinating multi-agency policy development and reporting groups are examples of achievements that should be described in this factor. Achieving change might require bringing perspectives of other agencies back to your organization and winning support for something that serves the public interest even if it encounters resistance within the agency.

Demonstrate your leadership in terms of speaking to state and local governments, or representing the U.S. on international working groups. This factor seeks for you to demonstrate your ability to convey a sense that you are in charge of an organization and an ability to convince others that your agency's positions on critical issues are well based. If you have testified before Congress or other legislatures, or participated in important staff-level meetings, these are the factors that should be brought to bear here. Again, the focus needs to be on the results that are realized from your efforts.

The Changing Competition for SES Positions

Competition for SES positions will become more intense in the next 10 years. Not only are numerous baby boomers seeking the promotions that will cap careers that began in the late 1960s, but the Clinton administration has promised to reduce the number of SES positions as a result of its National Partnership for Reinventing Government—the successor to the National Performance Review.

To date, most reductions were achieved by cutting the Department of Defense (closures of major installations resulted in many workforce cuts) or eliminating positions that were on the books but had not been filled. In other instances, agencies eliminated one position only to replace it with the creation of another—redesigned to conform to the changes that resulted from "reinvention." These changes, however, tend to be at the margins of the SES. Most SES positions are designated for the leadership of core programs that would require statutory changes. In an era of divided government, such major program changes are not very frequent, no matter how many proposals are advanced.

Appendix B contains samples of core qualifications statements developed to reflect the kinds of skills sought in different kinds of positions. Some are composites of real people—all of the positions are variations on positions that exist in different agencies of the federal government.

CHAPTER 12

Writing an Effective Cover Letter

Federal agencies rarely ask for cover letters as a required item in a job application because, on a federal resume, a job announcement number appears where the objective would be found on a private-sector resume. With that number so prominently displayed, no one should confuse your application with the mountains of other mail that pile into a personnel office every day.

To Send or Not to Send?

An effective cover letter can add important information and draw attention to elements of the application that you want to emphasize. As agencies increasingly move toward resumes as the most common form of application, a well-written cover letter can provide the margin separating yours from other applications that might have the same desired emphases.

Even a minimal cover letter can provide an opportunity to affirm information contained in the application and help to distinguish your application from others. A simple letter can make important distinctions that will ease the transition from application to acceptance. The most basic cover letter should guide reviewers through the material enclosed and be concise yet sufficiently detailed to stress the points important to the job. Cover letters also can be used to provide more information for senior positions.

Be sure to personalize the cover letter if a name is given on the job announcement. Before signing the letter, reread it carefully and make certain that it presents you as favorably as possible. Then review your completed application and make sure that all enclosures are ready for insertion into the envelope—in the order described in the cover letter. Then sign and seal, and it will be ready for delivery.

Here is an example of a stand-out cover letter.

Johnson Q. McKittrick
354 Hyattstown Boulevard
St. Louis, MO 63105
(314) 655-5578

February 27, XXXX

Director of Personnel
United States Secret Service
Law Enforcement Training Academy
Quantico, VA 22594

Dear Personnel Director:

This letter transmits my completed federal resume in response to your announcement of law enforcement officer positions, TREA/SS/1811/7-9, 98-345X. Thank you for your consideration of this application. I have dedicated my career preparation to law enforcement professions, and I am eager to build upon my military experience in your organization.

Let me direct your attention to my basic qualifications. After completing a bachelor's degree in the criminal justice program at the University of Missouri-St. Louis, I entered the U.S. Air Force and served a four-year enlistment as an Air Police Officer. I rose to the rank of sergeant (E-5) during those years and gained valuable street-level experience in law enforcement. I am fully dedicated to this profession.

In addition to the descriptions of my employment, I have included the following for your evaluation:

- A copy of my DD-214, indicating my service with the U.S. Air Force, and an honorable discharge, effective July 27, 1997. Part of this service included support of the U.S. Forces in Bosnia, which qualifies me for a five-point veteran's preference.

- A copy of the completion certificate from the Air Police Academy, reflecting previous training related to the position advertised.

- Five, one-page statements responding to the knowledge, skills, abilities and other factors identified on the job announcement.

Thank you for your consideration. I look forward to hearing from you.

Sincerely,

Johnson Q. McKittrick

Johnson Q. McKittrick

Emphasize Your Strongest Credentials

A good cover letter does more than outline an application for the officials reviewing the candidates. In responding to federal employment announcements, you want to make sure that your strongest credentials are emphasized and that reviewers have reason to focus on the critical information that separates your presentation from the others in the pile. A strong cover letter will focus the reviewers' attention on the most important parts of your file and help to place your application among the "most qualified."

In writing your cover letter, pay careful attention to the structure of the vacancy announcement. Write your strengths in terms that, within the limits of accuracy, meet or exceed the expectations described in the announcement. If your best falls short of the minimum required in the position announcement, and you believe that you can provide equivalent alternative experience, the cover letter can be structured to incorporate your claim. The cover letter is your best advertisement for favorable consideration of your application, as shown in the next example.

> The cover letter is your best advertisement for favorable consideration of your application.

MARISUE M. SWEETWATER

776 Horizon Terrace
Lincoln, NE 67798
May 22, XXXX

Federal Emergency Management Agency
500 C Street, SW, Room 1125
Washington, DC 20909

ATTN: Florence N. Smithson

Dear Ms. Smithson:

I am submitting this application for the position as a program specialist advertised in your announcement, FEMA-98-47326-MAJ. This announcement indicates that several positions will be filled in the GS-11-12-13 range. I would appreciate your consideration and believe that my education and experience make me qualified at the highest level.

This packet contains all information requested in the position announcement. I have included a complete federal resume as requested in the announcement. Allow me to elaborate upon the knowledge, skills, and abilities identified there.

My knowledge of federal, state, and local government operations has developed through both my college education (a political science minor) and seven years of progressively responsible work for both state and federal agencies with interwoven responsibilities.

(continued)

My knowledge of program analysis and evaluation also developed through college courses in business and economic analysis, policy evaluation, and mathematics. These skills were required in previous experiences at the GS-7 and GS-9 levels.

My ability to conduct research and develop reports is reflected in both a senior thesis, "The Legacy of Failure in Educational Policy," and in several reports prepared in junior positions at the Department of Housing and Urban Development. One of these was cited by my current supervisor in proposing me for the Secretary's Award, which I won this year.

My recent responsibilities included service on an interagency task force that required evaluation of national security contingency plans. Members of the working group included representatives of state and local governments. My college studies included courses in American history, constitutional politics and law, and American politics (including a section on national security policy).

I have prepared briefing materials for senior officials in two agencies, including responses to congressional correspondence that received a Cabinet Secretary's signature. I have included a copy of a recent memo that provides evidence of my writing abilities. My routine responsibilities include reporting to other members of the staff as requested by my current office director.

I have requested that my current supervisor, Mr. James D. Marshon, forward the supervisor's appraisal under separate cover. My performance ratings for the past four years have consistently exceeded "fully successful." This supervisor may be contacted at your convenience.

I have included a copy of my most recent Form 50, affirming my current status as a federal employee.

As requested, I have also submitted Standard Form 181, Race and National Origin Identification, with appropriate responses.

Thank you for your consideration, and I am eager to provide any additional information that you might need to evaluate this application.

Sincerely,

Marisue M. Sweetwater

Marisue M. Sweetwater

Cover Letter Formats

Cover letters can be presented in a variety of formats, with headers centered, flush left, or flush right. Margins may be justified or not. Paragraphs may be indented or blocked. Signature blocks can be flush left or centered. Federal agencies are relatively tolerant of different formats. Use common sense when deciding on your design.

The best type size to use for readability of your cover letter is 11 or 12 point. If you'd like to emphasize certain information, you can bullet key phrases and qualifications. The header on the letter can match the resume type font, size, and spacing so that the application will look like a package. Always include the announcement and vacancy title in the first paragraph of the letter.

Here are some additional format pointers:

☆ Maintain consistency in your style. If you indent the first paragraph, consistently use an indented style.

☆ If you are familiar with the *Federal Style Manual,* follow general guidelines in this regard. For example, a cover letter should be limited to a single page, but SES cover letters (see the next section) can require more detailed information. If a paragraph is spread over two pages, do not leave only one line on a page.

☆ Keep it simple. Remember, you are applying for a responsible public position, not an advertising sales opening. Target your presentation to the audience who will read it and hire you.

☆ Proofread everything (don't rely on a spell checker alone), and make certain that you sign the letter before sealing it.

Cover Letters for SES Positions

Responses to SES announcements require abundant supporting material–especially if applications are being considered from outside the federal workforce. OPM data indicates that SES members typically have at least 10 years of federal experience prior to the first SES position, and many SES positions require a level of background that is not available to younger professionals. Moreover, an SES position will commonly require unique experiences that few applicants will have.

An effective SES cover letter will assure the reviewer of the level of experience requisite to the SES (including a cursory summation of the Executive Core Qualifications) and then direct attention to the particular strengths that you bring to the position. The critical challenge in writing the SES cover letter is to emphasize that your strongest qualifications are most vital to the position advertised, while convincing the reader that other factors can be strengthened to exceed the hiring agency's requirements. Again, the letter must be concise and targeted to the position advertised.

The following cover letter was written for an SES position.

JOSEPH T. JOHNSON
147 Seven Locks Court
Raleigh, North Carolina 28509
(919) 549-9876

April 10, XXXX

Office of Executive and Technical Resources
U.S. Department of Energy
ATTN: Robert W. Sherman
1000 Independence Avenue, SW
Washington, DC 20585

Dear Mr. Sherman:

Enclosed is my application responding to your announcement #ERD-98-79, Associate Director for Research, Applied Sciences (ES-1301). This application contains the following:

A federal resume highlighting my accomplishments in a federal career that now spans more than 22 years. My current position, Director of Waste Disposal Technology Research for the Environmental Protection Agency's Air and Radiation Research Laboratory, demonstrates my ability to design and manage a program of the scope and complexity of the one envisioned in your announcement. In addition, my third previous position as Deputy Director of EPA's Office of Federal Facility Compliance required regular review of waste disposal plans developed by Department of Energy personnel. In that capacity, I assisted the approval process for several Environmental Impact Statements that would be relevant to the advertised position.

A summary of additional professional training relevant to this position. I earned my Ph.D. in mechanical engineering at Michigan State University and have more than ten years' experience directing major engineering research and development programs. These records also document my presentation of more than 50 technical papers at professional conferences including the American Physical Society, the American Academy for the Advancement of Science, and the Association of State and Territorial Air Pollution Control Officials. As the titles indicate, these papers include critical evaluations of current research and technology in the pollution control field that are especially relevant to the Department of Energy's nuclear disposal requirements.

Responses to the Executive Core Qualifications required for all members of the Senior Executive Service. As reflected on the enclosed federal resume, my three most recent positions have involved increased complexity, supervisory responsibility, and budget authority, even though all have been graded at the GM-15 level. I am scheduled to complete the course of study at the Federal Executive Institute in May, which would provide additional demonstration of my SES capabilities prior to the anticipated starting date of this position.

Detailed statements addressing both the mandatory and optional qualifications announced in the advertisement. In all cases, my extensive experience is especially suited to the engineering and physical science technical requirements identified as vital to this position.

I have requested that Mr. Robert Quinones, who served as my supervisor in my immediate previous position, complete the required supervisory appraisal. He will forward the form under separate cover. As indicated on this federal resume, I have not informed my current supervisor of my employment search, and I request that she should not be contacted until an offer is made.

A completed SF-181, Racial and National Origin Identification, as requested.

A copy of my DD-214, confirming three years of active duty in the United States Army and qualifying me for a five-point veteran's preference.

Thank you for your consideration. I will call your office in two weeks to confirm receipt of this material and to ascertain your procedures for evaluating applications and filling this position.

Sincerely,

Joseph T. Johnson

Cover Letters in Summary

An effective cover letter should not duplicate the plethora of material in your application. If done correctly, the cover letter should help HR professionals to identify the salient qualifications in your experience. Developing your experience and qualifications throughout your career is the topic of the next and final chapter.

CHAPTER 13

Federal Career Development: A Strategy Guide

H ow would you like to make an extra $150,000 during your career, part time, risk free, at the rate of $58 per hour? Sound too good to be true? It isn't.

That's what you'd make if you invested one hour each week in career development in government, leading to a new job or promotion every three years at a 10 percent raise. That's not hard to achieve. Many people will do and can do better, especially when combining career advancement with the cost of living increases and incremental raises that occur with increasing grade levels in government positions.

Many people don't do that well at all because they don't apply for new jobs or reach out for additional tasks and challenges. They risk downsizing, career setbacks, being dead-ended, being overlooked. They risk being outplaced into positions that are not acceptable to them. Thoreau reminds us, "The mass of men lead lives of quiet desperation." But he also said, "If one advances confidently in the direction of his dreams, and endeavors to live the life which he has imagined, he will meet with a success unexpected in common hours."

Setting Goals Makes the Difference

What is the difference? The difference is in setting goals, developing (and following) a plan, believing in yourself, and recognizing that no one is going to come along and just promote you or hire you away into your dream job. You'll find over and over in the literature of success that goal setting (in the words of success expert Brian Tracy) is "the threshold skill that underlies all advancement." Or, as Yogi Berra put it, "If you don't know where you're going, you're likely to end up somewheres else!"

> **To take charge of your career, invest an hour each week in long-term planning.**

A successful federal government career development strategy isn't merely about the money. In fact, it's not at all about the money, though that's what often motivates people to get serious in the first place. At the rate of 2,000 hours per work year, a career that lasts from age 21 to age 67 involves 92,000 hours spent at the office! That's 10½ years, 24 hours a day, seven days a week. That's way too much time to be underemployed, underappreciated, and miserable. A federal career development strategy first and foremost needs to be about you: your dreams, your talents, your goals, your needs, and your skills.

To take charge of your career direction, plan to invest an hour each week in long-term planning and career development. (Stephen Covey, in *The Seven Habits of Highly Effective People*, calls this kind of investment "Quadrant 2" time, for work that is important but not urgent. It's the best kind of time investment you can make.) You may spend this hour doing many things, from self-examination to sending out resumes.

Six Steps for Reaching Your Dreams

Here's a six-step process to help you live your dreams:

1. **Start with a statement of your dream job.** Don't worry that you probably aren't qualified for it right now–few of us are. Watch out for a job that's too specific. The problem with wanting to be President of the United States is that there's only one job, and it comes available no more often than once every four years. Think about the characteristics of the dream job rather than a specific job title. Examples: Uses my people skills, provides overseas travel, puts me on TV, helps other people, doesn't require computer savvy.

2. **Expand your picture.** What kinds of positions would have at least some, if not all, of the characteristics you like? The bigger the list, the better. If (as is likely) you can't make the jump from where you are to that dream job in one leap, consider interim jobs or situations that would move you in the right direction. If you want to be in national politics, for example, you might start in local politics or as a volunteer. If you want to manage a large agency, you might start lower on the management track.

3. **Consider the obstacles.** What stands in your way? There are always going to be obstacles between you and any dream you have, on the grounds that if there weren't, you'd have already achieved them. Are you missing certain credentials? Does your experience not fit your goals? Don't rush right out to get an extra college degree. While some jobs require specific educational qualifications, you'll find that some of the most successful people in almost every field don't possess "qualifications." They have skills.

4. **Make a plan for overcoming each obstacle.** You have to face the obstacles before you can overcome them. If you don't have the right degree or it's not from the right school, how can you get or demonstrate that you have the right skills some other way? If you had a bad experience in a previous job, how can you overcome it, learn from it, put it behind you, or turn it into an asset? If you don't know the right people or have the right contacts, how can you meet the people and develop the contacts? While a few lucky people are born with the right contacts, most of us have to go out and network to get our foot in the door.

> We tend to overlook the many sources of help.

5. **Look for help.** Zig Ziglar (in his book *Top Performance*) tells this story: A little boy tried in vain to move a heavy log to clear a path to his favorite hideout. His dad finally asked him why he wasn't using all his strength. The boy explained he was straining as hard as he could. But the father disagreed. "Son, if you were using all your strength, you'd have asked me to help."

We tend to overlook the many sources of help, forgetting that even the legendary self-made man or woman seldom made it on his or her own. We need the strength and resources of others to meet our goals. Besides, most important jobs require teamwork, and now is the time to get started.

Who can help: Survey your friends, acquaintances, supervisors, and business associates. Talk to them about your dreams and goals, and ask them what they might be able to contribute. You'll be surprised at the range of contacts and advice you'll get.

Attend courses, workshops, and seminars. Use your agency training budget to develop skills that make you upwardly mobile. Ask your supervisor about an agency-sponsored career development program that could help you advance in government. Take a few minutes to introduce yourself to the leaders or speakers. They always like to hear positive things about their presentation, and most of them are eager to share additional advice and tips with a participant who is willing to listen.

Get involved in professional associations and meetings where people in your desired field or industry hang out. Introduce yourself. Most people are happy to share; we all like a receptive audience. Use the "information interviewing" techniques developed by Richard Bowles in his seminal *What Color Is Your Parachute?* volumes, updated annually.

Write letters to people who've achieved what you want to achieve. Many will write back, and some will be happy to advise you.

Keep a list of your accomplishments at work. If the list is getting low, find something new to add to your responsibilities and create an accomplishment.

> **Break career development into simple steps, and focus on the immediate next step you have to do.**

Consider professional help, including career counselors, resume writers, and others who can look at your situation dispassionately and expertly, and give you advice and technical help you might not be able to get anywhere else.

Most of us need some morale help, too. Friends, family, loved ones, and partners of any sort can help keep our focus, energy, and positive feelings high.

6. **Go one step at a time.** It's often emotionally draining to look at the enormous work involved in career development, especially if you already have a demanding job. One way to help you through any difficult project, especially one without the urgent pressure of a deadline, is to break the job into simple steps and focus only on the immediate next step you have to do.

Set goals to apply for a certain number of jobs in a certain amount of time. Follow up with agencies and hiring officials. Try to build the kind of relationship that gets you considered for the next job.

Set a goal to meet one person from a different agency or department each week and ask what the person does. The knowledge will help you in your current job, and the networking will help you seek a future job.

One Hour a Week Can Pump Up Your Career

One hour a week doesn't seem like a lot of time, and it isn't a lot of time. That's all you need to focus on right now. In one hour, you could make a written draft of the six steps you've read here. In one hour, you could amplify and add to that draft. In one hour, you could read a couple of chapters in a good career development book. In one hour, you could have an introductory meeting with a career transition center counselor in your government agency or a career counselor. In one hour, you could attend an evening lecture by a notable in your field. In one hour, you could gather all the material you need for your resume. In one hour, you could search the Partnership for Reinventing Government's Web site at www.npr.gov for job announcements. In one hour, you could read your agency's Web site to review new programs and mission statements. In one hour, you could work on your federal resume draft. In one hour, you could skim some of the federal budget and look for agencies and programs that are adding and subtracting slots.

Nothing stops you from putting in more than an hour, but you don't have to. The advantage in doing an hour every single week is that it removes the pressure of urgency from your life. It takes you a few weeks before you start to feel the progress, but you can keep going. If there's a setback in your agency, you don't have to go into full-panic, job-hunting mode;

you're already on your way to something better. If you don't like a particular offer or a particular situation, you don't have to let desperation drive your decision; you can continue to develop yourself.

You don't have to settle for a "life of quiet desperation" in the federal job that has become mundane. You can be someone who dares to live the life that he or she has imagined, and you, as Thoreau says, "will meet with a success unexpected in common hours."

APPENDIX A

Federal Resume Examples

Full federal resumes appear in this appendix for your reference and inspiration.

College Resumes

B.S. in Economics, applying for Labor Economist, GS-9/11

GARY L. BLANKENBURG
SS# 225-68-6975
U.S. CITIZEN

8 WINDSWEPT LANE
COLUMBIA, MD 21030

HOME: (410) 744-4324
WORK: (410) 881-9943

VETERANS PREFERENCE: 5 POINTS

FEDERAL STATUS: N/A

OBJECTIVE:

Labor Economist, GS-0110-9/11, U.S. Department of Labor
Announcement: NCSC/ILAB 95-046

EDUCATION:

University of Tennessee, Knoxville, TN 32408
B.Sc., Economics, 1993
GPA: Overall: 3.4 Economics: 3.5

ACADEMIC AWARDS AND HONORS:

Fulbright Grant in Stockholm Sweden, August 1993 to May 1994
Research focused on efforts to improve the labor market in the United States by researching historical and current institutions in Sweden. Interviewed Swedish government officials, academicians, and business executives who provided volumes of data and anecdotal references. Researched, analyzed and interpreted economic data.

Utilized specialized methods such as sampling, statistics and economic forecasting to gather data. Tools of analysis included supply and demand, cost benefit, labor market, ISLM equilibrium, inter-temporal external balance methods, 1st and 2nd order condition optimization, and Lagrangian optimization techniques. Procedures for quantifying and measuring economic relationships included game theory, econometric forecasting, regression analysis, OLS methods, etc. Utilized Mini-Tab and SAS statistical programs.

Top Economic Award (Przygoda) at University of Tennessee for Exceptional Standard of Economic Scholarship, May 1993

International Honor Society in Economics: Omicron Delta Epsilon, April 1993

Macro Economics Award for Excellence, University of Tennessee, May 1992

Dean's List for Academic Excellence, University of Tennessee, May 1992

Graduate, Oak Ridge High School, Oak Ridge, TN, May 1982. Member, National Honor Society

PAPERS & PRESENTATIONS:

Federal Tax Receipts Associated with Two U.S. Labor Market Improvements: A Proposal. Summary proposal of Fulbright research conducted in Stockholm Sweden. May 1994. This work anchors itself in progressive labor economic concepts, innovative childcare modeling techniques, and specialized policies and programs regarding contemporary women's issues.

Economic Systems Analysis: A Case Study Comparing the Economies of Sweden and the United States. Conference paper presented at The Society for the Advancement of Socio-Ecomonics, New School for Social Research in New York City on March 27, 1993.

B.S. in Economics, applying for Labor Economist, GS-9/11

PAPERS & PRESENTATIONS (continued):

Economic Systems Analysis: A Case Study Comparing the Economies of Sweden and the United States. Conference paper presented at The Society for the Advancement of Scandinavian Studies, University of Texas at Austin in Austin Texas on April 22, 1993.

Structural and Political Analysis of European Economic and Monetary Union. Research paper. April 1993.

Two Labor Market Ideas to Strengthen the American Family: Lessons from Sweden. Research paper. March 1993.

Economic Systems Analysis: A Case Study Comparing the Economies of Sweden and the United States. Extensive 130-page symmetrical study which critically examined areas for cross-fertilization of economic and social ideas in Sweden and the United States. Academically supervised semester course, August-December, 1992.

Papers published in *Tennessean* (university newspaper), 1992-1993.

EMPLOYMENT HISTORY

Baltimore Savings Bank
21 N. Calvert Street, Baltimore, MD 21203   July 1994-Present
Assistant Branch Manager
Salary: $25,000 annually   40 hours/week plus overtime
Supervisor: Greg Summers (410) 244-3628   Please do not contact
    Assist with managing retail bank operations, including supervision of 10 tellers and customer service representatives. Train staff in policies, procedures, bank products, cash management and customer services. Provide account services, bank product sales and coordination of loan applications. Introduce consumer and mortgage loan services to customers. Assess customer financial and bank service needs and make appropriate recommendations.

Fulbright Commission
12-1 855 First Avenue, Stockholm, Sweden   June 1993-June 1994
Researcher
Salary: $1000 per month grant stipend   40 hours/week
Supervisor: Carol Lundstrom 011-46-08-107-2789

Learning Resource Center at Loyola Marymount University
55 Surrey Lane, Greeneville, NC 40840   January 1992-May 1993
Senior Writing Tutor
Salary: $400 per month   20 hours/week
Supervisor: Kevin O'Connor (310) 338-7702
    Provided writing support and course specific tutoring in economics, history and English to undergraduates.

United States Marine Corps Intelligence Field   January 1988-January 1992
Cryptologic Spanish Linguist
Salary: $1500 per month   40 hours/week
Supervisor: Edward A. Hall (202) 736-3259
Top Secret Clearance. Honorable Discharge, 1992.

B.S. in Economics, applying for Labor Economist, GS-9/11

MILITARY CLEARANCE AND AWARDS:

United States Marine Corps, 1988-1992.
Cleared for Top Secret information and granted access to Sensitive Compartmented information based on a special background investigation completed on 880802 under CCN #88132-1366.

Awards:
- National Defense Service Medal (Operation Desert Shield/Storm)
- Rifle Expert Award
- Good Conduct Medal
- Overseas Service Ribbon
- Letter of Commendation
- Letters of Appreciation

LEADERSHIP ACTIVITIES:

President of the Economics Society at University of Tennessee, 1992-1993.
Student Selection Committee, 1993.
> Special appointment by University Academic Vice President for the selection of the new Dean of Liberal Arts.
Student Advisory Council, 1993.
> Special appointment by the University Dean of Liberal Arts.
Vice President of the Sailing Club at University of Tennessee, 1986.
Vice President of the Oak Ridge High School Student Body, 1981-1982.

SUMMARY OF RELEVANT SKILLS:

Economics
- Utilize knowledge of economic relationships to advise senior researchers.
- Apply money, banking and foreign exchange principles to current research.

Econometrics
- Prepare economic and governmental forecasts.
- Provide information to support policy decision-making.

Computers
- Mini-tab and SAS statistical software.
- Data compilation, statistical analysis.
- Spreadsheet and report production.

Written Language
- Construct clear, concise, audience specific reports.
- Conduct extensive research to support team-oriented work projects.

Public Speaking
- Design and present informative, demonstrative or persuasive speeches.
- Deliver animated conference level presentations with visual aids.
- Interview specialized professionals and executives on economic research.

B.S. in Criminology, applying for Law Enforcement Officer, GS-7

Joe Friday

2500 Rolling Road
Baltimore, MD 21228
Home: (410) 555-1212 ♦ Office: (410) 844-1212

Social Security Number: 123-45-6789
Veteran's Preference and Federal Civilian Status: N/A
Country of Citizenship: U.S.A.
Vacancy Announcement Number: 96-0012-LE
Job Title: Law Enforcement Officer, GS-7

EDUCATION

University of Maryland - Baltimore County, Baltimore, MD 21228
B.S. Degree, *Magna Cum Laude,* May 1994
GPA: 3.85/4.0
Major: Emergency Health Services - Paramedic Track
Semester Academic Honors: Fall 1992, Spring 1993, and Fall 1993
Member of Phi Kappa Phi National Scholastic Honor Society

Calvert Hall College High School, Baltimore, MD 21286
College preparatory curriculum, received diploma, June 1989

PROFESSIONAL DEVELOPMENT

Specialized Training and Education in Controlled Dangerous Substances
University of Maryland - Baltimore County, Baltimore, MD, Spring 1993
University level course in Medical Emergencies covering drug identification, pharmacology of illicit and prescription drugs, and treatment of drug-related emergencies. Course included: Controlled Dangerous Substances lecture given by Maryland State Police Narcotics Division; the 1970 *Controlled Substances Act;* and, schedule stratification of drugs according to their medical use and abuse potential.

Basic Police Training Course
Eastern Shore Criminal Justice Academy, Salisbury, MD, May 1995
Intensive one-month law enforcement training program for Ocean City Police Department recruits. Topics covered, but not limited to: firearms, PR-24 Police Baton, restraining devices, DWI, criminal law/investigation, report writing, constitutional law, domestic violence, drug identification, and court testimony.

Introduction to Criminal Justice
Essex Community College, Baltimore, MD, January - May 1995
Semester long course dealing with current issues in Criminal Justice and police administration. Course combined theory and practice of current law enforcement techniques as illustrated by the instructor, a Captain in a local Police Department.

B.S. in Criminology, applying for Law Enforcement Officer, GS-7

Joe Friday, SS#123-45-6789   **Page 2**

Stevenson Volunteer Fire and Ambulance Company, Stevenson, MD, June 1992 - April 1995. Active volunteer in community, with the duty of providing quality medical care to the sick and injured, and preservation of life and property. Currently certified as a NREMT-P, Nationally Registered Paramedic, Registry 4PO855719. Also, currently certified by the American Heart Association in ACLS-Advanced Cardiac Life Support, PALS-Pediatric Advanced Life Support, and CPR-Cadiopulmonary Resuscitation and Emergency Cardiac Care. Certified in the State of MD, as an EMT-Emergency Medical Technician.

Harford County Fire Academy, Baltimore, MD, January - June 1991.
A six-month intensive course covering tactics and techniques of fire fighting, classroom instruction, and practical search and rescue. Currently certified under the National Professional Qualifications Board as a Firefighter 11.

Computer Related Skills and Training, Baltimore, MD, September 1991 - Present.
Familiar with personal computer operations for both the Apple Macintosh and IBM-PC compatible computers. Knowledge of software packages includes Microsoft Windows, Microsoft Works, WordPerfect, and a variety of multi-media application programs. Also familiar with modem communications, Internet, World Wide Web, and a variety of other on line services.

EMPLOYMENT HISTORY

Nordstrom Department Stores   11/95 – 2/96
  10400 Mill Run Circle, Owings Mills, MD 21117
  Christopher Troutman, Supervisor; Telephone: (410) 555-1212
  Salary: $8.00/hour
  Hours: 20-30 hours/week
  Employer may be contacted.

LOSS PREVENTION SPECIALIST
- Educated associates regarding external losses of merchandise.
- Ensured compliance with security procedures.
- Prevented external loss by using surveillance techniques, undercover operations, and physical deterrents.
- Provided a safe environment for both employees and customers.
- Controlled internal loss by monitoring physical inventory and financial transactions.
- When appropriate, investigated and arrested suspects for crimes such as theft, conspiracy, malicious destruction of property, and credit card/check fraud.
- As required, interacted with County law enforcement officers.

B.S. in Criminology, applying for Law Enforcement Officer, GS-7

Joe Friday, SS#123-45-6789   **Page 3**

Rehoboth Beach Police Department   4/95 – 11/95
    6501 Coastal Highway, Rehoboth Beach, MD 21842
    Sgt. John W. Kraemer, Supervisor; Telephone: (410) 555-1212
    Salary: $8.28/hour
    Hours: 40+ hours/week

PROBATIONARY POLICE OFFICER

- Enforced laws pertinent to the Maryland Annotated Code, Maryland Motor Vehicle Law, and local ordinances.
- Conducted vehicle patrols in and around the Town of Rehoboth Beach to observe for violations of traffic or criminal law. Issued citations or warnings when appropriate.
- Interacted with the public using interpersonal skills to explain the law, keep the peace, and promote safety in the community.
- Developed concise and detailed reports concerning criminal offenses and motor vehicle violations.
- Conducted surveillance activities, interviewed witnesses, interrogated suspects, and investigated violations of criminal law.
- Made arrests and testified in court on both the District and Circuit levels.

St. Agnes Shock Trauma Center   9/94 – 4/95
    22 Maiden Choice Lane, Baltimore, MD 21201
    Robbie Kramden, Clinical Specialist; Telephone: (410) 844-1212
    Salary: $7.25/hour, initially started as volunteer for five-month period.
    Hours: 20-30 hours/week

TRAUMA TRANSPORT TECHNICIAN

- As a paramedic and medical assistant, rendered aid to critically ill and injured patients.
- Worked in cooperation with other medical professionals (e.g.: paramedics, nurses, and doctors) to assist them in the care and treatment of patients.
- Used effective interpersonal skills to communicate with patients and medical personnel during emotionally and physically stressful situations.
- Understood the use of empathy in dealing with critically ill and injured population.
- Disseminated and acquired specialized knowledge and skills to further my career in the medical field.

B.S. in Aviation, applying for FAA Aviation Operations, GS-7/9

ROBERT M. GOODMAN
100 Willowbrook Circle
Gaithersburg, MD 21228

Home: (301) 744-4324	Work: (301) 719-4422

Social Security # 213-78-8077	Veteran's Preference: N/A
Country of Citizenship: USA	Highest Federal Civilian Grade Held: N/A

OBJECTIVE:

Department of Transportation, Federal Aviation Administration
Civil Aviation Security Specialist, Dangerous Goods/Cargo Specialist
FG-1801-7/9/11/12

EDUCATION:

Bachelor of Science, with Honors, AVIATION MANAGEMENT   June 1996
UNIVERSITY OF ARIZONA – PHOENIX

- **Aviation Planning:** Aviation Forecasting, Airport Master Plan Development, Environmental Impact Assessment
- **Airport Design:** Airport Capacity and Aircraft Delay, Runway Design, Taxiway and Apron Design, Aircraft Approach and Departures Paths, Airport Pavements, Terminal Building Development, Heliport Design
- **The National Airspace System**
- **Advanced Computer Applications** – SIMMOD and INM
- **Aviation Safety**
- **Airport Management** – NPIAS, Licensing and Certification, Maintenance, Emergency Plans, Security (FAR), Financial Management, Economics, Leases, Public Relations

Georgetown Prep, Rockville, MD; High School Diploma, 1986

LICENSES & CERTIFICATIONS:

Private Pilot, Instrument Rating
Held Secret Security Clearance
Advanced and Instrument Ground Instructor

COMPUTER SKILLS:

ATP, AIRPAC, FLIESOFT, A/P DIRECTORY, SOURCE BOOK, AVITAT, INM,
SIMMOD, Word, Excel, Powerpoint

EXPERIENCE:

AIRCRAFT OWNERS AND PILOTS ASSOCIATION   March 1997 to Present
800 Airport Blvd., Gaithersburg, MD 21229   38 hours/week
Supervisor: Ted Turnbill (301) 744-0112   Salary: $22,500/year
Supervisor may be contacted

Technical Specialist, Aviation Services Department
Department lead in airport issues for Aviation Services Department. Technical advisor to the organization's members and other trade associations in the development and planning of airports and the air traffic control system. Assist with preparation of presentations to local, state, and federal agencies, civic groups, and airport management.

B.S. in Aviation, applying for FAA Aviation Operations, GS-7/9

AIRCRAFT OWNERS AND PILOTS ASSOCIATION *(continued):*

Research and consult with members in the following areas:

- **Airport Operations,** including hazards to air navigation, zoning, compliance grants/assurances, federal funding, minimum standards, exclusive rights (noise).
- **Airside and landside project** research to ensure compliance with federal standards and the goals of AOPA.
- **Airport zoning** issues such as tower and building construction that pose a possible hazard to air navigation, lighting and marketing of tall structures, zoning laws and associated state and federal regulations.
- **Support international operations** in the Bahamas, Canada, Mexico, Caribbean, Customs and IFIMS.
- **FAA regulations** relating to airport development, design and funding.
- **Airport improvement projects**, obtaining federal funds through AIP and FAAP programs.
- **Economic benefit of airports**, establishing airstrips, proposed closing of airports, and compatible land uses.

Specialized Knowledge:
- Corporate Aviation: 91 vs. 135
- Aviation Regulations: 61, 91, 135 121,
  43, 45, 67, NTSB, 77, CFR General Overview
- Advisory Circulars
- FAA Orders
- Taxes: Sales/Use, Income
- FAA Enforcement Actions
- Airman Certification
- Maintenance: AD's, MPRM's
- Aircraft Valuations
- Insurance: Aircraft Pilots
- Legal Assistance: Accidents/Incidents
- Corporate Status/Legal Research
- Aviation Sales
- Title/Escrows and Liens
- Marketing Surveys

MILITARY EXPERIENCE:

COMPANY C, 1ST BATTALION, 20TH SPECIAL FORCES
Bel Air, MD 21228
Supervisor: SFC Doug Miller (410) 744-3772

Nov. 1991 – Nov. 1993
40 hours/week
Salary: $23,000/year

Administrative NCO　　　　　　　　　　　　November 1991 – August 1993
- Non-commissioned officer in both combat arms and support roles.
- Managed the pay, training and administration of a 130-member Special Forces Unit. Awarded for establishing a tracking and follow-up system for Army personnel experiencing problems with pay and injuries incurred in the line of duty.

Infantry Squad Leader　　　　　　　　　　　　January 1987 – November 1991
Maryland Army National Guard, Catonsville, MD

B.S. in Aviation, applying for FAA Aviation Operations, GS-7/9

PROFESSIONAL TRAINING:

- Strategic Communications: Influencing Business Outcomes, 1998
- FAA Enforcement Course, 1997
- Airport Management: FAR parts 107 (airport security), 108 (airplane operator security), 109 (indirect air carrier security), 129 (foreign air carriers), emergency planning, National Plan of Integrated Airport Systems, leases, public relations, maintenance, 1996
- International Air Commerce, 1996
- Aviation Law, 1995
- Air Carrier Management: FAR parts 121 (domestic air carriers), 135 (air taxi), 1995
- Aviation Safety, 1995
- Aviation Planning, 1994
- Airport Design, 1994
- The National Airspace System, 1994
- Flight, 1993-1994
- Primary Leadership Development Course, 1989

HONORS AND AWARDS:

- AOPA "Ace" award for contributions to the design and training of the department on a new computer operating system, 1997
- AOPA "Ace" award for background research for new aviation publications, 1998
- AOPA "Ace" award for representation of the organization at major trade shows, 1998
- Wrote "Business Use of Aircraft" published in November 1997 AOPA Pilot magazine
- Army Achievement Medal (one oak leaf cluster), 1993
- Good Conduct Medal, 1993

PROFESSIONAL AFFILIATIONS:

National Business Aviation Association
American Association of Airport Executives
Aircraft Owners and Pilots Association
University of Arizona School of Aeronautics Alumni Association

B.S. in Aviation, applying for FAA Aviation Operations, GS-7/9

Candidate:
ROBERT M. GOODMAN
SS # 213-78-8077

Position:
Department of Transportation, Federal Aviation Administration
Civil Aviation Security Specialist, Dangerous Goods/Cargo Specialist
FG-1801-7/9/11/12

KSAO #1 Ability to work independently and organize and set priorities.

As lead Technical Specialist for airports with the Aircraft Owners and Pilots Association (AOPA), duties include collecting and evaluating information received from the organization's members or other sources to decide whether further action is required on developing issues. Many issues are time critical and must be ranked accordingly for action, review by supervisor, or for further data collection.

All casework is done independently and with minimal supervision.

Investigated a proposed closure of Runway 15L-33R at Dulles International Airport due to installation of weather reporting equipment. Through research determined that alternative siting points were available and runway closure was postponed.

Examine incoming information from various sources to identify harmful legislation, trends or conditions.

Organize and write a current issue report using a variety of sources. Decide on priority issues that need to be brought to the attention of AOPA management and possible courses of action.

KSAO #2 Ability to influence others inside and outside the organization in order to achieve program objectives.

Cooperate with diverse segments of the aviation industry in the course of resolving casework to achieve AOPA objectives. Develop alternatives to proposed actions that meet the goals of the organization but are still acceptable to all parties involved.

Participated with Western Pacific Region ADO, ATC and AOPA Regional Representative in order to eliminate the requirement for VFR traffic to receive a clearance before taking off while still ensuring safety at Metropolis Airport. Solved the problem by implementing new ground traffic control procedures which enhanced safety yet was invisible to pilots affected.

Assisted pilot group in postponing a proposed closure of Runway 15L-33R at Dulles International Airport. The runway was slated to close due to the installation of weather reporting equipment. Coordinated between FAA and Virginia Department of Aviation to find alternative sites for placement of equipment. The shutdown has been postponed until a new study is completed.

Represent AOPA at trade shows and conferences in order to promote AOPA's goals and objectives and to make professional contacts for future use.

B.S. in Aviation, applying for FAA Aviation Operations, GS-7/9

KSAO #3 Ability to write inspection/investigations narrative reports.

Prepare written briefings for Aviation Services Department throughout the course of case investigations detailing significant findings, problems encountered, and progress being made.

Prepared 30-40 written responses per week to inquiries from members.

Researched and wrote two articles for *AOPA Pilot* magazine.

Prepared written technical assistance for staff writers for AOPA's newest publication, *Getting Recurrent.*

Researched and wrote responses for the President of AOPA on a variety of technical issues.

KSAO #4 Ability to interpret and apply a variety of regulations, orders and manuals in a regulatory environment.

Responsible for researching and answering questions on 49 CFR 175, air transportation of hazardous materials.

Completed formal training on security regulations 14 CFR parts 107, 108, 109 and 129 and airport regulations 139, 150 and 157.

Provide expertise in interpreting recent changes to FAR part 61.

Wrote requests for legal interpretation from FAA Chief Counsel on regulations.

Fluent in FAR parts 43, 61, 67, 77, 91 and 135.

Frequently use FAA Orders for questions on Air Traffic Control (7110.65, ATC Handbook), Terminal Instrument Procedures (8260.3, TERPS Manual), and General Aviation policies and procedures (8700.1, General Aviation Operations Inspector's Handbook).

B.A. in French with legal internships, applying for Paralegal Specialist, GS-7

ELAINE McCARTHY

1854 Arthur Street
Washington, DC 20055
SS#: 215-76-8066
U.S. Citizen

Day: (202) 812-8188
Evening: (202) 554-3372
Veteran's Status: None
Federal Eligibility Status: None

OBJECTIVE

To obtain the position of Paralegal Specialist (Ann. #GS-90, Grade 7) with the Civil Division of the U.S. Department of Justice.

EDUCATION

Loyola College, Baltimore, MD 20230
Bachelor of Arts Degree, May 1993
Majors: French, Psychology
- Top 10% (3.6 GPA)
- University of Paris Sorbonne, Summer Program, 1992

Glenelg Country School, Glenelg, MD 21228
Graduated, May 1988
- Vassar College Summer Program for Graduating Seniors, 1987

PROFESSIONAL EXPERIENCE

Davis & Lloyd, 1725 Connecticut Ave., NW, Washington, DC 20006
Legal Assistant, June 1983 - present; Full-time, $20,000 per year
Supervisor: John Jacobson (202) 872-9217, contact may be made
- Provide support services to assist civil litigation activities of a major Washington law firm.
- Review depositions of witnesses or experts providing testimony in a variety of civil proceedings.
- Prepare written summaries highlighting key points of testimony and identifying potential issues of importance.
- Generate charts demonstrating crucial points of evidence.
- Compile material necessary to prepare witnesses for trial.

D.C. Crisis Counseling Center, P.O. Box 30987, Washington, DC 20036
Counselor, May 1994 - present, 6 hours per week, volunteer
Supervisor: Carolyn Weeks (202) 872-9711
- Assist victims of sexual assault in an active rape crisis center operating in the District of Columbia.
- Provide counseling, information and referral.
- Completed 65-hour training program regarding services, local laws, and counseling techniques.

B.A. in French with legal internships, applying for Paralegal Specialist, GS-7

ELAINE McCARTHY **Page 2**

Columbia Theatre Festival, P.O. Box 772, Columbia, MD 21237
Box Office Manager, Summer of 1990 and 1991, Full-time, $250 per week
Supervisor: John Levin (410) 872-9874

- Managed box office operations during a busy three-month summer season.
- Responsible for handling as much as $700,000 in transactions each summer.
- Maintained records of more than 750 trustees and subscribers to ensure timely notification of upcoming events.

COMPUTER SKILLS

Word Processing: Microsoft Word, WordPerfect
Databases: Dbase IV, Paradox
On-Line Research: NEXIS/LEXIS and BASYS

TRAINING

- D.C. Crisis Counseling Center / May 1994 / 65 hours / training in counseling and in local laws.
- Davis & Lloyd / September 1994 / 10 hours / training in how to use on-line legal databases (LEXIS/NEXIS)

SKILLS

- Proficient with Dbase IV, Paradox, Microsoft Word and WordPerfect.
- Skilled in using legal research software: NEXIS/LEXIS and BASYS.
- Comfortable in either Macintosh or PC environment.
- Fluent in French.
- Type 60 WPM.

AWARDS

- Who's Who Among Students in American Universities and Colleges
- Red and Blue Honor Society
- Vassar College Summer Program for Graduating High School Seniors
- Nominated for Dean's Award
- Outstanding Member - Alpha Chi Sorority

Third-year Law Student, applying for Attorney Advisor, GS-9

JENNIFER T. HARRIS
U.S. Citizen
SS# 215-76-8066

School Address
2312 H Street, N.W., Apt. 2
Washington, D.C. 20037
(202) 000-0000

Home Address
535 East 85th Street, 10D
New York, New York 10028
(212) 000-0000

Veteran's Status: N/A

Federal Civilian Status: N/A

OBJECTIVE

Attorney Advisor, U.S. Department of Justice, Announcement Number J-1359

EDUCATION

The George Washington University National Law Center, Washington, D.C. 20006
J.D. expected May 1998; maintaining a B average
   Honors, Legal Research and Writing
   Member, International Law Society
   Westlaw Student Representative

The Johns Hopkins University, Baltimore, Maryland 21225
B.A. in Political Science, May 1992; GPA 3.4/4.0
   Member, Varsity Women's Tennis
   Tutor, Tutorial Project
   Committee Member, Spring Fair Publicity Committee

Syracuse University in Florence, Syracuse, New York 00000; Fall Semester, 1991
The Dalton School, New York, New York 00000; Graduated June 1988

EXPERIENCE

Office of the District Attorney
Street address, Queens, New York 00000
Supervisor: Martin Himless (212) 787-6767
LAW STUDENT INTERN, APPEALS BUREAU

Summer 1995
40 hours/12 weeks
Contact can be made

- Full responsibility for answering appellate briefs and motions
- Acted as Moot Court judge to prepare prosecutors for oral arguments
- Assisted prosecutor in trial preparation
- Performed various research assignments for Assistant District Attorneys
- Attended trials and appellate division arguments

Curtis, Mallet-Prevost, Colt & Mosle
Street address, New York, New York 00000
Supervisor: Thomas Colt (212) 676-4545
PARALEGAL

Summer 1994
40 hours/10 weeks

- Assisted attorneys with digesting depositions in the area of corporate law
- On behalf of the firm, met with paralegals from other law firms to confirm the accuracy of important financial data being used in a case

Third-year Law Student, applying for Attorney Advisor, GS-9

JENNIFER T. HARRIS   **Page Two**
SS# 216-76-8066

University of the Pacific, McGeorge School of Law   *Summer 1992*
Salzburg University, Austro-American Institute of Education   42 hours/5 weeks
Supervisor: Wyatt Newmann (212) 787-8989
- Received Certificate of International Legal Studies while studying under Professor A.W. Bradley and Justice Anthony Kennedy
- Studied "Fundamental Rights in Europe and the United States"
- Attended "The Supreme Court" lecture given by Justice Scalia

Center for National Policy Review   *Fall 1992*
Street address, Washington, DC 00000   15 hours/12 weeks
Supervisor: Edward Kramer (202) 444-7878
RESEARCHER
- Conducted research for institute on constitutional bases of affirmative action programs and performed statistical research on demographics of poverty.

Common Cause
Street address, Washington, D.C. 00000   *Summer 1991*
Supervisor: Kathryn Martien   (202) 454-8989   40 hours/8 weeks
SUMMER INTERN
- Contacted members by telephone keeping them informed and coordinated activities
- Established telephone network in the New York area to help combat "revolving door" practices in government
- Encouraged communication between constituents and elected officials

Senator Daniel Patrick Moynihan
Street Address, New York City Office   *Summer 1991*
Supervisor: Elizabeth Morgan (212) 787-4444   40 hours / 4 weeks
SUMMER INTERN
- Researched issues and wrote correspondence to constituents.
- Visited an animal shelter to assess quality of care and prepared a report for the Senator
- Interviewed an army official accused of rape and summarized findings for the Senator
- Attended hearings and wrote summary reports

COMPUTER SKILLS

Lexis/Nexis; Westlaw; WordPerfect 6.1; Word; Macintosh; Internet research

BACKGROUND AND INTERESTS

Proficient in French and Italian
Traveled throughout Europe, The Middle East, Africa and the Orient
Lived with families in Denmark and Sweden as participant in "The Experiment in International Living"
Active tennis player and runner and enjoy most sports
Avid photographer and guitarist

Example of College Course List with Description

Selected Courses with Descriptions

GEORGE WASHINGTON UNIVERSITY
Master of Aviation Technology

MAS 603	**Aircraft/Spacecraft Development**	Spring 1998

Overview of aircraft and spacecraft development, including vehicle mission, requirements directed by economics, military and defense considerations, and research and development process needed to meet vehicle requirements.

BA 521	**Global Information & Technology Management**	Spring 1998

Combination of technical and managerial material to develop knowledgeable users of information technology in aviation.

MS 201	**Principles of Management**	Winter 1997

Overview of relevant management principles/practices as applied in contemporary organizations. Focus on management theories, philosophies, and functions.

MAS 608	**Aerospace Accidents Investigation & Safety Systems**	Winter 1997

Critical analysis of selected aircraft accidents and an evaluation of causal factors.

BA 645	**Airport Operations & Management**	Winter 1997

Study of the management and operations of public use airports, traffic forecasting, revenues, passenger and cargo terminal building management, ground handling and access systems, and U.S. FAA regulations dealing with airport operations.

BA 632	**Labor Relations and Collective Bargaining**	Fall 1997

Study of union movement, labor legislation, representation elections, the collective bargaining process, contract administration, and conflict resolution.

MAS 613	**Airport Operations Safety**	Fall 1997

Study of airport operations safety as applied to day-to-day operations. Review and analysis of all federal regulations applicable to operations and safety are conducted.

MAS 604	**Human Factors in the Aviation/Aerospace Industry**	Summer 1997

Overview of the human factor in all aspects of the aviation and aerospace industries.

SS 305	**American Military History**	Winter 1993

Military history with emphasis on military policy, organization and technology as they relate to political, economic, and social developments from 1775 to the present.

AS 254	**Aviation Regulations**	Summer 1993

Survey of state, federal and international regulation of the aviation industry. Historical and current events, past and present legislation, conventions and treaties.

SF 320	**Human Factors in Aviation Safety**	Spring 1993

Examination of the major causative agent in aircraft accidents, the human being. Emphasis placed on psychological and physiologic factors that enhance the accident probability. Detailed analysis of ergonomics (human engineering) and its influence.

GS-8 and Below

Correspondence Analyst, GS-301-8 seeking Program Assistant, GS-301-9

DONNA M. STEPHENS
9006 Mill Court
Ft. Washington, MD 20744

Home: (301) 248-8831   Work: (703) 695-1647

Social Security No.:   215-76-8067
Citizenship: United States
Federal Status: Correspondence Analyst/Expediter, GS-8
Veterans Status: N/A

OBJECTIVE: Program Assistant, GS-301-09, Announcement No. C-8673-F

SKILLS SUMMARY:

Fourteen years of administrative experience with the Department of the Navy serving as Correspondence Analyst Leader, Research Assistant and Personnel Assistant. Skilled in assisting with program functions; supporting and communicating with senior managers; coordinating work load and projects; ensuring compliance and quality control. Effective at responsively serving customers and constituents regarding activities and information.

- Research, analyze, process and track files, documentation, correspondence and information.
- Communicate with government managers and staff.
- Maintain awareness of program and management functions in order to act as effective intermediary between managers.
- Coordinate office administrative functions.
- Train and delegate assignments to project staff.
- Troubleshoot PCs with Windows, communications and multiple applications.

EMPLOYMENT HISTORY

DEPARTMENT OF THE NAVY, Washington, DC 20350   9/80 to present
Secretary of the Navy (Administration Office)

CORRESPONDENCE ANALYST/EXPEDITER (GS-8)   2/92 to present
   Allan Grisolm, Supervisor (703) 744-4324   40 hours/week
   Supervisor may be contacted

Responsible for analyzing, prioritizing and making decisions for the appropriate handling of correspondence for professional staff within the Administrative Office of the Secretary of the Navy, the Department of Defense and other agencies.

- Maintain awareness of events, programs, priorities and issues in order to perform responsibilities.
- Create abstract of the correspondence using key words, cross-references and relationships to other correspondence and programs.
- Track documents and maintain information concerning action items and deadlines.
- Retrieve and update status of documents on computer tracking system.
- Review and ensure quality control of documents for the Secretary of the Navy's signature.

Correspondence Analyst, GS-301-8 seeking Program Assistant, GS-301-9

DONNA STEPHENS, page two
SS#: 215-76-8067

- Representative for an Information Systems Group. Provide information to users concerning system and application updates.
- Communicate with congressional offices, Department of Navy heads and other inquiries concerning correspondence and documents flowing through the Administrative Office.
- Utilize WordPerfect and Lotus 1-2-3 to produce correspondence, and to track and report statistics on documents and correspondence.

Additional Responsibilities
Representative and Assistant Secretary
NSSORA Recreation Association (1993-present)
- Represent the association with vendors providing services and products to employees of the Department of the Navy.
- Procure, negotiate prices and handle logistics of receiving clothing, movie and event tickets for employees.

TEAM LEADER (GS-7)   12/86 - 2/92
Ms. U. Schlegel, Supervisor (703) 695-1648   40 hours/week

Responsible for the efficient operations in the Outgoing Mail Records and Reference Branch and implementing new systems to increase efficiency and customer service.

- Provided direct supervision to student aides and clerical employees.
- Implemented training programs to improve efficiency and accountability.
- Enhanced job-related skills by cross-training and quality reviews.
- Improved efficiency of document control and processing
- Reviewed all final documents for procedural and format compliance with DoD guidelines.
- Provided input into staff performance reviews.

Accomplishments:
- Developed and implemented a basic internal hands-on training program for the installation of the electronic document archiving systems. Trained the staff, oversaw the archiving of all previously manually maintained files, and met project deadlines.
- Wrote job descriptions for summer hires manpower. Utilized this staff to handle the backlog workload and administrative processes.
- Improved daily operations, cutting down on duplication of efforts. Analyzed system and improved efficiency of paper flow within Outgoing Mail, Records and Reference Branch.

RESEARCH ASSISTANT (GS-6)   1/85 – 12/86
Mike James, Supervisor (703) 695-1648   40 hours/week

Responsible for reviewing and analyzing technical, policy and organizational material; applied classification number according to Standard Subject Instruction Manual.
- Maintained/integrated permanent correspondence with micrographics equipment.
- Maintained and compiled a dossier for the Secretariat and staff.
- Edited and modified data from automated correspondence control system.

Correspondence Analyst, GS-301-8 seeking Program Assistant, GS-301-9

DONNA STEPHENS, page three
SS#: 215-76-8066

Accomplishments:
- Performed job responsibilities during a time of reorganization and severe personnel and equipment shortages. Participated in quality control projects; provided special service to the executive director; and delegated activities to 10 new employees handling the administrative responsibilities of this office.
- Received a Sustained Superior Performance Award.

ASSISTANT FOR AWARDS AND PERSONNEL ACTIONS (GS-5)   1/84 - 1/85
Ms. B. Shephard, Supervisor (703) 695-1648   40 hours/week

Responsible for coordinating support for personnel actions and awards. Researched personnel actions and maintained files; retrieved data from automated system; answered personnel inquiries and requested from individuals and agencies.

MAIL & FILE CLERK, Naval Military Personnel Command (GS-3/4)   9/80 - 1/84
Ms. D. Sewell, Supervisor (703) 694-2821   40 hours/week

- Received and analyzed mail and materials to be placed into military personnel records. Verified documentation and reviewed correspondence for correctness.
- Researched information in the database and Bidex for personnel information. Responded to inquiries concerning personnel files and entries.

EDUCATION:

University of Maryland, College Park, MD 21205
Bachelor of Arts Degree, 1992
    Courses included:
    Personnel & Labor Relations (24 credit hours)
    Business Management (27 hours)
    Information Systems Management (12 hours)

Prince George's Community College, Largo, MD 21227
Associate of Arts Degree, 1990

Oxon Hill Senior High School, Oxon Hill, MD 21280; Graduated 1988

AWARDS:

Superior Scholastic Achievement Award, 1992
Quality Step Increases / Cash Awards, 1987 - 1992
Sustained Superior Performance Award, 1987
Naval Developmental Scholarship, 1982

Computer Operator, GS-7, seeking GS-8 Computer Specialist position

Rachel T. Jones
4000 – Eighth Street, SW
Washington, DC 20017

Home: (202) 888-8888   Work: (202) 666-6666

Social Security No.:	234-56-7890
Citizenship:	United States
Federal Status:	Computer Operator GS-7, 2/93 to present
	Office of the Secretary, U.S. Department of State
Veteran's Preference:	N/A

OBJECTIVE: COMPUTER SPECIALIST, GS-8; ANN. # 98-32-0001

PROFILE:

As a Computer Operator and member of computer support team, provide e-mail, computer system, hardware, software, networking management and upgrading to more than 300 users within the Office of the Secretary, Department of State. Hold **Top Secret Clearance.**

Provide System Solutions, Modifications and Problem-Solving:
- Assist with resolving critical problems in existing or planned systems/projects (LAN or e-mail)
- Anticipate systems changes and prepare users for changes
- Make minor modifications to computers, networks and e-mail systems
- Provide technical advice to management and program office officials seeking ADP support
- Use innovative methods and techniques for problem-solving
- Analyze interrelationships of pertinent components of the system

Member, Project / Support Service Team:
- Carry out project assignments, meeting deadlines, providing quality service to customers
- Determine sequence of actions necessary to accomplish the assignment
- Responsible for at least one segment of the overall project
- Assist in development and maintenance efforts

COMPUTER SKILLS:

Networks:	Networking with Novell Software 3.12, Windows NT
Operating Systems:	Windows NT, Windows 95, MS/DOS 5.0, Wang and IBM
Programs:	Word 6.0, Word Perfect, PageMaker, MultiMate, Lotus 1-2-3, VSO

EXPERIENCE:

U.S. Department of State
1988 to present

Computer Operator, GS-7   February 1993 to present
Office of the Secretary, 2201 C Street, NW, Washington, DC 20520 $26,069/year
Supervisor: John Smith; (202) 666-6666; may be contacted   40 hours/week
- Provide technical support for critical information systems for the Secretary of State and over 800 users at the Secretariat level. Manage the electronic mail system, imaging and Local Area Networks (LANs).
- Provide technical and troubleshooting assistance to hundreds of software application package users throughout the entire Department of State.
- Provide technical support for a vital electronic mail and telegram system: Principal Officer's Electronic Mail System (POEMS) and POEMS Automated Telegram Handler (PATH) in the Department of State.

Computer Operator, GS-7, seeking GS-8 Computer Specialist position

- Maintain a key Wang VS Imaging system, with local area network attached, housing the Secretary's inter-agency correspondence.
- Perform computer operations and systems functions such as tape mounts, backups, reboots, monitoring and repairing problems, rebuilding files, and network maintenance. Manipulate paper charts, imaging services, graphics, improved scanning software.

Accomplishments:
- Installation of NOVELL Netware 3.1 on LANs throughout the entire department.
- Standard plan for software required modifications to set-up and reinstall additional software.
- Installation of software works – PC hardware.
- Installation of e-mail micro-systems systems for new offices.
- Installation of 20 to 30 software works on PC hardware for reorganized department.

Information Assistant, GS-5   May 1989 to February 1993
2201 C Street, N.E., Washington DC 20520 $20,370/year
Supervisor: Ricardo Smith; (202) 647-2977   40 hours/week
- Received and analyzed telegrams and mail in the Office of Information Resources Management Remote Automated and Collating System (REARCS) at the Department of State. Distributed sensitive (limited use, official, confidential, top secret) incoming telegrams to State Department employees throughout the 25 Bureaus in the Department
- Developed and implemented a plan to process telegraphic backlogs.
- Operated the IBM computer system to retrieve information; trained staff on the use of the system, including keyboard, operator console, hardware configurations.

Microfilm Equipment Operator, GS-4   March 1988 to May 1989
Passport Agency, 1425 K Street, N.W. Washington, DC 20524 $15,171/year
Supervisor: K. Hawkins; (202) 326-6079   40 hours/week
- Coordinated a variety of priority projects and collaborated on special projects with the Deputy Assistant Secretary of Passport Services.
- Operated microfilm equipment in the Automated Records Branch, under supervision of the Deputy Assistant Secretary.
- Prepared master films of passport applications and all related documentation; set up Documate Microfilm cameras and microfilm processing equipment; indexed films for retrieval.
- Provided ongoing preventive equipment troubleshooting and maintenance, and performed routine repairs as warranted.

Sales Clerk   May 1985 to February 1988
Bloomingdale's Department Store, White Flint Mall, Rockville, MD
Supervisor: Randy McCleod; (301) 984-4515

EDUCATION:

Strayer College, Washington, DC   March 1995 to present
Major: Computer Information Systems Science (CISS)

University of the District of Columbia, Washington, DC   August 1984 to March 1994
Completed 115 of 130 credit hours toward B.S. degree in Computer Information Systems Science (CISS). Major courses of study included data processing; COBOL/JCL; business statistics. Attended college while working full-time.

St. Anthony's High School, Washington, DC; High School Diploma   June 1984

AWARDS:
Received cash awards for outstanding performance in 1990, 1991, and 1992

Executive Secretary, GS-318-8/10 seeking training or editing positions

Emily Anne Layton

310 Frederick Road
Ft. Worth, Texas 87987

Office: 604.333.2245	E-mail: ealayton@audit.navy.mil	Home: 604.988.3333

SSN: 215-52-7762	Federal Civilian Status: GS-8/10, 4/87
United States Citizen	SFC, US Army Reserve
Position Desired:	Security Clearance: SECRET

Profile

Executive secretary, office manager and instructor/writer with over 25 years Federal, National Guard and Army Reserve experience. Excellent communications, organizational and administrative skills. Valued by senior executives for ability to independently manage offices, improve systems, meet deadlines and implement new administrative procedures.

Office Reorganization and Design of Administrative Processes Experience

- As Executive Secretary, Naval Audit Service HQ (1989 to present) have developed improved office administrative systems for decreased staffing and growing audit report production requirements. Improved workflow, file management and communication methods which meet deadlines, maintain quality and ensure satisfaction by 10 audit managers plus the Director.

- As an Administrative Assistant to the Director of the Internal Security Division, IRS, wrote new procedures governing time keeping and processing requests for personnel actions, reducing errors and processing time. Successfully managed an extensive travel and premium pay budget for investigative staff.

- As a personal Assistant/Secretary for the Chief of Policy Liaison, Defense Contract Audit Agency, created, implemented and maintained and improved internal operating files, records storage and retrieval systems.

Writing and Editing Experience

- Edited the Department of Energy (DOE) *D.O.E. This Month,* a monthly newsletter distributed to all Departmental headquarters and field offices. (7 years)

- Edited the *Public Information Field Report* (on key programs, events and issues) for daily distribution to 50 top Headquarters officials and 300 field public information officers department-wide. Increased *Public Information Field Report* coverage 30% in one month.

Training Experience

- Senior instructor/writer for the 2970th U.S. Army Reserve Forces School, Ft. Belvoir, VA. Courses include: Basic Computer Operation and Concepts of the Tactical Area Army Computer System (TAACS), Document Security Methods, Office Management.

- Taught EEO for the Federal Women's Program.

Computer Skills

- MS Word, Power Point, Excel; Word Perfect; Lotus 1-2-3; Ventura; cc:Mail; GENUS; TAACS.

Executive Secretary, GS-318-8/10 seeking training or editing positions

Employment History

Executive Secretary, GS-318-8/10
Naval Audit Service HQ, 5677 Compton Blvd., Dallas, TX 78732
Supervisor: Andy McDowell, 604.681.6092; may be contacted

July 1989 - Present
40 hours per week
Starting Salary: $25,910
Current Salary: $38,199

Serve as principal assistant to the Director of Audit Operations, as well as sole administrative and audit support staff to 10 department management auditors. The Director is charged with monitoring worldwide audit activities within the Department of the Navy.

- Act as liaison to Congressional staff, government agencies, Navy components and the public.
- Direct office administrative activities including workflow, deadlines, correspondence, records, and appointments.
- Consistently meet audit report deadlines (3-5 per month).
- Receive audit updates by email and PC disk from audit managers.
- Produce detailed and timely audit reports and statements in the correct format.
- Research and respond to audit manager's questions for information, scheduling and coordination matters.
- Meet ongoing deadlines; manage multiple projects.
- Utilize knowledge of DOD procedures, policies and standard formats.
- Continually analyze and develop systems to meet changing administrative and reporting demands.
- Designed record-keeping systems, calendar and schedule of projects for audit staff and myself.

Administrative Assistant, GS-318-8
Internal Security Division, IRS, Dallas, TX 78987
Supervisor: Dan Moneybags, 604.387.8732

September 1986 - July 1989
40 hours per week
Starting Salary: $20,855
Ending Salary: $ 25,910

Served as administrative assistant to the Director of the Internal Security Division, a national office with 110 employees, 3 Branches and 7 Regional Offices.

- Provided supervision and management for all administrative functions in office including record keeping, appointments, travel, correspondence and special projects.
- Monitored travel and premium pay budget to support travel and overtime requirements of 15-25% of investigative staff. Keeping these accounts current was crucial in maintaining funding levels necessary for investigations to proceed in a timely manner.

Personal Assistant/Secretary, GS-318-6
Defense Contract Audit Agency, Andersonville, TX 78098
Supervisor: Dan Tanna, 606.378.8798

September 1984 - September 1986
40 hours per week

Managed office administration for the Chief, Policy Liaison Division. Executive Assistance included: staff supervision, prioritizing work flow to meet deadlines, correspondence review and disposition, record keeping, travel arrangements, voucher preparation, reception and appointments scheduling.

- Initiated, prepared, developed and edited documents, reports, analyses and correspondence from contributing staff elements.

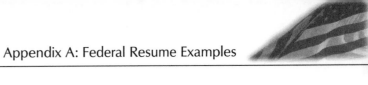

Executive Secretary, GS-318-8/10 seeking training or editing positions

Secretary/Editor, GS-318-7   October 1975 - November 1984
Department of Energy, Wallace, TX 78987   40 hours per week
Supervisor: Bob Newhart, 605.987.8782

Promoted rapidly during transition of U.S. Energy Research and Development Administration into the Department of Energy. Gained knowledge of energy issues and organizational mission that led to a position in the Office of Public Affairs.

- Supervised and managed all administrative and clerical functions in office including record keeping, appointments, travel, correspondence and special projects.
- Edited *D.O.E. This Month,* a monthly newsletter distributed to all Departmental headquarters and field offices.
- Edited the *Public Information Field Report* (on key programs, events and issues) for daily distribution to 50 top Headquarters officials and 300 field public information officers.
- Increased distribution of *Public Information Field Report* by 30% in one month.

National Guard & Army Reserve Service

Joined the 115th Infantry Unit of the Maryland National Guard in 1975 and was the first woman to serve in the Unit. Transferred to the U.S Army Reserves in 1977. Currently serving as a Senior Instructor/Writer with the 6th BN 80th Division, Dallas, TX. Current Supervisor: Daniel Jacobson, Unit Telephone: (604) 233-8777. (20 hours per week – current). Current annual salary: $5,000.

Education

48 Hours, *Education,* University of Texas, 1969, Lubbock, TX 98789
Diploma, Danville High School, 1966, Danville, TX 98787

Professional Development

Technical, Management, Business Training:
Writing, Office Management, Office Productivity Through Individual Leadership, Quality Improvement, Travel Voucher, Executive Secretarial, Instructor Training

Military Leadership Training:
Instructor Training Course, Ft. Worth, TX, 1990, with honors
Advanced Retention NCO Course, Ft. Worth, TX, 2-weeks, 1989
U.S. Army NCO Academic Graduate, Advanced, 1985
Pennsylvania Military Academy, Administrative NCO in Charge of Personnel, Texas National Guard, Danville, TX
Army Personnel Management

Honors & Distinctions

Outstanding Performance Evaluations, 1992 - 98
Navy Audit Performance Award, 1991
National Defense Service Medal
Army Achievement Medal w/ 4 Oak Leaf Clusters, 1984, 87, 89, 91, 92
Army Commendation Medal, 1983
Career Counselor Badge, 1987
Letters of Achievement and Commendation, 1975 - Present

GS-9 and Above

Special Assistant for Systems Development, GS-15 seeking SES position

NICOLE E. DAY
1012 Beaumont Avenue
Falls Church, VA 22123
Office: (202) 408-3423   E-Mail: nday@acf.dhhs.gov   Home: (703) 897-3243

Social Security No.: 219-32-3287
Citizenship: U.S.
Veterans Preference: N/A
Federal Status: GS-301/15
Special Assistant for Systems Development, 6/96 to Present

Objective

Profile

Senior program manager with twenty year background creating and managing innovative and cost effective large scale and long-term programs. Extensive governmental reengineering and streamlining experience. Strong strategic sense with the ability to balance short-term priorities against long term organizational mission and goals. Excellent communication, leadership and negotiation skills. National network of professional contacts in and out of government.

Employment History

U.S. Department of Health and Human Services (DHHS)   **6/77 to Present**
Office of Child Support Enforcement (OCSE)   40 hours/week
300 C Street, SW, Washington, DC 20432   Starting Salary: $80,323/year
Supervisor: Debbie Mazar (202) 408-2187   Present Salary: $76,878/year
Supervisor may be contacted.

SPECIAL ASSISTANT FOR SYSTEMS DEVELOPMENT, GS-301/15
SPECIAL ASSISTANT TO DIRECTOR OF PROGRAM OPERATIONS   6/96 TO PRESENT

- Work directly with the Director to develop the expanded Federal Parent Locator Service (FPLS), one of the largest databases in the country, consisting of over 275 million records.
- Serve as co-project officer on a $14 million contract to manage and monitor the activity of over 100 contracts responsible for developing the system. Review expenditures, approve hiring, and review the work of the contractors.
- Participate in negotiations and development of a Memorandum of Understanding and multi-million dollar cost reimbursement agreement with the Social Security Administration to jointly design, develop, and implement this system.
- Provide extensive briefings, training, and outreach to federal agencies, 50 state employment agencies, and 4.3 million employers in the U.S.
- Serve on the design team to delineate the systems requirements and consult with state partners on policy issues affecting the design and development of the system.
- Coordinate national security plan to safeguard the privacy and confidentiality of the data.

Special Assistant for Systems Development, GS-15 seeking SES position

Nicole E. Day, SS# 219-32-3287　　　　　　　　　　　　　　　**Page 2**

DETAIL TO THE OFFICE OF THE COMMISSION, OCSE　　　　　　　　1995 – 1996

- Established OCSE's Office of Reengineering. Responsible for identifying and introducing new and innovative management trends and practices such as Total Quality Management, Teams and Change/Transition Management.
- Council for Excellence in Government (CEG). Was one of 120 people competitively selected from across the country to participate in a yearlong leadership program to train mid-level federal executives to lead high performing agencies.
    - Participated in a series of monthly activities and daylong seminars on leadership styles and skills, benchmarking, coaching teams, and results-oriented management.
    - Met with top executives from private industry and learned how they transformed their companies, and how these skills could be used in the federal government.
- Led an innovative program improvement project sponsored by the Maryland State Legislature to determine if a public sector child support office (Washington County) could compete with a privately operated office (Lockheed/Martin).
    - Worked with a team consisting of managers and caseworkers that completely reengineered the office by introducing proven private sector business practices.
    - Within one year, the office was the highest producing child support office in the State of Maryland with an 87% collection rate.

DETAIL TO ACF'S CHIEF FINANCIAL OFFICE　　　　　　　　　　1993 – 1994

- Directed a task force of 20 managers and staff to consolidate and reorganize three offices under the auspices of the agency's Chief Financial Officer.
    - Developed a new organizational structure that incorporated the streamlining and managerial recommendations of the National Performance Review.
    - Provided the team with Myers Briggs and Change management to help facilitate the transition to the new organization.
- Led a work group responsible for merging three separate offices, and creating a new consolidated organization that met the requirements of the National Performance Review.
- Participated on the "ACF Video Conferencing Team" which was responsible for: researching current video conferencing technology and developing a strategic plan to implement video conferencing in both headquarters and the ten regional offices.
- Participated on the "ACF Staff Development and Training Workgroup." Provided top management with an overall strategy to develop a Training Resource Center and provide supervisory, managerial, and program specific training to ACF employees.
- Co-trained a "Training of Trainers" course for state and local CSE agencies.
- Conducted "Quality Awareness" seminars.

SUPERVISORY PROGRAM/MANAGEMENT ANALYST, GS-301/13　　　　1992 – 1993

- Directed the Philadelphia Performance Enhancement Program, a joint federal, state and court project to improve the overall effectiveness of the CSE office in the Philadelphia Family Court.

Special Assistant for Systems Development, GS-15 seeking SES position

Nicole E. Day, SS# 219-32-3287

SUPERVISORY PROGRAM/MANAGEMENT ANALYST (continued):

This project involved training key court staff in management analysis and reengineering techniques such as work simplification, job redesign, form analysis, and flow-charting. Using this training as a base, staff was able to develop recommendations to reengineer the way cases were processed in the office.

- The team redesigned the entire office: developed a new organizational structure and reduced the workflow by 50%.
- Redesign of the office resulted in a 40% increase in productivity.

BRANCH CHIEF, LOCATION AND COLLECTION SERVICES BRANCH 1986 – 1991

- Responsible for the day-to-day operation of the Federal Parent Locator Service (FPLS). Supervised approximately six staff in grades ranging from GS-7 through GS-13.
- Established and maintained effective liaison with seven Federal agencies and 50 State Employment Security Agencies (SESAs) to ensure accurate and timely transmission of data between the agencies and State and local CSE agencies.
- Acted as spokesperson for FPLS and Project 1099 at State and local CSE conferences.
- Successfully negotiated agreements with the Department of Labor and 50 SESAs to provide wage and unemployment data to the FPLS.
- Conducted a formal evaluation of the FPLS/SESA crossmatches to assess the cost-effectiveness of the program.
- Designed, developed and delivered training courses on the FPLS and Project 1099 at State and National CSE conferences.

MANAGEMENT ANALYST 1981 – 1986

- Conducted comprehensive analyses and studies management in nine state and local child support offices. Provided top management with and recommended organizational and procedural changes to improve productivity.
- Conducted studies concentrating on organization and staff development, resource allocation, administrative processes and procedures, and productivity evaluation.
- Developed alternative organizational structures and staffing allocations, revised floor plans and workflow in the office to improve the overall efficiency of the office.

PROGRAM ANALYST, NATIONAL HEALTH SERVICE CORPS
U.S. PUBLIC HEALTH SERVICE 1978 – 1981

- Coordinated the receipt and processing of over 8,000 applications for the National Health Service Corps. Scholarship Program that was responsible for recruiting doctors, dentists and nurses to serve in medically underserved areas of the country.
- Analyzed program accomplishments and presented recommendations for improvement.
- In conjunction with the American Medical Association, developed a socio-economic profile on scholarship recipients, which provided the Federal government with the first definitive analysis of scholarship recipients.

Special Assistant for Systems Development, GS-15 seeking SES position

Nicole E. Day, SS# 219-32-3287   **Page 4**

Education

MAS Management	George Washington University	1988
BA History	University of Virginia	1971

Frederick High School, Frederick, VA, graduated 1966

Professional Training

Team Building and Coaching Skills for Managers, 1996
Certified Trainer, William Bridge's Seminars on Managing Organizational Transitions, 1995
Appearing at Your Public Best, Georgetown University
Certified Trainer for Pritchett & Associates, Business as Unusual, 1994.
Seven Management and Planning Tools, Goal/QPC, 1993
Workshop for Team Leaders & Team, OPM, 1993
Management Effectiveness Seminar, Career Track, 1991
Front Line Leadership, Zenger-Miller, 1990
Training prior to 1990 available upon request

Honors and Awards

Cash Award for Outstanding Performance
Assistant Secretary's Excellence Award, 1997
Assistant Secretary's Excellence Award, 1995
Assistant Secretary's Teamwork Award, 1995
Assistant Secretary's Citation, 1995
Cash Award for Outstanding Performance, 1994
Federal Leadership Award, 1993
Deputy Director's Award, 1992
Special Service Award, 1990
Administrator's Citation, 1988
Quality Step Increase, 1988 and 1987
Cash Awards for Outstanding Performance, 1985 and 1984

Professional Associations / Leadership Positions

Former member of the Federal Managers' Association
Currently on Board of Directors and Past President, Hampton Townhouse Association
Past Member of Toastmasters International
Member of National Child Support Enforcement Association

Publications, Speeches, Articles

Frequent guest speaker/trainer at numerous state and local CSE conferences and workshops.
"Improving Program Performance Through Management Information," DHHS, 1986.

Inspector General for Investigations, GM-1811-15 seeking SES position

TIMOTHY HUTTON
13343 TRIADELPHIA MILL ROAD
WOODBRIDGE, VA 22191

HOME: (703) 744-4324   WORK: (202) 709-9874

Social Security No: 265-43-0987
Citizenship: U.S.A.
Federal Status: Supervisory Special Agent, GM-1811-15, 5/87 to present
Military Status: U.S.M.C., 1967-1978
Veteran's Preference: 10 Point Veteran (3 Purple Hearts and 1 Bronze Star WI Combat V)
                           Assistant Inspector General for Investigations, ES-1811

OBJECTIVE: Department of Transportation, Office of Inspector General
                   Announcement No: 1-95-30

PROFILE: Sixteen years with the General Services Administration, Office of Inspector
                   General (OIG). Responsible for managing Inspector General investigations,
                   developing and directing investigative programs which are comprehensive
                   and responsive to the Inspector General and ensuring the integrity of agency
                   programs and personnel and/or the administration of its affairs.

                   Skilled in managing complex investigations that involve alleged violations of
                   Title 18, United States Code. Experienced in establishing investigative priorities,
                   selectivity in case initiation, and performing case and office reviews.
                   Continually strive to improve investigative techniques, quality and
                   effectiveness of investigative programs and personnel. Represent the office in
                   conferences and meetings with congressional staff, agency officials, other
                   OIG staff and high level governmental officials on investigative matters.

                   Experienced manager of agents and support personnel. Effective at
                   implementing OIG training and workforce diversity programs. Currently
                   implementing training and development programs to implement National
                   Performance Review's goals of increasing workforce effectiveness and
                   controlling cost, as well as achieve the agency mission, vision, and goals.

EMPLOYMENT HISTORY

GENERAL SERVICES ADMINISTRATION
Office of Inspector General   May 1979 to present

Regional Inspector General for Investigations (RIGI), GM-1811-15   9/90 to present
        Washington Field Investigations Office   55-60 hours/week
        Regional Office Building, Room 1915   Beginning Salary: $66,125/year
        7th & D Streets, SW, Washington, DC 20407   Current Salary: $83,614/year
        Supervisor: Charles Vanderbilt (202) 432-4324
        Contact can be made

        Manage a staff of professional special agents ranging in grades from GM-14 to GS-7
        (have ranged between 8 and 18), as well as three support personnel. Responsible for
        hiring, staff and career development, reassignments, personnel and program
        evaluations. Management of the regional investigative program in the Washington Field
        Investigations Office covers both regional and national GSA programs and operations.

Inspector General for Investigations, GM-1811-15 seeking SES position

TIMOTHY HUTTON, SS# 265-43-0987

Regional Inspector General for Investigations (continued):

Managed the administrative (budget, personnel, office automation) and operational workload of the office and made long-range investigative plans. Provide technical advice to supervisors and special agents. Promote and require the use of information technologies in the investigative program.

Accept and reject highly complex and sensitive investigative work products. Work closely with OIG headquarters and regional management personnel to enhance and improve the investigative program. Conducted sensitive and complex investigations of the highest level employee in the agency.

Advanced the concept of cultural diversity in the OIG by hiring both minority employees and women. Promoted the first and currently only two female special agents to Assistant RIGI positions.

Accomplishments:

- Participated in a task group with AIGI Henderson and an outside consultant resulting in the development of the Office of Investigations Strategic Plan pursuant to the Government Performance and Results Act (GPRA) which links budget requests with performance goals and measurable outcomes. It results in mission-driven accomplishments. Issued in May of 1995.

- Also in May 1995, I developed for AIGI Henderson the Office of Investigations, Executive Management Report, an automated report for the Inspector General which reports on quarterly accomplishments.

- In September 1994, following the Office of Investigations Strategic Planning Conference, where downsizing and budget reductions were announced, initiated a training program in the Washington Field Investigations Office in accordance with US Vice President Al Gore's reinvention initiatives to make the government work more efficiently and cost less. Implemented training of the staff in Total Quality Management principles to encourage the use of self-directed work teams and employee involvement and empowerment.

- In order to accomplish my training objectives, became a trainer of a 4-day course by Dr. Stephen R. Covey entitled "The Seven Habits of Highly Effective People" in order to improve staff's personal effectiveness.

- Incorporated a customized Self-Directed Work Team course into our region's staff development program taught by the Human Resources Office of the Federal Aviation Administration in order to improve teamwork effectiveness and better utilize available staff following downsizing of our agency.

Director, Investigative Support (IS)
Programs and Projects Division, GM-1811-15   3/24/86 - 9/16/90
    GS Building, 18th & F Streets, NW, Washington, DC   50-60 hours/week
    Supervisor: Alfred H. Henderson (202) 401-9874

Managed the Office of Investigation's policy development, security, record maintenance, administrative and ADP technical support to field operations.

Provided technical operational guidance to the Assistant IG for Investigations; advised on a range of subjects including: budget/personnel matters, office automation/ADP support, uses of information technologies in an investigative environment.

Inspector General for Investigations, GM-1811-15 seeking SES position

TIMOTHY HUTTON, SS# 265-43-0987

Director, Investigative Support, Programs and Projects Division (continued):

Accomplishments:

- As the manager of the ADP Division, recognized the need to improve the ADP and management information systems within the Office of Inspector General and sub-offices (Office of Investigations and Office of Audits).

- Helped develop and prototype the Office of Audit's Audit Information System at the direction of the Inspector General and was assigned as the OIG Project Director for overall development of an OIG Management Information System. This assignment resulted in my supervising not only my division, but the OIG Systems Support and Development Division.

Acting Regional Inspector General for Investigations, GM-1811-14

Washington Field Investigations Office
Supervisor: Ralph Emery (202) 401-9874

8/85 - 3/86
40 hours/week

Managed an investigative staff of 18 agents and three clerical support personnel. Supervised and conducted highly technical and complex sensitive investigations involving the programs and operations of GSA. Provided technical advice to supervisors and agents.

Managed the administrative and operational workload of the office and long-range investigative plans. Developed and implemented budget and personnel actions. Evaluated office, supervisor and agent performance. Accepted and rejected work products.

Assistant Regional Inspector General for Investigations, GM-1811-14

Washington Field Investigations Office
Supervisor: Henry Blumfeld (202) 401-9873

1/85 - 8/85
40 hours/week

Supervised a group of agents and clerical staff in the accomplishment of all investigative activity including prevention.

Assisted the RIGI in managing the office and the investigative program. Analyzed Agency regulations, laws and policies affecting the investigative program. Accepted and rejected work products.

Criminal Investigator Staff Officer Assistant to DAIGI, GS-1811-13

Office of Investigations
GS Building, 18th & F Streets, NW, Washington, DC
Supervisor: Carroll Driscoll (202) 437-0987

12/83 - 1/85
40 hours/week

As the staff officer assistant to the Deputy AIGI, helped develop and coordinate nationwide Office of Investigations policies and procedures. Helped develop and prepare budgetary submissions and personnel actions. Analyzed and prepared statistical reports regarding nationwide office accomplishments.

Planned, organized and conducted sensitive and complex investigations and special projects related to enhancing and developing administrative management processes and management goals and objectives.

Inspector General for Investigations, GM-1811-15 seeking SES position

TIMOTHY HUTTON, SS# 265-43-0987

Criminal Investigator, GS-1811-13   6/82 - 12/83
    Office of Policy, Plans and Management Systems, Washington, DC   40 hours/week
    Supervisor: Jack Abrams (202) 576-9874

    Planned and evaluated functions of and for the Office of Investigations.
- Developed policy and procedures for that office by preparing the Investigations chapter of the OIG manual.
- Developed a guide for evaluating investigation headquarters and field components. Reviewed legislation, rules and regulations of the office and Agency as the OIG assistant clearance office.

Criminal Investigator, GS-1811-13   5/79 - 6/83
    Office of Special Projects, Washington, DC   40 hours/week
    Supervisor: Louis Corsy (202) 401-0987

- Conducted sensitive and complex criminal fraud investigations.

MILITARY EXPERIENCE:

U.S. Marine Corps (various locations throughout U.S. and Far East)   1/67 - 9/78
Conducted criminal investigations pursuant to Chapter 10 U.S. Code and other federal laws to include investigations of fraud against the government, homicide, rape and narcotic violations. Conducted white-collar crime investigations requiring knowledge of federal laws and federal accounting systems. These investigations required that I collect and preserve both physical and testimonial evidence, take statements and depositions under oath, analyze questioned documents and prepare and review highly technical criminal investigation reports.

EDUCATION:

GEORGE WASHINGTON UNIVERSITY, Washington, DC 20006
    Completed 45 credit hours in Political Science

PENSACOLA JUNIOR COLLEGE, Pensacola, FL
    Associate of Arts Degree, Political Science, 1974

FEDERAL EXECUTIVE INSTITUTE, Charlottesville, VA, 6/90 - 9/90
    Studied economics and Foreign Affairs Management Studies

GEORGE WASHINGTON UNIVERSITY, Washington, DC, 12/87 - 2/88
    School of Government & Business, Contemporary Executive Development Program

CENTER FOR CREATIVE LEADERSHIP DEVELOPMENT PROGRAM,
    Greensboro, NC, 1988
    GSA Meritorious Service Award, 1989
    GSA (IG) Commendable Service Awards (2), 1989, 1993
    OPM Honor Graduate, Federal Personnel Management Issues, Federal 171
    Executive Management Seminar, 1988

Construction Project Manager/Engineering Technician, WS-5402-10 seeking Team Leader position

KENNY KUCHINSKI

U.S. Citizen	53 Crownsville Road
SS: 210-99-8439	Baltimore, MD 21225
Veterans' Preference: 5 points	Home: (410) 555-1212
Highest Civilian Grade Held: WS-5402-12, 4/94-present	Work: (410) 222-1515

OBJECTIVE: Engineering Technician (Project Manager) GS-802-12
Announcement Number: N-905

SUMMARY OF QUALIFICATIONS:
- Project manager for new and renovation construction projects
- 15 years of experience as supervisor
- Skilled budget manager
- 30 years of technical construction knowledge regarding equipment, materials, design specifications, and environmental considerations
- Skilled as liaison between customers and contractors to assure proper implementation of changes.
- Extensive training in supervision, management, job skills, and EEO.
- 13 years experience as EEO counselor.

CERTIFICATIONS:
First Grade Engineer, State of Maryland, 1995

EMPLOYMENT EXPERIENCE:

Department of the Navy, Naval Surface Weapons Center	4/94 - Present
10910 New Hampshire Avenue	50 hours per week
Silver Spring, MD 20910-5000	$24.50 per hour
Supervisor: Mark Cohen (301) 744-0800	Present supervisor may be contacted

**ACTING PROJECT MANAGER, MINOR SPECIFIC CONSTRUCTION
CODE 580, WS-5402-12**

ENGINEERING TECHNICIAN, WS-5402-10
Project Manager for Washington District-wide projects ranging from **1,000** to **80,000** sf and with budgets ranging from **$25K to $700,OOOK.** Manage an average of 4 to 9 projects simultaneously on an ongoing basis. Customers include the U.S. Army, Navy, Marine Corps, Washington Naval District. Supervise an average of 20 to 40 tradesmen per project. Report to a zone manager concerning minor specifics. Responsible for all aspects of project from intake, construction analysis, planning, scheduling, managing budget, customer liaison, quality control, and **completing project on time and within budget.**

As Project Manager manage all active customer requests (CR-1s) for designated customers. Track customer requests from receipt into Public Work Center (PWC) through completion and closeout. Handle warranty issues; researching problems and ensuring customer satisfaction. Customer requests include the following: renovation of office space, remodeling of offices, heating, A/C, electrical power modifications, ceilings, lighting, floors, applications of flooring, painting, erection of doors, storage areas and modifications to specific construction.

Construction Project Manager/Engineering Technician, WS-5402-10 seeking Team Leader position

Kenny Kuchinski, SS# 210-99-8439   **Page Two**

DUTIES & RESPONSIBILITIES:

Construction Consultant –

Planning, Design and Management Stages:

- Technical supervisor of construction and engineering projects involving new construction design and management, repair, and modifications.
- Participate in pre-scoping and design conferences with A/E and customer representatives.
- Technical assistant and advisor analyzing construction, engineering and architectural aspects, complex technical specifications and special laws and regulations.
- Interact with designers and customers to determine the best needs to fulfill project. Review additional services for electrical, domestic and sanitation provisions to meet the needs and provide customer comfort throughout construction phases.

Project Management:

- Coordinate project schedules; ensure commitment of all parties including design, Specific Construction Engineering (SCE), PWC related departments, supply commitments and procurement needs.
- Plan work schedule and timetables and develop plans and solutions:
  - initial and final assessment for expenditures
  - environmental and safety procedures
  - quality of equipment and material
- Manage materials and equipment for projects.
- Experience in identifying risk for asbestos, hazardous waste, removal and disposal, and recommendations for alternative needs.
- Ensure that databases are maintained.
- Utilize best methods to accomplish any type of construction project.

Public Work Center Liaison:

- Monitor changes in workflow to improve operations and increase productivity within guidelines set by the Public Work Center, Washington Naval District.
- Coordinate all actions with appropriate PWC personnel. Ensure prompt and unified efforts are provided throughout project.
- Represent and handle problems for the customer within the PWC.
- Assisted with formulation of goals, budget and manpower requirements throughout construction projects, proposed engineering/architectural designs.
- Provide technical direction to constituent areas of study. Analyze results from project scope, funding and resolving problem areas.

Customer Relations:

- Communicate with customers throughout project in order to meet budget and project schedules. Attend weekly meetings to discuss project and resolve issues.
- Perform evaluations to ensure flow of work completions, monitor workload.
- Monitor customer's funded workload for Acquisition Planning.
- Coordinate surveys, inquiries and production records in order to resolve problems.

Recent project:

- Sole responsibility for the renovation of the Naval Inter-Agency Postal Service at Building 94, Anacostia Naval Station.

Construction Project Manager/Engineering Technician, WS-5402-10 seeking Team Leader position

Kenny Kuchinski, SS# 210-99-8439   **Page Three**

Naval Surface Warfare Center   1/81 to 4/94
10901 New Hampshire Avenue, Silver Spring, MD, 20903   40 hours per week
Supervisor: Carter Barnes (202) 294-1415 $12.60/hour to $16.94/hour

ACTING SUPERINTENDENT, PUBLIC WORKS SHOPS (1991, 6 months)

- Served as Acting General Foreman of Public Works maintenance shops.
- Responsible for the day-to-day operation of all public works functions including carpentry, machine, paint, pipe, refrigeration, boiler plant, roads and grounds, and trouble-center repair shops.

SUPERVISORY FOREMAN BOILER PLANT
ACTING GENERAL FOREMAN (1987-1988)

- Managed a main boiler plant and 35 boilers throughout facility.
- Supervised a staff of 86 tradesmen. Coordinated, scheduled manpower.
- Planned preventative maintenance programs.
- Led safety and training seminars.
- Prepared production reports on fuel consumption, cost and maintenance operations reports, equipment modifications/up-grade estimates.
- Maintained/updated instructions, regulation manuals, files, logs and equipment.
- Responsible for safe and efficient operation of all buildings/plants throughout the military complex, including: control of steam, hot water and humidity levels.
- Responsible for the electrical shop operations and served as troubleshooter during any storms or other mechanical problems.

Previous Experience:

Utility System Repairer and Operator, General Services Administration (1979-1981)
Boiler Plant Operator in Charge - Naval Surface Weapons Center (1977-1979)
Foreman, Heating Mechanics, Housing Authority, Baltimore City (1976-1977)

EDUCATION

Maryland GED Certificate, April 1975

ADDITIONAL TRAINING/EDUCATION

Community College of Baltimore, Math, 6 credits
Basic Electrical Maintenance, 96 hours, Dundalk Community College, 1974
Quality Assurance Manager, 40 hours, Washington Navy Yard, 1985

EEO training: Performance Appraisal Review, Preventive Discipline, Performance Evaluation and Appraisal Rating, Supervisor Development Program, Rights of Supervisors, Building Productive Labor-Management Relations, Prevention of Sexual Harassment, Top Quality Management Initiative Training.

Supervisor training: Practical Personnel Management, Preventive Discipline, FERS Training, Communications Skills, Internal Control, Career Planning, Legal Responsibilities, Timekeeping, Setting Goals, Supervisory Development.

Construction Project Manager/Engineering Technician, WS-5402-10 seeking Team Leader position

Kenny Kuchinski, SS# 210-99-8439   **Page Four**

Safety training: CPR, Supervisor Safety, Hearing Conservation, Protective Equipment Supervisor, Health and Safety, Confined Space and Rescue Techniques, Asbestos Removal and Protection, Hazardous Waste Handling, Elevator Safety Training, Safe Handling Compressed Gases, Ordinance Qualifications Certification.

Technical training:
Contracting Officer Technical Representative
Corrosion Control, Equipment Design and Usage, Fiberglass Facilities
Cleaver Brooks Boiler Construction
Energy Conservation
Bureau of Mines Feedwater Treatment
Fundamentals of Pneumatic Controls
Corrosion Control Underground Facilities and Equipment
Drew Feedwater Treatment and Watertowers
Mechanical Seals School
Power Principles Instructor Training
Mechanical Seal & Plumbing
Quality Assurance Evaluation

Areas of Technical Expertise:
Sheet metal, breaks, crimpers, seamers, Philia slip formers
Electrical amprobes, continuity tester, volt probes, ETC
Piping and plumbing, steamfitting, threaders, cutters, rollers, benders, light welding
Carpentry: planers, routers, joiners, skill/band saws, jug saw, lathe, all hand tools
Refrigeration: gauges, sweating tools, testers, hermitic analyzers, vacuum pumps
Masonry: brick laying, concrete forming, poured concrete, block
Lagging: wet and dry insulating material, seamers, cutters
Mechanical: Lathes, planers, shapers, millers, micrometers, calipers, drill presses.

Specification Reading and Writing:
Able to write, interpret specifications from: tech manuals, manufacturer's specifications, verbal instructions, schematic drawings and blueprints, standard operating instructions, security and safety pamphlets, equipment and personnel safety regulations.

SPECIAL SKILLS, HONORS, ACHIEVEMENTS

Superior Performance Award, 1981, 1982, 1983, 1987, 1988, 1991, 1992
Special Achievement Award, 1982
Public Works EEO Award, 1990
Public Works Safety Committee Chairman, 1984
Certificate of Recognition, Adult & Community Education for Peer Teaching & Basic Skills
        Teaching, Board of Education City of Baltimore, MD, 1987
Certificate of Appreciation for the National Committee for Employer Support of National
        Guard & Reserve
Member, National Association of Power Engineers
Notary Public for the City of Baltimore

Project Manager/Systems Engineer, GS-334-13, seeking GS-14 Supervisory Computer Specialist

DANIEL MINSON
1205 Orange Grove Way
Bedford, PA 32343

Business (717) 235-4332   Residence (717) 323-4324

Social Security #:   212-65-4324
Citizenship: United States
Veterans Preference: N/A
Federal Status: Project Manager/Systems Engineer, GS-334-13

OBJECTIVE: Supervisory Computer Specialist, GS-334-14, Ann. 97-06

QUALIFIED BY:

15 Years of Information Technology industry-related design, integration, software engineering, assessment, Life Cycle Management, requirement analysis, program development/management and implementation. Hold Bachelor of Science in Computer and Information Sciences. Proven ability to effectively analyze Information Technology, lead development and testing efforts, and implement in projected target areas for the highest return on investment.

EDUCATION:

Microsoft Certified Systems Engineer (MCSE)   1996
MS TCP/IP Product Specialist   Microsoft Networking Product Specialist
MS Exchange 4.0 Product Specialist   MS Windows 95 Product Specialist
NT Server 3.51   MS NT Workstation 3.51

CompuServe International, Philadelphia, PA
Certified Wide Area Network Professional   1994 - 1995
Certified Local Area Network Professional   1995

University of Pennsylvania, University College, College Park, PA
B.S. – Computer and Information Sciences   1986

Layton High School, Layton, PA 34298   1980

EXPERIENCE:

NAVAL INFORMATION SYSTEMS MANAGEMENT CENTER   1991 – Present
    4600 Navistar Way, Philadelphia, PA 32432   40 hours/week
    Supervisor: Vince Serio – (717) 235-4323   Salary: $59,917/year
    Supervisor may be contacted.

Project Manager/Systems Engineer (GS-334-13)
Lead Engineer defining and coordinating the technical efforts of a 6-man Development Team of Computer Analysts, technicians and support staff in the implementation of a state of the art Metropolitan Area Network (MAN) and data communications technology infrastructure based on the Institute of Electrical and Electronic Engineers (IEEE) standards.

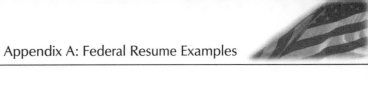

Project Manager/Systems Engineer, GS-334-13, seeking GS-14 Supervisory Computer Specialist

DANIEL MINSON, SS# 212-65-4324   **p. 2**

Accomplishments:

- Implemented multiple building IEEE 802.3 Ethernet LANS; 802.3 CISCO and 3Com Ethernet electronics; connected remote offices via ANSI FDDI Metropolitan Synchronous Optical Network topology provided by Bell Atlantic.

- Analyzed, defined and implemented organizational requirements for Enterprise computing. Effected and evaluated requirements for a campus implementation of low bit rate Video Teleconferencing.

- Administered the requirements and execution of a $1.3 million FY94-95 Organization Information Technology Infrastructure refreshment that included the purchase of FDDI Metropolitan circuits, Ethernet and FDDI cabling of a company building, LAN Servers, laptops, Intel client workstations, Windows 95 and NT client software, Microsoft ExChange groupware application software and Network Management Utilities.

- Direct the day-to-day operations of the Command's enterprise network to ensure operational readiness and timely support to the functional users. Established processes and procedures to monitor, troubleshoot and correct operational problems affecting network servers and communication links. Evaluate network usage to ensure the availability of operational capacity to user demands. Developed short and long-range network capacity plans for available bandwidth, hardware and software upgrades and enhancements.

- Maintain technical competence of changing technology and new product lines via trade publications, conferences and seminars.

- Utilized defacto and open communication and transport protocols, TCP/IP OSI, DLC, Appletalk, IPX/SPX, NetBEUI, and routing protocols of OSPF and RIP. Designed, developed and support a heterogeneous Metropolitan Network predicated on the Microsoft Windows NT 3.51 Server, Sun SPARC 20 workstation and Microsoft Exchange 4.0 Enterprise Message System.

- Accelerated the implementation of Internet Engineering Task Force RFC 1542 for the Dynamic Host Configuration Protocol across a multiple NT Domains.

- Secured and implemented multiple Class "C" IP addresses for the organization. Steered the organization toward the internet. Conceived and documented the requirements for an organization Internet Home Page. Defined the hardware and software operating requirements for the Home Page and Implemented DNS registration for name resolution broadcasting on the Internet.

- Evaluated the components of the Microsoft Back Office Suite to include NT Server 3.51, SQL Server 4.21, SMS Server 1.0 and the Exchange Client 4.0. (Received Cash Awards FY 1994, 1995 and 1996)

- Performed the technical review of the Compaq Proliant SMP 4500 mid-range server. Standardized the entire organization MAN on the Compaq Proliant line of SMP Servers.

- Standardized the entire MAN on the Microsoft NT 3.51 NOS, Microsoft Exchange 4.0 Groupware.

Project Manager/Systems Engineer, GS-334-13, seeking GS-14 Supervisory Computer Specialist

DANIEL MINSON, SS# 212-65-4324   **p. 3**

NAVAL DATA AUTOMATION COMMAND   1989 – 1991
    Philadelphia Navy Yard, Philadelphia, PA   40 hours/week
    Supervisor: Evan Burstein – (717) 235-4323   Salary: $43,835/year

Program Analyst (GS-334-12)
Conducted LCM reviews and approval of major (in excess of $10 million) ADP programs for Naval Aviation Systems Command. Coordinated and drafted formal Cost Analysis Studies and provided the results to Executive Management in reports and point papers.

Accomplishments:

- Participated in technical site visits to assess system performance of major Naval ADP system developments. Surveyed systems included the Naval Aviation Logistics Command Management Information System (NALCOMIS) and Shipboard Non-Tactical ADP Program (SNAP).

- Assisted the Navy Comptroller's Office (NAVCOMP) with annual ADP budget reviews and Navy IRM Budget audits to justify ADP program expenditures and out-year budget forecasts. Participated as a team component in Mission Assessment studies with management and Computer Specialist. Participated on a software evaluation panel to review and analyze software products produced by Navy central design activities. (NARDAC, Wash.) Managed the design, development and deployment of various small OA and IRM systems. Utilized ADP Project Management methodologies to monitor and track the development of projects and programs.

- Drafted reports and Gantt charts for forecasting and scheduling of development modules and program stages to management. Produced LCM documentation detailing and outlining necessary resources, hardware, software, and personnel to effectively support the development and deployment of a full-scale system life cycle effort. Reviewed and monitored ADP acquisitions approvals, operations, planning, and development of AIS programs and projects in the COMNAVAIR arena. (Received Promotion January 1990)

NAVAL WEAPONS ENGINEERING SUPPORT ACTIVITY   1985 – 1989
    Philadelphia Navy Yard, Philadelphia, PA 32343   40 hours/week
    Supervisor: Terry Richardson (Retired)   Salary: $37,743/year

Systems Analyst Software Engineer (GS-334-7/12)
Coordinated and participated in development teams for engineering applications and Office Automation (OA) requirements for the following systems: Security Authorization, Personnel Administration, Action Item Tracking, ADP Inventory, Training Tracking, Budget and Manpower systems.

Computer Specialist, GS-334-11, seeking GS-12 Computer Specialist

HAROLD L. WALTERSON
SS# 218-86-4321
U.S. Citizen

1008 Edmondson Avenue   Baltimore, MD 21228
Home: (410) 744-0112   Work: (410) 744-4324

Highest Federal Civilian Status: Veterans Preference: N/A
Computer Programmer Analyst, GS-334-11, 11/91 to present

OBJECTIVE

Information Technical Systems Development Programmer/Analyst, GS-334-12

SUMMARY OF QUALIFICATIONS

- Experienced in current mainframe systems environment
- IBM/MVS/ESA system architecture
- TSO, CICS/VS, COBOL/COBOL II experience
- Knowledge of NP, AIR and accounting principles
- Ability to perform detailed system analysis
- Experienced working independently

WORK EXPERIENCE

DEFENSE INVESTIGATIVE SERVICE   **11/83 to present**
Information Systems Management & Planning Directorate   Salary: $32,000
National Computer Center Systems Development Division
45 N. Charles Street, Baltimore, MD
Supervisor: Chris Troutman (410) 744-3762   Supervisor may be contacted

Computer Programmer Analyst, GS-334/11 (promoted 1991)
Duties & Responsibilities:
- Member of Computer Programmer Analyst team providing design, development, enhancement and maintenance services to application systems.
- Perform design activities including program specifications for development and modification tasks.
- Assist in cost and feasibility analysis to determine the best solutions that will meet immediate needs of the agency.
- Provide support to application systems including feasibility studies, cost benefit studies, resource requirement studies.

Projects:
- Developed a <u>label creation system for the mailroom</u>. System included CICS programs for: data entry, updating, deleting, selecting labels for printing System; also included batch program written in COBOL for actual printing of labels.
- <u>Member of conversion team managing system changeover from DOS to MVS</u>. Responsible for identifying differences, in establishing standards for the new environment, and running parallel to verify results.

Computer Specialist, GS-334-11, seeking GS-12 Computer Specialist

HAROLD L. WALTERSON, SS# 218-86-4321   **Page 2**

- <u>Member of conversion team</u> that took system in Ohio running in SAMSAM/ SAMTAM environment and adapted them to run in a <u>CICS/COBOL/VSAM</u> environment. Approximately 100 CICS programs and 125 batch COBOL programs had to be written to accomplish this task. Worked closely with the end-user development test data.
- <u>Created system to upload data from PC (off-site)</u>; ran data against mainframe files; downloaded results back to PC.

U.S. CUSTOMS SERVICE   1/81 – 11/83
Financial Management Division, Computer Section   Salary: $28,000
Customs House, Baltimore, MD
Supervisor: Andrew Shuster (410) 788-2780

(U.S. Customs is the only bureau that creates profit from tariffs, export fees, etc. The Financial Management Division was responsible for A/R, A/P, general ledger management and financial information management.)

Computer Operator/Programmer Trainee, GS-334/5
Duties & Responsibilities:
- Utilized an on-line system communicating with 3 out of 7 regional offices.
- Wrote programs to produce ad hoc financial reports for Comptroller.
- Maintained existing A/P and A/R programs.
- Performed detailed system analysis working independently.
- Maintained A/R data from import-export brokers.
- As requested by user, designed, developed, coded and implemented an on-line Inventory Control System for regional Logistics Management Branch.
- Wrote programs in Datashare language system; automated a manual system and generated reports used by both local management and HQ personnel.
- Prepared reports for Financial Management Branch.

EDUCATION
Howard Community College, Columbia, MD
Associate of Arts Degree, 1980
Major: Data Processing Technology   Minor: Accounting
Deans List 2 semesters

TRAINING
Job Control Language & Utilities, State of Maryland, Certificate
Datashare Programming Course, Datapoint Corporation, Certificate
CICS Application & Design, Advanced Technology Systems, Inc., Certificate
Introduction to IBM-PC, Dundalk Community College, Certificate

SPECIAL SKILLS, ACCOMPLISHMENTS, AWARDS
Superior Performance Award 1992
Quality Step Increases 1992 and 1993

Contract Specialist, GS-12 seeking General Business and Industry Specialist, GS-1101-12

STEVEN R. TYLER
1725 Greenview Drive
Silver Spring, MD 21209

Home: (301) 233-4333   E-mail: stevetyler@nismic.navy.mil   Work: (202) 789-9874

Social Security No.: 222-33-4444   Citizenship: United States
Federal Status: Contract Specialist, GS-12   Veteran's Status: N/A
Security Clearance: Secret

OBJECTIVE   General Business and Industry Specialist, GS-1101-12, Ann. # C-138F

EDUCATION

Master of Arts in Procurement and Acquisitions Management, 1996	**GPA: 3.8**

Wilshire University, Andrews AFB, Washington, DC
Honors: Distinguished Graduate
Thesis: Alternative Dispute Resolution

Defense Acquisition University, 1996	**GPA: 4.0**

Defense Acquisition Workforce Improvement Act Level I and Level II certified
Honors: Distinguished Graduate for Automated Information Systems
              Honor Graduate for Government Contract Law
              Distinguished Graduate for Intermediate Contracting

Bachelor of Science Degree in Political Science, 1992	**GPA: 3.5**

Morgan State University, Greenview, MN
Minor in Military Science
Honors: Dean's List
G.T.E. Academic All-American and scholar athlete award in college football

RECENT ACCOMPLISHMENTS

- Awarded $250 million dollar services contract using new innovative Blanket Purchase Agreement procedures (BPA). Using this streamlined process has saved the government hundreds of thousands of dollars and shortened the life cycle of putting a contract in place. EC/EDI was used throughout the process to simplify the acquisition. Other time and money saving tools used were integrated product teams, tele-conferencing, oral presentations and past performance questionnaires. The project has received praise from national media (copies of press clips available upon request), and the agency received the "Hammer Award" from Vice President Al Gore for its cost-effective use of BPA's. The General Services Administration refers to NISMC as the BPA experts when asked by industry or other federal agencies.

- Played an integral role in highly successful first annual Navy Contracting Intern Training Conference. Nominated by my supervisor and selected by the Department of the Navy leadership to be a team leader for the conference; served on the committee to organize, plan and coordinate the conference; responsible for developing the curriculum, agenda, format and speakers for over 400 participants; briefed the Under Secretary of Defense and the Assistant Secretary of the Navy on the progress of the conference. Received an award from the Assistant Secretary of the Navy and other top Navy officials.

Contract Specialist, GS-12 seeking General Business and Industry Specialist, GS-1101-12

STEVEN R. TYLER, SS # 222-33-4444   **Page 2**

- Selected for the United States Government's "Outstanding Scholar Intern Program," designed to attract the most outstanding students coming out of college. Assigned to the 1102 contracting series for a three-year internship, received high performance ratings and grade increases (GS-7 to GS-12) every year in the program. Graduated from the program with distinguished honors.

- Solid business and management background developed from the management of 1,000-acre grain and livestock family farm. Communicated effectively between farm owner, agri-businesses and seasonal employees. Served as team leader for 50 seasonal employees as well as the farm manager responsible for maintaining a tight, rigorous weekly schedule.

EMPLOYMENT HISTORY

DEPARTMENT OF THE NAVY, Washington Navy Yard, Washington D.C.   12/93 to present
Contract Specialist (GS-12)   45 hours per week
Supervisor: Tom Hanks (202) 666-3298   Contact may be made
Starting Salary: $22,717   Current Salary: $46,000

Introduction:

Over three years of contracting experience with the Department of the Navy serving as a Contract Specialist, Cost Team Leader, and Source Selection Evaluation Board member with the Naval Information Systems Management Center (NISMC). The central contracting office and center of excellence for the acquisition of information technology (IT), NISMC implements the strategic vision of the Department of Defense, Navy and Marine Corps by providing innovative contracting services and quality customer support. NISMC contracts for and acquires competitive and commercially available products/services for PCs, software, networks, data management, communications, video and data telecommunications and internet used worldwide on ships, at military bases and headquarters.

Projects:

Currently, serve as cost team leader and senior contract specialist on the ITSS project. This $250 million support services project will be awarded using streamlined Blanket Purchase Agreement (BPA) procedures. Served as contract specialist and SSEB member on the $700 million Tac-4 contract, a tactical and non-tactical hardware/software project. Also worked as the lead contract specialist for three months on the NTOPS contract, a hardware project worth over $100 million. Completed an extensive rotation administering nine post award contracts worth over $150 million. Served a six month rotation with the Fleet and Industrial Supply Center (FISC) responsible for managing over 20 contracts from pre-award to contract close-out.

Responsibilities:
- Facilitate integrated product teams and evaluation boards.
- Advise and assist Contracting Officer on the implementation of Federal, DoD, and other agency policy (FAR, FIRMR, DFAR).
- Stay current with and implement Congressional changes to procurement policy (FASA, ITMRA, FARA).

Contract Specialist, GS-12 seeking General Business and Industry Specialist, GS-1101-12

STEVEN R. TYLER, SS # 222-33-4444   **Page 3**

Responsibilities (continued):

- Implement electric commerce/electric data interchange (EC/EDI) into contracting process.
- Efficiently use the latest IT equipment and software.
- Create contract documents in HTML and upload to agency website for vendor use.
- Analyze Information Technology (IT) market conditions and conduct market surveys.
- Analyze proposed costs and prices and negotiate contract terms and conditions.
- Award Blanket Purchase Agreements (BPA) to GSA schedule holders.
- Evaluate all proposed terms and conditions. Determine competitive ranges.
- Research, prepare and write position papers for the contracting officer and contract file.
- Communicate with vendor and contractor community on a daily basis.

Specialized Training and Skills:
Defense Acquisition University, Small Business Contracting, Commerce Business Daily Transmissions using the Internet, Service Contract Act, Trade Agreements Act, HTML/Internet Programming and Usage, Defense Acquisition Workforce Improvement Act, Government Ethics, Security in the Workplace, Procurement Integrity Act, Blanket Purchase Agreements, Privacy Act and Freedom of Information Act, Communications with Congress and Department of Defense Heads. (All training took place from 1994 to 1997 and lasted from 2 hours to 4 weeks.)

UNITED STATES SENATE, SROB, Washington D.C.   Fall 1993
Congressional Intern for Senator Donald O'Sullivan   24 hours per week
Supervisor: Diana Swinson (202) 686-8734
- Responded to Congressional inquiries, reviewed and wrote general correspondence
- Researched and developed Senator O'Sullivan's 1995 Farm Bill Policy
- Managed 1,000 pieces of incoming constituent mail per day

SCHOOLDEN'S FARM SERVICE, Schoolden, MN   Nov 1992 to Sep 1993
Custom Applicator/Sales   50 hours per week
Supervisor: Willie Nelson (605) 333-2334
- Chemical and fertilizer management of 50,000 acres
- Recommended and implemented nutrient programs for area farmers

CARLSON HY-BRID COMPANY, Carlson, MN   Summers 1989 to 1992
Harvest Production, Wheelpuller Operator, Construction   45 hours per week
Supervisor: Daisy Duke (605) 233-4332
- Facilitated and trained inexperienced operators with emphasis on safety
- Production management of $500,000 in seed corn per day

C.A. TYLER FARMS, Three Rivers, MN   May 1991/92 to Aug 1991/92
Farm Manger   60 hours per week
Supervisor: Clarence Tyler (605) 322-8774
- Team leader of 50 seasonal employees
- Timeline and milestone management of 1,000 acre farm

Contract Specialist, GS-12 seeking General Business and Industry Specialist, GS-1101-12

STEVEN R. TYLER, SS # 222-33-4444   **Page 4**

MICHIGAN GAS COMPANY, Three Rivers, MN   Jun 1988 to Aug 1988
Drafter   40 hours per week
Supervisor: Ron David (605) 324-3442
- Coordinated gas service maps and assisted installation personnel
- Provided timely customer support/service for all of Southwest Minnesota

RELEVANT COURSE WORK:

Information Technology Contracting, Information Systems Security, Computer Resources and Information Management, Contracting Fundamentals, Contract Pricing, Government Contract Law, Intermediate Contracting, Intermediate Contract Pricing, Congressional Research training, Library of Congress training, Negotiations, Logistics, Pricing, Operations Management, Security Management, Analysis of Management Systems, Proposal preparation

COMPUTER SKILLS:

Internet (Microsoft Explorer and Netscape), HTML (hot dog), Microsoft Word, Excel, Powerpoint, Access, Schedule, Windows 95, Windows 3.01 and 3.11 for Work Groups, Adobe Acrobat, Harvard Graphics, Lotus 1-2-3, Word Perfect, EBBS, E-mail (cc-mail and Microsoft Exchange), CA Super Project, Delrina Form Flow, Macintosh

AWARDS:

- Outstanding Performance Appraisal Review System award, 1996, 1997
- Quality Salary (Grade) increase, 1994, 1995, 1996
- Tac-4 Contract Recognition award from Vice Admiral
- Tac-4 Protest Recognition award from Rear Admiral
- Outstanding achievement award for 1995 Navy Contracting Intern Training Conference
- Navy Intern Conference Letter of Commendation from Assistant Secretary of the Navy
- Distinguished graduate for Contracting 201, 211 and 241 courses
- United States Government Outstanding Scholar Program recipient
- Letter of Commendation from FISC executive officer for outstanding customer support
- G.T.E. Academic All-American, all-conference academic team in college football
- College Scholars of America
- Letter of appreciation from U.S. Senator Donald O'Sullivan for outstanding constituent support

LEADERSHIP AND ACTIVITIES:

Civilian Leadership Development Program, College Football team captain for over 100 players, National Contract Management Association, Ice Hockey team captain responsible for organization of 20 teammates, Benevolent and Protective Order of Elks, Friends of the National Zoo, Sons of the American Revolution, NISMC Blood Drive Coordinator, Soil and Water Conservation Society, Government Ethics Representative, High School class president responsible for class reunion of over 300 people, Morgan State University Alumni Association and Varsity Club

Secretary (Steno), GS-318-10, seeking Editor or Program Assistant

PATRICIA J. WINCHILD
3423 33RD AVENUE
LARGO BEACH, FL 54534
HOME: (408) 322-3222 • WORK: (408) 324-3243

Social Security No.:	226-56-0951
Citizenship:	United States
Veteran's Status:	None
Federal Status:	Secretary (Steno) GS-10, 07/90-present

OBJECTIVE: Assistant to the Deputy Administrator, Announcement No. 9-87-051-7

SKILLS SUMMARY:

Eighteen years experience in administration and program support with Animal and Plant Health Inspection Service (APHIS), Department of Agriculture. As an integral staff professional, assisted senior level managers with implementing important animal and plant health inspection service programs resulting in successful cooperation with private industry and states. Skilled in assisting with program functions; supporting and communicating with senior managers, private industry representatives, APHIS program managers. Coordinate program activities; coordination of workload and projects; ensuring compliance and quality control. Participate with management team supporting policy and program management decisions and issues. Research and compile information in support of studies; and act as interface with internal and external organizations.

EMPLOYMENT HISTORY:

U.S. DEPARTMENT OF AGRICULTURE
Animal and Plant Health Inspection Service
Federal Center, Sarasota, FL 56434
6/78 to present

SECRETARY (Steno) (GS-10) 7/90 to present
Ben Stratten, Supervisor (408) 323-4323 40 hours/week
Supervisor may be contacted Current salary: $43,000/year

Serve as personal assistant to the Associate Administrator and participate in the work of the Associate Administrator of APHIS. Perform administrative responsibilities required to effectively and efficiently manage the organization and its programs. The Associate Administrator serves in a coordinate capacity with the Administrator and is delegated the same authorities as the Administrator.

Programs:

Equine Piroplasmosis and the 1996 Atlanta Olympic Games. Supported the Associate Administrator in ensuring the veterinary regulatory oversight of international movements of horses into the U.S. for the 1996 Olympic Games in Atlanta, GA. Prepared written materials, reports, and supported policy and program management issues. Liaison between contacts in Atlanta and Associate Administrator.

Bovine Spongiform Encephalopathy (BSE) is a chronic degenerative disease affecting the central nervous system of cattle, commonly known as "mad cow disease." Supported the Associate Director with an extensive educational effort to U.S. cattle producers and veterinarians about the disease. Scheduled and coordinated briefings, produced fact sheets, and coordinated with public health service offices concerning inquiries. *continued . . .*

Secretary (Steno), GS-318-10, seeking Editor or Program Assistant

PATRICIA J. WINCHILD, 226-56-0951

Programs (continued):

Provided research and information dissemination regarding expedited programs for expanded surveillance efforts, training of veterinary inspectors, and enhanced education to producers, animal nutritionists and veterinarians.

Amended indemnity regulations for livestock exposed to tuberculosis. Provided support to changing regulations concerning this disease.

Increased disease surveillance to protect U.S. Poultry from highly pathogenic avian influenza outbreak in Mexico. Supported activities surrounding an increased surveillance program managed by APHIS. Coordinated schedules for evaluation team of veterinarians; served as liaison with Mexican officials; and prepared research reports and correspondence for this issue.

Regionalization Criteria for Imports of animal commodities. Supported the Associate Administrator with research and plans to regionalize commodities trade regulations. Researched information, acted as liaison, maintained status reports and information, and assisted with dissemination of information.

Supported the Associate Administrator's successes in APHIS' cooperative efforts with producers and the states for the implementation of new disease eradication programs:

Brucellosis: Reached a major milestone in the Cooperative State-Federal Brucellosis Rapid Completion Plan. The program successfully decreased the risk of Bison in Yellowstone National Park from transmitting brucellosis to animals in the surrounding States that are free of the disease.

APHIS Vision: Assisted the Associate Administrator with the dissemination, scheduling of meetings and support for the implementation of APHIS Vision throughout the organization.

Responsibilities:
- Maintain awareness of events, programs, priorities and issues.
- Coordinate schedules and contacts with Secretary's office, key Members of Congress, and APHIS Management Team members.
- Arrange meetings and conferences for Associate Administrator, including travel arrangements.
- Develop, implement, and adapt administrative procedures, controls, and reporting requirements necessary to coordinate and manage the Associate Administrator's office.
- Responsible for analyzing, prioritizing, and making decisions for the appropriate handling of correspondence within the Office of Administrator and subordinate units of APHIS.
- Track documents and maintain information concerning action items and deadlines.
- Retrieve and update status of documents on computer tracking system.
- Review and ensure quality control of documents for the Administrator's, Assistant Secretary's, and Secretary of Agriculture's signatures.
- Communicate with congressional offices, Department of Agriculture heads, and other inquiries concerning correspondence and documents flowing through the Administrator's Office.

SECRETARY (Steno) (GS-9)   2/89 - 7/90
World Agricultural Outlook Board   40 hours/week
James Brolin, Supervisor (408) 234-3243   Salary: $28,835/year

Served as personal assistant to the Chairperson; primary responsibility involved coordinating administrative functions to ensure the smooth and efficient operation of the Chairperson's office. *continued . . .*

Secretary (Steno), GS-318-10, seeking Editor or Program Assistant

PATRICIA J. WINCHILD, 226-56-0951   PAGE 3

Responsibilities:
- Participated in management of the Chairperson's office by performing secretarial and administrative duties.
- Provided direct supervision to student aides and clerical employees.
- Coordinated workflow of the office by shifting secretarial personnel to cover emergency situations with the office.
- Improved efficiency of document control and processing.
- Reviewed all final documents for procedural and format compliance with established guidelines.
- Provided input into staff performance reviews.
- Prepared and assembled charts, graphs, and appropriate background data for the Chairperson's use in presenting weekly briefings to the Secretary of Agriculture.

SECRETARY (Steno) (GS-8)   8/83 - 2/89
Office of the Deputy Administrator, Veterinary Services   40 hours/week
Johnny Depp, Supervisor (408) 432-9874   Salary: $25,000/year

Executive Secretary to the Deputy Administrator, Veterinary Services, with responsibility for assistance to the Deputy Administrator as well as office manager. Primary responsibilities involved managing all administrative operations of the office and serving as the chief liaison for the Deputy Administrator.

Responsibilities:
- Directed the preparation of correspondence, ensured quality control, coordinated all assignments, and ensured that all deadlines were met.
- Arranged staff meetings and conferences; obtained details of agenda and briefed the Deputy Administrator in preparation for the meetings.
- Attended and prepared minutes of staff meetings.
- Developed background information and coordinated preparation of speeches to be presented by the Deputy Administrator.
- Assessed and determined training needs of clerical staff.
- Researched and recommended secretarial training programs in support of office administration.

SECRETARY (Steno), GS-6   6/78 - 8/83
Cattle Diseases Staff, Veterinary Services   40 hours/week
Supervisor: Billy Ray Cyrus (408) 432-3432   Salary: $20,000/year

Senior secretary with responsibility for assistance to the Senior Staff Veterinarian as well as coordinating all administrative and secretarial services required by the Cattle Diseases Staff.

Responsibilities:
- Reviewed and determined the disposition of all office correspondence; determined priorities; ensured quality control.
- Directed the preparation of correspondence with a staff of five. Coordinated all assignments and followed up to completion on ongoing projects.
- Prepared responses to inquiries of a nontechnical nature.
- Reviewed outgoing correspondence and ensured accuracy of subject material, format, grammar; when required, edited and rewrote for clarity and organization.
- Trained and directed staff in the use of a new word processing system.   *continued . . .*

Secretary (Steno), GS-318-10, seeking Editor or Program Assistant

PATRICIA J. WINCHILD, 226-56-0951   PAGE 4

DEPARTMENT OF LABOR, Washington, DC   6/62 - 10/70
Manpower Administration

This office was responsible for developing, recommending, and issuing policies and standards relating to national manpower training programs. Served as Secretary to the Director of Job Corps (3/69-10/70), who directed the operational and financial aspects of the Job Corps programs operating throughout the United States. The Job Corps program is now part of the USDA Forest Service. At the time I worked for Job Corps, the functions were being transferred to the Department of Labor from the Office of Economic Opportunity.

Responsibilities:
- Managed and coordinated office activities during the difficult transition period; provided nonstop administrative and secretarial support to the Job Corps Director and State affiliates.
- Served as Director's key assistant for information, correspondence, and verbal communication with key government officials, Members of Congress, and White House officials.
- Provided information and served as liaison with State Governors, State education directors, and Government representatives concerning Job Corps programs and objectives.
- Developed new systems and procedures for handling Job Corps programs and trained all secretaries in Department of Labor systems and procedures.

EDUCATION:
Graduated Cabot Cove High School, Cabot Cove, Connecticut, 1962

TRAINING AND DEVELOPMENT:
Cabot Cove Community College: Supervisory Development I, Introduction to Business, Introduction to Data Processing, Basic Programming Language
USDA Graduate School: Decisionmaking for Secretaries, Letter Writing Workshop, GOP Style Manual and English Review, WordPerfect 6.1
USDA Personnel: Career Enhancement Program
APHIS Training Unit: Conflict Resolution

AWARDS:
Cash Awards, 1984 – 1995
Quality Step Increase – 1978
Numerous letters of commendation for outstanding service for the Job Corp, DOL

ACCOMPLISHMENTS/SKILLS:
- Performed job responsibilities in an outstanding manner during a time of reorganization and personnel shortages.
- Highly effective working under pressure
- High standards for writing and correspondence production; detail oriented
- Politically sensitive
- Ability to adjust to changing environment

Federal Government to Private Industry

Supervisory Auditor seeking high-energy and technically challenging private industry position.

WAYNE L. BOSETTI, JR.

320 South 61st Avenue
Clearwater, Florida 32506
(850) 444-4444 (h), (850) 444-4444 (w)
Email bosetti@mindspring.com

OBJECTIVE

Seeking to transition from government employment to a high-energy and technically challenging private industry employment experience in the area of financial, program or management analysis, auditing, acquisition, budgeting, or consulting.

PROFILE

- Diverse professional background in Audit, Government Contracts Analysis/Award/ Administration, Weapon Systems Financial and Program Analysis, Foreign Military Sales, Saudi Arabian Government Consulting, and Information Systems Management
- Recommended for Government Senior Executive Service Developmental Program
- Advanced computer skills with many software applications and personal computer hardware
- Possess strong desire and ability to identify, analyze, and solve problems
- Loyal, ethical, hard-working, and self-motivated professional

PROFESSIONAL EXPERIENCE AND ACCOMPLISHMENTS

Director of Production, Supervisory Auditor   *1997 - Present*
Department of the Navy, Naval Audit Service, Pensacola Office, 850-452-2611   *1986 - 1993*

Returned to this job after 4 year overseas assignment. Responsible for planning, coordinating, and managing the execution of difficult and complex audits of multi-billion dollar naval aircraft programs in accordance with generally accepted government auditing standards. ***Presented briefings of audit reports and program analysis issues to the Under Secretary of the Navy, the Assistant Secretary of the Navy for Research Development and Acquisition, the Vice Chief of Naval Operations, and the Comptroller of the Navy.*** Supervised audit team of 4 professional auditors. Utilized statistical analysis techniques to validate budgetary cost estimates. Designed and developed computer models to simulate the flow of aircraft through training and operational squadrons for projecting aircraft usage and maintenance requirements. Recommended Navy-wide policy changes and program revisions resulting in cost avoidance and savings in excess of $1 billion. Completed a research paper for the ASN (RDA) on the affordability, technical deficiencies, and Navy requirements for an advanced jet flight training aircraft.

Various Overseas Positions   *1993 – 1997*
Department of the Army, Saudi Arabian National Guard Modernization
Program (OPM-SANG), Riyadh, Saudi Arabia, 011-966-1-498-2480

Director, Information Systems and Telecommunications. Served as the Director of Information and Telecommunication mission areas throughout OPM-SANG. Exercised full responsibility for IS program management and directed 17 subordinate personnel performing technical and administrative functions. Developed and implemented program objectives, policies, plans, and projects. Defined and controlled information system configurations to include system status accounting, security, database management, system operability, and system maintainability

Supervisory Auditor seeking high-energy and technically challenging private industry position.

WAYNE L. BOSETTI, JR.   **Page 2**

and reliability. Developed in-house and external training plans. Performed cost analysis on information system requirements and developed alternative approaches for comparative analysis. Provided consulting services and advice to the leadership of the Saudi Arabian National Guard concerning plans for local area networking of their Directorate.

Light Armored Vehicle Program Analyst. Performed a complete and detailed cost analysis of an $800 million developmental LAV weapon system *fully relied upon by the U.S. Vice President and U.S. Army to support diplomatic negotiations with the Crown Prince of Saudi Arabia.* Executed a wide range of programmatic and analytical duties pertaining to the Saudi Arabian National Guard Modernization Program Foreign Military Sales Case. Responsibilities focused on analysis, evaluation and reporting of the $3.6 billion FMS sub-case for the procurement of 1,000+ Light Armored Vehicles (LAV), ancillary equipment, maintenance and training facilities and related support services. Measured resource estimates and utilization, intra-program and inter-program balances, potential problem areas, trends, and merit and deficiency situations. Excelled in utilization of statistics and advanced Microsoft Excel spreadsheet and database functions in analysis. Recommended program fiscal adjustments in response to program accelerations/delays, program changes, and cash availability.

Contract Cost & Price Analyst. Responsible for cost and price analysis of a $300 million dollar training contract in support of the Saudi Arabian National Guard Modernization Program. Assisted contracting officers in the evaluation, negotiation, award and modification of various types of contracts including Cost Plus Award Fee, Cost Plus Fixed Fee, and Firm Fixed Price. Designed and developed computer models to estimate contract costs based on correlation with past cost performance, contractor effectiveness, and anticipated changes in the contractor's labor mix of nationalities and productivity levels. Employed advanced analysis techniques such as regression analysis and cost probabilities. Consulted with contractors regarding establishing and maintaining reliable financial and management control systems. Advised the Saudi Arabian National Guard financial leadership in understanding cost analysis techniques.

EDUCATION AND TRAINING

Bachelor of Science, Accounting, Mississippi State University, December 1987
Honor Graduate, Defense Acquisition Institute Courses, 1994-1996
Numerous Specialized Audit, Finance, and Acquisition Courses, (400 Hours)

VOLUNTEER EXPERIENCE

Community Leader. Subsequent to a terrorist bomb attack on our office building in Riyadh, Saudi Arabia, November 13, 1995, recognized as the community leader for the organization of family support efforts, casualty visitation, donations, and counseling services.

Red Cross Volunteer. CPR Instructor, Water Safety Instructor, Blood Donor

AWARDS

Superior Civil Service Award. July, 1997. "Not many times in the history of OPM-SANG has one person performed so well in so many varied and important positions."

Letters of Appreciation, Commander, Saudi National Guard. 1995
Employee Special Act Awards. 1996, 1989
Sustained Superior Performance Awards. 10 of last 11 years
"Employee in the Spotlight," Naval Audit Service. 1989

Private Industry to Federal Government

The first resume here includes a cover letter and KSA set.

Food Manufacturer Marketer seeking Marketer, GS-9 for U.S. Postal Service

CANDACE A. GREENIER

4456 Charles Street
Baltimore, MD 21202
(410) 744-2334

August 1, 1998

U.S. Postal Service
Corporate Personnel Management
475 L'Enfant Plaza, SW, Room 1813
Washington, DC 20260-4261
Attn: VA# 97-48

To whom it may concern:

I have enclosed my Federal Resume and Knowledge, Skills and Abilities statement for consideration of the **MARKETING SPECIALIST** position with the U.S. Postal Service.

With my 18 years experience in marketing and account management for McCormick, I believe that I have the knowledge, expertise and corporate background to develop successful marketing, customer relations and product development programs for the U.S. Postal Service.

I accepted an early "retirement" from McCormick, and am available now for an interview or employment with the Postal Service. Thank you for your consideration. I look forward to your response.

Sincerely,

Candace A. Greenier

Food Manufacturer Marketer seeking Marketer, GS-9 for U.S. Postal Service

CANDACE A. GREENIER

4456 Charles Street
Baltimore, MD 21202
(410) 744-2334

Social Security No.:	215-88-8798
Citizenship:	U.S. Citizen
Veteran's Status:	N/A
Federal Civilian Status:	N/A

OBJECTIVE: Marketing Specialist # 97-46
U. S. Postal Service

PROFILE:

Experienced Account Manager and Marketer with 18 years experience with McCormick Inc. Positions included: Sales Representative, Account Manager, Retail Sales Specialist and Training and Recruitment Specialist.

EXPERTISE:

- Managing national accounts with outstanding success
- Meeting customer needs and acting as highly-effective sales consultant
- Analyzing historical, competitive, product and program sales
- Packaging, pricing and positioning successful product-mix
- Designing cooperative advertising and promotions
- Devising new ways of doing business and selling products
- Implementing new programs
- Training motivated sales representatives

CAREER HISTORY:

McCORMICK INC.
25 Spice Way, Baltimore, MD 21221
1979 to 1997

TRAINING & RECRUITMENT SPECIALIST (1/97 to 4/97)
Full-time: 40+ hours/week
Base Salary: $50,000; Bonus: $10,000
Supervisor: Dave Oregano (215) 555-1212; contact may be made.

Territory: Southern half of the Northeast Region of McCormick Inc.

- Recruited, interviewed and hired applicants for customer service and retail sales positions for 5 sales branches in MD, Northern VA and Washington, D.C.
- Developed and presented full- and half-day orientation programs for newly hired employees.
- Trained, supervised and evaluated sales force, enabling them to improve skills and meet organizational goals.
- Conducted on-going training sessions on company policies and programs.

Food Manufacturer Marketer seeking Marketer, GS-9 for U.S. Postal Service

CANDACE A. GREENIER, 215-88-8798   Page Two

MERCHANDISING SUPERVISOR (10/93 to 12/96)
Full-time: 40+ hours/week
Salary: $45,000; Bonus: $8,000
Supervisor: Basil St. John (410) 788-2780

Territory: Baltimore, MD, Williamsport, MD, Salisbury, MD and Landover, MD Sales Teams for McCormick Inc.

- Maintained flexible staffing requirements for four sales teams by scouting, hiring, training, administering, and scheduling full- and part-time merchandisers.
- Coached, trained and conducted performance appraisals for all direct reports.
- Supervised 225 employees.

RETAIL SALES SPECIALIST (6/93 to 10/93)
Full-time: 40+ hours/week
Salary: $42,500; Bonus: $8,000
Supervisor: Mike Curry (410) 788-2780

- Served as Retail Sales Specialist for the Washington DC Division of McCormick Inc..
- Obtained, organized, analyzed and communicated fact based data, brand/unit mix, merchandising programs, retail trends and competitive activity to assist in meeting sales objectives and field forecasting.
- Assisted in developing strategy sales meetings including program updates, account-specific programs, assigned objectives and retail analysis.

ACCOUNT MANAGER (10/86 to 6/93)
Full-time: 40+ hours/week
Salary: $40,000; Bonus: $12,000
Supervisor: Greg Allspice; (410) 788-7387

- Served as Account Manager for the Mid-Atlantic Division for McCormick Inc. Customers consisted of the Mid-Atlantic Division of A&P/Superfresh, B. Green Wholesalers, ACME Markets, Valu Foods Markets, Klein's Superthrift, Superpride Markets and Baines and E&S Stop, Shop and Save Markets.
- Met or exceeded sales objectives in all assigned accounts totaling $8 million in annual sales.
- Developed annual business plans through analysis of economic and competitive information.
- Created account specific sales proposals and marketing strategies.
- Managed overall account trade budget, including customer deductions and provided recommendations for expenditures to gain incremental volume and profit.

Special Projects:
- Among first to test and present Value Added Selling Techniques (VAST), a computer software based program to compile sales data and to customize sales presentations.
- Among first to test and use Marketing Development Project (MDP) a computer mainframe based program used to analyze market/scan data and project sales increases.

Food Manufacturer Marketer seeking Marketer, GS-9 for U.S. Postal Service

CANDACE A. GREENIER, 215-88-8798   Page Three

SALES REPRESENTATIVE (2/79 to 10/86)
Full-time: 40+ hours/week
Salary: $8,000 to $30,000 (includes Commission)
Supervisor: Janet Peppermill; (410) 788-2800

Territory: Baltimore Sales Branch

- Achieved total business objectives within assigned territories by using effective selling techniques and proper merchandising.
- Maintained sales, shelf space and display activity across all classes of trade.
- Promoted company/retail goodwill through personal contact with store managers.

Accomplishment:
- Increased Baltimore inner-city territory sales by 10% and was promoted to higher volume territory in Harford County, MD.

EDUCATION

BS., Psychology, TOWSON STATE UNIVERSITY, Baltimore, MD, 1978

Graduate courses in Marketing Management, TOWSON STATE UNIVERSITY, Baltimore, MD

Continuing Education:
- Computer skills in Microsoft Office including Word for Windows, Powerpoint, Excel and Microsoft Mail.
- Spanish as second language - intermediate level

SPECIAL TRAINING

Accountability Team Selling (December 1987)
Accountability Seminar/Sales Negotiations (October 1987)
Accountability Seminar/Strategic Planning (October 1987)
Effective Oral Presentations (November 1988)
Effective Business Writing (September 1991)
Licensed Maryland Real Estate Sales Person (June 1990)
Dale Carnegie Course (October/November 1995)
Dale Carnegie Graduate Assistant (November 1996/February 1997)

OTHER RELEVANT EXPERIENCE

Directed special events for social organizations
  -Fundraising committee of Kennedy Center for the Performing Arts, Washington, DC, 1996
  -Chaired adult education facet of Streetscape Festival, Annapolis, MD 1991
Baltimore Symphony Orchestra Community Outreach committee, 1990-1991
Youth Enrichment Program Tutorial program, Columbia, MD 1990-1991
National Aquarium exhibit guide, Baltimore, MD 1981-1983

Food Manufacturer Marketer seeking Marketer, GS-9 for U.S. Postal Service

CANDACE A. GREENIER
215-88-8798

U.S. Postal Service
Marketing Specialist # 97-46

KNOWLEDGE SKILLS AND ABILITIES

KNOWLEDGE OF:

Marketing Principles and Procedures

Innovative marketer for 18 years experience with McCormick Inc. Utilize hands-on knowledge of marketing, account management and business development to improve sales and marketing of McCormick products. Expert in both financial and sales analysis, as well as conceptual and creative aspects of marketing.

Skilled in devising new marketing programs and strategies; introducing new products; establishing sales goals and volumes; analyzing data for pricing and purchasing decision-making; negotiating merchandising and promotional incentives and programs; and providing consultative services to customers.

Develop revenue, volume and net contribution goals for products and services. Devise long (annual) and short-term (monthly) sales goals based on past performance, company goals. Outline ways to assist accounts in achieving profit, volume and cost effective sales goals. Review appropriate sources to identify appropriate actions for sales teams to take in order to achieve sales goals.

Serve as account marketing and sales consultant to introduce new products and enhance existing business.

Product Development and Management

NEW PRODUCT INTRODUCTIONS
Introduced many new products negotiating effective display and merchandising strategies for new product introductions. Examples have been Almost Home cookies and Snack-Wells products. Created excitement about new products, special promotions and a partnership with retailers in new product introductions.

Results:
- Effectively utilized corporate monies to fund special programs, effect pricing, obtain advertising displays.
- Developed competing programs based on competitive new products.
- Utilized allowances from invoices based on volume for rebates.
- Invested rebates into special promotions.

Food Manufacturer Marketer seeking Marketer, GS-9 for U.S. Postal Service

ABILITY TO:

Plan, develop and implement marketing programs and strategies

CREATED AN INNER CITY PROGRAM

Created market sensitive products, packages and prices to meet the needs of inner-city retail customers. Conceptualized and implemented the INNER CITY PROGRAM emphasizing the increased volume of product inventory and lower price for the first of the month. For instance, recommended to McCormick Buyers the packaging of a .9 oz. jar, instead of the 2.37 oz.

Results:
- Program kept the price down and sales up.
- Created a full calendar of events, products and prices to meet inner-city special purchasing needs.
- This became a national program utilized in other major cities throughout the U.S.

INNOVATIVE PUBLIC RELATIONS WITH RADIO AND TELEVISION ADVERTISING

Cooperated with Shop and Save to create a radio and local promotion – Stone Soul Picnic – the first of its kind in Baltimore, Maryland.

Results:
- The promotion has been held each year since and has given heightened visibility to McCormick and product loyalty.
- Increased display activity and cooperative advertising through radio station.
- Increased sales through promotion – 12 now.

PLAN, DEVELOP AND IMPLEMENT MARKETING PROGRAMS AND STRATEGIES

Participated in alternative cross-trade programs such as "For Sisters Only," "Stone Soul Picnic," and "Memorial Day/Bay Bridge Celebration" to leverage incremental business.

Develop revenue, volume and net contribution goals for products and services

CREATED A NEW MINI SPREADSHEET PROGRAM – A SYSTEM FOR SALES AND PRICING STRATEGIES

As an account manager, utilizing the pricing strategy from corporate McCormick, created new mini spreadsheet programs listing the sale of products within a certain time-frame, including:
Proposed price
Potential gross margin based on price
Historical sales information – one year ago
Differential in sales
Customer preferences

Results:
- Account decision-makers could see sales history and profitability quickly and make excellent purchasing and merchandising decisions for their stores.

Food Manufacturer Marketer seeking Marketer, GS-9 for U.S. Postal Service

---

Develop, test and coordinate the implementation of new products and services

CREATED A NEW BREATH OF LINE PROGRAM FOR McCORMICK

In 1992 as the National Account Team Member for A&P, introduced a product combination sales strategy with a Unit Mix price of $1.99. Selected products that added up to $1.99 retail and developed a rotating product-line with a consistent price.

Results:

- Purchasing and merchandising for retailers was easier because of the stable pricing system.
- Sales in my territory were higher because of the easy of product selection and ordering.
- Contributed to the corporate marketing plan with the Breath of Line program.
- The new program was introduced by McCormick's Marketing Director as an innovative new program to improve sales
- Corporation utilized the concept to establish an entire line of products and pricing strategy.

Collect, organize and analyze information used in developing pricing recommendations for products and services

CREATED A SALES AND PRICING ANALYSIS SHEET FOR RETAIL ACCOUNT CUSTOMERS

To help customers make buying decisions based on historic sales, devised a historical sales spreadsheet with products, pricing, gross margin for an entire year. The retailers were able to purchase a product mix with a combination of high and low profit items which increased their overall profit margin and took away some of the guesswork that accompanies retail merchandising and selling.

Results:

- Customers appreciated the new service and increased their overall profit by purchasing a stronger product mix.

Develop requirements for marketing information and for service analyses

THE INNER CITY PROGRAM RESULTED IN SATISFIED ACCOUNTS AND CUSTOMERS

- Sales figures and reports from inner city sales program resulted in increased sales and customer satisfaction. The retailers increased their sales volume by understanding the buying practices of their customers and responding to their needs.

NEW PRODUCT INTRODUCTIONS AND SALES TEAM SUPPORT

New products and programs required marketing information to be devised and produced for sales representatives. As a Merchandising Supervisor, ensured that four sales teams utilized available marketing information, advertising programs and sales analysis information to ensure their customers were purchasing the correct mix and volume of products.

Property Manager seeking Realty Specialist with GSA, GS-9

JESSICA L. HEIL

2122 Alberta Street • Greensboro, NC 90847 • (310) 456-0987

U.S. Citizen

SS#: 214-80-9990

Federal Status: Secretary, GS-4, 1968-69

Veterans Preference: N/A

Department of Transportation, FAA

PROFILE

Fourteen years experience as resident property manager of a luxury condominium in northwest Washington, D.C. Skilled in tenant relations, administration, and supervision of staff. Acted as construction liaison for a $10 million rehabilitation project that involved total post-tension reconstruction. Oversight of many capital improvement projects including corridor decoration, replacement of HVAC equipment and two roofs. Successfully managed restoration project after a $5 million fire in 1983.

Ten years experience in commercial real estate property administration, leasing administration and tenant liaison for Charles E. Smith Companies for office building and retail portfolio. Experienced with GSA leasing administration.

Experienced administrator/office manager with diversified background in supervising staff, contracting, accounting, budgeting and purchasing to manage building operations.

PROFESSIONAL EXPERIENCE

THE HAY-ADAMS

6/80- 11/94

4200 Massachusetts Avenue, NW

50 hours/week

Washington, DC 20016

Salary: $27,500/year

Supervisor: Jan McPherson (202) 872-9712

Supervisor may be contacted

Building Manager

Responsible for the on-site management of a luxury condominium with 126 units in Northwest Washington. Responsible for the supervision of a staff of 20, acting as contract manager for renovation and service contracts, and ensuring services and security to persons and property.

PERSONNEL SUPERVISION:
- Received, reviewed and delegated job orders to mechanical engineering (unit maintenance and central plant), property, service and landscape personnel. Reviewed job performance for quality workmanship and timeliness.
- Coordinated construction with owners; resolved problems surrounding construction noise, dust and traffic flow.
- Delegated assignments and motivated employees to perform job duties responsibly, efficiently in a spirit of teamwork. Increased customer service and employee morale resulting in low turnover of employees.

MANAGEMENT REPORTING:
- Attended and provided reports for monthly board of director meetings.
- Implemented new facility programs, policies and procedures.
- Made recommendations for improvements in services, control of cost and efficiency to property owners.

Property Manager seeking Realty Specialist with GSA, GS-9

FACILITIES MANAGEMENT:
- Managed the care and maintenance of entire building and landscaped gardens.
- Monitored inventory control of maintenance, janitorial and office supplies.
- Supervised mechanical engineering staff maintaining physical plant and HVAC.

ACCOUNTING & OPERATIONS:
- Managed an operating budget of $1.4 million.
- Maintained accounts payable, accounts receivable, prepared payroll information and prepared workpapers for accounting and taxes.

CUSTOMER SERVICES:
- Communicated with owners concerning all types of needs and problems; provided assistance to resolve resident problems.
- Negotiated and resolved problems surrounding construction projects.

CONTRACT MANAGEMENT:
- Acted as owner's representative for $10 million property renovation project over a term of 3 years involving a major structural project.
- Successfully restored facility after a $5 million fire in 1983.
- Reviewed contract performance, quality and authorized payments to contractors.
- Liaison between contractor, subcontractors, owners and board of directors.
- Negotiated changes in services, security and noise control during construction.

DAVID E. KELLY, INC.
Commercial Management Division
1101 17th Street, NW, Washington, DC 20036
Supervisor: Tom Davidson (202) 737-8637

1970 - 1980
40 hours/week
Starting salary: $24,500
Ending salary: $25,000

Executive Assistant, Executive Vice President, Commercial Management Division
- Hired, trained, and supervised all administrative personnel. Record-keeping responsibilities for staff included $6,000,000 per month in rental income.
- Involved in Division operations consisting of 40 office buildings and 8,500,000 square feet of shopping centers, hotels and recreation facilities.
- Served as contractor's representative in creating specifications and analyzing bids for annual contracts.
- Acted as Division representative for all inter-departmental coordination of day-to-day activities and special projects.
- Liaison between General Counsel, Computer Services, Leasing, Tenant Alterations and Account Payable/Receivable.
- Acted as Office Manager and Purchasing Agent for Division.
- Provided leasing and tenant support GSA-leased office space, who was a major tenant in several of the multi-use and commercial properties.
- Compiled GSA lease agreements and interacted with leasing specialists and tenants.

EDUCATION
Northern Virginia Community College, Arlington, VA 22304	1968 - 1971
George Washington University, Washington, DC 20006	1971 - 1978
Institute of Real Estate Management, Completed IREM 101, 201, 301	1984
John Kennedy High School, Arlington, VA 22304	Graduated 1970

Hold Active D.C. Real Estate License

Engineer, Scientist seeking Environmental Protection Specialist, GS-13

Bonita E. Dick, Ph.D.

1725 K Street, NW • Denver, CO 80526
(310) 877-9988

Social Security Number: 116-42-6006	Citizenship: United States
Highest Previous Federal Grade: GS-9; No reinstatement eligibility	Veteran's Preference: None

Position Desired: Environmental Protection Specialist, (AT0312)

Profile:

Experienced geochemical engineer and financial analyst with extensive environmental research skills. Broad experience includes seismic, geochemical, and business assessments of mineral development and agricultural properties, natural resource evaluations, oceanic and watershed research, and missile research abatement. Technological consulting includes innovative special effects for futuristic movies. Advanced law student seeking opportunities to apply scientific and business experiences in a position involving natural resource management responsibilities.

Employment History:

DICK CONSULTING	Denver, Colorado
President	1983 – 1996
Supervisor: None	Salary: $40,000 – 120,000

Developed and led firm conducting scientific, operational and economic assessments of natural resource and mineral sites. Performed financial assessment and strategic engineering evaluations of investment options. Reviewed assets and performance of over-the-counter oil and gas firms in the western U.S. and provided guidance to investors and firms. Supervised work of ten mineral engineers, financial analysts, and operations research professionals to produce analytical reports of resource capacities, extraction strategies, and operational factors. Comprehensive site evaluations included seismic assessments, optimization studies, strategic and operational plans incorporating environmental mitigation strategies. Wrote and presented reports providing strategic assessments, problem resolutions, and advice regarding management approaches to maximize performance. Developed and sustained corporate growth through twelve-year period.

- ▸ *Real estate investment and development.* Assessed wide array of oil and gas ventures, and managed acquisition, renovation, leasing, and sale of investment properties. Assisted in acquisition of properties for environmental management and multi-purpose developments.
- ▸ *Cinema support.* Researched scientific and technical factors to support development of special effects and to enhance plots of major motion pictures.

DRT ENVIRONMENTAL MANAGEMENT, INC.	Golden, Colorado
Lead Environmental Economist/Scientist	1994
Supervisor: Mary Poppins; (805) 999-8324	Salary: $60 per hour

Wrote draft Environmental Impact Statement for a major Southeast Asian project. Applied environmental site remediation requirements established by regulations under the Comprehensive Environmental Response, Compensation, and Liability Act (CERCLA, or Superfund) and the Resource Conservation and Recovery Act (RCRA). Incorporated factors derived from parallel state regulations to provide alternative strategies assessing minimum costs within strict compliance terms.

- ▸ Identified list of preferred list of industries to support economic development in Indonesia and provided research to assist securing of capital to finance major project development.
- ▸ Published financial analysis of innovative cleanup technologies for national conference.

Engineer, Scientist seeking Environmental Protection Specialist, GS-13

Bonita E. Dick, Ph.D.   **116-42-6006**   **2.**

EMPLOYMENT HISTORY
(Continued)

GLOBAL RESEARCH SYSTEMS   San Diego, California
Financial Analyst and Environmental Engineer   1981 – 1983
Supervisor: Karl Sagan; (302) 877-9877   Salary: $25,000 – 35,000

Provided scientific and economic consulting services for major industries. Analyzed financial potential and environmental effects of agricultural business opportunities in developing nations. Reviewed soil chemistry and evaluated farm sites of saline marshes of Mexico, conducted political risk assessments and developed economic strategies and provided reports to major U.S. corporations.

> ▸ *Agricultural research and innovation.* Analyzed opportunities for growing halphytes in salt marshes of Mexico as an exploratory venture funded by Coca-Cola. Conducted environmental and aquacultural evaluations of shrimp farming in closed ecosettings to develop additional food resources. Reports resulted in start-up investment and introduction of new cash crop in Mexico. Subsequently supported successful transition of shrimping farm to Hawaii.

BEECHWOOD CORPORATION   Redwood City, California
Environmental System Engineer   1978 – 1981
Supervisor: Michele McCarthy; (704) 332-8977   Salary: $26,000 – $32,000

Conducted chemical and engineering research assessing environmental effects of heavy missile testing at a major Air Force installation. Analyzed environmental reports, developed, and recommended mitigation strategies to ensure compliance with emergent health and safety standards. Prepared technical reports as preparation and support documentation for Environmental Impact Statements. Wrote trade studies assessing multiple basing concepts for complex missile technologies.

UNITED STATES GEOLOGICAL SURVEY   Denver, Colorado
Geochemist – Department of Uranium and Thorium   1977 – 1978
Supervisor: Andrew Anderson; phone unknown   Salary: $12,000 – 15,000

Developed innovative geochemical approaches using sulfides in trace elements to identify sources of roll-front uranium deposits. Based on research for master's and doctoral degrees, refined technologies for the extraction of trace minerals in mining operations. Analyzed dissolution of rock matrices to ascertain purification of resulting pyrite concentrates to confirm information yielded from trace mineral assessments.

EDUCATION

University of Denver School of Law
Denver, Colorado 80526   Juris Doctor   Expected, 1999

California School of Mines   Ph.D. in Mineral Economics   1982
Mineral City, CA 90099   Major: Operations Research   Minor: Geochemical Engineering

California School of Mines   Master of Science   1982
Mineral City, CA 90099   Geochemistry

University of Colorado   Bachelor of Science   1976
Ft. Collins, CO 80526   Chemistry

Engineer, Scientist seeking Environmental Protection Specialist, GS-13

Bonita E. Dick, Ph.D.	**116-42-6006**	**3.**

EDUCATION
(Continued)

Loyola University	Graduate Courses	1989
San Diego, CA 90292	Psychology – 16 credits	
University of Colorado	Graduate Courses	1981
Ft. Collins, CO 80526	Economics – 9 credits	

High School: *Culver City Senior High*, Culver City, CA 90872   1971

RECENT HONORS

University of Denver School of Law   1996 – 1998
- Ranked First in Law Class
- American Jurisprudence Bancroft-Whitney Award – Highest GPA in Criminal Law
- *Dean's Scholarship* Recipient – 1997
- Business Editor, *UD Law Review* (Volume 28)
- Assistant Editor, *UD Law Review* (Volume 28)
- Delta Theta Phi – Law School Honor Society Member
- Member, UD School of Law Student Advisory Commission, 1995 – 1997

SELECTED PUBLICATIONS

Financial Analysis of Innovative Site Clean-up Technologies, Twenty-First Annual National Energy and Environmental Quality Division Conference, *United States Quality Society*, 1994.

Forecast of Performance for Newly Issued Oil and Gas Stocks in the Los Angeles Over-the-Counter Market, Doctoral Dissertation, *California School of Mines*, 1982.

Analysis of the Abundance of Trace Elements in Iron Disulfides in the Buena Visa Roll-Front Uranium Deposit, Webb County, Tennessee, Master's Thesis, *California School of Mines*, 1976.

COMPUTER SKILLS
Word Processing: WordPerfect and Microsoft Word
Data Management: Wide array of Statistical Software and spreadsheets
Familiar with Basic and Fortran programming languages

LANGUAGE SKILLS
Spanish – Read, write, and speak proficiently   French – Read, write, and speak passably

PROFESSIONAL AFFILIATIONS
American Association for the Advancement of Science
American Chemical Society – Division of Geochemistry
American Bar Association – Science and Environmental Law Division
Trial Lawyers Association of America
Institute of Management Sciences

LICENSES
Real Estate License – State of Colorado

Military Computer Specialist seeking Computer Specialist, GS-9/11

Kevin Lee James
27 Beechwood Avenue / Alexandria, VA 22409 / (703) 244-8902

Social Security Number: 255-55-1212	Veteran's Preference: 5 points
Citizenship: United States	Highest Federal Civilian Position: N/A

OBJECTIVE: Computer Specialist, GS-9/11
Department of Commerce at the Census Bureau.

SKILLS SUMMARY:

Over 14 years of Desktop Support, User Support, Help Desk and Computer Operations experience while serving in the United States Navy.

Extensive experience with PC hardware, software and operating systems both in stand alone and networked environments. Able to communicate effectively with technical peers and end users to resolve technical issues.

- Supervised, managed and trained personnel for Desktop/PC and LAN Support, Help Desk, and Computer Operations, time management and production scheduling.
- Responsible for over $7,000,000 of equipment and software as well as liaison with Operations and Maintenance Division personnel.
- Effective team-builder with strong leadership skills and proven track record at setting and achieving realistic goals for self and others. Maintained mission of command and division in perspective at all times.
- Proactive EEO leader meeting all command EEO objectives. Effectively motivated and trained junior personnel contributing to unit cohesiveness.
- Provided top-notch customer service at all commands achieving 98+% satisfaction rate at the Naval Computer and Telecommunications Area Master Station.

EMPLOYMENT HISTORY:
UNITED STATES NAVY
1/83 - 3/98

Naval Computer and Telecommunications Area Master Station   9/95 - 3/98
25 Commander Way, Virginia Beach, VA 22832
Petty Officer 2nd Class, Data Processing Technician
Supervisor: CDR Ryan O'Neal; (804) 233-8798; contact may be made

Automated Data Processing Technician   48 hours/week
Responsible for installation, upgrade, maintenance, and repair of PC's, peripherals and associated software. Supervised five personnel providing desktop and user support to 5,000 users for MS Word 6.0, WordPerfect 5.0/6.0, MS-DOS (to v6.22), Windows 95, Windows 3.1, Norton Utilities, McAfee, cc:Mail and PC Tools in a Novell NetWare 3.x LAN environment. As Help Desk Supervisor personally handled 20-50 trouble calls on a daily basis.

Provided Level I and II Help Desk support for communications and COTS issues to seven sites on a global basis including Puerto Rico, Alaska, Italy and U. S. Naval vessels afloat. Help Desk handled over 300 trouble calls daily and was in operation 24 hours a day, 7 days a week. Provided routine hardware and software maintenance and changes to PC's, LAN, and all software as necessary.

Prepared and presented training lectures to station personnel on hardware, COTS software and proprietary software such as GATEGUARD, PCMT, NOW and NOWNET.

Military Computer Specialist seeking Computer Specialist, GS-9/11

Kevin Lee James - page 2

VQ-2 Reconnaissance Squadron   10/93 - 9/95
Electronic Warfare Department - ADP Maintenance Division
Naval Air Station Madrid, Spain
Petty Officer 2nd Class, Data Processing Technician
Supervisor: LTC Karl Kreissler; 011-98-77890-98

Automated Data Processing Technician   48 hours/week

Provided desktop and user support to 250 users for MS Word 6.0, WordPerfect 5.0/5.1/6.0, Windows 3.1/3.11, MS DOS 5.0-6.22, Novell NetWare 3.1x, and PC Tools.

Installed, upgraded, repaired and maintained PC's, software, printers, scanners, projectors, and associated peripherals. Assisted in installation and maintenance of a 1 server, 250 node Novell NetWare 3.1x network. Server was used as a repository of files and e-mail using cc:Mail.

Prepared lectures and trained personnel in automated data processing (ADP) security as well as use of computer applications and utilities.

USS Orion (AS-18) – Submarine Tender   5/91 – 10/93
Supply Department – Automated Processing Division
La Mena, Manata, Spain
Petty Officer 2nd Class, Data Processing Technician
Supervisor: CDR Joseph Garcella; 011-77-88888-99

Shift Supervisor   56 hours/week

Supervised the operation and monitoring of the Honeywell DPS-6 System and the AN/UYK 65 Tape Drive Unit. Provided technical assistance and software support to end-users.

Responsible for the daily work activities of four personnel including data entry, production control and production scheduling. Developed technical documentation for functional descriptions, maintenance and operation of equipment.

Prepared training lectures for technical personnel and end user on proper operating procedures.

Naval Headquarters Europe   2/89 – 5/91
Naval Operations Support Atlantic Command, London, England
Petty Officer 2nd Class, Data Processing Technician
Supervisor: LTC Howard Hessler; 011-09-99999-88

Senior Computer Operator   48 hours/week

Responsible for the operation and monitoring of a Honeywell DPS8/70 with an AUTODIN interface and associated peripherals for the WWMCCS (World Wide Military Communications Command System).

Provided technical assistance to end users and taught proper operating procedures. Supervised shift personnel and also had role as media librarian.

National Security Agency   9/87 – 4/88
Central Security Service, Fort Meade, MD
Petty Officer 3rd Class, Data Processing Technician
Supervisor: John Sykes (Retired)

Network Controller   40 hours/week

Monitored and controlled local and worldwide packet switching networks for the worldwide Signal Intelligence Generator Network Technology (SIGNT) system. Documented all outages and occurrences affecting network operations and maintained system software databases.

Kevin Lee James - page 3

Network Controller (continued):

Performed fault isolation and initiated corrective measures such as alternate routing of communication trunk lines, reconfiguring network nodes or executing emergency backup and restoration procedures.

Scheduled and coordinated maintenance activities for both local and remote sites and provided technical and software assistance to end users and network support personnel.

National Security Agency   3/86 – 9/87
Central Security Service, Fort Meade, MD
Petty Officer 3rd Class, Data Processing Technician
Supervisor: LTC Eugene Donaldson; (301) 778-9887

Computer Operator   40 hours/week

Operated, monitored, and performed system backups and restorations on three systems primarily the UNISYS 1100/84 and six UNISYS 1100/70's using the UNISYS OS1100 operating system. The other systems were the CDC 7600 using the IDA System Software with CDC 819 Disk Units, CDC 7639 Disk Controllers, Braegen 7110 Automated Tape Library and the CDC Cyber 176 using proprietary software with CDC 885 Disk Units, Braegen 7110 Automated Tape Library.

USS Sierra (AD-18)   6/83 – 2/86
Supply Department – Automated Data Processing Division, Charleston, SC
Seaman (Undesignated)

Data Entry Clerk/Computer Operator   56 hours/week

Performed duties as data entry clerk and computer operator on the Honeywell DPS-6 System with the AN/UYK-65 Tape Drive Unit, Card Punch/Reader and Paper Tape Punch/Reader.

Provided technical assistance to end users and performed daily and weekly inventories of media library catalog.

COMPUTER SKILLS:

Hardware:

IBM PC's, Micro-computers, HP LaserJet IV and DeskJet printers, ALPS Dot Matrix printers, HP Scanners and other peripherals and components (Memory, Network Interface Cards, Hard Drives, Floppy Drives, etc.).
Honeywell DPS-6 System and AN/UYK-65 Tape Drive Unit; Honeywell DPS-8/70 with AUTODIN Interface and associated peripherals for WWMCCS (World Wide Military Communications Command System); Platform Network; OPSN (Overseas Packet Switching Network); TESTNET (Multi-purpose network primarily for testing); Pluribus IMP (Multi-processor, multi-bus non-redundant mini-computer), C-30 IMP (Single processor non-redundant mini-computer), and C-70 IMP; NASI and NASII (PDP 11/34 Systems); UNISYS 1100/84 and 1100/70; CDC Cyber 176, CDC 819 and 885 Disk Units, and CDC 7639 Disk Controllers; Braegen 7110 Automated Tape Library; and various models of Cray Mini-computer Systems.

Software:

Novell NetWare 3.1x; Windows 95, Windows NT 4.0, Windows 3.1/3.11, MS Word 6.0-8.0, WordPerfect 5.0-6.0, McAfee, Norton Utilities, PC Tools, cc:Mail, MS DOS 5.0-6.22, Gateguard (Software used for secure message traffic); PCMT (Personal Computer Messaging Terminal); and NOW and NOWNET (Navy Order Wire Network)

Military Computer Specialist seeking Computer Specialist, GS-9/11

TRAINING:

1998   Microsoft Certified Software Engineer (MCSE) Old Dominion University/ ICTS, Alexandria, VA 223*14*.

1994   Harvard Graphics Human Resources Office Naval Air Station, Rota, Spain.

1991   SNAP *1* (Shipboard Naval Automated Processing) ADP System Enlisted Operator/Supervisor Fleet Training Center Naval Base, Norfolk, VA.

1989   WWMCCS (World Wide Military Computer Communications Systems) Computer Operator 3300 Technical Training Wing Air Force Base Keesler, MS/London, England.

1986-1987   Introduction to Computer Systems Operation, Univac *1108* Systems, CDC *76*00 System Software National Cryptologic School In-house Education Program for the Department of Defense, Fort Meade, MD.

1986   Data Processing "A" School (Data Processing fundamentals, and extensive training in operating various computers in shore, and sea environments) Service School Command Naval Base, San Diego, CA.

1979-1981   Business Data Processing Machine Operations and Business Data Processing Programmer (RPG and COBOL) Lake County Area Vocational Center, *195*25 West Washington Street, Grayslake, IL *60*030.

EDUCATION:

1994   University of Maryland, University College: European Division, Rota, Spain
                      Micros: Hardware and Software
                      Micros: Desktop Publishing
                      Micros: Networks and Communications
                      Advance Operating Systems

HONORS AND AWARDS:

1996   Good Conduct Medal – Third Award (previously awarded *1987* and *1991*)

March *1994*   Letter of Commendation for the Successful Installation of the Fleet Air Reconnaissance VQ-2 Local Area Network

CLEARANCE:

                      Held Top Secret (TS/SCI) Clearance for over *1*0 years which was deactivated October *1997*. Last investigation was completed May *1995*.

Resumix Scannable Resume

Executive Secretary, GS-318-8/10 seeking Public Affairs or EEO position

MARGARET T. RILEY
333-33-3333
7888 Front Avenue
Battle Creek, MI 22645
Home: (888) 999-8989
Work: (888) 787-8989
e-mail: margaret.riley@casc.gov
Vacancy Announcement: A-058-97-DRD
Lowest position that I will accept: GS-7

SKILLS SUMMARY:

EEO/Affirmative Action and Discrimination Complaint Processing, Writing, Analytical Skills, Fact-finding, Case Management, Oral Communications, Negotiations, Stress Management, Community Liaison, Public Affairs, Corps of Engineers Early Resolution Program, EEO Program Evaluation, Reports, EEO Executive Orders, Public Laws and Civil Rights Act; AR 690-600, CEERP, Career Program-28.

Cataloguing Acquisition Systems, Office of Public Affairs Representative and Recorder, Special Emphasis Program Committee; Member, Office Managers Advisory Committee; Recorder, Special Emphasis Training Committee

Office Management, Organization, Efficient Systems, Files Management, Systems Design: Exceptional Performance Rating and Cash Award (1990)

Town Planning Commission Chair, Battle Creek, MI (1981-1985). Sensitive Rezoning Hearings, Presentations, Fact-finding, Negotiations, Mediations, Hearings, Reports, Leadership.

WORK EXPERIENCE:

7/91 to present; **Executive Secretary** (Steno), GS-0318-8/10, Catalogue Acquisition Systems Center, Office of Public Affairs, Washington, DC 20314-1000; Supervisor: Wm. Monroe (909) 898-8989. Promoted to GS-8/6 on 7/21/91.

> Executive Secretary - Administrative Assistant to Chief of Public Affairs
> Principal EEO staff advisor to the MSC commander and senior management.
>
> Provide management assistance, as well as secretarial and administrative support to the Chief of Public Affairs.
> Maintain Chief's calendar and projected absences calendar.
> Ensure distribution of the "Early Bird" to the General officers, selected SES personnel, and the Executive Office.
> Prepare folders of fact sheets, pamphlets and pertinent information as handouts to visiting foreign officers.
> Draft and prepare outgoing correspondence.

Executive Secretary, GS-318-8/10 seeking Public Affairs or EEO position

Receive telephone calls and messages from reporters, Congressional offices, Pentagon officials, division and district Public Affairs Officers (PAOs), and the general public. Make all travel arrangements for Chief.

Process travel orders, vouchers and other financial documents.

Maintain and distribute updated public affairs roster for updating in Worldwide Public Affairs Directory

Career Program Manager for Career Program-28

Special Emphasis Committee, Public Affairs Primary Member

Member, Office Manager Advisory Committee

Manage and give career advice to SES careerist, interns and applicants.

Act as community liaison; represent the MSC commander; plan and implement outreach programs with regional, state and government organizations, including EEO employment issues.

Ensure that EEO training is planned and conducted within the agency.

Provide leadership and counseling concerning management policies, practices/procedures and issues that affect minorities and women.

Ensure consistent achievement of office EEO objectives.

Plan and implement the MSC EEO/affirmative action and discrimination complaint processing programs.

Conduct program evaluation to ensure compliance with legal and regulatory requirements.

Process allegations of discrimination, especially where there is a conflict of interest.

Act as community liaison; represent the MSC commander; plan and implement outreach programs with regional, state and government organizations, including EEO employment issues.

Ensure that EEO training is planned and conducted within the agency.

Completed CEFMS Training Courses

FEW Conference

9/86 to 7/91 Secretary (Steno), GS-0318-07 (promoted 9/86), CASC, Directorate of Real Estate, Washington, DC 20314-1000; Supervisor: Mr. A.M. Thomas (202) 222-9090

Administrative Assistant to the Chief, Management and Disposal Division.

Liaison and support to two branches with 10 attorneys, 2 realty specialists and 3 secretaries.

Reviewed incoming and produced outgoing correspondence.

Independently composed correspondence.

Responded to inquires from Secretariat offices, Corps District and Division offices, Federal Agencies, Congressional offices, White House and the general public

Managed appointments and meetings.

Independently made schedule commitments based on knowledge of schedule and subject matter.

Received cash award for managing office organization; improving correspondence; production and handing systems; developing an effective suspense system; and reorganizing office files.

Received Exceptional Performance Rating and $1,800 Cash Award.

Executive Secretary, GS-318-8/10 seeking Public Affairs or EEO position

9/83 - 9/86, **Secretary** (Steno), GS-0318-06 (promoted 9/83), HQ, CASC, Directorate of Civil Works, Washington, DC 20314-1000; Supervisor: Mr. M. Matthews (202) 222-2222.

12/82 - 9/83, **Secretary** (Typing), GS-318-05, Small Business Administration Office of Congressional and Legislative Affairs, Washington, DC 20416; Supervisor: Dr. D. M. Smith (202) 666-6666.

11/77 - 12/82, Associate Broker, Banneker Realty, Inc., 140 S. Main Street, Kellogg, MI 22645; Supervisor: Mr. M. Banneker (808) 999-9999.
   Real estate sales and brokerage for the sale, purchase or leasing of homes, farms, land and commercial property.
   Appraised homes, land, commercial property and farms.
   Counseled clients on financing options and processes.
   Negotiated contracts and coordinated settlements.
   Researched property records through county records.
   Realtor's License, 1977
   Broker's License, 1982

EDUCATION / PROFESSIONAL TRAINING:

Realtor's Institute, Real Estate Broker, Real Estate, State of Michigan.

Writing, MARKS Recordkeeping System, Effective English, Conflict Management, Stress Management, Office Management.

"Meeting the Challenge of a Changing Environment," Corps of Engineers Operating Budget Users Group, New Orleans, LA, 16 hours, 1993.

"Interacting and Communicating with the Public," Ft. Worth, TX, 16 hours, 1993.

APPENDIX B

KSA and ECQ Examples

This appendix provides examples of KSAs and ECQs. For more details on KSAs, see Chapter 10. For details on ECQs, refer to Chapter 11.

KSA Examples

Natural Resources Biologist, GS-9

A Natural Resources Biologist with a a recent M.S. in Environmental Science & Policy is seeking a position with the National Oceanic & Atmospheric Administration as a Fisheries Management Specialist.

Knowledge of the U.S. Commercial and Recreational Fishing Industries and their practices

As a Natural Resources Biologist in the Fisheries Division, Resource Management Unit, I have four years experience implementing the commercial striped bass harvest monitoring system and analyzing landing data for Maryland's commercial striped bass fisheries.

I monitor the six separate fisheries that make up the State's commercial striped bass fishery business: 1) Pound Net, 2) Haul Sein, 3) Commercial Hook and Line, 4) Chesapeake Drift Gill Net, 5) Atlantic Trawl, and 6) Atlantic Gill Net.

I am responsible for monitoring licensed seafood dealers in the Chesapeake Bay Region, and over the past two years have worked diligently to build a good working knowledge of the U.S. commercial and recreational fishing industries and their practices.

Material Examiner and Identifier, WG-6

This Material Examiner and Identifier is applying for a Working Leader position. The examples demonstrate her ability to communicate effectively, clearly and with urgency.

Ability to communicate orally and in writing with all levels.

In February 1996, I was responsible for shipping a prototype model from NSWC, Bethesda, MD to NBSWC, Bayview, ID. The model was 60 feet long, 8 feet wide and weighed 80,00 pounds. It required special handling with assistance and cooperation from the State and Park Police and Maryland Department of Transportation. I requested a waiver from the State of Maryland because of travel times. I received assistance from the Park Police in closing the parkway in order to move this model through the front gate. If the shipment was delayed, for any reason, it would have cost the center $10,000 per day.

Due to the forthcoming closure of the NSWC, Annapolis, MD detachment, I arranged for the excess steel to be moved to NSWC Bethesda, MD for reutilization. This required coordination with the commercial carrier, Military Traffic Management Command (MTMC), crane company and internal technical codes. I organized meetings with all participants to determine the best means of loading, transporting and unloading material. I coordinated with on-site personnel to perform inventory, measure, weigh and schedule each piece of steel for transport. I gave clear verbal instructions from Annapolis to Bethesda on what was en route and where it should be off-loaded.

In my previous position as the Assistant Manager for one of Prince George's County's taxi cab firms, I managed scheduling for 100 employees and 110 vehicles with a 24-7 operation. I communicated effectively with both drivers and customers, ensuring that a timely and accurate delivery service was made.

Secretary (Office Automation), GS-7

This Secretary is a "cutting-edge" secretary with outstanding computer skills. With detailed explanation of her expertise with software, including applications and designs of new forms, she should be able to increase her grade level.

Applies knowledge of word processing and computer software programs, including desktop and web-based publishing.

In my present position, I use **Microsoft Word or WordPerfect word processing software** on a daily basis. In MS Word, I recently completed a proposal for restructuring our Branch. Using a pre-existing template, I developed a ten-page proposal using chapter breaks, several levels of headings and footnotes. In addition, I was dissatisfied with some of the pre-defined styles, so I modified an existing style to incorporate a larger font and small capitals.

I also have prepared tables, merge letters, and columns, and have even created new templates in order to simplify some of my tasks. One template that I created and use daily defines the appropriate margins for our office's letterhead, and has date, address and signature blocks. I frequently use this template in conjunction with merge letters. For an award dinner, I developed a merge form using the letterhead template to send letters to all interested parties. Since we had most of this information in the Microsoft Access database I designed, I merged the information directly from that database to the Word form. I used similar procedures to address the 300 invitations for the dinner in a flowing script font. This substantially reduced the amount of time necessary for preparing the invitations that had been previously addressed by hand.

I have used **Microsoft Publisher** extensively for desktop publishing. When I first arrived at my office, the organization was not reaching its constituents and employees in other locations well. Using Publisher, I developed a new weekly publication that summarizes and reports on a wide variety of issues. The publication is normally two pages, and includes graphics, word art, shading and text components. I have also redesigned the Branch's information brochure in Publisher, developing the two-color shell as well as rewriting the text. I purchased existing shells from Paper Direct, and used Publisher to layout the text accordingly. Finally, my most recent desktop publishing achievement was completely recreating the Branch's annual award dinner program and guest list. In prior years, the program was a 4-page gray-scale brochure sent to the printer. The guest list was prepared in-house, 8½"x 11" black text on colored paper with color cardstock covers. It was clearly an in-house creation. This year, I combined the two publications into one that I designed using Publisher. While keeping the publication black text, I found a cream cover with a gold foil inlay. Using Publisher, I included the pictures of the honored guests, the complete table listings, the evening program, and information about our Branch. The program was still 8½" x 11" but folded to make it smaller and easier to use. I was very pleased when our awardee was showing it off, and the entire project cost no more than the prior year.

Supervisory Personnel Specialist, GS-8

With ten years experience as a GS-8, this outstanding personnel specialist is seeking a well-deserved promotion to a GS-9.

Ability to establish and maintain an effective administrative program, including computerized database and processing security data.

After just six months as a Supervisory Personnel Assistant in the Personnel Pay Programs and Administration office, I was tasked with organizing and managing a Centralized File system for all 5,000 ATF employees. Each employee would have four personnel files, creating a 20,000-paper centralized file system. Delegating tasks to a young and inexperienced staff, Stay-in-School and Intern employees, I supervised the workflow and established an efficient physical management system. I also designed and implemented a file sign-out form which was streamlined and improved control of the file tracking system. **Results:** We cut lost files by 30% by implementing the improved file tracking system. I am currently supervising the conversion of this massive and complex paper system into an automated database which will be more accessible to personnel officials and managers.

Other supervisory assignments include classifying and establishing hard copy filing systems for sensitive ATF employee medical files. For example, I established and maintain ATF's first environmental base line testing of employees' files. These sensitive analyses and exposure documents are considered High (2) under the Privacy Act 1974 code, and I ensure their security.

I make sure that all processing and filing of security data complies with the guidelines of ATF Subject Classification and Filing Order ATF O1310.1. I ensure that the correct subject codes are used on all ATF correspondence and records consistent with the classification system laid down by the Office of Primary Interest (OPI) – i.e., Personnel (2000); Inspections, General (8000); Investigations, General (8600); Integrity and other Investigations (8010); Personnel Security Investigations (8820).

Budget Analyst, GS-12

This GS-12 Budget Analyst with 16 years federal experience is applying for a promotion to GS-13.

Knowledge of the Federal budget process, procedures and requirements.

I have been working in various financial management components within the Office of the Chief Counsel of the IRS for the past ten years. I am currently serving as GS-560-12 Budget Analyst in the Financial Management Formulation Section. As such, I help formulate the budget processes, procedures and requirements used to develop and manage the overall budget requirements of the Chief Counsel.

I have expert knowledge of relevant OMB circulars and directives, Treasury, IRS and Chief Counsel instructions, and the IRS Service Manual. I use these rules and directives on a daily basis to guide my work and to provide the most current information possible on specific issues to my co-workers and superiors.

An example of my knowledge of the Federal budget process is demonstrated by my contributions as a member of the IRS's Nationwide Reimbursable Task Force. We spoke with staff persons across the country to determine the most efficient method of managing this reimbursable service, and then made recommendations for a standardized national process. I took the results of this work back to my office and created the Reimbursable Program for the Office of the Chief Counsel, *from the ground floor up,* in 1995. This program has streamlined the obligations and commitment process, controlled costs, and provided upper management with a refined management planning tool.

Transportation Specialist, GS-11 (Procurement Specialist Statement)

A career Army NCO, this Sergeant was applying for a civilian Department of Defense position in Europe as a GS-11 Transportation Specialist.

Demonstrated working knowledge of procurement and contracting regulations; quality assurance evaluation procedures and applicable laws and regulations; quality assurance evaluation procedures and applicable laws and regulations; and the development of performance work statements and quality assurance evaluations plans.

During my three years in the Command Group of US Army South, I served as Procurement NCO responsible for all materiel requirements of the Command Group. I provided liaison with the Contracting and Budgeting Offices, and assisted the Secretary of the General Staff in budget recommendations and procedures.

When I first took on my responsibilities as the Command Group Procurement NCO, supply personnel were burdened with an eight-step local-purchase process involving 13 signatures, and a wait of two to four weeks for an emergency walk-through O2 priority purchase for the Commanding General. It was necessary to plan for such emergencies with a sixth sense well ahead of time and greasing the wheels of progress was required through the use of office politics and the ability to make friends with the right people at the right time.

I identified systemic problems with the Government's Visa card purchasing program and then worked with the Directorate of Contracting to correct those problems.

I took corrective steps including writing a simplified but complete purchase card standard operating procedure (SOP) manual that could be understood and utilized by purchasing agents in each section throughout the command. I assisted the Director of Contracting in preparing and validating a four hour training tape on the new streamlined procedures. I conducted training programs with the personnel of associated sections of the Command Group. And I gave the IMPAC program coordinator at the Contracting office feedback on the current command-wide training program.

Recognition: For my work with the IMPAC program and simplifying the procurement process at Headquarters, I was awarded an **Army Achievement Medal.**

International Trade Specialist, GS-11 (Research/Writing KSA)

This KSA statement describes the steps involved in compiling information, researching and writing complex subject-matter.

Demonstrated ability to prepare speeches, briefing papers, technical reports, etc. both in writing and in person.

As a legislative fellow with Senator Carol Moseley-Braun, I prepared briefing memoranda for the Senior Legislative Assistant and Senator on the OECD Shipbuilding Agreement; the Trade Promotion Coordinating Committee; Holocaust Victim Accounts in Swiss Banks; and Sexual Harassment in the Military.

To prepare these reports, I collected and reviewed a variety of materials, performed independent analysis of Congressional hearing transcripts, discussed the issue with government agencies, other Congressional offices, foreign Embassies and industry associations. I would then consolidate the information into a concise memorandum, outlining the nature of the problem, the options, state impact, and recommendations to the Senator. I continued to follow the issues though the media and Congressional hearings.

During my fellowship, I researched and wrote more than 50 responses on a variety of issues ranging from country-of-origin markings and "Made in the USA" standards, to refugees in Vietnam and Hamas trials in the United States. In one instance, I substantially developed the Senator's position on the Supreme Court's decision regarding women attending the Virginia Military Institute. In another case, a friend of the Senator's and a constituent requested information regarding proposed changes in the "Made in the USA" standard. I reviewed the changes proposed by the Federal Trade Commission, and was then able to explain how this would affect the constituent, and what the Senator's position was on the changes. By the time I left, the Legislative Assistant I worked with had the least amount of constituent mail outstanding.

Computer Specialist, GS-11

This Computer Specialist is seeking a promotion to a GS-12 position.

1. Skill in Novell NetWare 3.x/4.x and Windows NT System Administration procedures.

Over four years experience as a Novell LAN administrator up to v4.11. Have performed upgrades from Novell 3.x to Novell 4.11 and possess detailed knowledge of the systems and procedures necessary for these upgrades. Extensive experience in daily LAN Administrator duties supporting over 500 users which include adding new users, deleting users, and establishing groups and appropriate rights. Responsible for addition of over 200 new PC Workstations to the Novell LAN as well as upgrades to the workstation operating systems from Windows 3.1/3.11 to Windows 95 and upgraded applications software to their latest version. This required detailed knowledge of the LAN, the operating systems and applications involved to ensure no conflicts occurred and system performance remained at the highest level possible.

Have completed training for Windows NT 4.0 Server Administration and Windows NT 4.0 Workstation operation.

Completed courses in Novell NetWare Administration and MS Windows 95 Product Specialist at the University of Maryland, University College and anticipate taking certification test in the Fall of 1998.

2. Knowledge of MS Office 97, WordPerfect for Windows 6.1, Quattro Pro for Windows, Paradox for Windows, Windows 3.1, MS-DOS, cc:Mail for Windows, Windows 95, etc. in a Novell NetWare/NT environment.

Very experienced in WordPerfect up to v7.0, Windows 95, Windows 3.1/3.11, MS-DOS to v6.22, MS Mail, MS Outlook and MS Exchange in a Novell NetWare environment. Have had training and personal use with MS Office 97 in a Windows 95 environment and training in HTML and the Internet. Have used and trained others in the use of Netscape Navigator up to v4.03.

Performed evaluations of new or upgraded software, tested the inter-activity of the new software with existing software located on the LAN. Conflicts encountered must be resolved in order to install new or upgraded software on the LAN without interrupting current work practices. Would troubleshoot to resolve these problems which requires knowledge of the LAN and the changes made during installations, as well as the overall setup of existing software located on the LAN. As the training room file server administrator, responsible for the overall setup and usability of that particular LAN which is subject to extensive changes made during training.

Computer Specialist, GS-11 (continued):

3. Ability to plan, develop, implement, and evaluate personal computer and network training programs for classroom and end user environments.

Currently maintain liaisons with vendors and educators for both software and hardware needs, as well as training needs. Convey to educators the type of training desired then determine which classes will best meet their needs. Assisted in the planning and implementation of new training classes such as Advanced Harvard Graphics for Windows and Netscape Version 1.1. The planning of these classes included outlining the information to be included in the class, writing and/or reviewing documentation, testing of documentation with a group of high-end users, making necessary adjustments to the documentation, and scheduling classes. Have conducted training classes in Netscape Version 1.1, teaching technical computer functions and uses to non-technical employees.

As Training Coordinator, Center-wide announcements for upcoming training events are issued. These announcements include details/descriptions about the upcoming events, as well as instruction on how to register for desired courses. A written activity report is then submitted to my supervisor for inclusion in his weekly report to the Division Director, as well as the Center Director and all Associate Directors.

4. Ability to effectively communicate technical computer information orally and in writing.

Part of my daily routine is to provide Technical Support via phone and in-person. This involves interacting with the end user, determining the problem, then providing a solution. Most users are not technical so having the ability to explain the solution to their problem so they can understand has made me very effective in providing technical support.

One of my responsibilities is to write "Technical Notes" which are used for resolution of Center-wide software and hardware problems. These "Tech Notes" are kept on the Network where all employees have access to them, and provide written technical information to non-technical people. When new software is received, technical instructions will be written which will provide step-by-step directions to non-technical users on how to use the new software.

As part of my Training Coordinator duties, it is necessary to communicate with all levels of the organization, from the Director to the newest student trainee. Announcements are routinely sent out concerning available training courses via E-mail. Will meet with employees to discuss the kind of training available and how it meets their needs, and hold registration sessions as required.

As the Office Automation Branch Training Coordinator, I write technical documentation for use in the computer training classes held at the Center. In addition to writing the training documentation, will frequently teach technical computer training courses for the users at the Center. These classes are open to all users of the Center and each class generally has a mix of different levels of end-user.

Clinical Nurse Manager, GS-12

A Nurse Practitioner in a critical care/research Immunotherapy ICU at NIH, she was applying for a position as a clinical manager at NIH.

Knowledge of clinical management of complex patient populations.

My first experience managing a complex patient population in a clinical setting was at a refugee camp on the Thai/Cambodian border. We diagnosed and treated 600-1000 Cambodian refugees daily and while I was there, we were confronted by a disastrous outbreak of measles. I set up and managed the epidemiological documentation and tracking system for the camp, authored the camp's nursing policy manual, and trained new medical relief volunteers in camp procedures and safety precautions.

When I was at the University of Colorado Health Science Center's Level I Trauma Center, I served as Primary RN and Assistant Head Nurse in the Trauma and Surgical ICUs, caring for patients with heart/liver transplant, trauma/head injury, craniotomy, open-heart, and other critical surgical conditions. I oversaw hiring, scheduling and staff evaluations. I initiated and set up a peer review program; served as Chair of the Primary Care Committee; served as a member of the Code Blue Committee; and as an Associate Researcher for the Infectious Disease Committee.

Program Analyst, GS-14

This GS-14 Program Analyst with 24 years experience was applying for a GS-15 Air Traffic Program Analyst.

Skill in program management.

In 1995, the Department of Transportation adopted the business and service standards outlined by the Government Performance and Results Act, and then asked the FAA to "reinvent" itself in order to comply with these new standards.

As part of FAA's response, I was recruited to serve on two teams to develop a business process reengineering plan for FAA's (former) Air Traffic Requirements and Airway Facilities Requirements organizations during the Agency-wide reorganization. Our study showed that these two organizations programs were redundant and we recommended that they be merged. Our plan was approved by senior FAA management and the two units were merged into the (new) Air Traffic Systems Requirements Service in 1996.

Some years ago, while I was serving in a different FAA unit, we were hit with an unfavorable OIG audit because we couldn't properly account for all the equipment assigned to us. To correct this problem, I created the FAA's <u>first</u> automated Property Inventory Control System (still being used Agency-wide). I developed the bid requirements and then collaborated with the winning vendors to develop and implement the system. After the system was installed, tested and debugged, I developed training material for FAA personnel, and then trained over 500 FAA employees in the use of the new system.

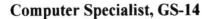

Computer Specialist, GS-14

Here is an example of the way you can set-up your KSAs with the name of the agency, title of position, announcement number and other announcement information centered on the page. Each of the KSAs would continue, or be printed on a separate page, depending on the length.

National Institute of Standards and Technology
Office of Human Resources Management

Position: Computer Specialist, ZP-0334-14
Announcement Number: NIST/98-3297/SGE

NAME
SS#: 999-99-9999

QUALITY RANKING FACTORS

1) **Skill, as evidenced by experience, in one or more of the following:**
    A) **Analyzing the need for and developing computer system requirements**
    B) **Designing computer systems**
    C) **Developing computer systems**

C) Developing computer systems:

After completion of 6 distinct systems database designs to meet unique application and user requirements, I developed 6 electronic document data repositories using Excalibur's Electronic Filing System software integrated with Oracle. They include 800,000+ Adverse Drug Reaction Reports, 35,000+ Drug Master File documents, 32,000+ Biopharmaceutic Division Files drug related reviews, 25,000+ Tobacco Activity documents, 20,000+ Advisory Committee Meeting documents, and 2,000+ Approved Drug Labels. I was the first person in FDA to successfully develop systems utilizing imaging software technology to store and retrieve electronic documents. Significant benefits to FDA were achieved as a result of the work I did to develop these systems including:

- Ease of access to documents and convenience of searching
- Information obtained was quite complete
- The ability to provide information quickly on a particular drug or NDA
- Users were able to produce high quality reviews in less time
- Made researching the history of a drug easy
- **Survey showed the average amount of time saved per person is 166.75 hours/year x 700 users is over 56 man years.**

Public Affairs Specialist, GS-14

This federal employee is seeking a GS-15 position in the same field of work. This KSA does not mention "endangered species conservation," but this writer does address very complex public relations activities on environmental subjects.

Skill in planning and executing communications activities such as print and broadcast media campaigns on behalf of sensitive and potentially controversial natural resource topics, for example, endangered species conservation.

In the Fall of 1996, EPA faced a huge public relations obstacle in convincing many reporters, politicians and citizens that we had to toughen the national air quality standards for ground-level ozone (smog) and particulates (soot, dirt, smoke) to protect human health and the environment. EPA estimated the cost would run from $6.6 to $8.5 billion annually by the year 2007, and we knew this cost estimate would result in dire predictions -- from opponents of tougher regulations -- of huge job losses and the imposition of a debilitating financial burden on industry, especially small businesses.

I was a member of the strategy team with high-level EPA officials in which we decided to create maximum publicity for a "kick-off" announcement of the proposed regulation. This would allow us to immediately take the offensive in helping sell our side of the story: *that the health and environmental benefits to Americans well outweighed the costs of the new regulation.*

We announced the proposal with a huge press conference at EPA Washington headquarters, attended by print and broadcast reporters from virtually all major national media organizations, along with 17 TV cameras. We also faxed a press release and other press conference materials to approximately 200 major media outlets in Washington and around the country.

This public relations offensive generated hundreds of generally favorable newspaper, magazine, radio and television stories throughout the nation. Despite strenuous opposition, EPA succeeded in issuing a final rule that contained no substantial weakening of the human health and environmental protections proposed the year before.

Based largely on my accomplishments in helping to sell the toughening of the particulate and ozone standards, I was recognized with Special Achievement Awards (cash) in 1996 and 1997.

Immigration, Naturalization Service – Detention & Deportation Officer, GS-12

An Air Force air operations staff officer, flight instructor, intelligence officer and DOD law enforcement mission coordinator with over twenty years of domestic and international operational experience successfully applied for a regional position managing prisoner and alien air transportation service. He got the position and was asked to apply for a higher grade (GS-13).

Ability to analyze information on, prepare written reports and present oral briefings.

For over 24 years, the success of many missions I have been assigned to turned primarily on the accuracy of my analysis of events surrounding the mission and the effectiveness and clarity with which I could present my findings to my counterparts, superiors and operational elements.

As a DoD Advisor to the United States Border Patrol (USBP) for example, I supported the Joint Task Force Six (JTF-6) counterdrug operations assigned to the USBP. I served as advisor to USBP to provide DoD support in formulating programs, policy planning, and command or direction of operations and application activities. My work consisted primarily of written reports, conducting briefings to counterparts and senior management, and training USBP agents in advanced intelligence methodologies and techniques.

Serving as the Tactical Analysis Officer for the American Embassy at Bridgetown, Barbados, I reported on the political-narcotic situation in the Eastern Caribbean region in support of U.S.-led counterdrug operations. My reporting ranged from face-to-face briefings with senior diplomatic, government and military officials to formal presentations and detailed written reports.

As the Intelligence Officer on the Joint Inter-Agency Task Force East, based in Key West, Florida, I coordinated a five-day international meeting and organized its technical working groups. The event hosted 270 interagency representatives from 40 countries and was considered *"outstanding."*

In a long term project for the U.S. Air Force, I was responsible for developing (from conception to delivery) new F-4 Phantom flight training systems. I kept my superiors current through detailed briefings and reports, trained other trainers to teach the new systems, and distributed complex technical data. I created manuals, developed curricula, wrote statements of work, mission goals and standard operating procedures. My efforts proved successful, and I was able to deliver 158 training projects worldwide.

ECQ Examples

Marsha. K. Pettifogger	789-01-2348	Executive Core Qualifications

1. **Leading Change -- The ability to develop and implement an organizational vision which integrates key national and program goals, priorities, values, and other factors. Inherent to it is the ability to balance change and continuity -- to continually strive to improve customer service and program performance within the basic Government framework, to create a work environment that encourages creative thinking, and to maintain focus, intensity, and persistence, even under adversity.**

My professional career has centered on developing the skills to provide sound counsel and to recognize effective operational practices through economic, legal, and political environments that accomplished a comprehensive change within the aviation industry. When the Airline Deregulation Act of 1978 changed the fundamental operating conditions of the nation's commercial air carriers, I played a pivotal role in facilitating the revisions of approaches to regulation and operation that would become required under new conditions. I fostered new approaches in critical arenas while serving in the Office of the General Counsel of the Department of Transportation.

First, I developed an effective litigation strategy for the Department of address potential threats from corporate executives who might attempt to create legal snares from changes in legal operations. Where the regulatory approaches under the Civil Aeronautics Board (CAB) had tolerated -- or institutionalized -- shared markets and monopolistic operations, the antitrust laws which govern competitive environments treat many similar actions as criminal violations of the law. In a series of public briefings, I outlined and explained appropriate legal arguments, and ensured that the industries learned that the Department was positioned to enforce implementation of the change in the law.

Second, I applied my understanding of emerging technologies to the series of regulations that would continue to influence the operations of air carriers until the sunset of the CAB For important safety regulations (for examples improved technologies for monitoring trains on tracks, better signaling and lighting systems at grade crossings, communications linkages between engineers and dispatchers, etc.) legal requirements to remain vigilant and promote continuous improvements in performance remain guiding elements of the industry. I participated in rulemaking proceedings involving the CAB, the Federal Aviation Administration, and the National Transportation Safety Board, to promote improvements in safety regulations and to ensure that enhanced technologies could be incorporated swiftly into effective operations.

Third, I dedicated a five-year period of my career to learning the marketing operations essential to success in the new commercial environment, taking on leadership of the Department's residual regulatory duties and managing them through the critical transition from regulation to competition. Not only did this managerial experience enhance my understanding of the business dimensions of the new environment, the operational experience acquired during this period has enhanced the caliber of representation that I have provided to the Department in subsequent negotiation of regulations, administrative proceedings, and litigation. This preparation assisted the shift from deregulation of rates and routes into an environment where the Department monitors on-time-performance and customer service. This knowledge was especially helpful in working within the framework of a revised Administrative Procedures Act and the Reagan Administration's Executive Order 12291, which created a regulatory framework designed to foster market change.

I believe that this integration of administrative and litigation experience in a regulated environment, development of legal perspectives on regulations that remain critical elements of continuing operations, and effective managerial experience combines to provide the strategic vision essential to the industry in the continuing competitive environment.

James K. Mitchelson   345-67-8910   **Executive Core Qualifications**

2.   **Leading People -- The ability to design and implement strategies which maximize employee potential and foster high ethical standards in meeting the organization's vision, mission, and goals.**

In 1997 the Administrator of the General Services Administration awarded me two Administrator's Awards for Excellence for activities that demanded team performance. I have been team-oriented throughout my public service, and these awards recognized the work of at least seven team members in each instance. My current supervisory responsibilities involve oversight of seven team leaders, and they receive effective leadership as they work to adapt the services provided by the GSA Information Technology Management Team to all federal agencies. Interagency liaison, and fostering interagency cooperation, are vital aspects of these continuing responsibilities.

Throughout my service I have sustained a commitment to the equal treatment of all employees and I have found that principle to provide the most effective foundation for ensuring successful implementation of merit systems principles, veterans' preference, the Americans With Disabilities Act, and other legislation enacted to address the nation's concerns about its management of its people. I have designed affirmative employment strategies, counseled individual employees to resolve workplace and personal issues that affect human performance, and have managed workforce reductions that required the elimination of as many as 40 percent of the people in my organization. I learned through these experiences that the greatest successes in managing people involve the difficult decisions associated with organizations in change.

Because all organizations must manage change in the current federal environment, I have made training a consistent part of my professional development. I have also directed persons under my supervision in courses of action that would prepare them for the next level of responsibility within the organization. This requires identifying where the opportunities for training might occur and ensuring that the work assignments of other team members are balanced to provide continuing opportunities for development. I have taken special measures to ensure that all employees understand the new requirements of the Information Technology Management Reform Act (Clinger-Cohen) and the Government Performance and Results Act (GPRA). When introducing innovative technologies in the federal work environment, I have included appropriate time to ensure that minimal training will be required to understand and operate "user-friendly" technologies, while ensuring that professionals who require complex services in an automated environment have capabilities to use the technologies available to them.

These abilities to relate technological requirements and human performance factors have been developed through extensive human resources management experiences in both civilian and defense agencies. I have managed information technology requirements analyses for complex organizations, assisted the reengineering of business processes (in other agencies as well as within GSA), and prepared people for emergent career challenges. I have adapted easily to the professional challenges associated with applying expertise in organizational analysis to the requirements of federal organizations that rely on a great range of skills, from cashiers and law enforcement officers to attorneys and environmental scientists.

My abilities to evaluate people, motivate effective performance, and achieve team results have been demonstrated repeatedly throughout my career. I have refined my abilities to work with a full range of talent, and I have a well-rounded perspective on evaluating organizations' personnel requirements and recruiting and training people to meet them. I am confident that my experiences in these areas and my success in managing in a team environment provide the foundation needed for success as a senior executive.

3.   **Results Driven -- Stresses accountability and continuous improvement. It includes the ability to make timely and effective decisions and produce results through strategic planning and the implementation and evaluation of programs and policies.**

When I arrived at the National Science Foundation as Director of Chemistry Programs in 1995, the agency perceived major threats to research funding associated with the change to Republican control of Congress and the Administration's commitment to other research priorities. The program was slated to take a 14 percent reduction in funding that resulted from a shift of research funds into areas that appeared to have more direct applications to life sciences and following scandals related to overcharges of administrative costs.

My first priority was to convey to the research community the strategic vulnerability that would be an inevitable consequence of any further mishandling of appropriated funds. In coordination with the General Accounting Office, I convened a national conference of university administrators, congressional staff, and prominent researchers, and ensured that all understood and committed to comply with the accounting standards associated with acceptance of federal research funds. In conjunction with this conference, I organized discussions that to identify a consensus for proceeding with substantive research.

In light of the importance of renewing public confidence before seeking additional appropriations, I proposed to redirect research funding into areas that provided greater assurance of applications within the near term (five to seven years). Building upon improvements in instrumentation technologies derived from enhanced computer software, I proposed and gained acceptance of a focus on research that would build upon refinements in measurements and validation of recent conceptual studies. The advances in instrumentation would provide a base of applications that held strong potential for interdisciplinary uses, and the replications would provide valuable information validating more promising research findings from recent years. This approach provided for the development of new organizations and researchers with effective methods for the future, while sustaining the professional credibility of long-term researchers.

This approach proved remarkably effective. The improvements in computerized instrumentation facilitated the evaluation of complex chemical compounds, with tremendous potential applications in the biomedical areas (especially pharmaceutical chemistry, narcotics bio- and physical chemistry, protein biochemistry, and energy applications). The integrated approach resulted in more than 30 new interdisciplinary projects, and enhanced developments associated with gas chromatography, mass spectroscopy, and nuclear magnetic resonance. These advances in instrumentation also attracted more than ten engineering departments to submit new applications promising further refinements of the technologies promoted in these efforts.

Working with GAO, and in cooperation with other federal funding agencies, we have monitored accounting within the major research universities, and prevented any recurrence of the expense scandals of the early portion of the decade. By keeping appropriations committee staff involved in both the accounting of funds and the results of projects, we have cultivated improved relations with affected constituencies, and realized a 17 percent increase in funding where significantly lower levels had been projected. Finally, by continuing to support researchers with innovative records -- even in replication and validation studies -- the programs have resulted in several innovative approaches to analytical techniques and the identification of significant new research questions. This commitment to a strategic approach advancing research built upon a solid knowledge of research progress and institutional practices, and reaffirmed my commitment to achieving sustained results even under adverse political and operating conditions.

Louis J. Stanton   890-12-3456   **Executive Core Qualifications**

4.   **Business Acumen -- The ability to acquire and administer human, financial, material, and information resources in a manner which instills public trust and accomplishes the organization's mission, and to use new technology to enhance decision making.**

I have demonstrated exceptional business acumen throughout my professional career. While managing the Joint FASTTRAK Test Force I conceived and implemented a program that grew from five personnel to more than 300 staff and administering a $125 million annual operating budget. The total procurement derived from this research and development program reached nearly $8 billion, and provided invaluable support for United States' air superiority during Operation Desert Storm. This record of success has been a consistent trait of my participation in every organization with which I have been affiliated.

Beyond my engineering training, I earned a master's degree in business administration early in my Navy career. I have applied emergent management techniques throughout my career, and have readily adapted to the efforts at reengineering business processes that derived from Total Quality Management approaches. I am a regular user of computerized spreadsheets to support program analysis, and have used data-based programs for analytical tasks ranging from assessment of flight test data to periodic reviews of budgets and spending plans. I have participated in the development of sophisticated air navigation and communications equipment and have administered cutting edge technological experiments.

I have maintained consistent awareness of resources that could be employed more efficiently, and gained certification as a level one manager in the Defense Acquisition System in 1992. I am familiar with a full variety of acquisition vehicles, and have worked extensively with flexible interagency agreements. By promoting EPA/DoD Partnership Councils, I facilitated the integration of management related to space operations for environmental assessment, and that partnership has already realized substantial savings in relation to preliminary estimates of research costs. These efforts contributed substantially to reducing observation and pollutant tracking satellite costs by $1.6 billion. My work with EPA's Satellite Observation Program Task Force has contributed to reducing average integration time from 24 to 18 months. When a joint NASA/DoD payload was stymied by the inability to acquire critical hardware, I led the acquisition of a free-flying spacecraft that saved $15 million while saving 36 months on the schedule that would have been required to produce alternative equipment. On another occasion I orchestrated an interagency transfer of a space payload canister that the owner agency had designated for surplus. Such novel acquisition approaches have been hallmarks of my career. When NATO encountered difficulty finding landing craft for a joint combat exercise, I identified suitable resources and acquired them through the Louisiana National Guard.

These managerial capacities stem from a solid understanding of the flexibilities available under current law. At the beginning of FY-1992, an unexpected cancellation of a critical support contract for the Joint FASTTRAK Test Force left the program without critical manpower support. I used a two-step procedure, first saving 60 jobs through a short-term bridge (sole source) contract that was developed in three weeks, then completing a full procurement to prevent a recurrence of this deficiency. The full acquisition -- which normally requires at least eleven months, was completed in six.

This consistent record of developing and managing material, contract, and human resources fully displays my ability to understand sound managerial practices and to seize the initiative necessary to provide the resources that are critical to program success.

5.   **Building Coalitions/Communication -- The ability to explain, advocate and express facts and ideas in a convincing manner, and negotiate with individuals and groups internally and externally. It also involves the ability to develop an expansive professional network with other organizations, and to identify the internal and external politics that impact the work of the organization.**

I am a well-organized leader with a capacity to provide policy direction and effective presentations to many forums. As Chair of the Department of State's Security Policy Board, I conduct monthly meetings of an interagency group that coordinates security issues among federal agencies. Through this venue, I frequently make policy presentations to senior officials at other agencies and provide guidance about the Security Policy Board's international concerns. I have a strong record of gaining interagency cooperation to resolve issues raised through this Committee. Among other accomplishments, we have raised the need to improve security training to the second highest priority for the Board, and secured improvements in funding from all major agencies.

I am thoroughly familiar with the process by which policy documents are approved as official statements, including legislative testimony, Statements of Administration Position on policy issues, Executive Orders, regulations, and other important legal and policy documents. I wrote and played an active role in the adoption of a Presidential Decision Directive outlining federal policy regarding sensitive telecommunications security issues. This Directive stood as national policy with minor modification over a period of nearly ten years. The Subcommittee of the Committee on Training Standards, which I chair, has developed new standards guiding security adjudications. Following a briefing that I organized, the Director of Central Intelligence recognized the need for standard adjudicator training as a high priority training activity for all federal agencies.

I am an effective public speaker who has served as a guest lecturer in professional courses taught through the American Society for Industrial Security. I have also made presentations to seminars conducted by the National Security Agency. While working to secure prohibited air space above sensitive facilities in the early 1990s, I worked effectively with the Department of Defense and the Federal Aviation Administration. Not only did I participate actively in agency meetings, I chaired a series of public hearings at twelve sites around the country to complete the notice and comment requirements of the Administrative Procedures Act. Each of these meetings provided opportunities to discuss relevant issues with print and broadcast media reflecting intense local interest in facilities such as Rocky Flats (CO), Savannah River (GA), and Hanford (WA). I represented the agency in several meetings with affected congressional delegations, and was able to secure adoption of necessary regulations without additional legislation. This record of effective participation in major agency meetings, dealing with other federal agencies, state and local governments, and congressional committees provides full demonstration of my ability to address a broad range of audiences and to build the coalitions needed for successful performance as a federal executive.

APPENDIX C

Federal Employment Forms

Several federal forms discussed in the book are reproduced here in their entirety. The forms are as follows:

☆ OF 510, Applying for a Federal Job

☆ OF 612, Optional Application for Federal Employment. See Chapter 1 for more information on this form.

☆ OF 306, Declaration for Federal Employment

☆ Form C, OPM's Qualifications & Availability Form

See Chapter 2 for information on how to obtain these forms.

**United States
Office of
Personnel
Management**

OF 510
(September 1994)

JOB OPENINGS

For job information 24 hours a day, 7 days a week, call **912-757-3000**, the U.S. Office of Personnel Management (OPM) automated telephone system. Or, with a computer modem dial **912-757-3100** for job information from an OPM electronic bulletin board. You can also reach the board through the Internet (Telnet only) at FJOB.MAIL.OPM.GOV.

APPLICANTS WITH DISABILITIES

You can find out about alternative formats by calling OPM or dialing the electronic bulletin board at the numbers above. Select "Federal Employment Topics" and then "People with Disabilities." If you have a hearing disability, call **TDD 912-744-2299**.

HOW TO APPLY

Review the list of openings, decide which jobs you are interested in, and follow the instructions given. **You may apply for most jobs with a resume, the *Optional Application for Federal Employment*, or any other written format you choose.** For jobs that are unique or filled through automated procedures, you will be given special forms to complete. (You can get an *Optional Application* by calling OPM or dialing our electronic bulletin board at the numbers above.)

WHAT TO INCLUDE

Although the Federal Government does not require a standard application form for most jobs, we do need certain information to evaluate your qualifications and determine if you meet legal requirements for Federal employment. If your resume or application does not provide all the information requested in the job vacancy announcement and in this brochure, you may lose consideration for a job. Help speed the selection process by keeping your resume or application brief and by sending only the requested material. Type or print clearly in dark ink.

Here's what your resume or application must contain

(in addition to specific information requested in the job vacancy announcement)

JOB INFORMATION

☐ Announcement number, and title and grade(s) of the job you are applying for

PERSONAL INFORMATION

☐ Full name, mailing address *(with ZIP Code)* and day and evening phone numbers *(with area code)*
☐ Social Security Number
☐ Country of citizenship *(Most Federal jobs require United States citizenship.)*
☐ Veterans' preference *(See reverse.)*
☐ Reinstatement eligibility *(If requested, attach SF 50 proof of your career or career-conditional status.)*
☐ Highest Federal civilian grade held *(Also give job series and dates held.)*

EDUCATION

☐ High school
   Name, city, and State *(ZIP Code if known)*
   Date of diploma or GED
☐ Colleges or universities
   Name, city, and State *(ZIP Code if known)*
   Majors
   Type and year of any degrees received
   (If no degree, show total credits earned and indicate whether semester or quarter hours.)
☐ Send a copy of your college transcript only if the job vacancy announcement requests it.

WORK EXPERIENCE

☐ Give the following information for your paid and nonpaid work experience related to the job you are applying for.
   (Do not send job descriptions.)
   Job title *(include series and grade if Federal job)*
   Duties and accomplishments
   Employer's name and address
   Supervisor's name and phone number
   Starting and ending dates *(month and year)*
   Hours per week
   Salary
☐ Indicate if we may contact your current supervisor.

OTHER QUALIFICATIONS

☐ **Job-related** training courses *(title and year)*
☐ **Job-related** skills, for example, other languages, computer software/hardware, tools, machinery, typing speed
☐ **Job-related** certificates and licenses *(current only)*
☐ **Job-related** honors, awards, and special accomplishments, for example, publica-tions, memberships in professional or honor societies, leadership activities, public speaking, and performance awards
   (Give dates but do not send documents unless requested.)

**THE FEDERAL GOVERNMENT IS
AN EQUAL OPPORTUNITY EMPLOYER**

VETERANS' PREFERENCE IN HIRING

❑ If you served on active duty in the United States Military and were separated under honorable conditions, you may be eligible for veterans' preference. To receive preference if your service began after October 15, 1976, you must have a Campaign Badge, Expeditionary Medal, or a service-connected disability. For further details, call OPM at **912-757-3000**. Select "Federal Employment Topics" and then "Veterans." Or, dial our electronic bulletin board at **912-757-3100**.

❑ Veterans' preference is not a factor for Senior Executive Service jobs or when competition is limited to status candidates (current or former Federal career or career-conditional employees).

❑ To claim 5-point veterans' preference, attach a copy of your DD-214, *Certificate of Release or Discharge from Active Duty*, or other proof of eligibility.

❑ To claim 10-point veterans' preference, attach an SF 15, *Application for 10-Point Veterans' Preference*, plus the proof required by that form.

OTHER IMPORTANT INFORMATION

❑ Before hiring, an agency will ask you to complete a *Declaration for Federal Employment* to determine your suitability for Federal employment and to authorize a background investigation. The agency will also ask you to sign and certify the accuracy of all the information in your application. **If you make a false statement in any part of your application, you may not be hired; you may be fired after you begin work; or you may be fined or jailed.**

❑ If you are a male over age 18 who was born after December 31, 1959, you must have registered with the Selective Service System (or have an exemption) to be eligible for a Federal job.

❑ The law prohibits public officials from appointing, promoting, or recommending their relatives.

❑ Federal annuitants (military and civilian) may have their salaries or annuities reduced. All employees must pay any valid delinquent debts or the agency may garnish their salary.

PRIVACY AND PUBLIC BURDEN STATEMENTS

The Office of Personnel Management and other Federal agencies rate applicants for Federal jobs under the authority of sections 1104, 1302, 3301, 3304, 3320, 3361, 3393, and 3394 of title 5 of the United States Code. We need the information requested in this brochure and in the associated vacancy announcements to evaluate your qualifications. Other laws require us to ask about citizenship, military service, etc.

❑ We request your Social Security Number (SSN) under the authority of Executive Order 9397 in order to keep your records straight; other people may have the same name. As allowed by law or Presidential directive, we use your SSN to seek information about you from employers, schools, banks, and others who know you. Your SSN may also be used in studies and computer matching with other Government files, for example, files on unpaid student loans.

❑ If you do not give us your SSN or any other information requested, we cannot process your application, which is the first step in getting a job. Also, incomplete addresses and ZIP Codes will slow processing.

❑ We may give information from your records to: training facilities; organizations deciding claims for retirement, insurance, unemployment or health benefits; officials in litigation or administrative proceedings where the Government is a party; law enforcement agencies concerning violations of law or regulation; Federal agencies for statistical reports and studies; officials of labor organizations recognized by law in connection with representing employees; Federal agencies or other sources requesting information for Federal agencies in connection with hiring or retaining, security clearances, security or suitability investigations, classifying jobs, contracting, or issuing licenses, grants, or other benefits; public or private organizations including news media that grant or publicize employee recognition and awards; and the Merit Systems Protection Board, the Office of Special Counsel, the Equal Employment Opportunity Commission, the Federal Labor Relations Authority, the National Archives, the Federal Acquisition Institute, and congressional offices in connection with their official functions.

❑ We may also give information from your records to: prospective nonfederal employers concerning tenure of employment, civil service status, length of service, and date and nature of action for separation as shown on personnel action forms of specifically identified individuals; requesting organizations or individuals concerning the home address and other relevant information on those who might have contracted an illness or been exposed to a health hazard; authorized Federal and nonfederal agencies for use in computer matching; spouses or dependent children asking whether an employee has changed from self-and-family to self-only health benefits enrollment; individuals working on a contract, service, grant, cooperative agreement or job for the Federal Government; non-agency members of an agency's performance or other panel; and agency-appointed representatives of employees concerning information issued to an employee about fitness-for-duty or agency-filed disability retirement procedures.

❑ We estimate the public burden for reporting the employment information will vary from 20 to 240 minutes with an average of 40 minutes per response, including time for reviewing instructions, searching existing data sources, gathering data, and completing and reviewing the information. You may send comments regarding the burden estimate or any other aspect of the collection of information, including suggestions for reducing this burden, to the U.S. Office of Personnel Management, Reports and Forms Management Officer, Washington, DC 20415-0001.

Send your application to the agency announcing the vacancy.

Form Approved: OMB 3206-0219   50510-101   NSN 7540-01-351-9177

*U.S. Government Printing Office: 1995 — 393-606/20008

Form Approved
OMB No. 3206-0219

OPTIONAL APPLICATION FOR FEDERAL EMPLOYMENT - OF 612

You may apply for most jobs with a resume, this form, or other written format. If your resume or application does not provide all the information requested on this form and in the job vacancy announcement, you may lose consideration for a job.

1 Job title in announcement

2 Grade(s) applying for

3 Announcement number

4 Last name   First and middle names

5 Social Security Number

6 Mailing address

City   State   ZIP Code

7 Phone numbers (include area code)
Daytime

Evening

WORK EXPERIENCE

8 Describe your paid and nonpaid work experience related to the job for which you are applying. Do **not** attach job descriptions.

1) Job title (if Federal, include series and grade)

| From (MM/YY) | To (MM/YY) | Salary $ | per | Hours per week |

Employer's name and address   Supervisor's name and phone number
( )

Describe your duties and accomplishments

2) Job title (if Federal, include series and grade)

| From (MM/YY) | To (MM/YY) | Salary $ | per | Hours per week |

Employer's name and address   Supervisor's name and phone number
( )

Describe your duties and accomplishments

50612-101   NSN 7540-01-351-9178   Optional Form 612 (September 1994)
U.S. Office of Personnel Management

GENERAL INFORMATION

You may apply for most Federal jobs with a resume, the attached *Optional Application for Federal Employment* or other written format. If your resume or application does not provide all the information requested on this form and in the job vacancy announcement, you may lose consideration for a job. Type or print clearly in dark ink. Help speed the selection process by keeping your application brief and sending only the requested information. If essential to attach additional pages, include your name and Social Security Number on each page.

- For information on Federal employment, including job lists, alternative formats for persons with disabilities, and veterans' preference, call the U.S. Office of Personnel Management at **912-757-3000, TDD 912-744-2299,** by computer modem **912-757-3100,** or via the Internet (Telnet only) at FJOB.MAIL.OPM.GOV.
- If you served on active duty in the United States Military and were separated under honorable conditions, you may be eligible for veterans' preference. To receive preference if your service began after October 15, 1976, you must have a Campaign Badge, Expeditionary Medal, or a service-connected disability. Veterans' preference is not a factor for Senior Executive Service jobs or when competition is limited to status candidates (current or former career or career-conditional Federal employees).
- Most Federal jobs require United States citizenship and also that males over age 18 born after December 31, 1959, have registered with the Selective Service System or have an exemption.
- The law prohibits public officials from appointing, promoting, or recommending their relatives.
- Federal annuitants (military and civilian) may have their salaries or annuities reduced. All employees must pay any valid delinquent debts or the agency may garnish their salary.
- Send your application to the office announcing the vacancy. If you have questions, contact that office.

THE FEDERAL GOVERNMENT IS AN EQUAL OPPORTUNITY EMPLOYER

PRIVACY ACT AND PUBLIC BURDEN STATEMENTS

- The Office of Personnel Management and other Federal agencies rate applicants for Federal jobs under the authority of sections 1104, 1302, 3301, 3304, 3320, 3361, 3393, and 3394 of title 5 of the United States Code. We need the information requested in this form and in the associated vacancy announcements to evaluate your qualifications. Other laws require us to ask about citizenship, military service, etc.
- We request your Social Security Number (SSN) under the authority of Executive Order 9397 in order to keep your records straight; other people may have the same name. As allowed by law or Presidential directive, we use your SSN to seek information about you from employers, schools, banks, and others who know you. Your SSN may also be used in studies and computer matching with other Government files, for example, files on unpaid student loans.
- If you do not give us your SSN or any other information requested, we cannot process your application, which is the first step in getting a job. Also, incomplete addresses and ZIP Codes will slow processing.
- We may give information from your records to: training facilities; organizations deciding claims for retirement, insurance, unemployment or health benefits; officials in litigation or administrative proceedings where the Government is a party; law enforcement agencies concerning violations of law or regulation; Federal agencies for statistical reports and studies; officials of labor organizations recognized by law in connection with representing employees; Federal agencies or other sources requesting information for Federal agencies in connection with hiring or retaining, security clearances, security or suitability investigations, classifying jobs, contracting, or issuing licenses, grants, or other benefits; public and private organizations including news media that grant or publicize employee recognition and awards; and the Merit Systems Protection Board, the Office of Special Counsel, the Equal Employment Opportunity Commission,

the Federal Labor Relations Authority, the National Archives, the Federal Acquisition Institute, and congressional offices in connection with their official functions.
- We may also give information from your records to: prospective nonfederal employers concerning tenure of employment, civil service status, length of service, and date and nature of action for separation as shown on personnel action forms of specifically identified individuals; requesting organizations or individuals concerning the home address and other relevant information on those who might have contracted an illness or been exposed to a health hazard; authorized Federal and nonfederal agencies for use in computer matching; spouses or dependent children asking whether the employee has changed from self-and-family to self-only health benefits enrollment; individuals working on a contract, service, grant, cooperative agreement or job for the Federal Government; non-agency members of an agency's performance or other panel; and agency-appointed representatives of employees concerning information issued to the employee about fitness-for-duty or agency-filed disability retirement procedures.
- We estimate the public reporting burden for this collection will vary from 20 to 240 minutes with an average of 40 minutes per response, including time for reviewing instructions, searching existing data sources, gathering data, and completing and reviewing the information. You may send comments regarding the burden estimate or any other aspect of the collection of information, including suggestions for reducing this burden, to U.S. Office of Personnel Management, Reports and Forms Management Officer, Washington, DC 20415-0001.
- Send your application to the agency announcing the vacancy.

9 May we contact your current supervisor?

YES [   ]   NO [   ] ▶ If we need to contact your current supervisor before making an offer, we will contact you first.

EDUCATION

10 Mark highest level completed.   Some HS [   ]   HS/GED [   ]   Associate [   ]   Bachelor [   ]   Master [   ]   Doctoral [   ]

11 Last high school (HS) or GED school. Give the school's name, city, State, ZIP Code (if known), and year diploma or GED received.

12 Colleges and universities attended. Do **not** attach a copy of your transcript unless requested.

Name / City, State, ZIP Code	Total Credits Earned		Major(s)	Degree - Year (if any) Received
	Semester	Quarter		
1) Name City State ZIP Code				
2)				
3)				

OTHER QUALIFICATIONS

13 **Job-related** training courses (give title and year). **Job-related** skills (other languages, computer software/hardware, tools, machinery, typing speed, etc.). **Job-related** certificates and licenses (current only). **Job-related** honors, awards, and special accomplishments (publications, memberships in professional/honor societies, leadership activities, public speaking, and performance awards). Give dates, but do **not** send documents unless requested.

GENERAL

14 Are you a U.S. citizen?   YES [   ]   NO [   ] ▶ Give the country of your citizenship. _____

15 Do you claim veterans' preference?   NO [   ]   YES [   ] ▶ Mark your claim of 5 or 10 points below.
     5 points [   ] ▶ Attach your DD 214 or other proof.   **10 points** [   ] ▶ Attach an *Application for 10-Point Veterans' Preference* (SF 15) and proof required.

16 Were you ever a Federal civilian employee?

     NO [   ]   YES [   ] ▶ For highest civilian grade give: Series   Grade   From (MM/YY)   To (MM/YY)

17 Are you eligible for reinstatement based on career or career-conditional Federal status?

     NO [   ]   YES [   ] ▶ If requested, attach SF 50 proof.

APPLICANT CERTIFICATION

18 I **certify** that, to the best of my knowledge and belief, all of the information on and attached to this application is true, correct, complete and made in good faith. I **understand** that false or fraudulent information on or attached to this application may be grounds for not hiring me or for firing me after I begin work, and may be punishable by fine or imprisonment. I **understand** that any information I give may be investigated.

SIGNATURE   DATE SIGNED

Optional Form 306
September 1994
U.S. Office of Personnel
Management

Declaration for Federal Employment

Form Approved:
O.M.B. No. 3206-0182
NSN 7540-01-368-7775
50306-101

GENERAL INFORMATION

1 FULL NAME
▶

2 SOCIAL SECURITY NUMBER
▶

3 PLACE OF BIRTH *(Include City and State or Country)*
▶

4 DATE OF BIRTH *(MM/DD/YY)*
▶

5 OTHER NAMES EVER USED *(For example, maiden name, nickname, etc.)*
▶
▶

6 PHONE NUMBERS *(Include Area Codes)*
DAY ▶
NIGHT ▶

MILITARY SERVICE

	Yes	No
7 Have you served in the United States Military Service? *If your only active duty was training in the Reserves or National Guard, answer "NO".*		

If you answered "YES", list the branch, dates (MM/DD/YY), and type of discharge for all active duty military service.

BRANCH	FROM	TO	TYPE OF DISCHARGE

BACKGROUND INFORMATION

For all questions, provide all additional requested information under item 15 or on attached sheets. The circumstances of each event you list will be considered. However, in most cases you can still be considered for Federal jobs.

For questions 8, 9, and 10, your answers should include convictions resulting from a plea of nolo contendere *(no contest)*, but omit (1) traffic fines of $300 or less, (2) any violation of law committed before your 16th birthday, (3) any violation of law committed before your 18th birthday if finally decided in juvenile court or under a Youth Offender law, (4) any conviction set aside under the Federal Youth Corrections Act or similar State law, and (5) any conviction whose record was expunged under Federal or State law.

	Yes	No
8 During the last 10 years, have you been convicted, been imprisoned, been on probation, or been on parole? (Includes felonies, firearms or explosives violations, misdemeanors, and all other offenses.) *If "Yes", use item 15 to provide the date, explanation of the violation, place of occurrence, and the name and address of the police department or court involved.*		
9 Have you been convicted by a military court-martial in the past 10 years? (If no military service, answer "NO".) *If "Yes", use item 15 to provide the date, explanation of the violation, place of occurrence, and the name and address of the military authority or court involved.*		
10 Are you now under charges for any violation of law? *If "Yes", use item 15 to provide the date, explanation of the violation, place of occurrence, and the name and address of the police department or court involved.*		
11 During the last 5 years, were you fired from any job for any reason, did you quit after being told that you would be fired, did you leave any job by mutual agreement because of specific problems, or were you debarred from Federal employment by the Office of Personnel Management? *If "Yes", use item 15 to provide the date, an explanation of the problem and reason for leaving, and the employer's name and address.*		
12 Are you delinquent on any Federal debt? (Includes delinquencies arising from Federal taxes, loans, overpayment of benefits, and other debts to the U.S. Government, plus defaults of Federally guaranteed or insured loans such as student and home mortgage loans.) *If "Yes", use item 15 to provide the type, length, and amount of the delinquency or default, and steps that you are taking to correct the error or repay the debt:*		

ADDITIONAL QUESTIONS

	Yes	No
13 Do any of your relatives work for the agency or organization to which you are submitting this form? (Includes father, mother, husband, wife, son, daughter, brother, sister, uncle, aunt, first cousin, nephew, niece, father-in-law, mother-in-law, son-in-law, daughter-in-law, brother-in-law, sister-in-law, stepfather, stepmother, stepson, stepdaughter, stepbrother, stepsister, half brother, and half sister.) *If "Yes", use item 15 to provide the name, relationship, and the Department, Agency, or Branch of the Armed Forces for which your relative works.*		
14 Do you receive, or have you ever applied for, retirement pay, pension, or other pay based on military, Federal civilian, or District of Columbia Government service?		

CONTINUATION SPACE / AGENCY OPTIONAL QUESTIONS

15   Provide details requested in items 8 through 13 and 17c in the continuation space below or on attached sheets. Be sure to identify attached sheets with your name, Social Security Number, and item number, and to include ZIP Codes in all addresses. If any questions are printed below, please answer as instructed (these questions are specific to your position, and your agency is authorized to ask them).

CERTIFICATIONS / ADDITIONAL QUESTION

APPLICANT: If you are applying for a position and have not yet been selected. Carefully review your answers on this form and any attached sheets. When this form and all attached materials are accurate, complete item 16/16a.

APPOINTEE: If you are being appointed. Carefully review your answers on this form and any attached sheets, including any other application materials that your agency has attached to this form. If any information requires correction to be accurate as of the date you are signing, make changes on this form or the attachments and/or provide updated information on additional sheets, initialing and dating all changes and additions. When this form and all attached materials are accurate, complete item 16/16b and answer item 17.

16   **I certify** that, to the best of my knowledge and belief, all of the information on and attached to this Declaration for Federal Employment, including any attached application materials, is true, correct, complete, and made in good faith. **I understand** that a false or fraudulent answer to any question on any part of this declaration or its attachments may be grounds for not hiring me, or for firing me after I begin work, and may be punishable by fine or imprisonment. **I understand** that any information I give may be investigated for purposes of determining eligibility for Federal employment as allowed by law or Presidential order. **I consent** to the release of information about my ability and fitness for Federal employment by *employers, schools, law enforcement agencies,* and *other individuals and organizations* to *investigators, personnel specialists,* and *other authorized employees of the Federal Government.* **I understand** that for financial or lending institutions, medical institutions, hospitals, health care professionals, and some other sources of information, a separate specific release may be needed, and I may be contacted for such a release at a later date.

16a   **Applicant's Signature** ▶   *(Sign in ink)*   Date ▶

16b **Appointee's Signature** ▶ *(Sign in ink)*	Date ▶	**APPOINTING OFFICER: Enter Date of Appointment or Conversion** ▶

17   **Appointee Only** *(Respond only if you have been employed by the Federal Government before):* Your elections of life insurance during previous Federal employment may affect your eligibility for life insurance during your new appointment. These questions are asked to help your personnel office make a correct determination.

	Date *(MM/DD/YY)*		
17a When did you leave your last Federal job?			
	Yes	No	Don't Know
17b When you worked for the Federal Government the last time, did you waive Basic Life Insurance or any type of optional life insurance? - - - - - - - - - - - - - - - - -			
17c If you answered "Yes" to item 17b, did you later cancel the waiver(s)? *If your answer to item 17c is "No," use item 15 to identify the type(s) of insurance for which waivers were not cancelled.* - - - - - - - - - - - - - - - - - - -			

Optional Form 306 (Back)   September 1994

U.S. OFFICE OF PERSONNEL MANAGEMENT

FORM APPROVED
OMB No. 3206-0040

QUALIFICATIONS & AVAILABILITY FORM

FORM C

DO NOT FOLD, STAPLE, TEAR OR PAPER CLIP THIS FORM.
DO NOT SUBMIT PHOTOCOPIES OF THIS FORM.
We can process this form only if you:
- Use a number 2 lead pencil.
- Completely blacken each oval you choose.
- Completely erase any mistakes or stray marks.

PRINT YOUR RESPONSE IN THE BOXES AND BLACKEN IN THE APPROPRIATE OVALS.

USE A NO. 2 PENCIL

EXAMPLES

CORRECT MARK

INCORRECT MARKS

1 YOUR NAME: _____

2 JOB APPLYING FOR: _____

3 ANNOUNCEMENT NUMBER: _____

**FOLLOW THE DIRECTIONS ON THE
"FORM C INSTRUCTION SHEET"**

4 OCCUPATION (OCC)

5 CASE NO. (CNO)

6 LOWEST GRADE (LAG)

7 EMPLOYMENT AVAILABILITY

ARE YOU AVAILABLE FOR:

	YES	NO			YES	NO
A) full-time employment		(FTE)	D) jobs requiring travel			(TRV)
-40 hours per week?	Y	N	away from home for			
			-1 to 5 nights/month?	Y	N	
B) part-time employment of		(PTE)	-6 to 10 nights/month?	Y	N	
-16 or fewer hrs/week?	Y	N	-11 plus nights/month?	Y	N	
-17 to 24 hrs/week?	Y	N				
-25 to 32 hrs/week?	Y	N	E) other employment questions			
C) temporary employment			(see directions)			(OEM)
lasting		(TMP)	Question 1?	Y	N	
-less than 1 month?	Y	N	Question 2?	Y	N	
-1 to 4 months?	Y	N	Question 3?	Y	N	
-5 to 12 months?	Y	N	Question 4?	Y	N	

8 (OSP) OCCUPATIONAL SPECIALTIES

1   2   3   4   5

6   7   8   9   10

9 (GFP) GEOGRAPHIC AVAILABILITY

1   2   3   4   5

6   7   8   9

4924858

OPM FORM 1203-AW
(2-98)

10 FIRST NAME (FNM) MI (MIN) LAST NAME (LNM)

11 SOCIAL SECURITY NUMBER (SSN)

12 TELEPHONE NUMBER (TEL) AREA CODE

CONTACT TIME (TCT)

○ Day

○ Night

○ Either

13 STREET, ADDRESS (HOUSE NUMBER AND STREET AND APT. NO., WHERE YOU WANT TO RECEIVE MAIL.) (ADR)

LEAVE BLANK COLUMN BETWEEN NUMBER, STREET, NAME, ETC.

14 CITY (CTY)

15 STATE CODE (STE)

IF OUTSIDE THE U.S.A. BLACKEN "OV" AND PRINT COUNTRY HERE

USE STANDARD STATE CODES

16 ZIP CODE + 4 (ZIP)

OPTIONAL

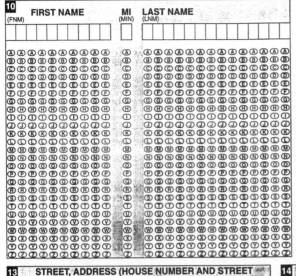

Page 2

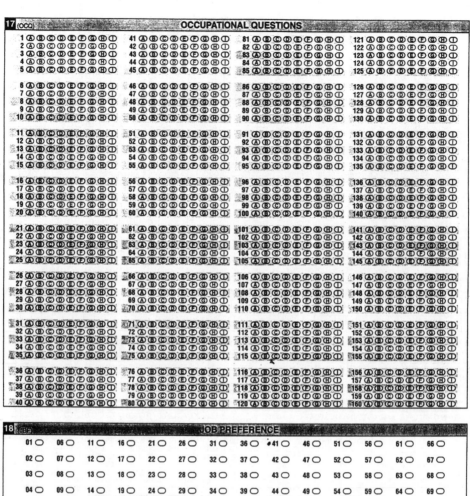

23 VETERAN PREFERENCE CLAIM
(VET)

○ No preference claimed

○ 5 points preference claimed

10 POINT PREFERENCE- You must enclose a completed Standard Form 15.

○ 10 points preference claimed (award of a Purple Heart or noncompensable service-connected disability)

○ 10 points compensable disability preference claimed (disability rating of less than 30%)

○ 10 points other (wife, widow, husband, widower, mother preference claimed)

○ 10 points compensable disability preference claimed (disability rating of 30% or more)

24 BACKGROUND INFORMATION
(SB1)

	YES	NO
1. Are you a citizen of the United States?	Ⓨ	Ⓝ
2. During the last 10 years, were you fired from any job for any reason or did you quit after being told that you would be fired?	Ⓨ	Ⓝ
3. Are you now or have you ever been: (Answer the following questions.)		
a) convicted of or forfeited collateral for any felony?	Ⓨ	Ⓝ
b) convicted of or forfeited collateral for any firearms or explosive violation?	Ⓨ	Ⓝ
c) convicted, forfeited collateral, imprisoned, on probation, or on parole, during the last 10 years?	Ⓨ	Ⓝ
d) convicted by a court martial?	Ⓨ	Ⓝ
4. Are you currently under charges for any violation of law?	Ⓨ	Ⓝ

25 DATES OF ACTIVE DUTY - MILITARY SERVICE

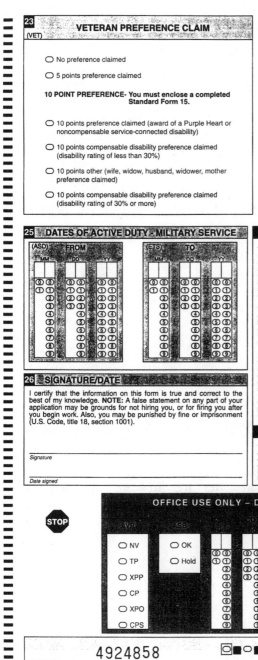

26 SIGNATURE/DATE

I certify that the information on this form is true and correct to the best of my knowledge. **NOTE:** A false statement on any part of your application may be grounds for not hiring you, or for firing you after you begin work. Also, you may be punished by fine or imprisonment (U.S. Code, title 18, section 1001).

_____
Signature

_____
Date signed

PRIVACY ACT

The Office of Personnel Management is authorized to rate applicants for Federal jobs under sections 1302, 3301, and 3304 of title 5 of the U.S. Code. Section 1104 of title 5 allows the Office of Personnel Management to authorize other Federal agencies to rate applicants for Federal jobs. We need the information you put on this form to see how well your education and work skills qualify you for a Federal job. We also need information on matters such as citizenship and military service to see whether you are affected by laws we must follow in deciding who may be employed by the Federal Government.

We must have your Social Security Number (SSN) to identify your records because other people may have the same name and birthdate. The Office of Personnel Management may also use your SSN to make requests for information about you from employers, schools, banks, and others who know you, but only as allowed by law or Presidential directive. The information we collect by using your SSN will be used for employment purposes and also for studies and statistics that will not identify you.

Information we have about you may also be given to Federal, State and local agencies for checking on law violations or for other lawful purposes. We may send your name and address to State and local Government agencies, Congressional and other public offices, and public international organizations, if they request names of people to consider for employment. We may also notify your school placement office if you are selected for a Federal job.

Giving us your SSN or any of the other information is voluntary. However, we cannot process your application, which is the first step toward getting a job, if you do not give us the information we request.

PUBLIC REPORTING BURDEN

The public reporting burden of information is estimated to vary from 20 minutes to 45 minutes to complete this form including time for reviewing instructions, gathering the data needed, and completing and reviewing entries. The average time to complete this form is 30 minutes. Send comments regarding the burden estimate or any other aspect of this collection of information, including suggestions for reducing this burden to: US Office of Personnel Management, Reports and Forms Management Office, 1900 E Street, NW, Washington, DC 20415.

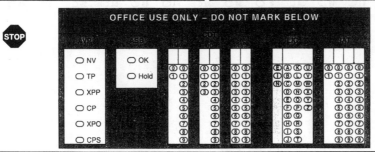

OFFICE USE ONLY – DO NOT MARK BELOW

STOP

4924858

APPENDIX D

Federal Occupational Information

This appendix reproduces interesting information on federal occupations:

☆ The first segment is from Dennis Damp's volume, *The Book of U.S. Government Jobs* (published by Bookhaven Press, 1996, and reprinted with permission).

☆ The second segment, called "Federal Occupational Groups," is reprinted from the OPM document EI-12 and lists the group and series numbers used to classify federal positions.

Book of U.S. Government Jobs Excerpt

by Dennis Damp

Federal workers are employed in almost every conceivable occupation. Approximately two out of every three federal workers are employed in *professional specialty, administrative support, or executive, administrative, and managerial occupations*. Secretaries are the largest administrative job series, employing over 100,000 workers.

College degrees are held by 37 percent of the total federal workforce. Certain jobs require a general four-year bachelor's degree and some positions require a specific concentration. A graduate or professional degree is necessary to enter some professional jobs. Since the Department of Defense employs over half of all non-postal federal workers, it employs some workers in almost every occupation.

Almost all professional specialty jobs require a four-year college degree or at least three years of non-clerical work experience. Some, such as engineers, physicians, and life and physical scientists, require a bachelor's or higher degree in a specific field of study. Engineers work in every department of the executive branch. Most are employed by the Department of Defense, a significant number work in the National Aeronautic and Space Administration (NASA) and the Department of Transportation.

Systems analysts and computer scientists are the largest professional specialty groups, employing about 50,000 workers throughout government. This specialty is needed to write computer programs, analyze data processing related problems, and to keep computer systems operating.

Almost 75 percent of all federal *health care workers* are employed by the Department of Veteran Affairs (VA) at one of their 172 VA hospitals, 233 outpatient clinics, and 120 nursing homes. The VA fills approximately 15,000 job vacancies each year due to retirements and to replace those who choose to leave. *Health Care Job Explosion! Careers In The 90's* is available from the publisher and it provides complete information on health care jobs in the public and private sectors. There are positions for audiologists, various technologists and technicians, medical records specialists, librarians, counselors, physicians, nurses, and dietitians. Other professionals include life scientists, including geologists, meteorologists, and physicists. The Department of Agriculture employs the majority of life scientists, but physical scientists are distributed evenly throughout the executive departments.

Executive, administrative, and managerial workers are primarily responsible for overseeing federal government operations. Because most people advance to these jobs from professional occupations, most have a bachelor's degree or at least three years of non-clerical work experience. Others provide management support. Accountants and auditors develop financial records and check operations for fraud and inefficiency. Inspectors and compliance officers enforce regulations, and tax examiners determine and collect taxes. In addition to the DOD, many of these workers are employed by the Department of the Treasury, and almost all of the tax examiners, inspectors, and compliance officers employed in the country work for the government. Other management support workers include purchasing agents, administrative officers, and management analysts.

Administrative support workers usually need only a high school diploma. They aid management staff and include secretaries, typists, word processors, and various clerks. All agencies hire administrative support workers.

Technicians and related support occupations aid professionals in research, analysis, or law enforcement, and often their tasks and skills are quite specialized. As a result, many technicians are required to have some vocational training or extensive work experience. Many have two-year associate degrees. Engineering technicians are most common. Others include health technicians, such as dental hygienists and radiologists, legal assistants, or air traffic controllers.

Most federal jobs in other occupations require no more than a high school degree, although some departments and agencies may prefer workers with some vocational training or previous experience. Over half of the precision production, craft, and repair occupations are mechanics, such as vehicle and mobile equipment mechanics, who fix and maintain all types of motor vehicles, aircraft, and heavy equipment, and electrical and electronic equipment operators, who repair electric items and telephone and cable television lines. Others include the construction trades, painters, plumbers, electricians, and other skilled trades.

Service workers are relatively scarce in the federal government. About half of all federal workers in these occupations are firefighters and police officers. The federal government employs relatively few workers in fabricator, operator, and laborer occupations; agriculture, forestry, fishing, and related occupations; and marketing and sales occupations.

Federal Occupational Groups

The U.S. Office of Personnel Management (OPM) has established occupational groups and series that are used to classify the work of positions. This classification is made in terms of the kind or subject matter of the work, the level of difficulty and responsibility, and the qualification requirements of the work. The classification is made to ensure similar treatment for positions within a class in personnel and pay administration.

Occupational groups have been established for both white collar and blue collar positions. The following is a list of occupational groups (bold type) and the specific series in each group. Use series "**9999**" for summer jobs.

WHITE COLLAR (General Schedule)

GS-0000	**MISCELLANEOUS OCCUPATIONS**
GS-0006	Correctional Institution Administration
GS-0007	Correctional Officer
GS-0011	Bond Sales Promotion
GS-0018	Safety and Occupational Health Mgt.
GS-0019	Safety Technician
GS-0020	Community Planning
GS-0021	Community Planning Technician
GS-0023	Outdoor Recreation Planning
GS-0025	Park Ranger
GS-0028	Environmental Protection Specialist
GS-0029	Environmental Protection Assistant
GS-0030	Sports Specialist
GS-0050	Funeral Directing
GS-0060	Chaplain
GS-0062	Clothing Design
GS-0072	Fingerprint Identification
GS-0080	Security Administration
GS-0081	Fire Protection and Prevention
GS-0082	United States Marshal
GS-0083	Police
GS-0084	Nuclear Materials Courier
GS-0085	Security Guard
GS-0086	Security Clerical and Assistance
GS-0090	Guide
GS-0095	Foreign Law Specialist
GS-0099	General Student Trainee
GS-0100	**SOCIAL SCIENCE, PSYCHOLOGY, AND WELFARE**
GS-0101	Social Science
GS-0102	Social Science Aid and Technician
GS-0105	Social Insurance Administration
GS-0106	Unemployment Insurance
GS-0110	Economist
GS-0119	Economics Assistant
GS-0120	Food Assistance Program Specialist
GS-0130	Foreign Affairs
GS-0131	International Relations
GS-0132	Intelligence
GS-0134	Intelligence Aid and Clerk
GS-0135	Foreign Agricultural Affairs
GS-0136	International Cooperation
GS-0140	Manpower Research and Analysis
GS-0142	Manpower Development
GS-0150	Geography
GS-0160	Civil Rights Analysis
GS-0170	History
GS-0180	Psychology
GS-0181	Psychology Aid and Technician
GS-0184	Sociology
GS-0185	Social Work
GS-0186	Social Services Aid and Assistant
GS-0187	Social Services
GS-0188	Recreation Specialist
GS-0189	Recreation Aid and Assistant
GS-0190	General Anthropology
GS-0193	Archeology
GS-0199	Social Science Student Trainee
GS-0200	**PERSONNEL MANAGEMENT AND INDUSTRIAL RELATIONS**
GS-0201	Personnel Management
GS-0203	Personnel Clerical and Assistance
GS-0204	Military Personnel Clerical & Technician
GS-0205	Military Personnel Management
GS-0212	Personnel Staffing
GS-0221	Position Classification
GS-0222	Occupational Analysis
GS-0223	Salary and Wage Administration
GS-0230	Employee Relations
GS-0233	Labor Relations
GS-0235	Employee Development
GS-0241	Mediation
GS-0243	Apprenticeship and Training

GS-0244	Labor Management Relations Examining	GS-0400	**BIOLOGICAL SCIENCES**
GS-0246	Contractor Industrial Relations	GS-0401	General Biological Science
GS-0249	Wage and Hour Compliance	GS-0403	Microbiology
GS-0260	Equal Employment Opportunity	GS-0404	Biological Technician
GS-0270	Federal Retirement Benefits	GS-0405	Agricultural Extension
GS-0299	Personnel Management Student Trainee	GS-0408	Ecology
		GS-0410	Zoology
GS-0300	**GENERAL ADMINISTRATION,**	GS-0413	Physiology
	CLERICAL, OFFICE SERVICES	GS-0414	Entomology
GS-0301	Miscellaneous Admin. and Program	GS-0415	Toxicology
GS-0302	Messenger	GS-0421	Plant Protection Technician
GS-0303	Miscellaneous Clerk and Assistant	GS-0430	Botany
GS-0304	Information Receptionist	GS-0434	Plant Pathology
GS-0305	Mail and File	GS-0435	Plant Physiology
GS-0309	Correspondence Clerk	GS-0436	Plant Protection and Quarantine
GS-0312	Clerk-OStenographer and Reporter	GS-0437	Horticulture
GS-0313	Work Unit Supervising	GS-0440	Genetics
GS-0318	Secretary	GS-0454	Range Conservation
GS-0319	Closed Microphone Reporting	GS-0455	Range Technician
GS-0322	Clerk-Typist	GS-0457	Soil Conservation
GS-0326	Office Automation Clerical	GS-0458	Soil Conservation Technician
GS-0332	Computer Operation	GS-0459	Irrigation System Operation
GS-0334	Computer Specialist	GS-0460	Forestry
GS-0335	Computer Clerk and Assistant	GS-0462	Forestry Technician
GS-0340	Program Management	GS-0470	Soil Science
GS-0341	Administrative Officer	GS-0471	Agronomy
GS-0342	Support Services Administration	GS-0475	Agricultural Management
GS-0343	Management and Program Analysis	GS-0480	General Fish & Wildlife Administration
GS-0344	Management Clerical and Assistance	GS-0482	Fishery Biology
GS-0346	Logistics Management	GS-0485	Wildlife Refuge Management
GS-0350	Equipment Operator	GS-0486	Wildlife Biology
GS-0351	Printing Clerical	GS-0487	Animal Science
GS-0356	Data Transcriber	GS-0493	Home Economics
GS-0357	Coding	GS-0499	Biological Science Student Trainee
GS-0359	Electric Accounting Machine Operation		
GS-0360	Equal Opportunity Compliance	**GS-0500**	**ACCOUNTING AND BUDGET**
GS-0361	Equal Opportunity Assistance	GS-0501	Financial Administration and Program
GS-0362	Elec. Accounting Machine Project Plan.	GS-0503	Financial Clerical and Assistance
GS-0382	Telephone Operating	GS-0505	Financial Management
GS-0385	Teletypist	GS-0510	Accounting
GS-0388	Cryptographic Equipment Operation	GS-0511	Auditing
GS-0389	Radio Operating	GS-0512	Internal Revenue Agent
GS-0390	Communications Relay Operation	GS-0525	Accounting Technician
GS-0391	Telecommunications	GS-0526	Tax Technician
GS-0392	General Communications	GS-0530	Cash Processing
GS-0394	Communications Clerical	GS-0540	Voucher Examining
GS-0399	Administration and Office Support	GS-0544	Civilian Pay
	Student Trainee	GS-0545	Military Pay
		GS-0560	Budget Analysis

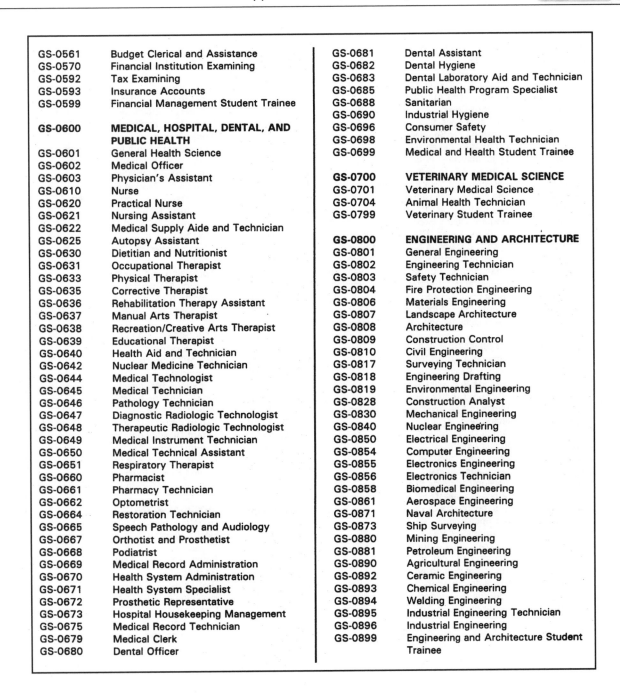

GS-0561	Budget Clerical and Assistance		GS-0681	Dental Assistant
GS-0570	Financial Institution Examining		GS-0682	Dental Hygiene
GS-0592	Tax Examining		GS-0683	Dental Laboratory Aid and Technician
GS-0593	Insurance Accounts		GS-0685	Public Health Program Specialist
GS-0599	Financial Management Student Trainee		GS-0688	Sanitarian
			GS-0690	Industrial Hygiene
GS-0600	**MEDICAL, HOSPITAL, DENTAL, AND**		GS-0696	Consumer Safety
	PUBLIC HEALTH		GS-0698	Environmental Health Technician
GS-0601	General Health Science		GS-0699	Medical and Health Student Trainee
GS-0602	Medical Officer			
GS-0603	Physician's Assistant		**GS-0700**	**VETERINARY MEDICAL SCIENCE**
GS-0610	Nurse		GS-0701	Veterinary Medical Science
GS-0620	Practical Nurse		GS-0704	Animal Health Technician
GS-0621	Nursing Assistant		GS-0799	Veterinary Student Trainee
GS-0622	Medical Supply Aide and Technician			
GS-0625	Autopsy Assistant		**GS-0800**	**ENGINEERING AND ARCHITECTURE**
GS-0630	Dietitian and Nutritionist		GS-0801	General Engineering
GS-0631	Occupational Therapist		GS-0802	Engineering Technician
GS-0633	Physical Therapist		GS-0803	Safety Technician
GS-0635	Corrective Therapist		GS-0804	Fire Protection Engineering
GS-0636	Rehabilitation Therapy Assistant		GS-0806	Materials Engineering
GS-0637	Manual Arts Therapist		GS-0807	Landscape Architecture
GS-0638	Recreation/Creative Arts Therapist		GS-0808	Architecture
GS-0639	Educational Therapist		GS-0809	Construction Control
GS-0640	Health Aid and Technician		GS-0810	Civil Engineering
GS-0642	Nuclear Medicine Technician		GS-0817	Surveying Technician
GS-0644	Medical Technologist		GS-0818	Engineering Drafting
GS-0645	Medical Technician		GS-0819	Environmental Engineering
GS-0646	Pathology Technician		GS-0828	Construction Analyst
GS-0647	Diagnostic Radiologic Technologist		GS-0830	Mechanical Engineering
GS-0648	Therapeutic Radiologic Technologist		GS-0840	Nuclear Engineering
GS-0649	Medical Instrument Technician		GS-0850	Electrical Engineering
GS-0650	Medical Technical Assistant		GS-0854	Computer Engineering
GS-0651	Respiratory Therapist		GS-0855	Electronics Engineering
GS-0660	Pharmacist		GS-0856	Electronics Technician
GS-0661	Pharmacy Technician		GS-0858	Biomedical Engineering
GS-0662	Optometrist		GS-0861	Aerospace Engineering
GS-0664	Restoration Technician		GS-0871	Naval Architecture
GS-0665	Speech Pathology and Audiology		GS-0873	Ship Surveying
GS-0667	Orthotist and Prosthetist		GS-0880	Mining Engineering
GS-0668	Podiatrist		GS-0881	Petroleum Engineering
GS-0669	Medical Record Administration		GS-0890	Agricultural Engineering
GS-0670	Health System Administration		GS-0892	Ceramic Engineering
GS-0671	Health System Specialist		GS-0893	Chemical Engineering
GS-0672	Prosthetic Representative		GS-0894	Welding Engineering
GS-0673	Hospital Housekeeping Management		GS-0895	Industrial Engineering Technician
GS-0675	Medical Record Technician		GS-0896	Industrial Engineering
GS-0679	Medical Clerk		GS-0899	Engineering and Architecture Student
GS-0680	Dental Officer			Trainee

GS-0900	**LEGAL AND KINDRED**	GS-1102	Contracting
GS-0904	Law Clerk	GS-1103	Industrial Property Management
GS-0905	General Attorney	GS-1104	Property Disposal
GS-0920	Estate Tax Examining	GS-1105	Purchasing
GS-0930	Hearings and Appeals	GS-1106	Procurement Clerical and Assistance
GS-0945	Clerk of Court	GS-1107	Property Disposal Clerical and Technical
GS-0950	Paralegal Specialist	GS-1130	Public Utilities Specialist
GS-0958	Pension Law Specialist	GS-1140	Trade Specialist
GS-0962	Contact Representative	GS-1144	Commissary Store Management
GS-0963	Legal Instruments Examining	GS-1145	Agricultural Program Specialist
GS-0965	Land Law Examining	GS-1146	Agricultural Marketing
GS-0967	Passport and Visa Examining	GS-1147	Agricultural Market Reporting
GS-0986	Legal Clerk and Technician	GS-1161	Crop Insurance Administration
GS-0987	Tax Law Specialist	GS-1162	Crop Insurance Underwriting
GS-0990	General Claims Examining	GS-1163	Insurance Examining
GS-0991	Workers' Comp. Claims Examining	GS-1165	Loan Specialist
GS-0992	Loss and Damage Claims Examining	GS-1169	Internal Revenue Officer
GS-0993	Social Insurance Claims Examining	GS-1170	Realty
GS-0994	Unemployment Comp. Claims Examiner	GS-1171	Appraising and Assessing
GS-0995	Dependents & Estates Claims Examiner	GS-1173	Housing Management
GS-0996	Veterans Claims Examining	GS-1176	Building Management
GS-0998	Claims Clerical Examining	GS-1199	Business and Industry Student Trainee
GS-0999	Legal Occupations Student Trainee		
		GS-1200	**COPYRIGHT, PATENT, AND**
GS-1000	**INFORMATION AND ARTS**		**TRADEMARK**
GS-1001	General Arts and Information	GS-1202	Patent Technician
GS-1008	Interior Design	GS-1210	Copyright
GS-1010	Exhibits Specialist	GS-1211	Copyright Technician
GS-1015	Museum Curator	GS-1220	Patent Administration
GS-1016	Museum Specialist and Technician	GS-1221	Patent Advisor
GS-1020	Illustrating	GS-1222	Patent Attorney
GS-1021	Office Drafting	GS-1223	Patent Classifying
GS-1035	Public Affairs	GS-1224	Patent Examining
GS-1040	Language Specialist	GS-1225	Patent Interference Examining
GS-1046	Language Clerical	GS-1226	Design Patent Examining
GS-1048	Foreign Language Broadcasting	GS-1299	Copyright and Patent Student Trainee
GS-1051	Music Specialist		
GS-1054	Theater Specialist	**GS-1300**	**PHYSICAL SCIENCES**
GS-1056	Art Specialist	GS-1301	General Physical Science
GS-1060	Photography	GS-1306	Health Physics
GS-1071	Audio-Visual Production	GS-1310	Physics
GS-1082	Writing and Editing	GS-1311	Physical Science Technician
GS-1083	Technical Writing and Editing	GS-1313	Geophysics
GS-1084	Visual Information	GS-1315	Hydrology
GS-1087	Editorial Assistance	GS-1316	Hydrologic Technician
GS-1099	Information and Arts Student Trainee	GS-1320	Chemistry
		GS-1321	Metallurgy
GS-1100	**BUSINESS AND INDUSTRY**	GS-1330	Astronomy and Space Science
GS-1101	General Business and Industry	GS-1340	Meteorology

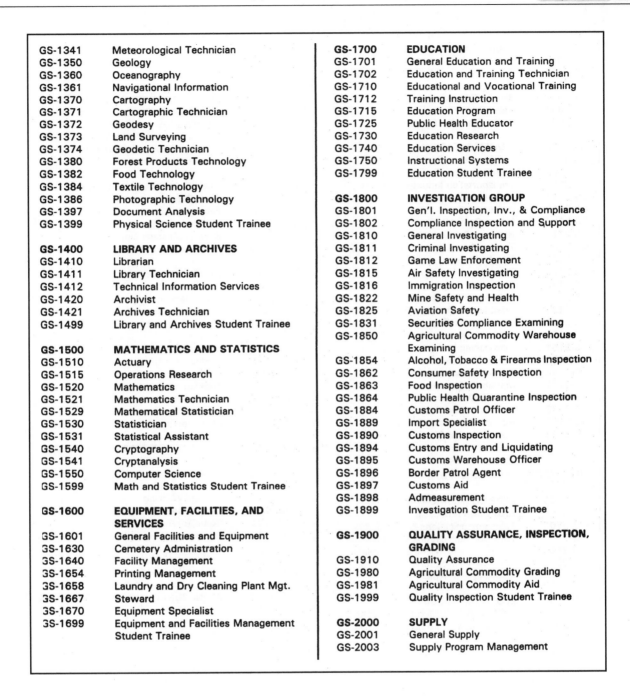

GS-1341	Meteorological Technician	
GS-1350	Geology	
GS-1360	Oceanography	
GS-1361	Navigational Information	
GS-1370	Cartography	
GS-1371	Cartographic Technician	
GS-1372	Geodesy	
GS-1373	Land Surveying	
GS-1374	Geodetic Technician	
GS-1380	Forest Products Technology	
GS-1382	Food Technology	
GS-1384	Textile Technology	
GS-1386	Photographic Technology	
GS-1397	Document Analysis	
GS-1399	Physical Science Student Trainee	
GS-1400	**LIBRARY AND ARCHIVES**	
GS-1410	Librarian	
GS-1411	Library Technician	
GS-1412	Technical Information Services	
GS-1420	Archivist	
GS-1421	Archives Technician	
GS-1499	Library and Archives Student Trainee	
GS-1500	**MATHEMATICS AND STATISTICS**	
GS-1510	Actuary	
GS-1515	Operations Research	
GS-1520	Mathematics	
GS-1521	Mathematics Technician	
GS-1529	Mathematical Statistician	
GS-1530	Statistician	
GS-1531	Statistical Assistant	
GS-1540	Cryptography	
GS-1541	Cryptanalysis	
GS-1550	Computer Science	
GS-1599	Math and Statistics Student Trainee	
GS-1600	**EQUIPMENT, FACILITIES, AND SERVICES**	
GS-1601	General Facilities and Equipment	
3S-1630	Cemetery Administration	
3S-1640	Facility Management	
3S-1654	Printing Management	
3S-1658	Laundry and Dry Cleaning Plant Mgt.	
3S-1667	Steward	
3S-1670	Equipment Specialist	
3S-1699	Equipment and Facilities Management Student Trainee	

GS-1700	**EDUCATION**
GS-1701	General Education and Training
GS-1702	Education and Training Technician
GS-1710	Educational and Vocational Training
GS-1712	Training Instruction
GS-1715	Education Program
GS-1725	Public Health Educator
GS-1730	Education Research
GS-1740	Education Services
GS-1750	Instructional Systems
GS-1799	Education Student Trainee
GS-1800	**INVESTIGATION GROUP**
GS-1801	Gen'l. Inspection, Inv., & Compliance
GS-1802	Compliance Inspection and Support
GS-1810	General Investigating
GS-1811	Criminal Investigating
GS-1812	Game Law Enforcement
GS-1815	Air Safety Investigating
GS-1816	Immigration Inspection
GS-1822	Mine Safety and Health
GS-1825	Aviation Safety
GS-1831	Securities Compliance Examining
GS-1850	Agricultural Commodity Warehouse Examining
GS-1854	Alcohol, Tobacco & Firearms Inspection
GS-1862	Consumer Safety Inspection
GS-1863	Food Inspection
GS-1864	Public Health Quarantine Inspection
GS-1884	Customs Patrol Officer
GS-1889	Import Specialist
GS-1890	Customs Inspection
GS-1894	Customs Entry and Liquidating
GS-1895	Customs Warehouse Officer
GS-1896	Border Patrol Agent
GS-1897	Customs Aid
GS-1898	Admeasurement
GS-1899	Investigation Student Trainee
GS-1900	**QUALITY ASSURANCE, INSPECTION, GRADING**
GS-1910	Quality Assurance
GS-1980	Agricultural Commodity Grading
GS-1981	Agricultural Commodity Aid
GS-1999	Quality Inspection Student Trainee
GS-2000	**SUPPLY**
GS-2001	General Supply
GS-2003	Supply Program Management

GS-2005	Supply Clerical and Technician
GS-2010	Inventory Management
GS-2030	Distribution Facilities and Storage Mgt.
GS-2032	Packaging
GS-2050	Supply Cataloging
GS-2091	Sales Store Clerical
GS-2099	Supply Student Trainee
GS-2100	**TRANSPORTATION**
GS-2101	Transportation Specialist
GS-2102	Transportation Clerk and Assistant
GS-2110	Transportation Industry Analysis
GS-2111	Transportation Rate & Tariff Examining
GS-2121	Railroad Safety
GS-2123	Motor Carrier Safety
GS-2125	Highway Safety
GS-2130	Traffic Management
GS-2131	Freight Rate
GS-2132	Travel
GS-2133	Passenger Rate
GS-2134	Shipment Clerical and Assistance
GS-2135	Tran. Loss & Damage Claims Examining
GS-2144	Cargo Scheduling
GS-2150	Transportation Operations
GS-2151	Dispatching
GS-2152	Air Traffic Control
GS-2154	Air Traffic Assistance
GS-2161	Marine Cargo
GS-2181	Aircraft Operation
GS-2183	Air Navigation
GS-2185	Aircrew Technician
GS-2199	Transportation Student Trainee

BLUE COLLAR* (Wage Grade)

WG-2500	**WIRE COMMUNICATIONS EQUIP. AND MAINTENANCE**
WG-2502	Telecommunications Mechanic
WG-2504	Wire Communications Cable Splicing
WG-2508	Comm. Line Installing and Repairing
WG-2511	Wire Communications Equipment Installing and Repairing
WG-2600	**ELECTRONIC EQUIPMENT INSTALLATION AND MAINTENANCE**
WG-2602	Electronic Measurement Equipment Mechanic
WG-2604	Electronics Mechanic

WG-2606	Electronic Industrial Controls Mechanic
WG-2608	Electronic Digital Computer Mechanic
WG-2610	Electronic Integrated Sys. Mechanic
WG-2800	**ELECTRICAL INSTALLATION AND MAINTENANCE**
WG-2805	Electrician
WG-2810	Electrician (High Voltage)
WG-2854	Electrical Equipment Repairing
WG-2892	Aircraft Electrician
WG-3100	**FABRIC AND LEATHER WORK**
WG-3103	Shoe Repairing
WG-3105	Fabric Working
WG-3106	Upholstering
WG-3111	Sewing Machine Operating
WG-3119	Broom and Brush Making
WG-3300	**INSTRUMENT WORK**
WG-3306	Optical Instrument Repairing
WG-3314	Instrument Making
WG-3359	Instrument Mechanic
WG-3364	Projection Equipment Repairing
WG-3400	**MACHINE TOOL WORK**
WG-3414	Machining
WG-3416	Toolmaking
WG-3417	Tool Grinding
WG-3422	Power Saw Operating
WG-3428	Die Sinking
WG-3431	Machine Tool Operating
WG-3500	**GENERAL SERVICES AND SUPPORT WORK**
WG-3502	Laboring
WG-3506	Summer Aid/Student Aid
WG-3508	Pipeline Working
WG-3511	Laboratory Working
WG-3513	Coin/Currency Checking
WG-3515	Laboratory Support Working
WG-3543	Stevedoring
WG-3546	Railroad Repairing
WG-3566	Custodial Working
WG-3600	**STRUCTURAL AND FINISHING WORK**
WG-3602	Cement Finishing
WG-3603	Masonry
WG-3604	Tile Setting
WG-3605	Plastering

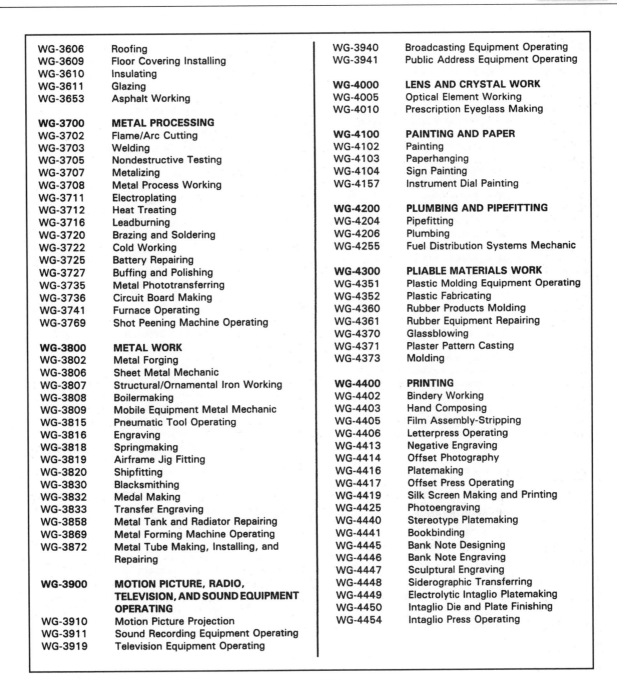

WG-3606	Roofing	
WG-3609	Floor Covering Installing	
WG-3610	Insulating	
WG-3611	Glazing	
WG-3653	Asphalt Working	

WG-3700 METAL PROCESSING

WG-3702	Flame/Arc Cutting
WG-3703	Welding
WG-3705	Nondestructive Testing
WG-3707	Metalizing
WG-3708	Metal Process Working
WG-3711	Electroplating
WG-3712	Heat Treating
WG-3716	Leadburning
WG-3720	Brazing and Soldering
WG-3722	Cold Working
WG-3725	Battery Repairing
WG-3727	Buffing and Polishing
WG-3735	Metal Phototransferring
WG-3736	Circuit Board Making
WG-3741	Furnace Operating
WG-3769	Shot Peening Machine Operating

WG-3800 METAL WORK

WG-3802	Metal Forging
WG-3806	Sheet Metal Mechanic
WG-3807	Structural/Ornamental Iron Working
WG-3808	Boilermaking
WG-3809	Mobile Equipment Metal Mechanic
WG-3815	Pneumatic Tool Operating
WG-3816	Engraving
WG-3818	Springmaking
WG-3819	Airframe Jig Fitting
WG-3820	Shipfitting
WG-3830	Blacksmithing
WG-3832	Medal Making
WG-3833	Transfer Engraving
WG-3858	Metal Tank and Radiator Repairing
WG-3869	Metal Forming Machine Operating
WG-3872	Metal Tube Making, Installing, and Repairing

WG-3900 MOTION PICTURE, RADIO, TELEVISION, AND SOUND EQUIPMENT OPERATING

WG-3910	Motion Picture Projection
WG-3911	Sound Recording Equipment Operating
WG-3919	Television Equipment Operating

WG-3940	Broadcasting Equipment Operating
WG-3941	Public Address Equipment Operating

WG-4000 LENS AND CRYSTAL WORK

WG-4005	Optical Element Working
WG-4010	Prescription Eyeglass Making

WG-4100 PAINTING AND PAPER

WG-4102	Painting
WG-4103	Paperhanging
WG-4104	Sign Painting
WG-4157	Instrument Dial Painting

WG-4200 PLUMBING AND PIPEFITTING

WG-4204	Pipefitting
WG-4206	Plumbing
WG-4255	Fuel Distribution Systems Mechanic

WG-4300 PLIABLE MATERIALS WORK

WG-4351	Plastic Molding Equipment Operating
WG-4352	Plastic Fabricating
WG-4360	Rubber Products Molding
WG-4361	Rubber Equipment Repairing
WG-4370	Glassblowing
WG-4371	Plaster Pattern Casting
WG-4373	Molding

WG-4400 PRINTING

WG-4402	Bindery Working
WG-4403	Hand Composing
WG-4405	Film Assembly-Stripping
WG-4406	Letterpress Operating
WG-4413	Negative Engraving
WG-4414	Offset Photography
WG-4416	Platemaking
WG-4417	Offset Press Operating
WG-4419	Silk Screen Making and Printing
WG-4425	Photoengraving
WG-4440	Stereotype Platemaking
WG-4441	Bookbinding
WG-4445	Bank Note Designing
WG-4446	Bank Note Engraving
WG-4447	Sculptural Engraving
WG-4448	Siderographic Transferring
WG-4449	Electrolytic Intaglio Platemaking
WG-4450	Intaglio Die and Plate Finishing
WG-4454	Intaglio Press Operating

WG-4600	**WOOD WORK**		WG-5026	Pest Controlling
WG-4602	Blocking and Bracing		WG-5031	Insects Production Working
WG-4604	Wood Working		WG-5034	Dairy Farming
WG-4605	Wood Crafting		WG-5035	Livestock Ranching/Wrangling
WG-4607	Carpentry		WG-5042	Tree Trimming and Removing
WG-4616	Patternmaking		WG-5048	Animal Caretaking
WG-4618	Woodworking Machine Operating			
WG-4639	Timber Working		**WG-5200**	**MISCELLANEOUS OCCUPATIONS**
WG-4654	Form Block Making		WG-5205	Gas and Radiation Detecting
			WG-5210	Rigging
WG-4700	**GENERAL MAINTENANCE AND**		WG-5220	Shipwright
	OPERATIONS WORK		WG-5221	Lofting
WG-4714	Model Making		WG-5235	Test Range Tracking
WG-4715	Exhibits Making/Modeling			
WG-4716	Railroad Car Repairing		**WG-5300**	**INDUSTRIAL EQUIPMENT**
WG-4717	Boat Building and Repairing			**MAINTENANCE**
WG-4737	General Equipment Mechanic		WG-5306	Air Conditioning Equipment Mechanic
WG-4741	General Equipment Operating		WG-5309	Heating & Boiler Plant Equip. Mechanic
WG-4742	Utility Systems Repairing-Operating		WG-5310	Kitchen/Bakery Equipment Repairing
WG-4745	Research Laboratory Mechanic		WG-5312	Sewing Machine Repairing
WG-4749	Maintenance Mechanic		WG-5313	Elevator Mechanic
WG-4754	Cemetery Caretaking		WG-5317	Laundry & Dry Cleaning Equip. Repairing
			WG-5318	Lock and Dam Repairing
WG-4800	**GENERAL EQUIPMENT MAINTENANCE**		WG-5323	Oiling and Greasing
WG-4804	Locksmithing		WG-5330	Printing Equipment Repairing
WG-4805	Medical Equipment Repairing		WG-5334	Marine Machinery Mechanic
WG-4806	Office Appliance Repairing		WG-5335	Wind Tunnel Mechanic
WG-4807	Chemical Equipment Repairing		WG-5341	Industrial Furnace Building and Repairing
WG-4808	Custodial Equipment Servicing		WG-5350	Production Machinery Mechanic
WG-4812	Saw Reconditioning		WG-5352	Industrial Equipment Mechanic
WG-4816	Protective and Safety Equipment		WG-5364	Door Systems Mechanic
	Fabricating and Repairing		WG-5365	Physiological Trainer Mechanic
WG-4818	Aircraft Survival and Flight Equipment		WG-5378	Powered Support Systems Mechanic
	Repairing		WG-5384	Gasdynamic Facility Installing
WG-4819	Bowling Equipment Repairing			and Repairing
WG-4820	Vending Machine Repairing			
WG-4839	Film Processing Equipment Repairing		**WG-5400**	**INDUSTRIAL EQUIPMENT OPERATING**
WG-4840	Tool and Equipment Repairing		WG-5402	Boiler Plant Operating
WG-4843	Navigation Aids Repairing		WG-5403	Incinerator Operating
WG-4844	Bicycle Repairing		WG-5406	Utility Systems Operating
WG-4845	Orthopedic Appliance Repairing		WG-5407	Electric Power Controlling
WG-4848	Mechanical Parts Repairing		WG-5408	Wastewater Treatment Plant Operating
WG-4850	Bearing Reconditioning		WG-5409	Water Treatment Plant Operating
WG-4851	Reclamation Working		WG-5413	Fuel Distribution System Operating
WG-4855	Domestic Appliance Repairing		WG-5414	Baling Machine Operating
			WG-5415	Air Conditioning Equipment Operating
WG-5000	**PLANT AND ANIMAL WORK**		WG-5419	Stationary-Engine Operating
WG-5002	Farming		WG-5423	Sandblasting
WG-5003	Gardening		WG-5424	Weighing Machine Operating

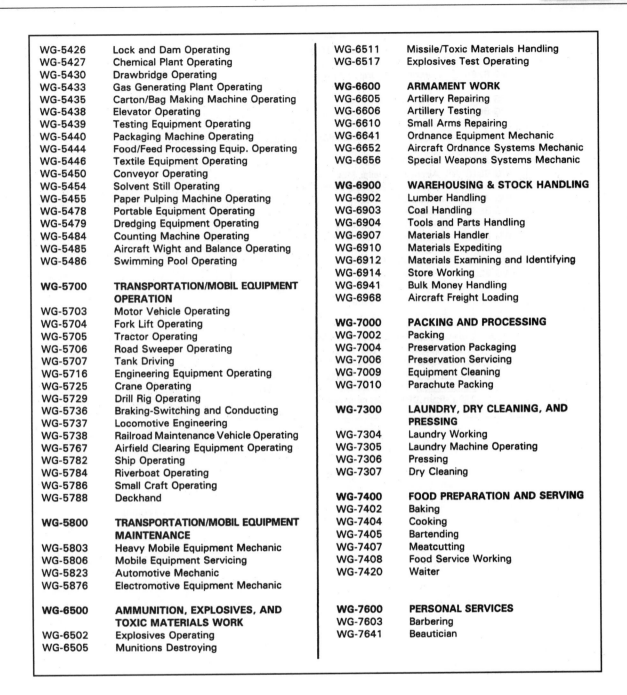

WG-5426	Lock and Dam Operating
WG-5427	Chemical Plant Operating
WG-5430	Drawbridge Operating
WG-5433	Gas Generating Plant Operating
WG-5435	Carton/Bag Making Machine Operating
WG-5438	Elevator Operating
WG-5439	Testing Equipment Operating
WG-5440	Packaging Machine Operating
WG-5444	Food/Feed Processing Equip. Operating
WG-5446	Textile Equipment Operating
WG-5450	Conveyor Operating
WG-5454	Solvent Still Operating
WG-5455	Paper Pulping Machine Operating
WG-5478	Portable Equipment Operating
WG-5479	Dredging Equipment Operating
WG-5484	Counting Machine Operating
WG-5485	Aircraft Wight and Balance Operating
WG-5486	Swimming Pool Operating

WG-5700   **TRANSPORTATION/MOBIL EQUIPMENT OPERATION**

WG-5703	Motor Vehicle Operating
WG-5704	Fork Lift Operating
WG-5705	Tractor Operating
WG-5706	Road Sweeper Operating
WG-5707	Tank Driving
WG-5716	Engineering Equipment Operating
WG-5725	Crane Operating
WG-5729	Drill Rig Operating
WG-5736	Braking-Switching and Conducting
WG-5737	Locomotive Engineering
WG-5738	Railroad Maintenance Vehicle Operating
WG-5767	Airfield Clearing Equipment Operating
WG-5782	Ship Operating
WG-5784	Riverboat Operating
WG-5786	Small Craft Operating
WG-5788	Deckhand

WG-5800   **TRANSPORTATION/MOBIL EQUIPMENT MAINTENANCE**

WG-5803	Heavy Mobile Equipment Mechanic
WG-5806	Mobile Equipment Servicing
WG-5823	Automotive Mechanic
WG-5876	Electromotive Equipment Mechanic

WG-6500   **AMMUNITION, EXPLOSIVES, AND TOXIC MATERIALS WORK**

WG-6502	Explosives Operating
WG-6505	Munitions Destroying
WG-6511	Missile/Toxic Materials Handling
WG-6517	Explosives Test Operating

WG-6600   **ARMAMENT WORK**

WG-6605	Artillery Repairing
WG-6606	Artillery Testing
WG-6610	Small Arms Repairing
WG-6641	Ordnance Equipment Mechanic
WG-6652	Aircraft Ordnance Systems Mechanic
WG-6656	Special Weapons Systems Mechanic

WG-6900   **WAREHOUSING & STOCK HANDLING**

WG-6902	Lumber Handling
WG-6903	Coal Handling
WG-6904	Tools and Parts Handling
WG-6907	Materials Handler
WG-6910	Materials Expediting
WG-6912	Materials Examining and Identifying
WG-6914	Store Working
WG-6941	Bulk Money Handling
WG-6968	Aircraft Freight Loading

WG-7000   **PACKING AND PROCESSING**

WG-7002	Packing
WG-7004	Preservation Packaging
WG-7006	Preservation Servicing
WG-7009	Equipment Cleaning
WG-7010	Parachute Packing

WG-7300   **LAUNDRY, DRY CLEANING, AND PRESSING**

WG-7304	Laundry Working
WG-7305	Laundry Machine Operating
WG-7306	Pressing
WG-7307	Dry Cleaning

WG-7400   **FOOD PREPARATION AND SERVING**

WG-7402	Baking
WG-7404	Cooking
WG-7405	Bartending
WG-7407	Meatcutting
WG-7408	Food Service Working
WG-7420	Waiter

WG-7600   **PERSONAL SERVICES**

WG-7603	Barbering
WG-7641	Beautician

WG-8200	FLUID SYSTEMS MAINTENANCE
WG-8255	Pneudraulic Systems Mechanic
WG-8268	Aircraft Pneudraulic Systems Mechanic
WG-8600	ENGINE OVERHAUL
WG-8602	Aircraft Engine Mechanic
WG-8610	Small Engine Mechanic
WG-8675	Liquid Fuel Rocket Engine Mechanic
WG-8800	AIRCRAFT OVERHAUL
WG-8810	Aircraft Propeller Mechanic
WG-8840	Aircraft Mechanical Parts Repairing
WG-8852	Aircraft Mechanic
WG-8862	Aircraft Attending
WG-8863	Aircraft Tire Mounting
WG-8882	Airframe Test Operating
WG-9000	FILM PROCESSING
WG-9003	Film Assembling and Repairing
WG-9004	Motion Picture Developing/Printing Machine Operating

* = Those occupational groups not listed have yet to be established. The data for Blue Collar occupational groups originated from the Job Grading System for Trades and Labor Occupations, Transmittal Sheet No. 68, May 1993, from OPM's Office of Classification.

APPENDIX E

Resumix Job Kits

Each federal agency that scans resumes publishes an instructional "job kit" explaining its scanning requirements. Scannable resumes are "read" by Resumix software, which extracts skills and other information. This appendix reproduces the job kits of the following three agencies:

☆ Human Resource Services Center, National Capital Region (This center services OSD, Defense Agencies, and DoD field activities.)

☆ Immigration and Naturalization Service (including a self-nomination form referred to earlier in the book)

☆ Central Intelligence Agency

For more information on writing a scannable Resumix resume, see Chapter 9.

HUMAN RESOURCE SERVICES CENTER
NATIONAL CAPITAL REGION
Servicing OSD, Defense Agencies & DoD Field Activities

CIVILIAN JOB KIT

IT IS IMPORTANT TO READ THESE INSTRUCTIONS COMPLETELY

BACKGROUND:

The National Capital Region (NCR) Human Resource Services Center (HRSC) is now using an automated system to fill vacancies. The patented artificial intelligence software reads information in your resume and extracts your skills and other significant information. **Why is this important to YOU?** With one properly prepared resume, the HRSC will consider all your skills for many jobs. You no longer have to submit a separate application for each vacancy! Once you are notified your resume is in our database, you self nominate yourself for vacancies for which you wish to be considered·   One-stop job shopping has never been easier. This automated system will accept applications through the HRSC web site. Resumes may also be submitted through the regular mail or E-mail. Preparing a resume is easy. Remember to focus on format and content. This job kit contains all the information you need to successfully complete your resume and apply for employment. **Only resumes will be accepted. The SF-171 and OF-612 will no longer be accepted.**

HOW THE AUTOMATED SYSTEM WORKS:

The computer "reads" your resume and identifies information such as your name, address, education, and unique skills. Summarize your most important skills first. You might list specific skills. For example, if you have office clerical experience, you might list skills such as proofing, word processing, secretarial, shorthand, mail, filing, typing, etc. Below the summary of skills, describe your work experience. (Refer to the sample resumes following these instructions.) List only the skills that you feel are relevant to your career.

WHO MAY APPLY:

- Resumes are being accepted for all vacancies filled by the NCR HRSC. Please refer to individual vacancy announcements for specific information on the area of consideration.
- NOTE: Current or former displaced employees who are eligible for consideration under the Interagency Career Transition Assistance Plan (ICTAP) will be provided priority consideration for those vacancies for which they are well-qualified within their commuting area. Candidates must submit proof of eligibility (as identified in 5 CFR 330.707 (2)) with their resume to receive this priority consideration. Contact your servicing agency for more information about the ICTAP program.

RESUME PREPARATION INSTRUCTIONS:

- The best method is to visit our web site at: http://www.hrsc.osd.mil/. Applicants will find our Resume Writer - a resume preparation program that will assist them in preparing their resume. The web site also allows applicants to submit their resume directly on line.

- If you do not have access to a browser, prepare the resume according to the format and sample in this job kit.

DO

- Follow all instructions <u>carefully</u> and <u>completely</u> (resumes will be scanned so this is important).
- Limit your resume to three pages. **Resumes that are longer will only have the first 3 pages scanned**.
- **TYPE** your resume, ensuring it is clear and legible. Typewriters or word processors may be used. <u>Handwritten resumes will NOT be accepted</u>. A typewritten original or a high quality photocopy is acceptable.
- Provide a laser printed original if possible. **Avoid** dot matrix printers, bubble jet printers, and low quality copies.
- Type with black ink on 8.5" x 11" white bond paper printed on one-side only.
- **E-mail** your resume to: **resume@hrsc.osd.mil** (Note: the word **"resume"** must be in the subject line of your E-mail message; include a string of 10 "@" symbols immediately before the start of your text; type your resume in the body of the E-mail message, do **not** send as an attachment) and remember to use hard returns at the end of each line; **or, Mail** your resume and all other documentation as required by the vacancy announcement unfolded in an envelope 9.5" x 12" or larger.
- Use a minimum margin of one (1) inch on all sides of your printed resume.
- Use standard business type fonts such as courier (10 to 12 point); or, times new roman, etc., in 12 point. A smaller or larger point will result in poor scanning and extraction.
- Use boldface and/or all capital letters for section headings as long as the letters do not touch each other.
- Include a summary of your job-related skills at the beginning of your resume after your name, address, and phone number. In the experience portion of your resume, describe in detail how these skills are/were used. Remember to type your name and social security number in the top left corner of each page of your resume.
- Proofread for any errors. Pay particular attention to spelling.
- Be specific when naming the computer software or types of equipment, etc., with which you have experience. (e.g., Microsoft Word, Lotus 1-2-3, Excel, computer-assisted design equipment, etc.)
- Describe your experience with specific words rather than vague descriptions.
- Be truthful! Falsification of your resume could result in termination of, or withdrawal of, an offer of Federal employment, and may be punishable by fine or imprisonment. **If selected, you will be required to sign a statement that all application materials are true, correct, complete, and made in good faith**.

DON'T

- Staple, fold, bind or punch holes in your resume.
- Use vertical or horizontal lines, graphics, or boxes.
- Use two-column format or resumes that look like newspapers.
- Use fancy treatments such as italics, underlining, shadows, or bullets.
- Use acronyms or abbreviations. Only use acronyms that are well established and commonly understood.
- Submit your resume on colored paper.
- Submit your resume as an attachment to an E-mail.
- Submit any documentation not specifically requested.

- Expect your resume or any documents submitted to be returned.

WHAT TO SUBMIT WHEN APPLYING:

- A properly prepared resume (<u>samples</u> included with this job kit).
- Any other documentation specifically required by the vacancy announcement.

HOW TO SUBMIT YOUR RESUME:

Use any one of the following methods to submit your resume:

1. Upload your resume on our web site at: <u>http://www.hrsc.osd.mil/</u>
2. E-mail to: <u>resume@hrsc.osd.mil</u> (Note: "resume" must be in the subject line; include a string of 10 "@" symbols immediately before the start of your text; type your resume in the body of your mail message, DO NOT send as an attachment.)
3. Or mail to:

   Resume
   Washington Headquarters Services
   NCR Human Resource Services Center
   5001 Eisenhower Avenue, Room 2E22
   Alexandria, VA 22333-0001
   NOTE: DO NOT FAX YOUR RESUME

HOW YOU WILL KNOW YOUR RESUME IS ACTIVE:

You will be notified within two weeks of receipt and disposition of your resume package. **You will not be considered for employment unless all information requested in this job kit is received and processed. RESUMES THAT ARE UNSCANNABLE AND/OR HANDWRITTEN WILL BE DESTROYED. Please note the 2 week resume processing period and the connection to the closing date of vacancies – get your resume in early.**

WHEN TO SUBMIT A NEW RESUME:

New resumes will be accepted at any time, however, updated resumes will only be processed on the first workday of each month. Hence, if your updated resume is received after the first workday, it will be updated only on the first workday of the succeeding month. This does not mean postmarked before the first workday of the month – the updated resume must be in the HRSC by COB prior to the first workday of the month. Revised resumes must be accompanied by a cover letter indicating the desire to replace the resume on file in the database. If you fail to provide the cover letter, the resume will be destroyed and you will be notified that you already have a resume on file. For updating resumes electronically submitted, this can be accomplished by providing this cover memo before the 10 "@" symbols.

GENERAL INFORMATION AND HELPFUL HINTS:

For ideas on where you might obtain INTERNET access, resume preparation assistance, or typing services, contact your state employment service, local schools, colleges, universities, public libraries, or look in the telephone book under Data Processing Services, Typing Services, etc. Newspapers often list these services in the classified section. You should bring a copy of this job kit with you. **The sender**

PRIVACY ACT INFORMATION

The Office of Personnel Management is authorized to rate applicants for Federal jobs under Sections 1302, 3301, and 3304 of Title 5 of the U.S. Code. Section 1104 of Title 5 allows the Office of Personnel Management to authorize other federal agencies to rate applicants for Federal jobs. We need the information you put on your resume and associated application forms to see how well your education and work skills qualify you for a Federal job. We also need information on matters such as citizenship and military service to see whether you are affected by laws we must follow in deciding who may be employed by the Federal Government.

We must have your Social Security Number (SSN) to keep your records straight because other people may have the same name and birthdate. The SSN has been used to keep records since 1943, when Executive Order 9397 asked agencies to do so. Giving us your SSN or any other information is voluntary. However, we cannot process your application if you do not give us the information we request.

ALL QUALIFIED RESUMES WILL RECEIVE CONSIDERATION FOR POSITION VACANCIES WITHOUT REGARD TO POLITICAL, RELIGIOUS, LABOR ORGANIZATION AFFILIATION OR NON-AFFILIATION, MARITAL STATUS, RACE, COLOR, SEX, NATIONAL ORIGIN, NON-DISQUALIFYING PHYSICAL HANDICAP, OR AGE. SELECTION SHALL BE BASED SOLELY ON JOB RELATED CRITERIA.

****

THE WASHINGTON HEADQUARTERS SERVICES NCR HRSC
IS AN EQUAL OPPORTUNITY EMPLOYER

IMMIGRATION AND NATURALIZATION SERVICE
STAFFING PILOT PROGRAM
JOB APPLICATION KIT

The Human Resource office is conducting a pilot project to test and evaluate a new software product called Resumix which automates the personnel staffing process.

> **_The instructions in this job application kit must be followed when applying for all announcements that are designated "Resumix Announcement"._**

The key points that affect the applicant are:

RESUMES ARE REQUIRED:

- Resumes are limited to 3 pages (one-sided). **NO other form of application will be accepted.**
- Resumes should discuss the applicant's overall education, work experience and background.
- Resumes must be typed and plainly formatted exactly as described in the job kit.
- Once in the database, a resume may be re-used for subsequent vacancies.

APPLY AS FOLLOWS:

- Submit a self-nomination form as well as the additional documentation specified in the vacancy announcement, in order to receive maximum consideration. A self-nomination and the additional documentation must be submitted for **each** vacancy announcement for which the applicant wishes consideration.
- All supplemental material must be identified with the applicant's name, social security number, and the vacancy announcement number.

INQUIRIES: phone: (202) 514-2530
cc: Mail: Resume-Questions
cc: Mail Bulletin Board: Resume Assistance

FOR MORE SPECIFIC DETAILS PLEASE READ THIS JOB APPLICATION KIT

TAKE A STEP INTO THE FUTURE—APPLY TO THE RESUMIX DATABASE

Version 1.0

What Is Resumix?

Resumix is an automated Human Skills Management system that uses state-of-the-art optical character recognition software, and a patented skill and education extraction system, to "read" your resume and extract information about you and your experience history. To be sure that you receive maximum consideration for vacancies, it's important to follow the instructions in this job kit in preparing and submitting your resume.

Resume Format

Since we are using an automated system, it is important that your resume be "machine readable" or "scannable". To maximize the computer's ability to read your resume, provide a clean, typed or computer-generated, spell-checked original and use standard size paper. (Hand-written resumes cannot be "read" by the computer and will **not** be accepted.) If you fail to follow the format suggested in this job kit, you risk losing consideration for placement because the computer may not properly extract your skills and/or other information. For best results:

- Use **white** 8 ½" X 11" paper, **printed on one-side** only.
- Summarize your skills at the beginning of your resume (See attached sample).
- Provide a **laser-printed** original, if possible. A typewritten original or a high-quality photocopy is acceptable. Do not submit resumes printed on dot-matrix printers.
- **Do not fold or staple** the resume.
- Use **standard typefaces** such as Helvetica, Arial, Optima, Universe, Times New Roman, Palatino, New Century Schoolbook, and Courier.
- Use a **font size of 12 to 14 points**.
- **Don't condense** spacing between letters.
- **Limit the use of boldface** or all capital letters to section headings only.
- **Do not use fancy font treatments** such as *italics*, underlining, shadows, and reverse (white letters on black background).
- **Do not use** vertical and horizontal **lines, graphics, and boxes**.
- **Do not use two-column format** or resumes that look like newspapers or newsletters.
- **List each telephone number on its own line**. Be sure to include all area codes and provide extensions when needed.

Resume Content

(Note: a sample resume appears following these instructions.) Include the following information on separate lines at the top of your resume (be sure to put your name at the top of each page):

- **Full Name** (First name, Middle Initial, Last Name)
- **Address**
  - Street address with apartment number if appropriate
  - City, state, zip code
- **Home telephone with Area Code**
- **Work telephone with Area Code**
- **Social Security Number**

SKILLS SUMMARY: Include a summary of all work-related skills you possess. Describe each skill (e.g. budget formulation, system design) in one or two words. List only the skills that are applicable to the occupations which meet your career goals and interests.

WORK EXPERIENCE: Be sure to include:
- Start and end dates (month/day/year)
- Hours worked per week, (month/day/year)
- Job Title
- Pay plan, series and grade (if Federal civilian position)
- Current salary (if non-Federal)
- If describing Federal civilian experience at different grade levels, include month, day and year promoted to each grade. [List the date of grade, not the date of your last with-grade (step) increase]
- Organization and address
- Supervisor's Name and telephone number
- Description of work performed

FORMAL EDUCATION: If a degree was competed (e.g. AA, BA, MA) list:
- Degree
- Major, minor
- College or University
- Year of Degree

If your highest level of education was high school, list either highest grade completed, year graduated, or date you were awarded a GED. If you have some college level work, list the number of years and semester/quarter hours completed.

SPECIALIZED TRAINING, LICENSES, and CERTIFICATES: List specialized training, including government-provided training, licenses and certificates that are pertinent to your career goals. Include month and year of training and date awarded the licenses or certificates. List typing speed if applying for a position requiring typing or office automation proficiency.

AWARDS: List any appropriate awards received.

Writing Your Resume

To receive maximum consideration of your knowledge, skills and abilities, please provide a comprehensive resume. The comprehensive resume is used primarily to get your skills and other pertinent information into the Resumix database. You should focus your resume on defining and identifying all the key skills you possess, which support your qualifications for all possible positions in which you are interested. Things you should remember:
- Place **your name at the top of <u>each</u> page**;
- Use simple sentences and **emphasize nouns instead of verbs**. Instead of describing what your **responsibilities** were, describe exactly what you **did**, and any tools, software, equipment, etc. you used.
- Don't say: "Performed the full range of project management duties for a new information system."

- Do say: "Used Microsoft Project to develop timelines, prepared budget requests, hired staff, selected vendors, negotiated contracts, and designed and implemented new client-server information system."
- Don't say: "Responsible for administrative and computer support in a publishing firm."
- Do say: "Used Microsoft Word, Excel, PowerPoint and Access in support of a large publishing firm. Familiar with many operating systems, including DOS, Windows 3.1 and Windows 95, Macintosh. Used Adobe Photo shop."
- Avoid using jargon, abbreviations, and acronyms, and spell out at least once the meanings of any abbreviations and acronyms you use. Remember that ADA may mean American Dental Association, Americans with Disabilities Act, or Ada, Oklahoma.
- Use the active voice! It is better to write, "I managed a project team", rather than "The project team was managed by me."
- Be concise! Don't repeat skills over and over. There is no extra credit. Once a skill such as "management" is pointed out, it is not necessary to restate the skill. The system will only give you credit once.
- Keep it simple! Use plain language whenever possible. The information system, the personnelist or the hiring manager may not understand what you are trying to communicate if you use very obscure words or phrases.

General Information

The Office of Personnel Management is authorized to rate applicants for Federal jobs under Sections 1302, 3301, and 3304 of Title 5 of the U. S. Code. Section 1104 of title 5 allows the Office of Personnel Management to authorize other federal agencies to rate applicants for Federal jobs. We need the information you put on your resume and associated application forms to see how well your education and work skills qualify you for a Federal job. We also need information on matters such as citizenship and military service to see whether laws we must follow in deciding whom the Federal Government employs affect you.

We must have your Social Security Number (SSN) to keep your records organized properly. Other people may have your same name and birth date. The SSN has been used to keep records since 1943, when Executive Order 9397 asked agencies to do so. Giving us your SSN or any other information is voluntary. However, we cannot process your application if you do not give us the information we request.

All qualified resumes will receive consideration for position vacancies without regard to political, religious, labor organization affiliation or non-affiliation, marital status, race, color, sex, national origin, non-disqualifying physical handicap, or age. Selection shall be based solely on job related criteria.

SAMPLE RESUME

Susan A. Sample
3270 House Road
City, VA 99999-9999
Home Telephone: (703) 555-1234
Work Telephone: (202) 555-1234
E-mail address: ssample@location.gov
SSN: 123-45-6789

SKILLS SUMMARY
Systems Analysis, Software Testing, Software Design, Visual C++, Oracle, Database
Administration, Database Design. Novell LAN certified. MS Office.

WORK EXPERIENCE
1 /1/95 to Present. 40 hours per week. Computer Specialist, GS-334-13, Department of the
Treasury, Washington DC, 20002-2000, Ms. Mary Smith, (202) 555-6731.

I analyze system requirements, prepare work plans, conduct design reviews, and perform
validation testing, draft documentation and install software systems. I designed and directed
development of a five-year information system plan and supervised the maintenance of the
supporting mainframe DB2 database.

9/1/89 to 12/31/94. 40 hours per week. Computer Specialist, GS-334-7 9/89 to 9/90, GS-9 9/90
to 9/91, GS-11 9/91 to 9/92, GS-12 9/92 to 9/94, Department of Justice, Washington DC, 20003-
2003, Mr. Robert Jones, (202) 555-4321.

I managed a project to improve software development procedures and design. I developed
implementation procedures for DOJ software engineering improvement requirements. I also
maintained databases and processed output requests including files, reports, and graphics.

7/15/88 to 8/31/89. 40 hours per week. Computer Programmer, ABC Systems, Fairfax, VA
21212-2121, Mr. William Brown, (202) 555-4343.

I developed various automated software packages using Visual C++. Functional areas covered
were Federal supply system and accounting management automation.

FORMAL EDUCATION
B. S., Computer Science, Minor in Mathematics, George Washington University, 1988.
M. S., Information Management, American University, 1994

OTHER
Certificate in Project Management, George Mason University Adult Education Program, 1996

AWARDS: Superior Performance Award 1996

Updating Your Resume

We will maintain only <u>one</u> resume at a time on you in the Resumix database. If you submit a new resume, it will replace the old resume and all information previously extracted on your skills and experience. Do not submit a new resume unless your experience and/or skills have changed in some way. Use the attached resume update form to tell us about changes in your address, phone numbers, education, etc.

> **All Information Included In Resumes Is Subject To Review And Verification.**
> **Authorized Legal And Regulatory Penalties May Be Imposed On Employees**
> **Submitting False Information.**

How Do I Apply For Jobs?

Applicants must have a resume on file in the database. **Only resumes of 3 pages** *(one-sided)* **or less will be accepted for vacancies covered by the pilot.** One comprehensive resume will allow you to be considered for <u>many</u> jobs. You no longer are required to submit a separate application for each vacancy. If you are an INS employee, your resume will remain active as long as you are an employee of the Service. If you are not an INS employee, your resume will be maintained for a period of **6 months.** After that, external applicants may either request an extension for an additional 6 months of consideration or submit a new resume. Once you have a resume on file, you need only to watch for announcements and self-nominate yourself when you are interested in being considered for a particular position. Vacancies that are part of the pilot will be identified in the job announcement.

You may submit your resume by hand delivery or U.S. Mail. INS employees may also submit their resume by cc-mail. If you choose to cc-mail your resume, be sure to follow the directions in this job kit. Any supporting documentation required in the announcement, such as a proof of veterans preference, should be faxed, mailed, or hand-delivered. All supplemental documents should be clearly marked with the applicant's name, social security number, and vacancy announcement number. Each applicant will be notified the resume has been received. **Be advised: resumes and supporting documentation will not be returned.**

> **Forms such as the OF-612 or SF-171 will not be accepted for consideration**
> **for INS Pilot vacancies.**

Self-Nomination

If you have been notified that we have your resume on file, use the attached self-nomination sheet to nominate yourself for any announced vacancy. As with resumes, you may hand carry or use fax, U.S. Mail, (or cc-mail for INS employees), to submit the form. See the directions below. <u>Self-nomination forms must be received by 5:00 PM on the closing date of the announcement, unless otherwise stated in the job vacancy announcement.</u> Applicants who are or have worked for the Federal government in a civilian capacity **must** submit a copy of their **most recent** performance appraisal and a copy of the **latest** SF-50 which reflects service on a career or career conditional appointment with the Federal government with the self-nomination form.

Supporting Documentation

Applicants who are current and former Federal employees **must** submit a copy of their **most recent** performance appraisal and the **latest** SF-50 which reflects service on a career or career conditional appointment with the Federal government with the resume and each self-nomination form.

If you are not an INS employee, include the following information in your resume:
(Failure to provide this information may result in the loss of appropriate consideration.)
- Social Security Number
- Date of Birth
- Highest permanent grade held in the competitive service, the pay plan, and number of months at that grade level.
- Your current or prior employment status: (i.e., career, career-conditional, temporary, excepted).

Military service and veterans' preference: (Only if the vacancy announcement requires it.) You must provide copies of appropriate DD-214 so we may verify this information. In addition, if you claim a compensable disability or other 10-point preference you must provide a SF-15, "Application for 10 point Veterans' Preference," and the supporting documentation listed on the reverse of the SF-15.

If you were discharged from the military service under honorable conditions, list **dates and branches** of service for all active duty military service. If all your active military duty was after October 14, 1976, list the **full names and dates** of all campaign badges or expeditionary medals you received or were entitled to receive. If you retired from the military, indicate the rank at which you retired and your date of retirement.

If you claim veterans' preference, indicate eligibility:
- **TP** - 5 Point,
- **CP** - 10 Point Compensable,
- **XP** - 10 Point Other,
- **XP** - 10 Point Disability,
- **CPS** - 10 Point Compensably Disabled 30% or more.

Citizenship: Indicate if you are an U. S. citizen.

Race/Ethnicity/Sex: (Note: This is optional information collected for statistical purposes only and is not used as a factor for employment consideration.) Providing this information is voluntary. No individual personnel selections are made based on this information. **(Failure to provide this information will not affect your chances for employment.)** Please identify one of the following:
Race/Ethnicity:
- American Indian or Alaskan Native
- Asian or Pacific Islander
- Black, not of Hispanic origin
- White, not of Hispanic origin
- Hispanic
  Sex. Indicate if you are (M)ale or (F)emale

SAMPLE ADDITIONAL INFORMATION SHEET
(For External to INS Applicants)

Susan A. Sample

SSN: 111-11-1111 (SSN)
DOB: 11-23-55 (DOB)
Highest Permanent Grade Held: GS-13, 18 months
Status: Career Conditional
Veteran Preference Claimed: XP 10 point other, widow of a 10-point veteran.
U. S. Citizen
Race: American Indian
Sex: Female

INS SELF-NOMINATION

NAME: _____

ADDRESS: _____

SOCIAL SECURITY NUMBER: _____

WORK PHONE: _____

HIGHEST PERMANENT PAY PLAN, SERIES, AND GRADE:_____

ANNOUNCEMENT NUMBER: _____

GRADE LEVELS FOR WHICH YOU WISH TO BE CONSIDERED: _____

IF THE VACANCY ANNOUNCEMENT IS FOR "ALL SOURCES", AND YOU ARE A STATUS CANDIDATE, DO YOU WANT TO BE CONSIDERED BOTH THROUGH MERIT PROMOTION AND COMPETITIVE PROCEDURES? YES_____   NO _____

If you are a current or former Federal government employee, please submit a copy of your most recent performance appraisal and a copy of a SF-50 which document or verifies service on a career or career conditional appointment with the Federal government.

Your self-nomination may be hand delivered, faxed, sent by cc-mail or mailed. Please be sure that your nomination is submitted in accordance with the instructions in the vacancy announcement. Follow the same instructions for any other supplemental documentation required in the announcement. **FAILURE TO PROVIDE ALL REQUIRED INFORMATION MAY RESULT IN YOUR LOSING CONSIDERATION FOR A VACANCY.**

 You may send your resume or self-nomination by any of the following methods:

By U.S. Post Office Mail: Human Resources Division
                                    Recruitment and Employment Services
                                    Immigration and Naturalization Service
                                    P.O. Box 50129
                                    Washington DC 20091

By Internal Mail or Hand Delivery to: Human Resources Division,
                                                Recruitment & Employment Services, Room 2038
                                                425 I Street, NW, Washington, D.C. 20536
By Fax to: 202-305-7817   Attn: Resumix

For cc-Mail Delivery of Resumes send to: Resume - (*INS Employees Only*)

- Put the words "Resumix resume" in the subject line;
- Prepare your resume as a Microsoft Word file and attach it to your message; or prepare the resume as an ASCII text file, and paste into the body of the message.   Be sure to include the vacancy announcement number if you are applying for a current job opening.

For cc: Mail Delivery of Self Nominations Send to: Resume-Self Nomination

- Put the words "Resumix Self Nomination " in the subject line

ITEM/DATA UPDATE SHEET

DO NOT USE THIS INFORMATION SHEET TO UPDATE YOUR EXPERIENCE OR SKILLS

NAME:

_____

ADDRESS:

_____

_____

WORK PHONE: _____

Identify the item/data that needs to be changed in your resume. Be specific.

(This form should not be used to update experiences or skills. Use it to update education or training, address, phone numbers, etc.)

FROM: _____

_____

TO: _____

_____

_____

You may send your Item/Data Update Sheet to us by any of the following methods:

By Internal Mail or Hand Delivery to: **Human Resources Division,**
Recruitment & Employment Services, Room 2038
425 I Street, NW, Washington, D.C. 20536
Attn: Resumix

By cc-Mail to: Resume (*INS Employees Only*)

- Put the words "Resume Update" in the subject line;

Or By Fax to: 202-305-7817

CENTRAL INTELLIGENCE AGENCY JOB KIT
AND RESUME PREPARATION GUIDE

INTRODUCTION

This guide is intended to help you prepare your resume for employment consideration by the Central Intelligence Agency (CIA). The CIA has implemented new human resources technology that will process your resume electronically. To receive employment consideration by the Agency, you should read this guide carefully and follow all instructions when preparing your resume.

OUR ORGANIZATION

Established in 1947, the Central Intelligence Agency is a key element of the U. S. Government Intelligence Community. The Agency advises the National Security Council; collects, evaluates, and produces finished reports on foreign intelligence; and provides senior U. S. policymakers with the most accurate, comprehensive, and objective intelligence. Additional information about the Agency can be found on the CIA's home page at http://www.odci.gov/cia.

HOW WE FILL JOBS

The Agency now uses an automated system to identify candidates for employment consideration. This patented software uses the latest in scanning technology, optical character recognition, and artificial intelligence to process your resume and extract information about your skills and other significant information. We will only accept resumes of one to two pages, prepared in accordance with the instructions in this job kit. **DO NOT submit an application form, such as an SF-171 or OF-612.**

HOW THE AUTOMATED SYSTEM WORKS

The computer "reads" your resume and identifies information such as your name, address, education, and skills. **Summarize your most important skills** as shown in the resume example contained in this kit. List specific skills that are relevant to your career goals.

WHO MAY APPLY

U.S. citizenship is required. You can access employment opportunity information through the CIA home page at www.odci.gov/cia, or through the On-Line Career Center at www.occ.com. The CIA is an equal opportunity employer.

RESUME PREPARATION INSTRUCTIONS

Since the Agency uses an automated system that scans your resume, it is important your resume be "machine readable" or "scannable." To maximize the computer's ability to read your resume, provide a typed original and use the standard 8.5″ by 11″ page size.

In addition, follow all instructions below carefully and completely.

- Limit your resume to no more than two pages.
- Provide a laser quality printed or typed original. A high quality photocopy is acceptable. **Do not** submit a dot matrix printed or a low quality photocopied resume.
- Use black ink on 8.5″ x 11″ **white** bond paper printed on one side.
- Use a minimum margin of one inch on all sides.
- Use plain type fonts. Helvetica or Arial scan well; you may also use Courier or Times New Roman. Use a font size of at least 10; 12 to 14 is preferable. **Do not** use fancy fonts such as italics, underlining, shadows, vertical or horizontal lines, graphics, boxes, two-column format, or a column set that looks like newspaper column.
- Include your name at the top of both pages.
- Include a summary of your job-related skills at the beginning of your resume after your education. In the experience portion describe how you have used those skills.
- Be specific when naming the computer software or types of equipment, etc., with which you have experience.
- Mail your resume **unfolded** in an envelope 9.5″ x 12″ or larger, with the word "RESUME" printed on the lower left-hand corner of the envelope. **Do not** staple, fold, bind or punch holes in your resume.

HOW TO SUBMIT YOUR RESUME

In order to ensure that your resume reaches the right place within the Agency, it is **essential** that you use the address on the advertisement to which you are responding. The address includes information that will direct your application to the Directorate or Office in which you are interested. If you are not responding to a specific advertisement, please send your resume to:

Recruitment Center
P.O. Box 12727
Arlington, Virginia 22209-8727

Your cover letter should indicate the position or work for which you are applying, whether you are willing to travel overseas, an acceptable salary range, and any other information you feel will make you a competitive candidate. We will respond within 45 days to those deemed to be of further interest.

RESUME FORMAT

Name: Prefix, first, middle, last name, title
Citizenship
* SSN

Mailing Address
City, State, Zip Code
Home Telephone Number
Work Telephone Number

Education:
Include in this portion the name and address of your high school and the year you graduated or were awarded a GED. Use the following format to describe your college, university, or technical school qualifications: degree awarded (e.g., AA, BS, MA), major field of study, name and address of college, university or technical school, year awarded or anticipated, and GPA.

Skill Summary:
Include a summary of the skills you possess. Describe these skills in one or two words. It is not necessary to list all of your skills. Emphasize those skills most relevant to your career goals.

Foreign Languages:
Include any foreign languages you speak as well as your level of proficiency in speaking and reading, using the descriptors: slight, proficient, or fluent.

Foreign Area Knowledge:
Include specific area of expertise e.g., politics; economics.

List any countries in which you have traveled or gained substantive knowledge as a result of residence, work, assignment, or study. Do not include travel as a tourist.

Experience:
    Start and end dates
    Full or part time
    Position title
    Annual salary
    Name and address of employer
    Name and telephone number of supervisor
    Major duties and accomplishments
    For military service, list branch or service; rank,
      grade, or rate; military occupational
      specialty and title; and dates of service.
    Reason for leaving.

Other:
List any other job-related information (e.g., licenses/certificates, including date certified and state, awards, professional associations).

* Your Social Security number is needed to keep accurate records, because other people may have the same name. Executive Order 9397 also asks Federal agencies to use this number to help identify individuals in agency records. Although disclosure of your Social Security number is not mandatory, failure to do so could cause delay in processing your resume.

EXAMPLE

Name: Mr. John Q. Doe Jr.
Citizenship: U.S.
SSN: xxx-xx-xxxx

23 Elm Street Apt #321
Any City, VA 99999
Home Telephone Number: (202) 555-4567
Work Telephone Number: (703) 555-1234

Education:
Any High School, Any City, VA 22203, 1981
BS, Computer Science/Accounting, Any University, Any City, VA 20194, 1985, GPA 3.5.

Skill Summary:
Systems analysis, software testing, software design, database administration, and database design.

Foreign Languages:
Mandarin Chinese: proficient speaking; slight reading.

Foreign Area Knowledge:
East Asia politics.

Foreign Travel:
China, study Aug 94-Jun 95; Mali, work/residence 93-95.

Experience:
September 1990 to present. Full time. Computer Specialist, $38,990, Any Company, Fairfax VA 22213, Ms. Jane Doe, (703) 555-9999. Assisted with project improvement of software development procedures and design for large-scale accounting systems. Maintained databases and processed output requests including files, reports, and graphics. Also developed database development training course for new employees of the company.

Other:
Certified Public Accountant, 1992;
Any Honor Society, 1985

APPENDIX F

Agency Employment Information

Many government agencies provide career information for students who are researching internships and occupations. Information from the following agencies is reprinted in this appendix:

☆ Environmental Protection Agency

☆ NASA

☆ Bureau of Alcohol, Tobacco, and Firearms

☆ Department of State (partial reprint of an internship application)

CAREERS

✓SCIENTISTS:
- ◆ Biologist
- ◆ Microbiologist
- ◆ Ecologist
- ◆ Toxicologist
- ◆ Environmental
- ◆ Hydrologist
- ◆ Chemist
- ◆ Geologist

✓ENGINEERS:
- ◆ Environmental
- ◆ Mechanical
- ◆ Chemical

✓ENVIRONMENTAL
  PROTECTION
  SPECIALISTS
(EPS)

✓ADMINISTRATIVE:
- ◆ Accountant
- ◆ Human Resources
- ◆ Computer
- ◆ Economist
- ◆ Program Analyst
- ◆ Admin. Specialist
- ◆ Budget Analyst
- ◆ Public Affairs
- ◆ Contracts

✓LEGAL:
- ◆ Attorney
- ◆ Paralegal

✓ENFORCEMENT:
- ◆ Investigator

✓SUPPORT:
- ◆ Office
- ◆ Technical

ENVIRONMENTAL CAREERS
United States Environmental Protection Agency (EPA)

Our Mission:

*"...to protect
human health and
to safeguard the natural
environment, air, water, and
land upon which life depends."*

About the EPA

Founded in 1970, EPA is a dynamic organization which brings together people from diverse backgrounds and is dedicated to improving and preserving the quality of public health and the environment. Our nation's continuing growth and prosperity depends on our ability to find effective, creative solutions to public health and environmental problems and make them work.

EPA Headquarters, located in Washington, D.C., is divided into thirteen offices. These offices develop environmental policies, set standards, manage complex research and development programs, and develop regulations for pesticides, toxic substances, hazardous waste, air, radiation, and water. Many EPA offices are dedicated to the development of new technologies to prevent pollution. Ten Regional Offices administer EPA programs and provide technical assistance to state, local and tribal governments. Several nationwide research laboratories perform risk assessment and risk management to remediate environmental and human health problems.

EPA offers a comprehensive compensation package. A competitive salary combined with a full menu of benefits makes working at EPA as fulfilling and rewarding as possible. Employee benefits include Quality of Worklife Programs, such as Career and Personal Development programs, Flexible Work Hours and Alternative Work Schedules.

Common EPA Career Groups

EPA employs almost 17,500 people with approximately 38% located in Washington, D.C. and 62% in regional offices and research laboratories. The chart below describes the major career groups at EPA; the side bar to the left lists the most typical fields within those groups.

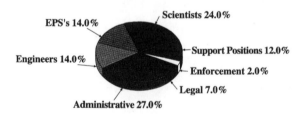

Special Student Opportunities

Student Career Experience Program - Gain valuable work experience directly related to your academic field of study while you are in school. You must be enrolled at least part-time and maintain a good academic standing.

Outstanding Scholar - A special hiring authority for entry-level administrative positions. You must graduate with a GPA of 3.45 or higher for all undergraduate course work, OR graduate in the upper 10% of your class or major university subdivision.

Presidential Management Intern (PMI) Program - Targeted towards graduate students completing or expecting to complete a master's or doctoral-level degree during the current academic year. You must be nominated for the PMI program by the dean, director, or chairperson of your graduate academic program.

For Job Information

For specific information about the career fields you are interested in and their qualification requirements, contact one of the EPA Human Resources Offices listed below:

United States Environmental Protection Agency Human Resources Offices			
Ann Arbor, MI	(313) 668-4220	Las Vegas, NV: (Includes Washington, DC; Montgomery, AL)	(702) 798-2401
Atlanta, GA	(404) 562-8182	New York, NY	(212) 637-3550
Boston, MA	(617) 565-3714	Philadelphia, PA	(215) 566-5240
Chicago, IL	(312) 353-2027	Research Triangle Park (RTP), NC: (Includes Duluth, MN; Gulf Breeze, FL; Narragansett, RI; Athens, GA; Corvallis, OR; Las Vegas, NV)	(919) 541-3072
Cincinnati, OH (Includes Ada, OK; Edison, NJ; RTP, NC)	(513) 569-7801	San Francisco, CA	(415) 744-1300
Dallas, TX	(214) 665-6563	Seattle, WA	(206) 553-2959
Denver, CO	(303) 312-6190	Washington, DC	(202) 260-6000
Kansas City, KS	(913) 551-7041		

Joblines & Internet Addresses

For current EPA vacancies you can use the following sources:

Office of Personnel Management (OPM) Homepage: www.usajobs.opm.gov.
EPA Homepage: www.epa.gov.

EPA Locations with jobline numbers:

Boston, MA:	(617) 565-3719	San Francisco, CA:	(415) 744-1111
Seattle, WA:	(206) 553-1240	RTP, NC:	(919) 541-3014
Kansas City, KS:	(913) 551-7068	Cincinnati, OH:	(513) 569-7840
Denver, CO:	(303) 312-6259	Washington, D.C.	(202) 260-6000

Career America Connection: (912) 757-3000
Automated Telephone System: (912) 757-3000 or TDD (912) 744-2299

All applicants for Federal employment receive consideration without regard to race, religion, color, national origin, sex, political affiliation, age (with authorized exceptions), sexual orientation, or any other non-meritorious factors. U.S. Citizenship is required.

STUDENT EMPLOYMENT

A Quick Guide to Student Employment Programs at NASA Ames Research Center

There are 9 different student employment programs available at NASA Ames Research Center. This Guide summarizes each program and lists a number to contact for further information.

High School Programs

❖ *SHARP (Summer High School Apprenticeship Research Program)*

SHARP is designed to provide research work experience for underrepresented high school juniors. Applicants must be U.S. citizens residing within commuting distance of NASA Ames Research Center. This is an 8-week summer program. The application deadline is March 1 of each year.
Contact: **Brenda Collins at (650) 604-3540.**

❖ *Space and Biology Research Program*

This program provides an opportunity for high school seniors to do science and engineering work at NASA Ames. We do not accept applications directly, but solicit nominations of one candidate per school from the local high schools. This is a volunteer program, and students work 6-8 hours per week.
Contact: **Tom Clausen at (650) 604-5544.**

❖ *Student Temporary Experience*

Ames serves as a model employer in providing training and work opportunities. These employees must be over 16 years old, U.S. citizens, and at least half-time students (high school or college).
Contact: **Patricia Powell at (650) 604-6988.**

College Programs

❖ *Student Career Experience Program*

The SCEP/COOP Program provides paid work experiences for undergraduate and graduate students who attend accredited universities. There is both a full-time and part-time SCEP/COOP Program available to meet individual needs. Students are U.S. citizens studying Electrical, Mechanical, or Aerospace Engineering; Computer Science; Physics; Math; or Business Administration.
Contact: **Patricia Powell at (650) 604-6988.**

❖ *Student Temporary Experience Program*

Ames serves as a model employer in providing training and work opportunities. These employees must be over 16 years old, U.S. citizens, and at least half-time students (high school or college).
Contact: **Patricia Powell at (650) 604-6988.**

Higher Education

❖ *Summer Faculty Fellowship Program*

This 10-week summer program is conducted in conjunction with Stanford University and is designed to offer selected college and university faculty members an opportunity to enhance their career development in the engineering and science disciplines. Each Fellow works with a Center colleague on a project of mutual interest.
Contact: **Marilyn Jackson at (650) 604-6937.**

❖ *Graduate Student Researchers Program*

These fellowship programs are designed to increase the supply of highly trained scientists and engineers to meet the continuing needs of the national aerospace program. Students have an opportunity to conduct their thesis research in conjunction with a NASA technical monitor for up to three years.
Contact: **Marilyn Jackson at (650) 604-6937.**

❖ *National Research Council Resident Research Associateship Program (NRCs)*

The NRC Program provides postdoctoral scientists and engineers of unusual promise with opportunities to conduct their own research which is intended to contribute to the research effort of Ames Research Center. Applications are accepted on a continuing basis and must be received by January 15, April 15, and August 15 for reviews in February, June, and October.
Contact: **Marilyn Jackson at (650) 604-6937.**

❖ *Graduate Degrees for Minorities in Engineering (GEM)*

The purpose of the GEM program is to provide opportunities for minority students to obtain master's and doctorate degrees in engineering, and doctorate degrees in science through a program of paid summer engineering internships and financial aid. Eligibility requirements include U.S. citizenship and ethnic identity of American Indian, Black American, Mexican American, or Puerto Rican; Ames sponsors 4–8 GEM Fellows each summer. Applicants must complete a master's degree in three semesters.
Contact: **Patricia Powell at (650) 604-6988.**

The TDD Number for Employment Information is (650) 604-4584

For more information on Ames Research Center check out our Web home page at: http://www.arc.nasa.gov

BUREAU OF ALCOHOL, TOBACCO AND FIREARMS	FACT SHEET		
EMPLOYMENT BRANCH	**HOT LINE** 202-927-8423	**TDD** 202-927-8423	**INTERNET** *www.atf.treas.gov*

Outstanding Scholars

What is the Outstanding Scholar Program?

The Outstanding Scholar Program is a special hiring authority established for entry-level administrative positions at the GS-5 and GS-7 grade levels. The Outstanding Scholar Program is authorized under the terms of a consent decree (Luevano vs. Newman) and can only be used for the specific series and job titles listed on the reverse side of this information sheet. It is not applicable for other entry-level professional jobs such as accountants, engineers, physical science careers, or jobs in the biological sciences or mathematics. The Outstanding Scholar Program is also not applicable at grades below GS-5 or above GS-7.

If you meet the requirements below, you may be offered a direct appointment by a Federal agency without having to go through the normal competitive hiring procedures. The direct appointment process cuts through all of the red tape and can save you weeks of time.

Requirements For the Outstanding Scholar Program

To qualify for consideration, you must be a college graduate and have maintained a grade-point average (GPA) of 3.45 or better on a 4.0 scale for all undergraduate course work, or have graduated in the upper 10 percent of your class or major university subdivision.

A college degree in any major is qualifying for most of the career fields covered by the Outstanding Scholar Program. A few, however, require some course work in subjects related to the job. You may apply a few months before graduation, but you must have the GPA or class standing at such time as you are offered a job.

How to Apply as an Outstanding Scholar

You should contact Personnel Offices of Federal agencies directly to inquire about their hiring needs. Send a resume or the Optional Application for Federal employment (OF 612), attach a transcript and a cover letter identifying yourself as an Outstanding Scholar applicant. Frequently, Federal recruiters will visit college campuses, giving you an additional opportunity to make contact.

Bureau of Alcohol, Tobacco & Firearms

RECRUITMENT REGISTRATION FORM

Recruitment Site:	Date:

Name: _____

SSN: _____ **(Optional)**

Address: _____

_____

Day Time Telephone No.: _____ **/Evening Telephone No.:** _____

High School Graduate: YES OR NO. If yes, give month/year _____

College/University Graduate: YES OR NO. If yes, list school(s):

_____

_____

Undergraduate Major: _____ **Grade Point Avg. :** _____
Type of Degree: _____ **Date of Graduation:** _____

Appointment Availability:

☐ Permanent	☐ Temporary	☐ Summer	☐ Student Programs

Area(s) of Interest:
(Check all that apply)

_____ Special Agent	_____ Inspector
_____ Chemist	_____ Contract Specialist
_____ Computer Specialist	_____ Clerical Support
_____ Management/Administrative	

Are you available for travel? YES OR NO. If so, how often? Explain.
(example 2 weeks per month, etc.)
_____

Are you willing to relocate? YES OR NO. If yes, list geographic locations of interest:
_____

STUDENT INTERN PROGRAM

The Most Interesting Work...
In The World

1997 - 1998

United States
Department
of State

INTERNSHIP
APPLICATION
DEADLINES

Applications must be *postmarked* or *hand delivered* by the applicable deadline below:

SUMMER INTERNSHIP - NOVEMBER 1
FALL INTERNSHIP - MARCH 1
SPRING INTERNSHIP - JULY 1

The Department of State is committed to equal opportunity and fair and equitable treatment of all without regard to race, color, national origin, sex, religion, age, sexual orientation, disabling condition, political affiliation, marital status, or prior statutory, constitutionally protected activity.

Federal Recycling Program
Printed on Recycled Paper

INTRODUCTION

The U. S. Department of State is the official international relations arm of the President of the United States and is the oldest executive department of the Federal Government. It is responsible for carrying out U.S. foreign policy and for maintaining diplomatic relations with other countries throughout the world.

The Department of State annually sponsors internships in which highly qualified college or university junior, senior, and graduate students have the opportunity to gain firsthand knowledge of American foreign affairs. These internships are open **only** to American citizens who are currently-enrolled, and are full-time and part-time students in accredited educational institutions who will return to school immediately following the internship.

Numerous internships are located at the Department of State in Washington, D.C., but we have had an increasing number of openings at various embassies and consulates overseas, at the U.S. Mission to the United Nations in New York, and at several locations in the U.S. with the Office of Foreign Missions. Depending upon the skill needs of the Department, interns are assigned para-professional duties which may include research, report writing, correspondence, information systems, analysis of international issues, and assistance in cases related to domestic and international law. Most interns are unpaid.

INTERNSHIP OBJECTIVES:

- To encourage students to consider careers in foreign affairs;

- To provide students with valuable work experience in a foreign affairs agency; and

- To aid the Department in achieving its mission.

ELIGIBILITY

To be eligible for an internship, a student must:

- Be a continuing college or university junior, senior, or graduate student. An applicant is considered a junior if he/she will have completed all sophomore credits (60 or more semester hours or 90 quarter hours) by the time the internship begins and will be entering at least the junior year immediately following completion of the internship; *****

- Be a U.S. citizen; and

- Be in good academic standing in an accredited institution.

In accordance with the Federal Equal Opportunity Recruitment Program, the Department encourages women and minority students with an interest in foreign affairs to apply for these positions.

Students must be available to begin their internship within the timetable described on page 6 (Interns Enter on Duty) and work a minimum of 10 weeks.

* IMPORTANT: If you are applying for an internship after receiving an undergraduate degree, you must indicate in your Statement of Interest and on the Employment Data Form that you will be a continuing student immediately upon completion of your internship. **If this is not indicated,** it will be assumed that you are not a continuing student and your application will not be considered. Proof of acceptance into a graduate school may be required.

APPENDIX G

Guide to Senior Executive Service Qualifications

The following information is reprinted from the OPM's 1998 instructional booklet, *Guide to Senior Executive Service Qualifications*. Refer to Chapter 11 for more information on applying for the SES.

Introduction

As we move into the 21st century, Government executives face special challenges. They must be visionary leaders with a strong commitment to public service. They must be able to apply "people skills" to motivate their employees, build partnerships, and communicate with their customers. Finally, they need solid management skills in order to produce optimum results with limited resources.

The Office of Personnel Management helps make sure the Government selects strong leaders by developing the core qualifications used to test new career appointees to the Senior Executive Service (SES) and by administering peer review boards which evaluate whether candidates possess these essential leadership qualifications. The Executive Core Qualifications (ECQ's) and the underlying competencies described in this publication were issued in September 1997. The new ECQ's are based on extensive research of the attributes of successful executives in both the private and public sectors; they are a collaboration, reflecting the best thinking of many senior executives and associations, as well as agency human resources professionals.

Replacing the ECQ's described in the August 1994 issue of *Guide to SES Qualifications*, the new ECQ's are:

- Leading Change
- Leading People
- Results Driven
- Business Acumen
- Building Coalitions/Communication

Senior Executive Service candidates will find this publication useful as they assess and describe their executive qualifications, in preparation for review by selection officials.

In addition to helping applicants, the *Guide* will be useful to individuals charged with reviewing executive qualifications, including agency personnel and executive development specialists and members of agency Executive Resources Boards.

Additional information about the SES is available in *The Senior Executive Service*, which summarizes how the SES operates, and *Federal Executives and Managers: Critical Resources in Review*, which provides an update on SES positions, incumbents, and activities.

Current vacancies at departments and agencies appear in the Governmentwide automated employment information system:

World Wide
Web Site . . . . http://www.usajobs.opm.gov

Electronic Bulletin
Board System . . . . (912) 757-3100
(computer)

By telephone . . . . (912) 757-3000

Touch Screen Kiosks . . Located at Office of Personnel Management offices and some Federal buildings

Internet to USAJOBS Bulletin Board System:

Telnet. . . . . . . fjob.opm.gov

FTP . . . . ftp.fjob.opm.gov

Executive Qualifications

The law requires that the *executive qualifications* of each new career appointee to the Senior Executive Service (SES) be certified by an independent Qualifications Review Board based on criteria established by the Office of Personnel Management (OPM). The Executive Core Qualifications (ECQ's) describe the leadership skills needed to succeed in the SES; they also reinforce the concept of an "SES corporate culture." This concept holds that the Government needs executives who can provide strategic leadership and whose commitment to public policy and administration transcends their commitment to a specific agency mission or an individual profession.

Executives with a "corporate" view of Government share values that are grounded in the fundamental Government ideals of the Constitution: they embrace the dynamics of American Democracy, an approach to governance that provides a continuing vehicle for change within the Federal Government.

OPM has identified five fundamental executive qualifications. The ECQ's were designed to assess executive experience and potential—not technical expertise. They measure whether an individual has the broad executive skills needed to succeed in a variety of SES positions—not whether he or she is the most superior candidate for a particular position. (The latter determination is made by the employing agency.)

Successful performance in the SES requires competence in each ECQ. The ECQ's are interdependent; successful executives bring all five to bear when providing service to the Nation.

Executive Core Qualifications:

1. Leading Change

The ability to develop and implement an organizational vision which integrates key national and program goals, priorities, values, and other factors. Inherent to it is the ability to balance change and continuity—to continually strive to improve customer service and program performance within the basic Government framework, to create a work environment that encourages creative thinking, and to maintain focus, intensity, and persistence, even under adversity.

2. Leading People

The ability to design and implement strategies which maximize employee potential and foster high ethical standards in meeting the organization's vision, mission, and goals.

3. Results Driven

The ability to stress accountability and continuous improvement, to make timely and effective decisions, and to produce results through strategic planning and the implementation and evaluation of programs and policies.

4. Business Acumen

The ability to acquire and administer human, financial, material, and information resources in a manner which instills public trust and accomplishes the organization's mission, and to use new technology to enhance decision making.

5. Building Coalitions/Communication

The ability to explain, advocate, and express facts and ideas in a convincing manner, and negotiate with individuals and groups internally and externally. It also involves the ability to develop an expansive professional network with other organizations, and to identify the internal and external politics that impact the work of the organization.

Key Characteristics and Leadership Competencies

To write an effective Senior Executive Service (SES) application, candidates need to understand the relationship between Key Characteristics and Leadership Competencies.

Key Characteristics are the activities or behaviors associated with the Executive Core Qualifications (ECQ's). Candidates should use these as guideposts as they describe relevant experience. This experience may be reflected through professional and volunteer work, education and training, awards, and other accomplishments, in addition to Federal Government service. Candidates do not need to address all of the Key Characteristics under each ECQ. The goal is to show an overall record of the knowledges, skills, and abilities needed to succeed in the SES.

Leadership Competencies, shown in Appendix A, are the personal and professional attributes that are critical to successful performance in the SES. They are based on extensive research of Government and private sector executives and input from agency Senior Executives and human resources managers. A well-prepared ECQ statement reflects the underlying Leadership Competencies (e.g., "Leading Change" reflects creativity and innovation, continual learning, external awareness, etc.) Experience and training that strengthen these Leadership Competencies will enhance a candidate's overall qualifications for the SES.

Merit Competition

Initial career appointments to the Senior Executive Service (SES) must be based on merit competition. The law (5 U.S.C. 3393) requires agencies to establish an Executive Resources Board to conduct the merit staffing process. Within this framework, an agency has considerable flexibility in structuring the SES merit staffing process to meet its unique needs. Generally, this process includes preliminary review of applications by a personnel specialist, rating and ranking of applicants by a panel with in-depth knowledge of the job's requirements, evaluation of each candidate's qualifications by an Executive Resources Board, and making recommendations to the appointing authority.

After the agency merit staffing process is completed and the appointing authority has selected the candidate he or she believes is best qualified for the position, the agency forwards the candidate's application to the Office of Personnel Management (OPM) for consideration by a Qualifications Review Board.

SES Merit Staffing Process

1. Agency advertises the position through the Governmentwide automated employment information system for a minimum of 14 days. The area of consideration is:

   – Qualified Federal Employees Only (only current Federal employees may apply); or

   – All Qualified Persons (anyone may apply).

2. Candidates submit their applications to the agency.

3. Agency rating panel reviews and ranks candidates.

4. Agency Executive Resources Board recommends the best qualified candidates to the selecting official.

5. Selecting official makes a choice and certifies that the candidate meets both the technical and executive qualifications (ECQ's) for the position.

6. Agency submits candidate's application package to an OPM-administered Qualifications Review Board (QRB) for certification of executive qualifications.

7. Following QRB certification, agency appoints the candidate to the SES position.

Qualifications Review Board Certification

The Office of Personnel Management convenes weekly Qualifications Review Boards (QRB's) to provide an independent peer review of applications for initial career appointment to the Senior Executive Service. The Board consists of three executives; at least two members must be career appointees. Board members review each application and decide if the candidate's experience meets the Executive Core Qualifications (ECQ's) requirements. The QRB does not rate, rank, or compare the candidate's qualifications against those of other candidates. Rather, Board members judge the overall scope, quality, and depth of a candidate's executive qualifications within the context of the five ECQ's.

QRB Certification Based on Announcement of a Specific Vacancy:

Criterion A—Demonstrated executive experience.

Candidates must demonstrate executive experience in all five ECQ's. While they don't need to have in-depth experience in each Key Characteristic to demonstrate possession of an ECQ, their applications should reflect an overall record of the knowledges, skills, and abilities necessary to succeed in the SES. This record may include professional and volunteer experience, education, training, and awards, in addition to Federal experience.

QRB members review each candidate's resume or Federal application form, executive qualifications statement, and other documents provided by the agency.

Criterion C—Possession of special or unique qualities which indicate a likelihood of executive success.

The candidate must possess special or unique qualifications which support the ability to perform the duties of the position and the potential to quickly acquire full competence in the ECQ's (e.g., an individual who is exceptionally familiar with an agency's programs through high-level staff experience, or who has had a significant impact on the highest policy levels of the agency). Criterion C

cases are very rare and appropriate only when exceptional candidates with demonstrated experience are not available.

QRB members review several documents for each candidate:

- an evaluation of the candidate's background as related to the ECQ's;
- at least one written reference by someone familiar with the candidate's managerial qualifications; and
- an Individual Development Plan (IDP) that includes developmental assignments and/or formal training, focused on the specific ECQ's that need to be enhanced.

The IDP must show the training and development the candidate will receive following appointment.

QRB Certification Based on Completion of a Candidate Development Program:

Criterion B—Successful participation in an Office of Personnel Management-approved Candidate Development Program (CDP).

Candidates who compete Governmentwide for participation in a CDP and successfully complete the program are eligible for non-competitive appointment to the Senior Executive Service (SES). In some cases, CDP openings are announced within a single agency rather than Governmentwide; these graduates must compete for SES positions. Either way, CDP graduates are not entitled to placement in the SES.

The agency's Executive Resources Board chair must certify that the candidate has successfully completed all CDP activities. OPM staff and an "ad hoc" Qualifications Review Board (QRB) review each candidate's training and developmental experience to assure that it provides the basis for certification of executive qualifications. QRB members assume that if the candidate has completed all CDP requirements, then he or she possesses the executive qualifications for initial career appointment to the SES.

Writing Executive Qualifications Statements

The key to a well-written qualifications statement is to give readers—executive resources staff, rating and selecting officials, and Qualifications Review Board (QRB) members—specific information about your achievements. Be sure to include professional and volunteer experience, education, training, and awards that demonstrate your skills in a particular Executive Core Qualification (ECQ).

Begin your ECQ statement with a brief summary of your executive experience. Then use the following approach to describe your accomplishments.

Challenge–Context–Action–Result Model

An ECQ statement may include one or more examples of relevant experience. The number of examples is not as important as assuring that your experience matches the ECQ criteria. Use the Key Characteristics as guideposts as you describe the challenges you have faced in your career. Keep in mind that the QRB is looking for specific challenges, actions and results.

Follow this model in writing your qualifications statements.

Challenge. Describe a specific problem or goal.

Context. Talk about the individuals and groups you worked with, and/or the environment in which you worked, to tackle a particular challenge (e.g., clients, co-workers, members of Congress, shrinking budget, low morale).

Action. Discuss the specific actions you took to address a challenge.

Result. Give specific examples of the results of your actions. These accomplishments demonstrate the quality and effectiveness of your leadership skills.

Other Suggestions

- Use clear, concise statements (1 – 1½ pages for each ECQ) written in the first person.
- Spell out all acronyms.
- Describe recent education and training that enhanced your skills in a particular ECQ.
- Include non-Federal experience (e.g., private sector, volunteer and professional organizations) if it demonstrates executive qualifications.
- Don't forget to include special assignments (e.g., details, task forces, committees) if they are relevant to an Executive Core Qualification (ECQ).
- Avoid statements that describe your personal beliefs or philosophies; focus on specific challenges and results.
- Include awards that relate specifically to an ECQ.
- If possible, quantify/qualify your accomplishments.

Examples of Qualifications Statements

The following examples illustrate good qualifications statements for Senior Executive Service candidates being certified under *Criterion A*, demonstrated executive experience. They include examples of private sector and volunteer work in addition to State and Federal Government experience.

The examples feature the Challenge-Context-Action-Result (CCAR) model. One of these four words appears after select sentences in the examples to show how the model works. Candidates should keep the CCAR model in mind as they write their qualifications statements but they should not annotate these statements with "Challenge," "Context," "Action," or "Result."

In short, good qualifications statements:

- Use the Challenge-Context-Action-Result model;

- Include specific examples of experience; and

- Focus on results.

These examples, from actual Qualifications Review Board cases, have been modified to protect the privacy of the SES candidates.

ECQ 1

Leading Change

This core qualification encompasses the ability to develop and implement an organizational vision which integrates key national and program goals, priorities, values, and other factors. Inherent to it is the ability to balance change and continuity—to continually strive to improve customer service and program performance within the basic Government framework, to create a work environment that encourages creative thinking, and to maintain focus, intensity and persistence, even under adversity.

Key Characteristics:

a. Exercising leadership and motivating managers to incorporate vision, strategic planning, and elements of quality management into the full range of the organization's activities; encouraging creative thinking and innovation; influencing others toward a spirit of service; designing and implementing new or cutting edge programs/processes.

b. Identifying and integrating key issues affecting the organization, including political, economic, social, technological, and administrative factors.

c. Understanding the roles and relationships of the components of the national policy making and implementation process, including the President, political appointees, Congress, the judiciary, State and local governments, and interest groups; formulat-

ing effective strategies to balance those interests consistent with the business of the organization.

d. Being open to change and new information; managing ambiguity; adapting behavior and work methods in response to new information, changing conditions, or unexpected obstacles; adjusting rapidly to new situations warranting attention and resolution.

e. Displaying a high level of initiative, effort, and commitment to public service; being proactive and achievement-oriented; being self-motivated; pursuing self-development; seeking feedback from others and opportunities to master new knowledge.

f. Dealing effectively with pressure; maintaining focus and intensity and remaining persistent, even under adversity; recovering quickly from setbacks.

Leadership Competencies

Continual Learning

Creativity & Innovation

External Awareness

Flexibility

Resilience

Service Motivation

Strategic Thinking

Vision

Example: Leading Change

Unlike traditional career paths, where one position leads naturally to the other, I have followed a course in which a combination of factors have led me to envision and launch novel and non-traditional enterprises. The most important illustration of this core competency is my work as a pioneer in the field of technology transfer.

Technology transfer—the successful commercialization of inventions and innovations that arise from the not-for-profit sector—was virtually unknown 15 years ago. Indeed, the notion of promoting collaborations between scientists in Federal laboratories or academia and their industrial counterparts was an anathema. Common wisdom dictated that technology transfer was doomed to fail, even if legislation was enacted to encourage such interaction. *(Context)* A handful saw it differently. I was among them.

I shared this vision with the top administrators of two research campuses. I met weekly with these officials and successfully argued that a Center for Technology and Development (CTD) should be created and given responsibility for all patenting and licensing activities. *(Challenge)* My vision for the CTD, including its mission, policies, and administrative structure, was adopted on both campuses. I proposed, lobbied for, and succeeded in including the phrase "transfer of knowledge and technology" as part of the new mission statement for the campuses, making technology transfer a sanctioned university activity. *(Action)*

My ability to communicate my expectations of the CTD as an economic engine for the State allowed me to garner the support of the local business community. *(Context)* The community rallied and provided the CTD with counsel on legal, technical, market, and economic development issues *pro bono*. Their backing was key in obtaining support from the State Legislature. Within 6 months, I had established the CTD as an important member of the technology transfer community and assembled strong networks with national and international

biotechnology and pharmaceutical companies, venture firms, investors, and service providers. These networks have proven vital to this day. *(Result)*

Later in my career, I moved from the academic world to the Federal Government as head of the Office of Technology (OT). This office was created to implement the requirements of the Federal Technology Transfer Act. The OT is charged with the successful and appropriate commercialization of technology developed in Federal Laboratories. *(Challenge)* With an annual operating budget of $5 million, patent prosecution expenditures of over $7.5 million and a royalty revenue stream of $30 million, the OT is, arguably, the largest and most influential not-for-profit technology transfer operation in the world.

When I was recruited to head the Office of Technology (OT) it was fighting for survival, plagued with tremendous unrest as to the direction and future of technology transfer. There was widespread discontent with the performance of the OT, giving rise to numerous investigations and the need to address 75 Corrective Actions. The OT was viewed with suspicion and concern by insiders and outsiders, It was clear something had to change. *(Context)*

In my first staff meeting, I set forth my vision for the OT. I embarked on a process of evaluation and strategic planning for every unit, gathering advice from staff at all levels within the organization. Working together, we wrote a new mission statement, established policies and procedures, reorganized the Office, appointed key personnel, reassigned some staff members, and opened an important dialogue with our customers to assess their needs and requirements. *(Action)*

Under my leadership the OT's performance has improved dramatically. Productivity has increased by 40 percent and is at an all-time high. In the last fiscal year, we have signed a record number of license agreements, reached a record level of royalty income, patented important new technologies, and systematically reviewed our portfolio to eliminate obsolete cases. From a management perspective, the OT has accomplished a remarkable turnaround. We have attracted and hired competent and energetic staff, and they are working as a cohesive group. The OT has successfully completed all but two of the 75 Corrective Actions. Most pre-existing EEO and personnel grievances have been resolved, and employee morale has improved significantly. In short, the OT is a well-run, proactive and productive organization. *(Result)*

Example: Leading Change

As Chief, Office of Security, I led the reinvention of my agency's personnel security process. *(Challenge)* In the year before my appointment, a high-profile hiring initiative had resulted in about 400 selections. However, at the end of the fiscal year the agency had not made any appointments because of a backlog in security investigations. By the time the security clearances were processed, the best candidates had found other jobs. *(Context)* I was asked to serve as Security Chief because I had a reputation as a manger who could achieve results quickly.

The agency's priorities included strengthening border enforcement and improving immigration services. These priorities had national ramifications because they related to policies backed by the White House and Congress. We requested and received additional resources to hire Border Officers and support staff to implement the immigration strategies. The White House and Congress expected the agency to demonstrate results in border enforcement and naturalization within the fiscal year. *(Context)* The recruitment, security clearance, and training of staff had to be accomplished expeditiously without sacrificing quality in the security process. Due to the Government

shutdown and furloughs in the first quarter, the agency had only 6 months to hire and appoint 4,000 employees. *(Context)*

At that time, personnel security investigations averaged 8 months. I led a comprehensive review of the process and identified four major systemic problems: severe delays in screening applicants for entry on duty; less than state-of-the-art software; lack of resources in field security offices; and no written guidance on procedures for security clearance decisions. *(Action)* All aspects of the process had to be revamped.

To address the system delays, I delegated entry on duty and suitability adjudication authority to the Field Officers, and provided adjudication training to ensure that employment decisions would be consistent throughout the agency. *(Action)* I worked with the Office of Personnel Management (OPM) to automate case files transmissions, which eliminated an average of 3 months from the process. *(Action)* Further, the new agreement with OPM gave us on-line access to investigative information as it was reported, and made it possible to grant waivers to permit entry on duty in as little as 2 weeks. Automated linkages are now in place in all four of our Field Centers. *(Result)*

I then negotiated and entered into an agreement with the Director of the U.S. Office of Federal Investigations, which agreed to provide fingerprint results within 8 calendar days of their receipt. *(Action)* Previously, the process had taken as long as 3 months. In addition, I directed the development, issuance, and implementation of Standard Operations Guidance for entry on duty decisions. *(Action)* This was the first written guidance to be published in 20 years.

None of this would have been possible without my leadership, which earned the full cooperation and support of my staff. *(Context)* I encouraged them to share my vision of a streamlined personnel security process. All of my employees joined the effort and we formed a truly effective team. Working together, we implemented new security investigations methods and gained the respect and trust of employees within our agency and throughout the Federal investigations community. *(Result)*

As a result of my efforts, 4,003 permanent and part-time employees were hired. Processing time for entry on duty security decisions was reduced from 195 to 20 days, on average. This streamlined process made it possible to screen 14,000 prospective candidates for law officer positions nationwide. *(Result)* I received the agency's Meritorious Service Award for these achievements.

ECQ 2

Leading People

This core qualification involves the ability to design and implement strategies which maximize employee potential and foster high ethical standards in meeting the organization's vision, mission, and goals.

Key Characteristics:

a. Providing leadership in setting the workforce's expected performance levels commensurate with the organization's strategic objectives; inspiring, motivating, and guiding others toward goal accomplishment; empowering people by sharing power and authority.

b. Promoting quality through effective use of the organization's performance management system (e.g., establishing performance standards, appraising staff accomplishments using the developed standards, and taking action to reward, counsel, or remove employees, as appropriate).

c. Valuing cultural diversity and other differences; fostering an environment where people who are culturally diverse can work together cooperatively and effectively in achieving organizational goals.

d. Assessing employees' unique developmental needs and providing developmental opportunities which maximize employees' capabilities and contribute to the achievement of organizational goals; developing leadership in others through coaching and mentoring.

e. Fostering commitment, team spirit, pride, trust, and group identity; taking steps to prevent situations that could result in unpleasant confrontations.

f. Resolving conflicts in a positive and constructive manner; this includes promoting labor/management partnerships and dealing effectively with employee relations matters, attending to morale and organizational climate issues, handling administrative, labor management, and Equal Employment Opportunity issues, and taking disciplinary actions when other means have not been successful.

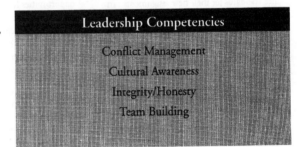

Leadership Competencies

Conflict Management

Cultural Awareness

Integrity/Honesty

Team Building

Example: Leading People

As a manager for the past 14 years, I have developed performance and training plans, counseled, appraised and hired employees, worked with unions, and taken disciplinary actions. I have gone from supervising five employees to managing 170 headquarters and field employees.

As head of the department's Office of Discrimination Resolution, I inherited a 4-year backlog of Equal Employment Opportunity (EEO) complaints and a 15-member staff. At the same time, the department issued a mandate requiring us to reduce the complaints backlog within 60 days and to eliminate it within 4 months. *(Challenge)* I had neither the funds nor the time to hire additional staff so I set out to make the maximum use of the human resources I had on board. *(Context)*

My first step was to review the complaints inventory to determine which complaints could be quickly moved through the system and which ones required in-depth review. I then reorganized the office by defining the structural needs of the EEO program and assessing the skill levels of my employees. I created five teams, using my own staff as well as field staff, and ensured that work was evenly distributed to each group. I worked closely with my employees to develop appropriate performance standards for their new assignments. In addition, we discussed the training that would be needed to enhance their performance. *(Action)*

I ensured that each employee understood the importance of his or her contribution to the project. Throughout the transition to teams, I kept an open-door policy and listened closely to employees' suggestions. As a result, the teams developed a remarkable "can do" attitude toward this overwhelming workload. The spirit and determination with which we worked together enabled us to meet the department's goal of eliminating the complaints backlog within 4 months. *(Result)*

During this period, I saw that several minority employees had potential far above their grade levels. *(Challenge)* I reclassified these support positions into positions with career ladders to the GS-13 level. I provided on-the-job training, specialized classroom training, and day-to-day supervision to give them the necessary experience to compete for the new positions. *(Action)* Four of the employees are now working successfully as GS-13 Senior Specialists. *(Result)* I received the agency's "EEO Manager of the Year" award for my upward mobility efforts.

My next step was to establish fair and neutral mechanisms for the selection and promotion of my employees. *(Challenge)* I selected minorities, women, and non-minorities for vacant positions within the office and, for the first time, provided two upward mobility opportunities for professional staff members. I placed two employees in field positions to accommodate a compassionate transfer, and canceled a field-to-headquarters transfer that would have imposed a severe personal hardship. *(Action)*

Training was another area that had been neglected before I came on board. *(Context)* I developed formal policies and plans to provide training opportunities for the staff, and established a budget for external and internal training. To observe supervisory potential, I established a policy of allowing senior staff members to rotate through vacant supervisory positions in order to gain experience. *(Action)*

In a few instances, I have taken disciplinary actions when employees have not responded to constructive coaching and counseling. *(Challenge)* For example, one of my senior managers who was a skillful technician was not dealing well with her supervisory and managerial responsibilities. *(Context)* I developed a performance improvement plan outlining the managerial skills that she needed to work on and then counseled her on how to reach those goals. *(Action)*

Unfortunately, the employee's performance did not improve and she was removed from her position. *(Result)* On the positive side, my staff knew that they would be protected from inappropriate and arbitrary behavior by their managers, and the office's productivity and morale have improved since the manager's departure. *(Result)*

Example: Leading People

Throughout my career, I have recognized the value of motivating and rewarding employees. In my current position as the agency's Director of Information Resources, I lead a very competent staff of 17 senior technical professionals and 90 contractors. These employees design and manage the agency's local area network and telecommunication systems.

Our office was recently tasked with leading a project to upgrade a critical agency-wide network. *(Challenge)* The project required knowledge and expertise beyond that held by a majority of my staff. *(Context)* I worked with employees to identify their individual training needs and talked with new employees about the possibility of using this project as a developmental opportunity. *(Action)* I saw the project as a unique opportunity to encourage cooperation among staff members and to place our office on the cutting edge of information technology. *(Context)*

Approximately three-quarters of the staff was trained in the complex technical concepts necessary to upgrade the network. Through my leadership, we were able to develop and implement a new system that will carry the agency's network into the 21st century. The upgrade was completed 3 months ahead of schedule. *(Result)* Throughout the project, productivity and morale were high despite increased workloads.

As a result of my employee performance appraisals, 90 percent of my staff received cash awards for their work on this critical project. In addition, I received the agency's Meritorious Service Award for Management Excellence for my ability to set the office's expected performance level.

Before joining the Federal Government, I was chief of the Information and Technology Office at a large private sector law firm. I led a 25-member staff of managers and senior technicians who were responsible for developing and managing the firm's information technology systems. I rebuilt the staff by filling vacant positions, motivating unproductive staff, reducing high absenteeism, and improving morale. As part of the rebuilding, I actively pursued a diverse workforce by hiring females and minorities to fill 60 percent of the office's vacant positions, including four key management and three staff positions.

When I joined the law firm, most of the staff had not had annual performance reviews for two years. *(Challenge)* Morale and productivity were very low, and there had been a high turnover of staff in recent months. *(Context)* I immediately set out to change this situation.

I met individually with employees to talk about performance expectations and to design tailored work plans for the following fiscal year. In addition, I used these sessions to learn about employees' interest in training and developmental assignments, and offered my assistance as a mentor. *(Action)* I served as a mentor for two new employees, and they showed great potential for moving into mid-management positions.

After 9 months under the new work plans, I saw a significant improvement in morale as well as cooperation among staff members who previously had not worked well with their colleagues. *(Result)*

As the office's senior manager, I served as the primary buffer between my staff and our customers—the firm's attorneys. In one case, I was able to diffuse an explosive situation that developed when one of my employees felt he was being unfairly pressured to design a new software program within a very short deadline. *(Challenge)*

The two employees had engaged in several shouting matches within ear shot of several attorneys and members of my staff. The entire firm was on edge, and the relationship between the attorneys and my staff had deteriorated as a result of this two-man battle. *(Context)*

I urged the men to meet with me and talk about the project and the attorney's expectations. *(Action)* After two long sessions, the attorney agreed to stop monitoring my employee's progress and to extend the deadline date. *(Result)* The tension in the office dropped significantly after this situation was resolved. In addition, my employee produced an excellent new software program for his client. *(Result)*

ECQ 3   Results Driven

This core qualification stresses accountability and continuous improvement. It includes the ability to make timely and effective decisions and produce results through strategic planning and the implementation and evaluation of programs and policies.

Key Characteristics:

a. Understanding and appropriately applying procedures, requirements, regulations, and policies related to specialized expertise; understanding linkages between administrative competencies and mission needs; keeping current on issues, practices, and procedures in technical areas.

b. Stressing results by formulating strategic program plans which assess policy/program feasibility and include realistic short- and long-term goals and objectives.

c. Exercising good judgment in structuring and organizing work and setting priorities; balancing the interests of clients and readily readjusting priorities to respond to customer demands.

d. Anticipating and identifying, diagnosing, and consulting on potential or actual problem areas relating to program implementation and goal achievement; selecting from alternative courses of corrective action, and taking action from developed contingency plans.

e. Setting program standards; holding self and others accountable for achieving these standards; acting decisively to modify standards to promote customer service and/or the quality of programs and policies.

f. Identifying opportunities to develop and market new products and services within or outside of the organization; taking risks to pursue a recognized benefit or advantage.

Leadership Competencies

Accountability

Customer Service

Decisiveness

Entrepreneurship

Problem Solving

Technical Credibility

Example: Results Driven

During my 10-year residence in Springfield, IL, I did volunteer work for the Citizens Budget Committee, and was later appointed to the city's Zoning Commission. I acquired a broad-based knowledge of city planning regulations and policies and an understanding of how local politicians vote on particular issues. Because of my successful track record in those positions, the Mayor asked me to lead a citizens group in planning and implementing a City Improvement Program. *(Challenge)*

I recruited approximately 50 volunteers and educated them in the areas of public and municipal finance and capital improvement planning. *(Action)* The team was committed to serving their customers—fellow residents—and to meeting the Mayor's high expectations for improving the quality of life in Springfield. *(Context)* I led the volunteers in a local election campaign to increase the city sales tax from 4 to 5 cents. I marketed the idea by talking to citizens groups and local politicians, describing the benefits of an attractive city and better access to recreational facilities. *(Action)* These meetings were covered by local TV and radio stations, which helped to spread our message.

In the local election, citizens voted to increase the sales tax to 5 cents. The additional $1.5 million raised annually through the tax increase was used to establish additional parks, athletic fields, walking and bike trails, and other recreational facilities. *(Result)*

I have a proven track record of getting results in the Federal sector as well, through careful planning that includes anticipating problems. After becoming Budget Director, I was immediately faced with implementing a congressional mandate to cut the agency budget by $25 million before the start of the next fiscal year. *(Challenge)* To reach this goal, I knew we would have to make major reductions to funding, facilities, programs and staff, particularly scientists and engineers. The cuts would be made at a time when agency managers were putting more of a demand on technical support from these specialists. *(Context)*

I organized task groups of functional and program staff from the field and headquarters and assigned specific priorities to each group. *(Action)* Over the next 4 months, these employees developed various options to accommodate the reductions, taking into consideration the interests of our scientists and engineers, managers who rely on these professionals, congressional demands, and the agency head's interest in complying quickly with Congress. *(Context)* Under my leadership, the task groups prepared several different plans for making the budget cuts.

At the same time, I developed and maintained computerized spreadsheets that allowed managers to immediately see the impact of their funding decisions. *(Action)* Later, we used this system and related processes to continually adjust the reduction targets as cost savings information was refined, allowing almost instantaneous mid-course corrections to the list of reduction targets.

Well before the start of the new Fiscal Year, we presented several alternatives to the agency head, who selected one of the options with few modifications. He praised the entire team for its hard work and innovation in designing a plan that would enable us to absorb the heavy reductions with minimal impact on the agency's mission. *(Result)*

Example: Results Driven

As Director of the Office of Hazardous Waste Management, I have had extensive experience in program direction and evaluation. For example, I led the revamping of our agency's HazMat Program to deal with the mismanagement of hazardous waste materials at sites throughout the country. *(Challenge)* This program was established to ensure that all U.S. companies involved in hazardous waste management assumed responsibility for safely disposing of these dangerous materials.

When I took over as Director, it was clear that the current program was unacceptably slow in addressing cleanup problems at many of these facilities. *(Context)*

I took the lead in redefining the HazMat Program's goals. Working closely with my agency's 10 Regional Directors as well as dozens of State hazardous waste program managers, I developed an outline of national goals: initiate risk-based cleanups, emphasize results over process, address problems at the worst sites first, stabilize immediate threats, comply fully with Federal regulations, and strengthen partnerships with the States. *(Action)* Our strategy received broad support from the agency's top management and from external stakeholders, including State managers and the General Accounting Office. *(Context)*

To implement this plan, I initiated a series of corrective action reviews. *(Action)* Headquarters and regional staff spent two weeks in each region reviewing files and discussing policy issues with regional and State managers. To ensure cross-regional coordination and to provide valuable perspective, we swapped staff between regions to serve on review teams. These reviews gave us a detailed understanding of how well each region was handling its oversight of hazardous waste facilities in its jurisdiction.

Next, I developed a system for ranking these sites, to ensure that the regions and States were giving

priority to problems at the worst-managed sites. In addition, we hosted several national meetings to encourage regional and State managers to exchange technical information on hazardous waste management. *(Action)* Also, we provided training and technical assistance in topics such as site assessment and collection of environmental statistics. *(Action)*

My actions to redesign the HazMat Program have significantly improved the conditions at our nation's hazardous waste management facilities. Both workers and local residents are pleased with the safer conditions at these sites. All of the 3,500 facilities have been assessed and prioritized, and the problems at 85 percent of the high priority sites have been corrected. *(Result)*

At the same time, I realized it was essential to ensure program accountability at all of the facilities. *(Challenge)* I developed indicators that stress the importance of stabilizing worst-managed facilities and limiting human exposure to hazardous waste at all sites. I asked Regional Directors to begin collecting information on their progress in dealing with these critical areas. *(Action)* All but one Regional Director reacted negatively to my request because of the cost implications. *(Context)* I convened a headquarters meeting of all Regional Directors to discuss their concerns; I convinced them of the need to measure results as we attacked these problems. *(Action)*

Regional Directors are now providing this valuable information for inclusion in our office's data base, and it is being used to set program objectives under the Government Performance and Results Act. *(Result)* In addition, I have championed a new relationship with the States which allows our agency to imitate many of the effective State-managed cleanup programs. *(Result)*

ECQ 4   Business Acumen

This core qualification involves the ability to acquire and administer human, financial, material, and information resources in a manner which instills public trust and accomplishes the organization's mission, and to use new technology to enhance decision making.

Key Characteristics:

a. Assessing current and future staffing needs based on organizational goals and budget realities. Applying merit principles to develop, select, and manage a diverse workforce.

b. Overseeing the allocation of financial resources; identifying cost-effective approaches; establishing and assuring the use of internal controls for financial systems.

c. Managing the budgetary process, including preparing and justifying a budget and operating the budget under organizational and Congressional procedures; understanding the marketing expertise necessary to ensure appropriate funding levels.

d. Overseeing procurement and contracting procedures and processes.

e. Integrating and coordinating logistical operations.

f. Ensuring the efficient and cost-effective development and utilization of management information systems and other technological resources that meet the organization's needs; understanding the impact of technological changes on the organization.

Leadership Competencies

Financial Management

Human Resources Management

Technology Management

Example: Business Acumen

As Director of Policy for the New Jersey Department of Transportation, I manage a $1.2 million budget and play a leadership role in setting manpower levels for all Department offices. These decisions are based on the Department's 10-year Mission and Values Statement, which follows the New Jersey Secretary of Transportation's goals.

As chair of the seven-member Executive Committee, I determine expenditures for the Department's divisions and programs—an annual budget of $3 billion. We set priorities by monitoring expenditures relative to forecasts for each program and the prior year's expenditures.

For example, several years ago during a particularly bad winter we made a decision to spend additional money on snow removal and to reduce funding for lower priority maintenance such as spring/summer grass cutting along the highways. *(Challenge)* Before making this decision, I met with Committee members to review upcoming expenditures and how this budgeting shift would impact various office budgets. *(Action)* In previous years, the Department had been severely criticized for not responding quickly and appropriately to hazardous road conditions. *(Context)*

As a result of our decision, we had the fewest weather-related traffic accidents in 12 years, and the Department received very high marks from New Jersey citizens. *(Result)*

I have designed budget strategies to support Departmental priorities. These strategies include coordinating with other executive agencies and outside stakeholders, and targeting State legislators as patrons. When key interest groups oppose the Department's legislation, I negotiate with them to achieve consensus, where possible.

For example, the Department was interested in clarifying the law with respect to payment when utilities must be moved from a Transportation Department right-of-way. *(Challenge)* Two major utility companies were opposed to the proposal. *(Context)*

I selected a General Assembly committee chair to introduce a study resolution requiring the Department, the utility companies, and other stakeholders to collaborate, develop a proposal, and report back to the General Assembly the next session. *(Action)* The Department negotiated with all of the interest groups and designed an acceptable approach. *(Context)* The same legislator introduced the resulting legislation the following year and it was passed by the General Assembly. Companies must now pay for moving their utilities from rights-of-way; this savings is reflected in the Department's budget. *(Result)*

As a member of the Department's Steering Committee, which is composed of Department heads from the internal audits and finance offices, and a team from the information systems office, I led the development of a new information management system. *(Challenge)* The Fiscal Management System was designed to ensure that financial and manpower reports would be accessible to all senior managers and that the information would be used in the Department's strategic planning process; this was not the case with the older system. *(Context)* The new system has been in place for two years and has been praised by managers throughout the Department. *(Result)*

Example: Business Acumen

I have gained extensive experience in managing financial, human, and information resources while working at the Veterans Affairs Medical Center in Arlington, VA.

Currently, as the Medical Center's Budget Director, I am responsible for managing a $150 million budget. This role has included making some tough financial decisions. For example, several years ago I led the development of a controversial plan to close a Veterans Affairs (VA) nursing home that had been in the neighborhood for 40 years. *(Challenge)* The nursing home had been losing money for several years. In addition, the Medical Center's 5-year budget did not include funding for much needed repair work at the aging facility. *(Context)*

I spent 6 months negotiating with union representatives, VA patients and their families. *(Action)* These emotionally charged sessions were held weekly; input from all of the stakeholders appeared in the final plan. The plan to close the nursing home was accepted by VA headquarters after intense negotiations with union officials, congressional offices, patients, and the affiliated university. *(Result)* In addition to saving the Department approximately $4 million annually, we found new Federal positions for all displaced employees and received minimal complaints from VA patients and their families. *(Result)*

Recently, I envisioned and implemented changes to our Medical Center's Funds Management Program. *(Challenge)* Under my leadership, our Financial Officer automated the program, creating spreadsheets that use macros to automatically extract payroll data from the system. *(Action)* This information is distributed over our network to Service Chiefs for use in managing their salaries and expenses budgets.

This decentralized budget program, which is updated every week, has been very popular with our Service Chiefs. *(Context)* They cite it as an invaluable tool in achieving their goals. Last year, this automation tool saved the Medical Center $3 million. *(Result)*

Earlier in my career, I was the Medical Center's Senior Supply Officer. I led 15 District Supply Officers in designing several innovative contracts with community hospitals. *(Context)* For example, we contracted with a local hospital to acquire their stand-alone Women's Outpatient Clinic. *(Challenge)* The contract included $230,000 to purchase the clinic and an annual recurring cost of $300,000.

After weeks of negotiating with hospital employees and their union representatives, I developed a plan to staff the Clinic with community hospital employees. *(Action)* This action minimized hardships on the hospital employees and saved time by avoiding the longer process of announcing the Clinic vacancies. *(Result)*

The result has been a 45 percent increase in the number of female VA patients treated in the area. In follow-up surveys, patients and their families report that they are very pleased with the care and facilities at the Clinic. *(Result)*

ECQ 5

Building Coalitions/Communication

This core qualification involves the ability to explain, advocate and express facts and ideas in a convincing manner, and negotiate with individuals and groups internally and externally. It also involves the ability to develop an expansive professional network with other organizations, and to identify the internal and external politics that impact the work of the organization.

Key Characteristics:

a. Representing and speaking for the organizational unit and its work (e.g., presenting, explaining, selling, defining, and negotiating) to those within and outside the office (e.g., agency heads and other Government executives; corporate executives; Office of Management and Budget officials; Congressional members and staff; the media; clientele and professional groups); making clear and convincing oral presentations to individuals and groups; listening effectively and clarifying information; facilitating an open exchange of ideas.

b. Establishing and maintaining working relationships with internal organizational units (e.g., other program areas and staff support functions); approaching each problem situation with a clear perception of organizational and political reality; using contacts to build and strengthen internal support bases; getting understanding and support from higher level management.

c. Developing and enhancing alliances with external groups (e.g., other agencies or firms, State and local governments, Congress, and clientele groups); engaging in cross-functional activities; finding common ground with a widening range of stakeholders.

d. Working in groups and teams; conducting briefings and other meetings; gaining cooperation from others to obtain information and accomplish goals; facilitating "win-win" situations.

e. Considering and responding appropriately to the needs, feelings, and capabilities of different people in different situations; being tactful and treating others with respect.

f. Seeing that reports, memoranda, and other documents reflect the position and work of the organization in a clear, convincing, and organized manner.

Leadership Competencies

Influencing/Negotiating

Interpersonal Skills

Oral Communication

Partnering

Political Savvy

Written Communication

Example: Building Coalitions/Communication

As a senior manager at Amtrak, I represented the corporation at many community activities. On one occasion, I was chosen to represent the entire railroad industry on a special task force to revitalize the city's transportation industry. *(Challenge)*

To succeed in this critical assignment, I called on talented managers from different sectors of the transportation community. *(Context)* In addition to my own management team and other Amtrak managers, I networked with colleagues in the airline, waterway, and trucking industries. These managers interviewed hundreds of private and public sector transportation executives to gather information on "best practices" for efficient and profitable systems.

I met bi-weekly with many of the above managers to compare notes and to draft a plan that would address our city's transportation needs. *(Action)* The result was the creation of a new approach to analyzing transportation needs as well as a plan for making our city "number one" in the transportation business. On the day we published the report, I was interviewed by both print and television media concerning the report's impact on city transportation policies. Within 6 months, the plan was adopted nationally as a blueprint for transportation management in the 21st century. Our city is now on its way to becoming the most convenient, customer-friendly travel city in the country. *(Result)*

Currently, as a Federal manager with the National Railroad Agency, I speak for the Agency at rail labor conferences, management seminars, and supplier workshops. Most recently, I was the keynote speaker for the winter meeting of the National Association of Railroads.

I work regularly with State government managers through the Federal-State Participation Program. This program was established to facilitate communication between Federal and State transportation managers. Since no Federal funding is provided for this program, I must rely on the good will of State managers and a spirit of cooperation to keep them interested in Federal rail transportation issues. Almost daily, I talk with my State regulatory partners, and we meet quarterly to ensure that the Agency is being responsive to their needs. In addition, we provide technical training for all State safety personnel in my region; once certified, these officers can give training on behalf of the Agency.

My current relationship with my home State is especially rewarding. When I first joined the Agency, I inherited a dispute over sharing sensitive Federal transportation safety documents with State transportation officials. *(Challenge)* The problem arose from a lack of communication between the principle players on both sides. *(Context)* I worked to rectify the situation through daily contact with my State counterparts, and by negotiating with my agency to share portions of these documents. *(Action)* The State representatives were very pleased with the documents we provided, and the negative feelings on both sides have disappeared. *(Result)*

Example: Building Coalitions/Communication

Throughout my career as a private sector attorney, I have represented the interests of a wide variety of organizations, including Fortune 500 companies, small businesses, homeless groups, and local government. This work requires a broad array of verbal and written skills in advocacy, negotiation, and mediation.

An example of this representational skill is my work on behalf of a local homeless clinic. *(Challenge)* I became aware of a pattern and practice by the city government of purposefully frustrating the orders of the local court system to avoid providing a wide variety of social services for the poor and homeless. *(Context)* While the government's failures were obvious in individual cases, little attention was paid to the fact that, when viewed broadly, this malfeasance occurred in virtually every local program designed to aid poor people. I decided that the only way in which this wide scale problem could be brought to light was by preparing a detailed report describing the city's misconduct in approximately 15 cases.

Working with three associates from my firm, we compiled information on the cases filed against the city by various plaintiffs (e.g., homeless individuals, public interest groups). *(Action)* In addition, we gathered facts from the plaintiffs' attorneys, talked to other legal service providers to identify relevant documents for the cases, and recruited a dozen local lawyers to write chapters for the final report. *(Action)*

Over the 10 months we spent writing the report, we were continuously required to represent the clinic to many diverse groups throughout the city (e.g., lobby groups for the homeless and poor, workers at other homeless clinics) whose cooperation was needed to complete the report. We were often required to make presentations to management officials of those groups, to gain their support. *(Action)*

In drafting and editing the report, we were constantly required to work with these groups to be sure that the report was accurate and reflected everyone's interests. During the writing phase, there were serious conflicts among the groups as to what the report should be addressing; we were frequently required to mediate these disputes without sacrificing the report's quality. *(Context)*

After publishing the 450-page report, we received hundreds of phone calls and letters praising our efforts. The report was covered on local radio and television stations, and the demand for copies prompted a second printing (500 copies) of the document. As a result of our findings, the Mayor established an oversight office to assure that the homeless would receive appropriate social services. *(Result)* Based on information from employees at various clinics and many homeless individuals, we know that the city's needy population is receiving these services. *(Result)*

In addition to my regular attorney duties, I head the firm's *pro bono* committee. *(Challenge)* Committee members spend a considerable amount of their time representing individuals who cannot afford to pay for legal services. Despite the negative attitude toward *pro bono* work held by some of the firm's attorneys, I have encouraged six co-workers to join the committee. I did this by "marketing" committee participation as a way to serve the public and to gain valuable experience working on cases that will have a substantial impact on the community. *(Context/Action)*

Approximately 75 percent of the firm's attorneys are now involved in *pro bono* work, and we have argued four *pro bono* cases in the last three terms of the Supreme Court. *(Result)* In addition, the firm has gained a reputation as a public service-minded company. *(Result)*

Leadership Competency Definitions

Leading Change

Continual Learning – Grasps the essence of new information; masters new technical and business knowledge; recognizes own strengths and weaknesses; pursues self-development; seeks feedback from others and opportunities to master new knowledge.

Creativity and Innovation – Develops new insights into situations and applies innovative solutions to make organizational improvements; creates a work environment that encourages creative thinking and innovation; designs and implements new or cutting-edge programs/processes.

External Awareness – Identifies and keeps up to date on key national and international policies and economic, political, and social trends that affect the organization. Understands near-term and long-range plans and determines how best to be positioned to achieve a competitive business advantage in a global economy.

Flexibility – Is open to change and new information; adapts behavior and work methods in response to new information, changing conditions, or unexpected obstacles. Adjusts rapidly to new situations warranting attention and resolution.

Resilience – Deals effectively with pressure; maintains focus and intensity and remains optimistic and persistent, even under adversity. Recovers quickly from setbacks. Effectively balances personal life and work.

Service Motivation – Creates and sustains an organizational culture which encourages others to provide the quality of service essential to high performance. Enables others to acquire the tools and support they need to perform well. Shows a commitment to public service. Influences others toward a spirit of service and meaningful contributions to mission accomplishment.

Strategic Thinking – Formulates effective strategies consistent with the business and competitive strategy of the organization in a global economy. Examines policy issues and strategic planning with a long-term perspective. Determines objectives and sets priorities; anticipates potential threats or opportunities.

Vision – Takes a long-term view and acts as a catalyst for organizational change; builds a shared vision with others. Influences others to translate vision into action.

Leading People

Conflict Management – Identifies and takes steps to prevent potential situations that could result in unpleasant confrontations. Manages and resolves conflicts and disagreements in a positive and constructive manner to minimize negative impact.

Cultural Awareness – Initiates and manages cultural change within the organization to impact organizational effectiveness. Values cultural diversity and other individual differences in the workforce. Ensures that the organization builds on these differences and that employees are treated in a fair and equitable manner.

Integrity/Honesty – Instills mutual trust and confidence; creates a culture that fosters high standards of ethics; behaves in a fair and ethical manner toward others, and demonstrates a sense of corporate responsibility and commitment to public service.

Team Building – Inspires, motivates, and guides others toward goal accomplishments. Consistently develops and sustains cooperative working relationships. Encourages and facilitates cooperation within the organization and with customer groups; fosters commitment, team spirit, pride, trust. Develops leadership in others through coaching, mentoring, rewarding, and guiding employees.

Results Driven

Accountability – Assures that effective controls are developed and maintained to ensure the integrity of the organization. Holds self and others accountable for rules and responsibilities. Can be relied upon to ensure that projects within areas of specific responsibility are completed in a timely manner and within budget. Monitors and evaluates plans; focuses on results and measuring attainment of outcomes.

Customer Service – Balancing interests of a variety of clients; readily readjusts priorities to respond to pressing and changing client demands. Anticipates and meets the need of clients; achieves quality end-products; is committed to continuous improvement of services.

Decisiveness – Exercises good judgment by making sound and well-informed decisions; perceives the impact and implications of decisions; makes effective and timely decisions, even when data is limited or solutions produce unpleasant consequences; is proactive and achievement oriented.

Entrepreneurship – Identifies opportunities to develop and market new products and services within or outside of the organization. Is willing to take risks; initiates actions that involve a deliberate risk to achieve a recognized benefit or advantage.

Problem Solving – Identifies and analyzes problems; distinguishes between relevant and irrelevant information to make logical decisions; provides solutions to individual and organizational problems.

Technical Credibility – Understands and appropriately applies procedures, requirements, regulations, and policies related to specialized expertise. Is able to make sound hiring and capital resource decisions and to address training and development needs. Understands linkages between administrative competencies and mission needs.

Business Acumen

Financial Management – Demonstrates broad understanding of principles of financial management and marketing expertise necessary to ensure appropriate funding levels. Prepares, justifies, and/or administers the budget for the program area; uses cost-benefit thinking to set priorities; monitors expenditures in support of programs and policies. Identifies cost-effective approaches. Manages procurement and contracting.

Human Resources Management – Assesses current and future staffing needs based on organizational goals and budget realities. Using merit principles, ensures staff are appropriately selected, developed, utilized, appraised, and rewarded; takes corrective action.

Technology Management – Uses efficient and cost effective approaches to integrate technology into the workplace and improve program effectiveness. Develops strategies using new technology to enhance decision making. Understands the impact of technological changes on the organization.

Building Coalitions/Communication

Influencing/Negotiating – Persuades others; builds consensus through give and take; gains cooperation from others to obtain information and accomplish goals; facilitates "win-win" situations.

Interpersonal Skills – Considers and responds appropriately to the needs, feelings, and capabilities of different people in different situations; is tactful, compassionate and sensitive, and treats others with respect.

Oral Communication – Makes clear and convincing oral presentations to individuals or groups; listens effectively and clarifies information as needed; facilitates an open exchange of ideas and fosters an atmosphere of open communication.

Partnering – Develops networks and builds alliances, engages in cross-functional activities; collaborates across boundaries, and finds common ground with a widening range of stakeholders. Utilizes contacts to build and strengthen internal support bases.

Political Savvy – Identifies the internal and external politics that impact the work of the organization. Approaches each problem situation with a clear perception of organizational and political reality; recognizes the impact of alternative courses of action.

Written Communication – Expresses facts and ideas in writing in a clear, convincing and organized manner.

Tips for Writing Effective ECQ Statements

Stay Focused

- Focus on leadership rather than managerial and technical abilities; all three are important, but leadership is more important.

- Show your experience in all 5 Executive Core Qualifications (ECQ's).

- Follow the Challenge-Context-Action-Result model.

- Each ECQ should contain specific, job-related experiences with specific accomplishments.

- It's not necessary to have experience in every Key Characteristic—your overall record should show that you have the qualifications needed to succeed in the Senior Executive Service.

- Be sure your statement reflects the Leadership Competencies underlying each ECQ.

- Never combine any of the ECQ's.

- Never address an ECQ by referring the reader to other parts of your application (e.g., SF-171).

- Avoid using an identical example for more than one ECQ.

- Avoid a "laundry list" of activities without context, actions, or accomplishments.

- Avoid statements that simply parrot the Key Characteristics.

- Focus on your vision for the organization not your personal vision.

- Focus on recent experience, education, and training. Some reviewers consider experience that's over 10 years old to be stale.

- Highlight awards or other forms of recognition that relate specifically to an ECQ, e.g., "Human Resources Manager of the Year."

- Include non-Federal experiences (e.g., private sector, volunteer and professional organizations) if they support the ECQ.

- Include relevant formal education or training that has enhanced your skills in a particular ECQ.

- Don't forget to include examples of special assignments and details.

- Include special qualifications: public speaking, publications, languages spoken, membership in related professional organizations or scientific societies, or expertise in a technical area (e.g., budget, information technology).

- Show measurable results, especially in terms of improved customer service, increased efficiency productivity, or money saved.

- Avoid vague statements.

  Good: I produce two weekly radio shows, one monthly television program, and a bimonthly newsletter to 10,000 employees located in 12 regional offices.

  Bad: I manage various communication processes to field offices.

English 101 Revisited

- Absolutely no typos or grammatical errors.

- Use personal "I" instead of third person.

- Write in short, complete sentences (subject, verb, proper tense agreement).

- Use common words and expressions instead of bureaucratic ones.

- Economize on words and expressions, but not to a cryptic extreme.

  Good: I briefed Congress.

  Bad: I conducted a briefing to key Congresspersons and their staffs. (10 words.)

- Avoid acronyms, unless you spell them out several times in the application.

Format

- Keep length 1 - 1¹/₂ pages for each Executive Core Qualification (ECQ).
- Material should be easy to read:
  - Use paragraphs or bullets to separate items.
  - Use headings and subheadings to indicate categories.
  - Use all capital letters, **bold** or *italics* to highlight important information.
  - Leave some white space; don't type margin to margin.
  - Avoid using small size type.
- Don't make reviewers hunt for experience (e.g., "see attachments"). Put all relevant information in the ECQ write-up.
- Application should be neat, clean, and typed.
- Make sure photocopies are legible.
- Don't attach copies of training certificates, awards, or position descriptions.
- Number all pages.
- Don't assume Spell-Check and Grammar-Check will catch all the errors; review every word.

Tone

- Be friendly and professional, not stilted, formal, or chatty.
- Avoid passive verbs; use active verbs with the personal "I."

  Good: I established a new team structure that eliminated the need for six supervisors (only 13 words; concise, clear, good use of personal "I" with an active verb).

  Bad: The establishment of a new team structure was considered one of my best accomplishments in that it reduced the need for six supervisory positions (too long—24 words; stilted, awkward sentence structure, too passive).

References

- Make sure that individuals you reference can attest to your ability to perform the Senior Executive Service job and can speak to your specific competencies in the Executive Core Qualifications.
- Contact references and tell them about positions for which you have applied.
- Be sure reference information is current (e.g., telephone numbers, addresses).

More Tips

- Avoid statements that describe your personal beliefs, philosophies, or commitment to social or political causes unless you can show bottom line results.
- Don't reveal information about your political affiliation or activities unless you are using experience as a political appointee to qualify.
- Don't identify your race, sex, national origin, color, religion, age, marital status, physical or mental disability, sexual orientation, or any other non-merit factor.

And Finally. . .

- When you're finished, ask three people (preferably dispassionate and knowledgeable individuals) to review your application.

About the Author and Contributing Authors

Author Kathryn Troutman is the founder and president of The Resume Place in Washington, D.C., and Baltimore, Maryland. The Resume Place was established in 1971 and specializes in writing, designing, and typesetting professional resumes, SF 171s, and now federal resumes. In 1978, Kathryn published *The 171 Reference Book,* written with Patricia Wood (now Director of Communications for Partnership for Reinventing Government). It was the most popular publication on ways to write an outstanding SF 171 and promoted the use of expanded job blocks. When the OPM eliminated the SF 171 in 1995, Kathryn created the format for the new "federal resume" that became the accepted standard in government. Within seven months, she wrote and published the first edition of *The Federal Resume Guidebook*. The book has become the model for federal resume instruction. This second edition was published by JIST Works, Inc., in Indianapolis.

Because The Resume Place is located in the nation's capital, the service has written thousands of job applications for federal employees. Kathryn is now a popular federal resume- and KSA-writing workshop leader. She has trained more than 5,000 federal employees in three years, primarily for Faith Williamson, Ed. D., Coordinator of the Work/Life Center at the Department of Health and Human Services in Washington, D.C., as well as for more than 20 other agencies and federal offices.

Kathryn now directs The Resume Place, Inc., primarily from the Baltimore location, where she receives e-mails and faxes from federal applicants throughout the U.S. and internationally. Her popular Web site, www.resume-place.com, receives more than 3,500 visitors per day who study the federal resume formats and write for help.

Kathryn's sister, Bonny Kraemer Day, has been a principal part of The Resume Place for 16 years. The federal resume samples in Appendix A were formatted and designed by Bonny, who specializes in creating outstanding visual resume presentations. Bonita Kraemer, Kathryn and Bonny's mother, has been a resume editor, typesetter, and business advisor. The family aspect of The Resume Place is appreciated by the thousands of clients who return for resume updates and rewrites.

The Baltimore office is across the street from Kathryn's home, where she lives with her 16-year-old daughter, Lauren, and where son, Chris, and daughter, Emily, come home from college as much as possible. From the experience of mentoring three high school students toward college majors and careers, Kathryn wrote her third book, *Creating Your High School Resume*, published by JIST Works. This is the first resume book specifically written for high school students and is used as a textbook in English, business, and career-tech programs.

Kathryn's next resume book addresses welfare-to-work job applications and will help the applicants write the best resumes possible.

Contributing Authors

Michael Singer Dobson is an author, consultant, and popular seminar leader in management, communications, and personal success, who brings a unique practical perspective to what works in the real world. He has trained people in well over 1,000 organizations on three continents on topics ranging from career strategies to project management. He has published six business books, including *Practical Project Management, Juggling Multiple Projects, Management Strategies for Technical Professionals, Exploring Personality Styles, Managing UP!*, and *Coping with Supervisory Nightmares,* as well as video and audio training programs. He was a contributing author for *The Federal Resume Guidebook,* first edition, and *The 171 Reference Book.*

His down-to-earth style and practical advice come from his management career positions, including vice president of Discovery Software, Inc., vice president for marketing and sales of Games Workshop, Inc., and director of marketing and product development for TSR, Inc. He has also been director of writing and senior writer for The Resume Place. Michael was a member of the research team that created and opened the Smithsonian National Air and Space Museum, the world's most popular museum.

Brian Friel is the assistant editor for *Government Executive* magazine and its companion Web site, GovExec.com. Brian has written more than 500 articles on federal government management issues, including downsizing, outsourcing, career development, technology, and human resources. He is also charged with the day-to-day management of GovExec.com. Outside the world of government, Brian enjoys running, volleyball, reading, and playing the piano.

Tom Kell is a Los Angeles-based freelance writer and public relations consultant. From 1972 through 1995 he was a writer, editor, and public affairs specialist with the U.S. Office of Personnel Management and an active member of the Public Employees Roundtable and the National Association of Government Communicators. He lives in Redondo Beach, California, and works for clients such as the Hermosa Beach Film Festival and California State Polytechnic University at Pomona. Tom also works with several clients "back home" in Washington via e-mail (twkell@AOL.com).

Edward J. Lynch, Ph.D., currently serves as a senior researcher with the Subcommittee on Civil Service of the House Committee on Government Reform and Oversight. He is also professor and lecturer on immigration policy at the Institute of World Politics. He served in senior policy and public affairs positions during the Reagan and Bush administrations, including the Immigration and Naturalization Service, the Federal Aviation Administration, the President's Commission on Privatization, and the Environmental Protection Agency. His articles have been published in the *Public Interest, Policy Review, Los Angeles Times, Washington Post,* and *Christian Science Monitor.*

Alan Cross is a senior writer at The Resume Place. He offers 20 years' public relations, public affairs, and journalistic writing experience. Alan has been published in national journals and has written material for award-winning exhibits. Alan's expertise at The Resume Place is creating outstanding federal resumes and KSAs for federal applicants who want to avoid bureaucratic language. His advertising and public relations background helps him write succinct, accomplishment-focused federal and private industry job search packages.

Index

citizenship, 54
e-mail address, 54
federal civilian status/reinstatement eligibility, 54
name and address, 54
samples, 56–57
Social Security number, 54
special instructions, 54–55
veterans' preference, 55–56
physical demands, 105
position descriptions (PDs), 14–16
for last two positions, 97
previous experience, 12
Private-Industry Applicant Applying for First Federal Job, 68–69
Private-Industry Applicant for GS-13 Sanctuary Manager, 80
Private-Industry Professional Pursuing First Position in Government, 68
private industry resumes, 3, 49
converting for work experience section, 113–117
federal resume differences, 4
other qualifications and skills, 76
professional journals, 22
professional memberships, 84–89
profile and accomplishments, 138
Profile Highlighting Education, Travel, and Languages, 134
profile section, 12
profile statements, 14, 124
biochemical research director, 129
business and marketing executive, 130
career changes, 131–132
classroom teacher changing to government educational program management, 131
environmental expert, 130
examples, 129–132
executive with experience doing business with government, 131
FBI agent, 130
geochemical engineer and financial analyst, 130

information system specialist, 132
JD candidate interested in legislative work, 131
vacancy announcements, 126–127
Program Analyst vacancy announcements, 31–47
promotional potential, 27
proofreading tips, 145–146
public speaking, 90
public speaking and presentations, 84–89
publication lists or written works, 84–89

Q

Qualification Standards for General Schedule Positions, 99
Qualifications Standards Operating Manual, 98
Quality Ranking Factors, 167
Quick and Easy software, 5
quotes, 90
Quoting Supervisor in Profile, 136

R

reading newspapers, 23
recent college graduates, 63–67
Registered Nurse and Federal Applicant, 81
researching federal agencies, 98–99
results, 2
emphasizing, 14–16
Resumix job kits, 325-342
Resumix resumes, 2, 151–164
agencies using, 160–161
brevity without cramming, 159
concrete examples, 157
e-mailing, 161–164
following instructions, 159–160

U

Z

List of Appendix A's Complete Federal Resume Examples

College Student Federal Resumes

GS-8 and Below

GS-9 and Above

List of Appendix B's KSA and ECQ Examples

KSA Examples

ECQ Examples

PC DISK AND CD-ROM
Federal Resume Guidebook
Federal Resume Samples/Templates
Designed by Kathryn Troutman and Bonny Day

All New Stand-Out Federal Resumes/Templates to Help You Write Your Federal Resume

PC Disk–$19.95 + $3.00 shipping (individual user)
All samples on the PC disk are for Windows 95 in Word 6.0 *and* WordPerfect 6.0

***New Digital Format:* CD-ROM–$29.95 + $3.00 shipping** (individual user)
Choose your operating system format: Macintosh, Power Mac, Windows 95, Windows 98, Windows 3.0, Windows NT 3.5, 4.0, Sun OS, Solaris, HP-UX, Linux, IBM AIX, OS/2. Samples are in Word 7.0 and WordPerfect 7.0.

License for multiple use for LAN, WAN, or Career Center PCs available.
Call for price list or quote: (888) 480-8265.

WHAT'S ON THE DISK?

Fourteen outstanding 3-to-5-page federal resume examples, as seen in Appendix A: college to federal, federal to federal, and private industry to federal.

College Federal Resume Samples:
- B.S. in Economics, applying for Labor Economist, GS-9/11
- B.S. in Criminology, applying for Law Enforcement Officer, GS-7
- B.S. in Aviation, applying for FAA Aviation Operations, GS-7/9
- Third-year Law Student, applying for Attorney Advisor, GS-9
- B.A. in French with legal internships, applying for Paralegal Specialist, GS-7
- Example of college course list with description

Federal Resume Samples:
- Military Computer Specialist seeking Computer Specialist, GS-9/11
- Computer Operator, GS-7, seeking GS-8 Computer Specialist. Great format for career change, advancement.
- Executive Secretary, GS-318-8/10, seeking training or editing positions.
- Correspondence Analyst, GS-301-8, seeking Program Assistant, GS-301-9. Favorite format from 1st edition.
- Special Assistant for Systems Development, GS-15, seeking SES position. Outstanding executive presentation.
- Secretary (Steno), GS-318-10, seeking Editor or Program Assistant
- Project Manager/Systems Engineer, GS-334-13, seeking GS-14 Supervisory Computer Specialist
- Contract Specialist, GS-12, seeking General Business and Industry Specialist, GS-1101-12

Entire Federal Resume, KSA, Cover Letter Package: Private industry to federal government application of a Food Manufacturer Marketer seeking Marketer, GS-9, for U.S. Postal Service.

How to Use the Samples on the PC Disk

☆ Open the files and choose the sample you like the most.
☆ Simply "save as" your name and insert your copy into the resume format.
☆ Move resume sections easily in your favorite word processor.

How Can the Samples on Disk Help You Write Your Resume?

☆ Just seeing a great-looking federal resume on your PC screen will help you start writing your resume.
☆ Select a format and resume on the disk and use it as your format.
☆ Save formatting and setup time!
☆ Easy to cut-and-paste your text into an existing format.

Who's Using the PC Disk and Sample Federal Resumes?

More than 10,000 PC disks have been sold and are being used by federal career transition centers and applicants for federal jobs. This simple PC disk has been a popular and valuable part of *The Federal Resume Guidebook* since its first printing.

(ORDER FORM ON NEXT PAGE)

ORDER FORM

Five ways to order The Federal Resume Guidebook
PC Disk or CD-ROM, Second Edition

1. Online at www.resume-place.com, go to the order form. There's an easy drop-down list for the selection of Operating System for CD-ROM.

2. E-mail to resume@ari.net: 24-hour delivery to your e-mail address.

   Got a tight deadline? Just send credit card number, expiration date, name, address, phone and word processing program preference. We'll send the files within 24 hours.

3. Toll-free telephone orders: 888-480-8265, 9 to 5:30 EST.

4. Mail: 310 Frederick Road, Baltimore, MD 21228.

5. Fax a copy of this order form to (410) 744-0112.

Number of PC disks ordered: _____

Number of CD-ROMs ordered: _____

Operating system for CD-ROM: _____

Total to be billed (include shipping): $ _____

Name: _____

Agency/Office: _____

Ship to Address: _____

City, State, Zip Code: _____

E-mail Address: _____

Daytime Phone Number: _____

Evening Phone Number: _____

Method of Payment: _____

Credit Card Number: _____

Expiration Date (m/d/y): _____

Purchase orders accepted from government agencies and educational institutions.

Purchase order number: _____

Visa, MC, Amex, Discover accepted. Make checks payable to The Resume Place, Inc.

THE RESUME PLACE, INC. IS A SMALL, WOMAN-OWNED BUSINESS. FEIN: 52-1905079

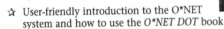
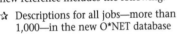
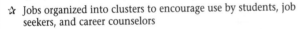

JIST Order Form

Please copy this form if you need more lines for your order.

Purchase Order #: _____ (Required by some organizations)

Billing Information

Organization Name: _____

Accounting Contact: _____

Street Address: _____

_____

City, State, Zip: _____

Phone Number: ( ) _____

Shipping Information with Street Address (If Different from Above)

Organization Name: _____

Contact: _____

Street Address: (We *cannot* ship to P.O. boxes) _____

_____

City, State, Zip: _____

Phone Number: ( ) _____

Phone: 1-800-648-JIST
Fax: 1-800-JIST-FAX
World Wide Web Address:
http://www.jist.com

Credit Card Purchases: VISA____ MC____ AMEX____

Card Number: _____

Exp. Date: _____

Name As on Card: _____

Signature: _____

Quantity	Order Code	Product Title	Unit Price	Total
			Subtotal	
			+5% Sales Tax Indiana Residents	
			+Shipping / Handling / Ins. (See left)	
			TOTAL	

JIST Works, Inc.
8902 Otis Avenue
Indianapolis, IN 46216

Shipping / Handling / Insurance Fees

In the continental U.S. add 7% of subtotal:
- Minimum amount charged = $4.00
- Maximum amount charged = $100.00
- FREE shipping and handling on any prepaid orders over $40.00.

Above pricing is for regular ground shipment only. For rush or special delivery, call JIST Customer Service at 1-800-648-JIST for the correct shipping fee.

Outside the continental U.S. call JIST Customer Service at 1-800-648-JIST for an estimate of these fees.

Payment in U.S. funds only!

Practical, self-directed tools and training for career explorers and job seekers of all ages!

JIST thanks you for your order!